*Athenian Political Thought
and the Reconstruction
of American Democracy*

Athenian Political Thought and the Reconstruction of American Democracy

EDITED BY

J. Peter Euben, John R. Wallach, and Josiah Ober

Cornell University Press

ITHACA AND LONDON

Copyright © 1994 by Cornell University

All rights reserved. Except for brief quotations in a review,
this book, or parts thereof, must not be reproduced in any
form without permission in writing from the publisher. For
information, address Cornell University Press, Sage House,
512 East State Street, Ithaca, New York 14850.

First published 1994 by Cornell University Press.
Library of Congress Cataloging-in-Publication Data

Athenian political thought and the reconstruction of American
  democracy / edited by J. Peter Euben, John Wallach, and Josiah Ober.
    p. cm.
  Includes bibliographical references and index.
  ISBN 0-8014-2980-3 (cloth : alk. paper).—ISBN 0-8014-8179-1
(paper : alk. paper)
    1. Democracy—Greece—Athens—History. 2. Democracy—United
States. 3. Democracy. 4. Elite (Social sciences)
5. Representative government and representation. 6. Political
participation. 7. Political stability. 8. Legitimacy of
governments. I. Euben, J. Peter. II. Wallach, John. III. Ober,
Josiah.
JC79.A8A86 1994   94-18797
321.8—dc20
Printed in the United States of America

⊗ The paper in this book meets the minimum requirements
of the American National Standard for Information Sciences–
Permanence of Paper for Printed Library Materials, ANSI Z39.48-1984.

CONTENTS

*Athenian Political Thought
and the Reconstruction
of American Democracy*

J. PETER EUBEN, JOHN R. WALLACH,
AND JOSIAH OBER

Introduction

"I know of no safe repository of the ultimate power of society," Thomas Jefferson wrote, "but the people themselves, and if we think them not enlightened enough to exercise their control with a wholesome discretion, the remedy is not to take it from them but to inform their discretion."[1] A generation later, John Stuart Mill insisted that because "the first element of good government" was "the virtue and intelligence of the human beings composing the community, the most important point of excellence which any form of government can possess is to promote the virtue and intelligence of the people themselves."[2] Yet the idea that the rulers should educate the people so they can rule and educate themselves is not a widely held view in the United States today. Despite the oft-heard paeans to democracy and "the American people" sung by politicians as well as talk-show hosts from all parts of the ideological spectrum, a more widely shared sentiment is that "the people" are best able to rule themselves when led by "responsible elites,"[3] drawn from politics, journalism, education, and

1. Letter to William Charles Jarvis, September 28, 1820, in *The Collected Works of Thomas Jefferson*, ed. Paul Ford (New York: Putnam, 1905) 12:1630. Jefferson's belief in a natural aristocracy did not undermine this conviction, as he thought that only an attentive and active citizenry could keep aristocrats from becoming voracious wolves. On the extent and ways Jefferson was or was not a democrat, cf. Hannah Arendt, *On Revolution* (New York: Viking, 1963) with Thomas Pangle, *The Spirit of Modern Republicanism* (Chicago: University of Chicago Press, 1988).

2. John Stuart Mill, *On Representative Government*, vol. 2 (Everyman), 193.

3. The phrase and sentiment are from Trilateral Commission, *The Crisis of Democracy* (New York: New York University Press, 1975). The report's authors are merely echoing democratic revisionists, who sound very much like Athenian antidemocrats.

business. Because of their position, experience, and expertise, such elites lay claim to be the true defenders of democracy—whatever the administration in power—because they save the people from their worst selves while recognizing current political complexities and engaging in the rational analysis the people do not or cannot manage. Such elites should "inform" the people's discretion, so that the people, thus informed, can then legitimate the elites' exercise of power to the degree of accepting their own alienation from the democratic political process. When such elites talk about public education, their emphasis is on making America economically competitive in the global capitalist economy.

Even if one shares the sentiments of Jefferson and Mill, hard questions remain. For who is Jefferson's "we" who promote the virtue and intelligence of the citizenry? How can such education be accomplished and in what institutional forms and forums? Hannah Arendt has argued that all education must begin by initiating the young and new into the habits and ways of their people.[4] Is there a uniquely "democratic" way of doing this? Or conversely, are there modes of education that democracies cannot engage in without contradicting their animating principles? And who, especially in a society as diverse as ours, constitutes "the people"? How we think about such matters depends on how we regard citizenship, democracy, and politics as well as the relationship between education and political education.

Citizenship today primarily signifies a legal status that accrues to all individuals born into a society. In turn, that society guarantees them rights against both the state and other individuals. But if this is all that citizenship implies, then nonparticipation in politics is simply a choice made by people who have more pressing things to do. Similarly, where political activity is considered merely one way of achieving gratification, which may be more efficiently attained, as Robert Dahl put it, by "working at a job, moving to another neighborhood or city, or coping with an uncertain future,"[5] then politics has no moral priority, and the reasons for educating democracy as the aim of education in a democracy are less pressing. If the obligation of citizenship is epitomized in the choice of representatives from among competing elites whose shared commitment is ensuring domestic tranquility, the rights of property, and national security, then all the political education we need is to know which party or leader will do these tasks best. And if the system "works," if the checks and balances indeed preclude anar-

4. Hannah Arendt, "The Crisis in Education," in *Between Past and Future*, enlarged ed. (Baltimore: Penguin, 1968), 143–72.
5. Robert A. Dahl, *Who Governs?* (New Haven: Yale University Press, 1960), 224.

chy and tyranny, then there is really no need for civic virtue or political education at all, except perhaps the education that brings us to admire the system that would be able to do without it.

The editors of this book regard citizenship as a set of practices as well as a legal status, practices that involve public action as much as private rights. From this perspective, the frequently used phrase "private citizen" and chapter titles such as "Citizenship without Politics" tend to become oxymora.[6] For when members of a community are called to tasks that in important ways sustain their political identity, and if the absolute absence of power corrupts as much as its absolute monopoly (because those without it become clients, subjects, or members of a despairing underclass[7]), then the failure to participate, even if it is the result of a "free choice," cannot be so easily dismissed in a democracy. This is especially true if participation is not only an expression of private interests but a way in which individuals come to think of themselves as citizens. A necessary condition for speaking and acting in public as a citizen is being recognized as a (relatively) equal presence in whatever shared deliberation is taking place. To be silenced or ignored is a kind of public erasure and oblivion, as feminists understood when they demanded that women's voices be heard. Teachers know that students in a classroom are more involved in the class, more willing to offer opinions, and more likely to be independent thinkers and think of themselves that way, if what they say receives the respect of their colleagues. Something similar can happen in democratic politics.

Though hardly an ardent democrat, Aristotle is usually credited with the first theoretical articulation of this view of citizenship. It is he who insists that citizenship is the active sharing of power based on the equality of friendship rather than either familial relations appropriate to the household or the language of rights and obligations fundamental to a society of strangers. It is also Aristotle who insists that the polis is the highest community (though not the highest activity)[8] because it is in public that "we" deliberate about what is highest, including what should be regarded as public and what is private. And it is Aristotle

6. That is the title of Dahl's *Who Governs?* chap. 25. See the discussion of republican and liberal conceptions of citizenship in Adrian Oldfield, *Citizenship and Community: Civic Republicanism in the Modern World* (New York: Routledge, Chapman and Hall, 1990).

7. See, e.g., John Gaventa's discussion of Appalachian miners, *Power and Powerlessness: Quiescence and Rebellion in an Appalachian Valley* (Urbana: University of Illinois Press, 1980).

8. Because we have a spark of the divine, politics cannot be, as Book 10 of the *Ethics* makes clear, the highest activity of all. But no one can be entirely outside the polis, because even the man capable of contemplation cannot *be* a contemplative man. He remains, as Plato's philosopher-kings do not, a man among men, with needs like those of other men.

who suggests that political participation changes the character of the participants in ways that educate them both morally and intellectually;[9] for it makes them less parochial in their speech and understanding and forces them to give reasons in support of their proposals in terms of public purposes, rather than simply to express their interests (which is not to deny the frequent conflation of the two). Though Aristotle certainly does distinguish public and private by activities, he also suggests that they can be distinguished by ways of speaking, as in the difference between "I want" and "we need."

But even if we are committed to a kind of "strong democracy" and regard citizenship as a privileged status and activity,[10] there are problems with the idea of political education in a democracy. For one thing, education usually involves a hierarchy between teacher and pupil or parent and child which is inappropriate in a political realm of equals. For another, political education conjures up ideas of indoctrination whereby the state dictates what can be taught, how, to whom, and by whom. Political education as we mean it is reciprocal in order to honor the equality democratic citizenship requires and is different from a politicized education in so far as that implies indoctrination.

The editors of this book believe that there resides in Athenian political practice and classical political theory an enormous potential for providing such education. That is why we turn, in the face of intense controversy over the place of classical literature in the canon, to Athenian political thought and practices as a primary source for educating democracy.[11] We are aware of the sometimes sordid consequences of Hellenic nostalgia and polis envy and of how Athenian society marginalized women, relied on slaves, embraced a highly suspect ethic of glory and conquest, and permitted social and economic inequalities to persist even among full citizens. Even A. H. M. Jones's qualified claim that "prima facie Athenian democracy would seem to have been a perfectly designed machine for expressing the will of the people" seems exaggerated,[12] let alone von Humboldt's idealization of Greek history, which became the inspiration for young German leaders to

9. Aristotle *Politics* 1253a10–12, 1280b11–12.
10. See Benjamin Barber, *Strong Democracy: Participatory Politics for a New Age* (Berkeley and Los Angeles: University of California Press, 1984), as well as his *An Aristocracy of Everyone: The Politics of Education and the Future of America* (New York: Ballantine, 1992).
11. Bernard Knox's recent argument for the enduring enlightenment offered by Greek culture, perhaps especially in our increasingly multicultural society, deserves mention, even if we find it insensitive to the exclusive character of that culture; see *The Oldest Dead White European Males* (New York: Norton, 1993).
12. A. H. M. Jones, *Athenian Democracy* (Oxford: Blackwell and Mott, 1957), 3. It is not necessarily either, *if* one translates people into demos and acknowledges that the people's will can oppress and dominate.

remake themselves. "Knowledge of the Greeks is not merely pleasant, useful or necessary to us," wrote von Humboldt, but embodies an "ideal of that which we ourselves should like to be and produce." Although every part of history enriches people with its wisdom, the Greeks alone are "almost godlike."[13] Any responsible appropriation of Athenian democracy must attend to such excess as well as to the stark incompleteness of that democracy and to the undemocratic "uses" to which the study of antiquity has been put.

The question is not only *why* we Americans would want to take such a turn but *how* we could, given a global economy, regimes of infinitely greater size and complexity, mass media, and the fact that "democratic Athens" seems as much a projection shaped by contemporary political controversies as a political society defined by scholarly attention to the facts. The latter complaint has been common. In 1960, Dahl asserted that "the primacy of politics in the lives of citizens of a democratic order" is a "myth" perpetuated by the idealization of the city-state, the "human tendency to blur the boundaries between what is and what ought to be," and the "dogma" that democracy would not "work" if citizens were not concerned with public affairs. From that dogma he derives the position that inasmuch as "democracy works," it "follows that citizens must be concerned. . . . The assumption, based on uncritical acceptance of scanty and dubious evidence, [is, then,] that whatever the situation may be at the moment, at one time or in another place the life of the citizen has centered on politics." This "ancient myth" is certainly wrong about America; whether it was a reality in Athens "will probably never be known."[14] We believe this judgment too easily dismisses the contemporary significance of Athenian democracy by reducing democracy to the conventional understanding of it in American political science and to a particular reading of American politics.

II

Despite the work of contemporary theorists such as Hannah Arendt and Alasdair MacIntyre, the democratic polis has not been a primary object of praise or blame in the discourse of theory or the practice of politics since the nineteenth century. Many theorists believe that Athe-

13. *An Anthology of the Writings of Wilhelm von Humboldt*, ed. and trans. Marianne Cowan (Detroit: Wayne State University Press, 1963), 78–98.
14. Dahl, *Who Governs*, 280–81. Dahl studied New Haven, but he extrapolates his conclusions to include the United States and politics itself.

nian democracy is more projection than description and, as Dahl now argues, that its exclusivity, its inability to articulate universal moral principles, and its sense of place make the experiences of the polis largely irrelevant to contemporary discussions of politics, democratic or otherwise.[15] Given the long history of critical engagement by western theorists (from Plato and Aristotle through Machiavelli to Rousseau and Mill) with the model of the polis, it is worth asking why it was that, about the time liberal democracy became the dominant political model for the western world, western theorists no longer found the democratic polis particularly "good to think with." The answer is complex, but two phenomena seem particularly germane: the changing place of classical studies in the intellectual arena, and the rise of a tradition of Marxist socialism as the primary countermodel to democratic liberalism.

The period encompassing the second half of the nineteenth and the early twentieth centuries was the great age of professionalization in the academy. And with the emergence of disciplinary professionalization, the study of the classical texts of Greece and Rome, at one time regarded as the core of the gentleman's cultural education, slowly lost its central educational role. In the latter part of the nineteenth century, classicists founded several professional societies (including the American Philological Association in 1869 and the American School of Classical Studies at Athens in 1881) and thereby joined the general movement to the professionalization of academic disciplines. In classics, as in other newly self-conscious disciplines, professionalization went hand in hand with specialization. Thus there was an increased concern for the "scientific" (*wissenschaftlich*) approach to the study of the past and its literatures. As a result, certain issues and approaches were canonized as appropriate to the field; those approaches and issues that fell outside the canonical bounds were, by disciplinary definition, regarded as some other discipline's business. And thus, classical political theory became the business of disciplinary philosophers or political scientists.[16]

There was, of course, resistance to the professionalizing movement. Some people continued to believe (for whatever set of reasons) that

15. See Stephen T. Holmes, "Aristippus in and out of Athens," *American Political Science Review* 73 (1979): 113–28, and Robert A. Dahl, *Democracy and Its Critics* (New Haven: Yale University Press, 1989).

16. On the professionalization of academic disciplines, see, e.g., Peter Novick, *That Noble Dream: The "Objectivity Question" and the American Historical Profession* (Cambridge: Cambridge University Press, 1988). For classics as a discipline, see Phillis Culham and Lowell Edmunds, eds., *Classics: A Discipline and Profession in Crisis?* (Lanham, Md.: University Press of America, 1989).

the cultural heritage of the classical past should not be partitioned and allowed to become the preserve of disciplinary hierophants. The resistance and its ultimate failure is well illustrated by Nietzsche's challenging *Birth of Tragedy* and the devastating criticism leveled against it by the grand master of professional and scientific classical philology, Ulrich von Wilamowitz-Moellendorff. The latter was clearly the victor, at least as far as the long-term direction of the field of classics was concerned.[17] Some classical scholars continued to give public lip service (at least when confronted with a "nonprofessional" audience, such as undergraduates or university administrators) to the notion that the study of the classics was good training in civic values. But from the late nineteenth century onward, few works of scholarship by "amateurs" would be taken seriously by professional classicists (except in England), and relatively few works by the latter would attempt to promote a serious engagement between the disciplinary material of classical studies and the "outside world" of contemporary political thought and practice.

By most measures, at least, this strategy did not prove a great success. In the ongoing intra-academy battle of the disciplines over turf (resources, students, faculty appointments, and clout in general), classics has fared relatively badly; the philological focus dictated by Wilamowitz-Moellendorff and text critics such as A. E. Housman proved very narrow indeed. So, in the course of the twentieth century, classics dropped out of the intellectual mainstream. By the latter part of the century, the subject had become quite peripheral, both within and outside of the academy.[18]

Not all the blame for this situation (if blame there be) need be placed on disciplinary classicists, because the outside world was for its own part becoming less and less interested in anything classicists might have to say about politics. By the early twentieth century, intellectuals and political activists increasingly saw their world as "modern" and modernity as a cultural, social, and political entity utterly distinct from everything that had gone before. To the modern sensibility it was clear that the distant past was irrelevant and that the future would be decided by a debate not between the polis and the liberal nation-state, but between the liberal state and the socialist state. Marx's revolutionary vision of class struggle seemed to many to have demonstrated "scientifically" and "objectively" why the classical past was utterly foreign to the present: antiquity as a whole was charac-

17. On the Nietzsche–Wilamowitz-Moellendorff debate, see Steve Nimis, "Fussnoten: Das Fundament der Wissenschaft," *Arethusa* 17, no. 2 (1984): 105–33.
18. See the essays collected in Culham and Edmunds, *Classics*.

terized by a mode of production that had been decisively ousted by
modern capitalist productive systems. Furthermore, the concern of
the classical polis with "the virtue of the citizen" was shown to be epiphenomenal and ideological. The reality of history was economic: the
evolution of modes of production and the struggle for the control of
its means. Real politics was concerned with the distribution of the surplus value of labor, not with pseudo-issues such as civic education. Despite Marx's own classical training, the considerable effort that Engels
put into revising the theories of Carl Bachhoven regarding the organization of the ancient family, and the respect for classical education on
the part of twentieth-century Marxists Georg Lukács and Antonio
Gramsci, the polis and its experience of politics was consigned to the
ashheap of history.

Opponents of Marxism quickly learned to discuss the modern
world in equally materialist and "realist" terms, arguing that liberalism, with its focus on the market and the individual, was a more natural and efficient system for distributing the scarce resources of wealth,
liberties, and power. Most Marxists and liberals tended to ignore the
Athenian democratic ideal of open communal debate and collective
decision making in favor of an elite-dominated political order based
on secrecy and hierarchy: for the Marxist it was the Communist party
as vanguard, for the liberal cold warrior it was "democratic elitism"
justified by some version of Robert Michels's "iron law of oligarchy."
The aim of education in both cases was efficiency, not civic identity;
the primary desired product was a producer and consumer of goods,
rather than an actively participatory citizen. In these visions of politics
and education, the classics and Athenian democracy had no real
place.[19] Thus, for a century or more, professional classicists turned
away from the world of debate about politics, and the world returned
the favor by turning its back on the classical past.

But, to put it mildly, times have changed. The party as vanguard
has been thoroughly discredited, and with the end of the Cold War,
democratic elitism no longer seems the only alternative to it. We have
moved from a future-oriented modernist world into a postmodernism
that has become hyperaware of the multiplicity of ways in which the
historical present is composed of overlapping citations and iterations
of the past. The great socialist dream of the late nineteenth and early
twentieth centuries has now to confront the reality of the suffering

19. On democratic elitism, see, e.g., Peter Bachrach, ed., *Political Elites in a Democracy* (New
York: Atherton, 1971). An important exception to this generalization is the concern with
ideas such as *phronesis* and *praxis* by "neo-Aristotelians" such as Martha Nussbaum, Alasdair
MacIntyre, Jürgen Habermas, and Hans Georg Gadamer.

caused by the entrenched elites who were to have led the ignorant masses to a future utopia.[20] Meanwhile, liberal democracy, victorious over its secular rival, faces a crisis of faith in its own ideals, confronted as it is with seemingly intractable problems of poverty, drugs, meaningless work, industrial stagnation, homelessness, environmental degradation, racial and sexual discrimination, random and not so random violence, rising crime rates, unconscionable disparities of wealth, and not least, the disrepute of public education. But if beating the enemy has not led to a well-ordered society and if the Marxian dream (at least in its original form) has failed, where is liberalism to find the interlocutor with which it might work dialogically toward new solutions? Reenter the polis and Athens.

They are available because some areas of classical studies in the second half of the twentieth century have changed almost as thoroughly as the world itself. Probably quite coincidentally, beginning in the mid-1970s, there has been a major resurgence in the study of the history of democratic Athens by professional classicists.[21] Both classical Athenian institutions and ideologies are being investigated with renewed vigor. Part of this renaissance can be traced to the discovery of new sources of evidence, notably the mass of inscriptions that have come to light in the American excavations of the Athenian agora, part of it to the reassessment of well-known sources of evidence (comedy, tragedy, and the corpus of political and legal speeches by classical Athenian orators) in light of new analytic paradigms. These new paradigms stress the evolution and practical function of institutions, the experience and identity of the citizen, and sociocultural discourse, not motives and doings of putative "leaders" or "parties."[22] Moreover, classical historians have of late become more self-consciously interdisciplinary. It is now much more common for sober-minded classicists to cite sociological and anthropological studies, literary and political theory—both as *comparanda* and as a source of analytic models.[23] A

20. See John Dunn, "Property, Justice, and the Common Good after Socialism," in *Transitions to Modernity: Essays on Power, Wealth, and Belief,* ed. John A. Hall and I. C. Jarvie (Cambridge: Cambridge University Press, 1992), 281–96.

21. For good summaries, see R. K. Sinclair, *Democracy and Participation in Athens* (Cambridge: Cambridge University Press, 1988), and Mogens H. Hansen, *The Athenian Democracy in the Age of Demosthenes: Structure, Principles, and Ideology* (Oxford: Blackwell, 1991).

22. E.g., Moses I. Finley, *Politics in the Ancient World* (Cambridge: Cambridge University Press, 1983); Christian Meier, *The Greek Discovery of Politics,* trans. David McLintock (Cambridge: Harvard University Press, 1990), original German ed. (1980); and Josiah Ober, *Mass and Elite in Democratic Athens: Rhetoric, Ideology, and The Power of the People* (Princeton: Princeton University Press, 1989).

23. Sarah C. Humphreys, *Anthropology and the Greeks* (London: Routledge and Kegan Paul, 1978) led the way, at least in the English-speaking world. Cf., more recently, Philip Brook

few historians of classical Athens have attempted to reenter the intellectual mainstream, by suggesting that the study of the classical polis
has something important to say to citizens of postmodern, postliberal,
postsocialist states and societies. At the same time, several scholars
who are not professional classicists have produced serious assessments
of the classical polis and its relationship to modern society.[24] Athens
and its political thought hardly provide a biblical vocabulary for progressive thinking about democracy today, but its importance tran-
scends its position as the first link in the historical chain of democratic
practices and ideas in western political and intellectual traditions.[25]

III

The critique of democratic Athens is often as much a "projection"
as the more positive view of Athens being criticized. "Athens," then, is
a politically contested idea as well as a historically defined entity—
which helps explain why debates over reform of the British Parliament and the French Revolution found conservatives criticizing the
politics of their own day in terms of the excesses of democratic Athens
and why *The Federalist Papers* did likewise to justify their redefinition
of republicanism and the need for a distant federal government.[26]
The critical influence of contemporary political debates on the
construction of the classical past can be seen in the present controversy over Martin Bernal's argument that "the" classical tradition
was reshaped by nineteenth-century racialists and anti-Semites as a

Manville, *The Origins of Citizenship in Ancient Athens* (Princeton: Princeton University Press,
1990), and Barry S. Strauss, *Fathers and Sons in Classical Athens* (Princeton: Princeton University Press, 1993).

24. Moses I. Finley, *Democracy Ancient and Modern* (New Brunswick: Rutgers University
Press, 1973) was innovative in this respect (and others). See also Mogens H. Hansen, *Was
Athens a Democracy? Popular Rule, Liberty, and Equality in Ancient and Modern Political Thought*
(Copenhagen: Royal Danish Academy of Sciences and Letters, 1989), and Kurt A. Raaflaub,
"Democracy, Oligarchy, and the Concept of the 'Free Citizen' in Late Fifth-Century Athens,"
Political Theory 11 (1983): 517–44. Notable works by nonclassicists: I. F. Stone, *The Trial of
Socrates* (New York: Doubleday, 1988); Eli Sagan, *The Honey and the Hemlock: Democracy and
Paranoia in Ancient Athens and Modern America* (New York: Basic Books, 1991); J. Peter Euben,
The Tragedy of Political Theory: The Road Not Taken (Princeton: Princeton University Press,
1990); and Orlando Patterson, *Freedom in the Making of Western Culture*, vol. 1 of *Freedom* (New
York: Basic Books, 1991).

25. In this respect, our emphasis differs from the more historicist treatment of the Athenian contribution to "democracy" that appears in John Dunn, ed., *Democracy: The Unfinished
Journey, 508 B.C. to A.D. 1993* (Oxford: Oxford University Press, 1992).

26. See the discussion in Frank M. Turner, *The Classical Heritage in Victorian Britain* (New
Haven: Yale University Press, 1981), chaps. 1 and 5, and *The Federalist Papers*, nos. 8–10, 14,
55, 63.

justification and consequence of European economic and military hegemony.[27]

Our own political agenda in this book has two aims. The first is to challenge the co-optation of classical political theory by conservatives who use that theory to denigrate Athenian democracy. We want to recontextualize the work of Classical Theorists by reading them with and against a living democratic tradition to which they owe substantial debts, even in critique. The second is to insist on the significance of classical political theory and Athenian democracy for contemporary democracy against the position that *both* need to be "de-privileged" as part of a system of white male cultural hegemony insensitive to or dismissive of the contributions or voices of women and "people of color." Such critics too often assume that the readings of classical texts found in canonists whose politics they oppose (such as Allan Bloom) are in fact canonical and that such readings justify dismissing those texts.[28] This attitude not only hypostatizes texts; it ignores the way canons change, thereby discouraging historical studies of how, why, and by whom a particular text is canonized. There is an odd symmetry between the Plato-loving, Athens-hating conservatives who abstract their canonical texts from the context of real politics and their anti-Plato, anti-Athens critics who assume that ancient political thinkers and practices were part of a homogeneously unregenerate ideological system.

Hypostatizing canonical texts has the paradoxical consequence of underestimating the contribution to our appreciation of Athenian democracy and classical political thought which critics, including those from the perspectives of Marxism, feminism, poststructuralism, and gay studies, have made. Criticism of the masculine warrior ethic in the *Iliad* and Pericles' Funeral Oration, studies of the homoerotic dimension of Athenian citizenship as well as the play of *eros* in Platonic dialogues, debate over Plato's attitude toward women in the *Republic* and Aristotle's division of household and polis in the *Politics*, have inspired more textured, resourceful, and inventive appreciations of those texts.[29] Similarly, challenges to Athenian democracy as being "based

27. See Martin Bernal, *Black Athena* (New Brunswick: Rutgers University Press, 1987), and "Black Athena Denied: The Tyranny of Germany over Greece and the Rejection of the Afroasiatic Roots of Europe, 1780–1980," *Comparative Criticism* 8 (1986): 3–70.

28. As Henry Louis Gates, Jr., put it in "Campus Forum on Multiculturalism," *New York Times*, December 9, 1990, E5: "After all the shouting is over, is it too much to hope that the real conversation, long deferred, may begin?"

29. See David M. Halperin, John J. Winkler, and Froma I. Zeitlin, eds., *Before Sexuality: The Construction of Erotic Experience in the Ancient Greek World* (Princeton: Princeton University Press, 1990), and the provocative debate between Gregory Vlastos and Mary Lefkowitz on

on" slavery, mysogyny, and a discrepancy between formal equality and informal inequalities have led to more historically attentive interpretations of Athens, which will again, paradoxically, permit a more realistic referent for educating us about democracy and about educating democracy itself. Thus, our appeal to Athenian democracy constitutes more a set of guidelines than a political program, one that will help us find our way between a moral relativism that disables judgment and a philosophical absolutism that insulates it from history.[30]

To acknowledge that our book has a politics is not to claim that everything is always political. Nor is it to claim that we can dispense with the search for evidence because such endeavors are all ideological anyway; for lack of respect for evidence leads to two kinds of error. One is mining the past for what is useful and relevant instead of permitting past practices and thought to interrogate our own (including our emphasis on relevance and our conception of use). The second is positing some transcendent moment that we can use to disparage our own time for it lacks luster compared with "the glory that was Greece." To acknowledge our politics is to claim what thinkers (from Plato and Machiavelli to Nietzsche, Michel Foucault, and historians concerned with the debate over the Ancestral Constitution in Athens and over the Ancient Constitution in England) have recognized: that every construction of the past, every story told, origin uncovered, or telos invoked, is partly strategic. Present political concerns shape any reading of the past (as well as how the idea of a past is understood), and readings of the past are part of contemporary controversies about collective identity.

A political education is not the same as a politicized one, any more than the cultivation of judgment can be equated with indoctrination, or educational blueprints can produce independent thinkers and citizens. The Socrates of Plato's *Apology* helps make these distinctions. He tells us that he roams the streets talking to anyone he meets, whether slave or free, man or woman, using everyday language, trying to get them to think about the moral and political implications and presuppositions of what they are doing. He goes to the men of political power and to the men with cultural power, the poets, only to discover that they know less than they suppose and that they exaggerate the signifi-

Plato and feminism: Gregory Vlastos, "Was Plato a Feminist?" *Times Literary Supplement*, March 17–23, 1989, 276, 288–89; Mary Lefkowitz, "Only the Best Girls Get To," ibid., May 5–11, 1989, 484, 497.

30. For related perspectives on how to appropriate the past in general and our ancient Greek ancestors in particular, see Clifford Geertz, "The Uses of Diversity," *Michigan Quarterly Review* (Winter 1986): 105–23, and Bernard Williams, *Shame and Necessity* (Berkeley and Los Angeles: University of California Press, 1993).

cance of what they do know. Yet even as he does all this, he denies that he is a teacher. In part that is because others assume that teachers have doctrines in the sense he does not and because his claim that the unexamined life is not worth living precludes having someone accept any doctrine, even that one, without reflection. In this book, we propound a conception of democratic political education that is committed to this Socratic enterprise, however difficult and allusive it may be (which is perhaps part of its point).

The question of political identity in the United States has special urgency now because of three developments, two largely national, the other international. The first is the rise of the politics of identity, in which "identity" is seen as an unstable amalgam of particular identities based on race, class, ethnicity, gender, and sexual preferences and in which "citizen" is regarded as a suspect abstraction. From this perspective, every "we" must be explicit about who is included and what is privileged and who or what is not; every polarity (such as those between male and female, gay and straight, writing and speech) must be "deconstructed" to reveal the hierarchy it disguises; and every boundary must be scrutinized for its construction of a center and a norm that marginalizes those pushed to the periphery and outside the normal.

The second—in part an extension of, in part a reaction to, the first—is the emergence of the new "communitarian movement" dedicated, in Amitai Etzioni's words, to "an awakening of values, of caring and commitment."[31] Concerned with the sorry state of our public life, the unchecked greed of the 1980s, the increase in crime, recession, drugs, broken families, and voter apathy and inspired by Robert Bellah and his colleagues' *Habits of the Heart*, these communitarians talk about balancing rights with responsibilities and call for sacrifice, social renewal, and "moral education" in the schools.[32] Whatever the dangers of the movement, there is no denying its influence on President Clinton's rhetoric and programs (such as the proposal for national service) or the fact that in proclaiming the need for the revitalization of citizenship, it has touched a responsive chord beyond the academics and lawyers who initated the movement.

31. For a statement of the communitarian agenda, see Amitai Etzioni, *The Spirit of Community: Rights, Responsibilities, and the Communitarian Agenda* (New York: Crown, 1993). On these issues, see also Robert Booth Fowler, *The Dance with Community: The Contemporary Debate in American Political Thought* (Lawrence: University of Kansas Press, 1991).

32. Robert M. Bellah et al., *Habits of the Heart: Individualism and Commitment in American Life* (Berkeley and Los Angeles: University of California Press, 1985).

The third development, already alluded to, is the end of the Cold War and the growth of democratic movements in Eastern Europe, South Africa, and China. For at least fifty years "we" Americans have defined ourselves in terms of antagonisms and alliances and by the fact that we were not totalitarian and communist. But this definition has lost its point and hold. Although some revel in the triumph of "West over East" as a victory of goodness over evil and see the United States as the apotheosis of history, that very triumph contributes to a crisis of national identity. And while the takeover of democratic movements by raw nationalisms, free-market ideology, and bureaucratic imperatives can hardly leave one complacent about the prospects for democracy in Eastern Europe, still, the democratic revolutions there and elsewhere have unsettled the easy assumption that we are, to adapt Seymour Martin Lipset's phrase from the 1960s, "the good democracy itself in operation."[33] These events, together with the rise (and partial fall) of deconstruction, bring into question the fundamental assumptions that have shaped western thought since the Enlightenment and open the possibility of turning back, without nostalgia, to pre-Enlightenment traditions.

The challenge to respect difference posed by the politics of identity, the dissolution of the admittedly tepid unity rendered by the Cold War, and examples of democratic activism abroad provide an opportunity to pose, and have taken seriously, questions first raised by the Athenians: What is involved in being a citizen of a democratic polity? How does a democratic culture provide the experience of and education for democratic politics? If we take these questions as primary, our first concern about the process and substance of any decision should be whether it enhances or diminishes the capacity of democratic citizens to take their place in the deliberative forums of their society and share the responsibility of sovereignty.

To make these questions and issues central to our public life would itself be an important step in democratizing it. Analyzing the origins of the polis, Jean-Pierre Vernant describes how politics became a public matter as decisions affecting the whole were brought before the people rather than remaining the private preserve of kings, priests, and nobles. Where the city had been centered around a royal palace ringed by fortifications, it was now centered on the agora, the common space and public hearth where problems of general interest to the entire community could be debated. (Of course, the "entire" community did not encompass women, slaves, and metics.) This redefini-

33. Seymour Martin Lipset, *Political Man* (New York: Doubleday, 1960), 403.

tion of public space was also a redefinition of mental space; the expansion of who could talk and the multiplication of places where such talk could occur was matched by an enlargement of what could be talked about. As the public domain emerged as an area of common interest and an arena for public discussions (rather than secret or private ones), there was a progressive appropriation by the people as a whole (i.e., by male citizens) of the conduct, knowledge, and procedures that originally were the exclusive prerogative of the kings and nobles who held power.[34] As knowledge, values, and techniques became elements of a common culture, and thus submitted to public criticism and controversy, and as those who exercised authority were subject to a rendering of accounts (*euthunai*), public life became more democratic and more politicized. If, despite the best intentions of those who, like President Clinton, invoke Jefferson's belief that every new generation of Americans must construct their identity anew, our politics is in danger of becoming the preserve of postmodern kings and priests, of professors, professionals, and media mavens, and not the subject of widespread public debate—if fewer things are brought before the commons and more are claimed as the exclusive domain of experts who reappropriate knowledge while forming a caste of initiates—then we may be in danger of reversing the democratizing process that distinguished Athenian political development.

Athenian political practice and the philosophers who were sometimes critical of it agreed that the quality of public life and the possibility of political wisdom depended on the quality and accessibility of education. They disagreed (how much is in dispute) about where, how, and when such education should take place and who was capable of learning what from whom. In Plato's *Republic*, Socrates claims that only a few rare individuals can be educated sufficiently to possess knowledge and be wise rulers; the masses must be instructed, as much as possible, by whatever means are useful. Though it too relied on hierarchy (built on polarities between men and women, slave and free, Hellene and barbarian), Athenian practice assumed that thousands of ordinary citizens with no specialized knowledge or professional education could set a rational policy for a complex city-state. It also assumed that political education in the sense of the cultivation of the wisdom, character, and judgment necessary for political deliberation and debate came from the living of a public life, including participation in religious festivals, in the armed forces, and as spectators in

34. Jean-Pierre Vernant, *The Origins of Greek Thought* (Ithaca: Cornell University Press, 1982), 51–52.

the theater. Herodotus suggests that the sharing of power in Athens gave it a singular energy and freedom and that civic responsibility and lawfulness were as much the consequence of citizen participation as a precondition for it.[35]

One contemporary response to this vision is, as we have already seen, to deny that Athens was a direct democracy either because of its exclusion or because it is a myth invented by those who value political activity highly. Another is to admit that Athens was a direct democracy and either criticize it for being overly democratic and illiberal or insist that because of historical differences, what it was is of no particular relevance to what we are or could be. Whatever the role of the common man may have been in the simple world of the Greek city-state, goes that line of argument, ordinary people cannot now handle the political issues that confront a modern polity, particularly one of our size and responsibilities.

It is true that, at least on the surface and in some ways, the political issues confronting us are more complex than those confronting the ordinary Athenian. Yet it is not clear that the public life of the city-state was simpler in the political dilemmas it faced: whether to go to war in some far-off land; how to lessen the inequalities between, or reconcile, the rich and poor; how to decide on who could be a citizen and what that status entailed; how far democratic practices such as rotation in office and selection by lot should extend, how to administer an empire. What Athenians did not have was a complex technology and an intricate, corporate-dominated economy based on highly sophisticated instruments of credit. Although such issues require expertise and professional education, they are largely technical matters, whereas the wisdom, judgment, and character necessary to judge their importance or place is not. (The question of whether there is a technique of politics analogous to the expertise of medicine or shoe-making is a major issue in the Platonic dialogues.)

The argument against the people governing themselves rests on the claim or assumption that they are too irrational, narrowly self-interested, or ignorant to do so. Yet if one looks at Watergate and Irangate and the Savings and Loan scandal, critically examines our Vietnam or Iraq policies, or concentrates on the subtexts of George Bush's Willie Horton ad, Dan Quayle's comments on Murphy Brown and criticisms of the cultural elite, or Pat Buchanan's speech at the 1992 Republican National Convention, one might wonder where irrationalism and

35. Herodotus is discussing the origins of democratic practices in the reform of Cleisthenes and the defeat of the Spartan proxies. See also the argument by Otanes in Herodotus *Histories* 3.80–83.

narrow self-interest lie. If political leaders teach by example as well as by precept, who is primarily responsible for the problems that plague American public life? Perhaps here, as at Athens, the greatest political abuses are those perpetrated by the "responsible elites." Surely the failure of those elites should make us uneasy with their complaints about the people "overloading the system" because they want economic equality and direct participation and about "value-oriented intellectuals" who are a "challenge to democratic government which is, potentially at least, as serious as those posed in the past by aristocratic cliques, fascist movements and communist parties."[36] The uneasiness grows when we remember that those who claimed to be responsible elites in Eastern Europe and the Soviet Union dismissed *their* "value-oriented intellectuals," who eventually led (as in Czechoslovakia) or aided (in Poland and East Germany) the revolutions our responsible elites now celebrate.

Because politics is not equivalent to state action and is found in other places or sites such as local governments, social movements, neighborhood associations, battered women's shelters, the New Highlander Center in Appalachia, or wherever there are publics, the appropriation of Athenian democracy and classical political theory could challenge the undemocratic aspects of our democratic institutions and discourse and alert us to democratic experiments in our midst and in our past.

If we could suspend our tendency to regard ourselves as the culmination of all that went before, we might allow Athenian thought and practice to disturb those "necessary" features of modernity or postmodernity by politicizing them in the sense that they are matters amenable to human design. For instance, insofar as the Greeks thought that political education involves the living of a public life— that people seek to participate in order to be seen and heard by others with whom they share power and assume responsibility and that there are intrinsic rewards to such participation because it promotes an enlarged understanding of common predicaments—they make us a little less comfortable about defending the "need" for apathy.

We should not minimize either the difficulty of educating democracy or the failures of democratic experiences (including that of Athens). The draw of democracy as an order of governance, a field of cultures, and a plurality of ethics is both a promise and a set of possibilities. The promise is that, when the people decide, their judgment

36. Trilateral Commission, *Crisis of Democracy*, 7.

is practically effective, politically sound, and morally defensible. Yet we know, as critics have been eager enough to emphasize, that the people may, as individuals and as a collectivity, fall short of the promise. Putative democrats have bridged this gap between promise and practice by relying on a set of categories such as false consciousness, manufactured consent, and the "general will," by setting themselves a task of "forcing" people to be free, by providing moral tutelage, or by ascribing to themselves a place in a vanguard party in a transitional state. The task, instead, should be to keep faith with democracy by acknowledging the gap between promise and practice without succumbing to the elitist temptations to close it. Educating democracy is crucial to this task. Such an education would mandate the study of the history of democratic experience (for both its exemplars and object lessons) and the elaboration of a democratic tradition in which Athens prominently figures.

Insofar as democracy rests on majority rule or a collective will, it seems inimicable to the authority of critical intelligence that is often associated with education. And insofar as Tocqueville was right that democracy rests on an equality that isolates individuals from the beliefs and practices of their predecessors, it seems that the idea of a "democratic tradition" is oxymoronic. Yet in the "art of association" particularly characteristic of American democracy, Tocqueville thought he found a partial remedy for this animus against critical intelligence and the excesses of democratic equality. Here was an experience that would connect citizens in endeavors that, however small or narrowly self-interested their beginnings, might issue in an enlarged sensibility that enabled Americans to resist the despotism of state and society. Here men and women would not merely market their self-interest in cloistered lobbies; they could learn to deliberate about the shared predicaments that confronted their communities, thereby learning responsibility in the exercise of power while thinking more critically about their status as citizens. Because democratic citizens are not infallible, such deliberations must be continuous. Because they are different, disagreement and conflict always are the heart of politics rather than a pathology to be remedied. Political deliberation is always a complex process of negotiation.[37] All the more essential, then, that democrats be able to draw on traditions of critical reasoning and on previous democratic practices, including Greek political thought and Athenian political practice.

37. Of late, enthusiastic references to "democratic deliberation" have proliferated in the scholarly literature of political theory, but what its authors mean by the phrase differs at various points from what we mean.

A direct way for democratic societies to educate themselves, and help constitute a democratic tradition, is studying other societies that took democracy seriously in order to discover how specific social practices inhibited or developed democratic virtue and what material circumstances best realize the ideals of freedom, equality, and the sharing of power. The sustained study of such states, however incompletely democratic or otherwise flawed they may be, may enhance democracy's capacity for justice by chastening its potential for arrogance.

Self-education also requires critical appreciation of those scholars who have celebrated or chastised various aspects of Athenian democracy, even when one disagrees with the politics and (often implicit) historical assumptions of their positions. It means reading Leo Strauss and Alasdair MacIntyre, who have used the antidemocratic attitudes of Athenian theorists against the democratic politics of the city, arguing that democratic excesses and moral relativism destroyed the aristocratic traditions essential for maintaining Athenian freedom and power, as well as Moses Finley, who honors the widespread participation of ordinary Athenians rather than the philosophical discourse of democracy's critics.[38] It involves reading Hannah Arendt's celebration of Athenian greatness, which she uses dramatically to reveal the bureaucratic structure of the administrative state as well as the banality or superfluity of life such a state requires, as well as Nicole Loraux, who finds, in the speech of Pericles that Arendt most admires, the source of continued domination of aristocratic ideals over the demos.[39] Each of these writers has broadened our awareness of Athenian democracy and, so, of our own and has in that regard provided an example for this book.

IV

The editors of this book outlined these ideas to those writers who have contributed essays to it, but in asking for their good work we prescribed no constraints on their subject matter, analytic categories,

38. See Leo Strauss, *The City and Man* (Chicago: University of Chicago Press, 1964); Alasdair MacIntyre, *After Virtue: A Study in Moral Theory*, 2d ed. (Notre Dame: University of Notre Dame Press, 1984), and *Whose Justice? Which Rationality?* (Notre Dame: University of Notre Dame Press, 1988); and Finley, *Politics in the Ancient World* and *Democracy Ancient and Modern*.

39. Hannah Arendt, *The Human Condition* (Chicago: University of Chicago Press, 1958); Nicole Loraux, *The Invention of Athens: The Funeral Oration in the Classical City*, trans. Alan Sheridan (1981; Cambridge: Harvard University Press, 1986).

or perspectives. The diversity of perspectives and concerns in these
essays constitutes their response. A volume of such contributions presents special problems of unity and diversity. Our commonality derives from our belief that critical thinking about the myriad facets of
Athenian political thought can help reconstitute our own and that
contemporary political conservatives have wrongfully claimed the virtues of Athenian practices and thought as their own. In addition, the
contributors all reject anachronistic praise that undervalues the distinctiveness of our practical problems and intellectual choices, ignores
the democratic aspects of our democracy, and uncritically or ahistori-
cally reifies Athens as a model. And finally, we all eschew a pro-
gressivist romanticism that exaggerates that distinctiveness as a way of
insulating America from the critiques of our democratic insufficiencies which taking Athenian democracy seriously can provide. But we
have carried out this shared impulse and commitment differently.
Some essays (such as those of Rocco and Lane and Lane) have taken
classical themes or ideas as the occasion to reflect on contemporary
texts or ideas. Others (Raaflaub, Hedrick) have focused on classical
materials and largely confined their contemporary concerns to allusions. Still others have explicitly compared ancient and modern democracy. Most essays deal with political and social aspects of Athenian
democracy, but a few (Monoson and Euben) deal with classical political theory. Readers will find as much discord as harmony, but discord,
as Marx said, defines democracy.

The essays (unbeknown to the contributors) have fallen into three
categories. In the first, "Democracy and Regimes of Power," belong
essays that situate the Athenian democracy in relation to various regimes of power: the imperial power of fifth-century Athens, the
forms of government contemplated by the framers of the American
Constitution, democratic political orders as conventionally understood
through history, and the order of constitutionalism itself. Three of
the four authors in Part I have explored how Athenian democracy
affected the conscience of later politicians and theorists, forcing them
to contrast, if not oppose, their own political orders to it. All show
how our engagement with Athenian democracy creates critical perspectives on subsequent political orders that claim in one way or another to be democratic. Exploring the meaning of Athenian democracy as these authors have—in terms of its own significations and
those of its subsequent reconstructions—illustrates the particular and
contingent character of later democracies. It disturbs conventional
understandings of what makes them democratic and provokes reflection not only on Athenian democracy itself but also on what other
past, present, or future democracies might involve.

Sheldon Wolin, in "Norm and Form: The Constitutionalizing of Democracy," points out how modern conceptions and practices of democracy typically constrain, more than enhance, the actual exercise of popular political power. He finds that modern democracies have domesticated our memory of ancient democracy by envisioning it as a threat to institutional stability and the power of elites. But he goes on to claim that one of the reasons that Athenian democracy is so troubling to theorists of contemporary democratic regimes is that the wellsprings of democracy, particularly those of fifth-century Athens, overflow and undermine any institutionalization of democracy. Democracy bears within it a moment of revolution, and Wolin argues that for any political order to remain genuinely democratic, it must nurture, rather than suppress, the seeds of its own transformation. Democracy violates constitutions, and constitutional democracies need to welcome their own violation if they would continue to be democratic.

In the two essays that follow, Ellen Wood and Jennifer Roberts unravel important aspects of the vexed traditions of the ideas of democracy in general and of Athenian democracy in particular. Wood's "Democracy: An Idea of Ambiguous Ancestry" reveals the dual ancestry of modern conceptions of democracy. The original one is indeed Athenian. It emphasizes both the power of the DEMOS, which signified the ordinary citizenry, and the POWER of the *demos*, namely, its ability to exercise actual political authority. The more recent ancestry is, by way of Victorian liberals such as George Grote and John Stuart Mill, the memory of Athenian democracy recomposed in a favorable frame. It presupposes the alienation of actual political authority from the demos and its transferral to a representative elite. This conceptualization of democracy made it compatible with capitalist social relations. The Athenian conception, by contrast, cannot readily complement such social relations, and Wood suggests that remembering democracy's Greek origins can foster a democratic critique of capitalism.

Roberts notes how the tension between ancient and modern democracy was exploited in the rhetoric of early American republicanism. In "The Creation of a Legacy: A Manufactured Crisis in Eighteenth-Century Thought," she highlights the ways in which eighteenth-century theorists of modern republics, particularly that of the United States, justified their fear of contemporary democrats by portraying ancient democracy in a particularly unflattering light. Democracy, in the view of modern republicans, threatened stability, and so their portrayal of Athenian democracy became a metonym for what they feared. She notes that calmer times and less anxious politicians have

been responsible for picturing Athenian democracy as a more stable
and exemplary political order. Her essay points out how understandings of the past wear the colors of the present and raises the question
of how the historical understanding of Athenian democracy actually
factored in the minds of the American Framers, as well as how it
might educate our own democracies today.

Kurt Raaflaub's essay, "Democracy, Power, and Imperialism in
Fifth-Century Athens," adds an interesting twist to these three narra-
tives and arguments. The previous writers see the memory of Athenian democracy challenging the authority and legitimacy of contemporary elites and regimes. Raaflaub shows how the historical
conditions of the emergence of Athenian democracy indeed reveal
the extraordinary dynamism of an empowered citizenry that successfully challenged the more oligarchic practices of its predecessor.
But he also points out the linkage of this dynamism to expansive imperialism. His article challenges those who would equate Athenian democracy with a naturally pacific or automatically salutary way of life.

The next set of essays, grouped under the heading " Critical Discourse in Athenian Democracy," explores how discourse in democratic Athens displayed an awareness of democracy's limitations. In
the 1950s, A. H. M. Jones shaped the way that many still view critical
discourse in Athenian democracy when he stated that Athens lacked
any democratic theory or theorist.[40] That encouraged the view that
the Athenian democracy—in part because it *was* democratic—was insufficiently self-critical. But the essays in Part II show in different
ways how the critical discourse of Athens was not simply antidemocratic. In "How to Criticize Democracy in Late Fifth- and Fourth-Century Athens," Josiah Ober notes that one of democracy's virtues is its
revisability, or capacity to reform itself. He argues that this feature
not only fosters institutional adaptation but also depends on the existence of critical outsiders. Employing interpretive tools provided by
J. L. Austin, Antonio Gramsci, and Michel Foucault, he shows how
elite texts from ancient Athens that typically are read as antidemocratic tracts function also as part of democracy's own literature of
resistance. In our age, one that has been characterized by "the disappearance of the outside," the critical discourses of Athenian democracy can then be read not as a storehouse of antidemocratic views but
as a set of rich resources for resisting hegemony and renewing democracy. They may well have performed that function in their own
time; they certainly can do so now.

Sara Monoson and Peter Euben venture into the belly of the whale

40. Jones, *Athenian Democracy.*

to point out the democratic potential in critical discourse that traditionally is viewed as virulently antidemocratic. Although Plato has often been condemned as the founder of totalitarian thought, Monoson
finds him, in a variety of his dialogues, honoring that eternal enemy
of totalitarianism, free and frank speech (*parrhēsia*). In "Frank Speech,
Democracy, and Philosophy: Plato's Debt to a Democratic Strategy of
Civic Discourse," she notes how parrhesia often served as a code word
for democracy in the more conventional discourse of Athens, and
then she proceeds to identify how Plato dialogically positions that idea
in a way that almost transforms it into an ideal. Her essay makes one
wonder whether Plato had democratic skeletons in his closet. Euben
also focuses on Plato. In "Democracy and Political Theory: A Reading
of Plato's *Gorgias*," Euben points out how Socrates' opposition to the
characters and views of both Gorgias and Callicles actually reveals the
conditions of a kind of democratic dialogue that Athens had not realized. He notes how the harsh criticism of the Athenians' political
heroes by Plato's Socrates seriously criticizes Athenian democracy on
one level but, on another, elevates our understanding of its greatest
potential.

The last essays are grouped under the category "Athenian Ideals
and Contemporary Issues." They create more direct dialogues between the discourse of Athenian democracy and that of contemporary
practices and thought by comparing texts and perspectives of Athenian democracy with critical or established paradigms of modernity,
politics, and America. Christopher Rocco's "The Tragedy of Critical
Theory" opens this dialogue by showing the porousness of the boundaries between Athenian thought and our own. Within Max Horkheimer and Theodor Adorno's seminal text of Critical Theory, *Dialectic of Enlightenment*, Rocco reveals a wide array of express and indirect
resonances with central themes of Athenian tragedies. Not only does
he find these German-Jewish philosophers echoing the content of
Sophocles' critique of Oedipus's arrogant rationalism in their own
text, written during the ascendance of Hitler's Reich. He also points
out how the formal structure and language of *Dialectic of Enlightenment*, like that of many Greek tragedies, undermines all discourses of
closure, which in our time range from those of "the systems of bureaucratic domination and economic production of late capitalism" to
those of "method, technique, and calculative reason." Yet even as he
identifies resemblances between these works, Rocco acknowledges the
differences in their form, content, and temporality. For this text of
Critical Theory, like the tragedies of the ancient Greeks, assures us
only that with suffering will wisdom come.

Three essays address directly the exclusions of democracy—in both ancient Athens and contemporary democracies. Barry Strauss makes exclusion the centerpiece of his essay, "The Melting Pot, the Mosaic, and the Agora," taking the reader on an extraordinary voyage into the terrain of multiculturalism. Does cultural unity require the domination of minorities? Did the Athenians only hold their political community together by purifying their democracy? Strauss begins by noting the anxiety among various Americans that the old melting pot is cracking under the weight of new immigration, new assertions of ethnic identity, and new intellectual emphases on cultural diversity. For some Americans these developments threaten the possibility of shared participation in a common life. He reflects on how the unity of Athenian democracy has been attributed to its racial and cultural homogeneity, signified by the Athenians references to themselves as "autochthonous"—self-generated from the earth, from nowhere or no one else. Modern beliefs about the autochthony of ancient Athenians have bolstered the arguments of those who believe that we can find political unity only if we don cultural blinders. Strauss acknowledges the exclusionary features of Athenian democracy. Not only were women, slaves, and metics subjugated; their subjugation was crucial for the exclusivity of citizenship. But he shows how Cleisthenes' democratic reforms, which mixed together Athenians from various tribes and traditions in a new political framework, drew strength from a civic myth of autochthony that diminished the potential for cultural domination. By positing this mythical picture of their essential cultural and political origins, Athenians constructed a vision of themselves that removed the privileged status of any particular cultural group. The myth indeed was ideological; it disguised the actual diversity of the Athenians and probably contributed to later efforts to eliminate the opportunities for naturalized citizenship. But it also indicates that the Athenians had no "natural" cultural unity and that their commonality, though artificial, was not thereby weakened. Strauss allows himself to hope that we might find some myths of community, similarly unnatural, to create a more harmoniously heterogeneous democratic society that is essentially enriched by no single culture but by many.

Like Strauss, Warren Lane and Ann Lane find surprising resources in ancient Greek thought for enriching equality and diversity in our society. In recent years, Athenian culture has frequently symbolized the ineradicably patriarchal character of western civilization. Feminists have sought to emphasize the many ways in which Athenian texts and practices degrade the experiences of women. But in "Athenian Political Thought and the Feminist Politics of Poiesis and Praxis," the Lanes point out that much feminist discourse operates within its own

set of limitations, many of which stem from the more immediate ideological context of liberalism. They argue that the Aristotelian discourse of praxis, as opposed to poiesis, can be used to invigorate contemporary feminism. Within that variegated discourse, writers and
activists often emphasize the importance of "caretaking" and "networking." But at times these emphases carry with them assumptions
about the relative permanence of social hierarchies that consign these
activities to subordinate social roles. Without denying Aristotle's thor-
oughgoing prejudices against women, Lane and Lane indicate how
the Aristotelian discourse of "doing" rather than " making" can provide a critical, egalitarian perspective on these feminist practices, helping them to avoid the reproduction of social structures they otherwise
would transform.

Charles Hedrick is much more skeptical than either Strauss or the
Lanes about the capacity of Athenian discourse or practice to provide
positive aid for rethinking and renewing our democratic society. He
points out that the internal exclusions from the privilege of full citizenship in the Athenian democracy—women, "slaves," and metics—
were not unfortunate imperfections of an essentially estimable political community. Instead, he argues that the notions of freedom, equality, and citizenship were generated by and with their opposites: slavery (and slaves), difference (the inequalities experienced by women),
and foreigner (non-Athenian–born Athenian workers, i.e., metics).
Using the language and theory of Aristotle as his basis for evaluation,
he maintains that there is no positive core to the democratic values of
Athens. Consequently, freedom, equality, and citizenship in classical
Athens comprise nothing more than, in the words of the essay's main
title, "The Zero Degree of Society." In every instance, they are maintained by and through domination. Casting a comparative eye, he
notes that modern conceptions of liberty, such as that of Isaiah Berlin,
similarly derive their content only in opposition. The existence of constraint is the precondition for Berlin's primary conception of "negative liberty." While Hedrick believes that the steady elimination of
exclusionary conditions for the privileges of citizenship represents an
unqualified advance over ancient Greek standards of political value,
he finds no solace in modernity. Instead, for he wonders whether the
dilution of contemporary citizenship has mostly resulted in shifting
the principal sources of political power away from the much larger
numbers of individuals now entitled to its exercise.

The last essay, "Two Democracies and Virtue" by John Wallach,
provokes a dialogue between Athenian and American democracy by
focusing on a particular feature of each society that sheds light on the

other. He attends, however, less to the structure of Athenian or American society than to their animating ideals: equal individual opportunity in the United States and arete in ancient Athens. He notes that the myth and ideology of equal opportunity in America is not a myth of community; on the contrary, it more often than not breeds centrifugal social forces. The result has been an outbreak of intellectual efforts to find a new language of civic virtue. This project, however, is more vexing than it may appear. For the language of virtue tends to diminish the value of democracy. This certainly was the case among the major Greek political theorists. Aristotle, for example, believed that democracy was hostile to the notion of desert. But then how can democracies constitute ideals for their political orders? How might citizens educate themselves in a way that also improves their democracy? Wallach believes that some parts of Greek discourse warn contemporary democrats of the obstacles to answering these questions while others open up avenues of inquiry that may relieve the perpetual tension between democracy and virtue. In this way, he believes that a serious encounter with Athenian political thought can indeed educate democracy today.

V

We stand at an exciting moment in the history of studying the polis—a moment that the editors of this book hope will be seen as a turning point. Not that we desire a turning back, either to the approaches of the predisciplinary nineteenth century or the polis itself. Such desires are as silly as they are potentially dangerous. Rather, we hope for the renewal of a pluralistic, critical dialogue between, on the one hand, a variety of modern and postmodern approaches to political theory and practice and, on the other, a persistently fertile classical political tradition. Thinking about and with the democratic polis, along with its ancient and modern critics, will not ipso facto supply us with solutions to contemporary dilemmas. But it may help us to reeducate ourselves as citizens who recognize a responsibility to perform and reconstitute a democratic culture. As citizens of a participatory, self-critical, revisable democratic culture, we might have a better chance of finding our way through the troublesome times in which we live.

I

DEMOCRACY
AND
REGIMES
OF POWER

SHELDON S. WOLIN

1 *Norm and Form: The Constitutionalizing of Democracy*

A constitution [is] an organization of offices in a state, by which the method of their distribution is fixed, the sovereign authority is determined, and the nature of the end to be pursued by the association and all its members is prescribed.

ARISTOTLE, *Politics*

My concern in this essay is with the political uses of "democracy" in relation to two diametrically opposed notions that symbolize two equally opposed states of affairs. One is the settled structure of politics and governmental authority typically called a constitution, and the other is the unsettling political movement typically called revolution. Stated somewhat starkly: constitution signifies the suppression of revolution; revolution, the destruction of constitution. The two notions, though opposed, are connected by democracy. The English revolution of 1688, the American one of 1776, and the French of 1789 are generally considered major milestones on the road to modern democracy. The first two have long been interpreted as culminating in constitutional settlements that, in effect, justified and fulfilled the prior revolutions. In France the most common criticism of the Great Revolution was that it failed to produce a lasting constitution, with the result that France suffered a series of revolutions throughout much of the nineteenth century, and the French continue to look back on their

The quotation from Aristotle's *Politics* that opens this essay is from the translation by Barker (see below, n. 46), and that at the head of Section I from that by Sinclair and Saunders (see n. 40).

29

revolutionary past with far more ambivalence than either the British or Americans.[1]

While preparing *Democracy in America*, Tocqueville complained that he found it difficult "to distinguish what is democratic from what is revolutionary . . . because examples are lacking."[2] The question is If democracy is rooted in revolution, what of democracy is suppressed by a constitution? Violence? Or is revolution politically richer than that, especially when contrasted with coups and putsches, the alternative methods of overthrow favored by oligarchs and would-be dictators? When a democratic revolution leads to a constitution, does that mark the fulfillment of democracy, or the beginning of its attenuation?

Lest this seem solely a question of terminology, recall the two different associations of democracy during the "revolutions" that led to the overthrow of communist tyrannies in the Soviet Union and in central and Eastern Europe. When the revolutions were under way in Poland, Czechoslovakia, Hungary, East Germany, and the Soviet Union, they were described as "democratic." When they succeeded, most of the constitutions subsequently adopted were characterized as "democratic." Yet a vast change had taken place in the character of politics from the revolutionary to the constitutional moment.[3]

During the revolutions, politics was primarily the affair of "civil society," not of conventional political parties or parliamentary processes. Various extralegal groups of workers, teachers, intellectuals, artists, students, religious dissidents, and ordinary citizens energized and sustained revolutionary movements whose internal politics was remarkably participatory and egalitarian. After the success of those movements, a different politics began to take shape, a politics of organized parties, professional politicians, and economic interest groups. Above all, it was a politics in which the overriding problems were declared to be economic. Suddenly Solidarity was rendered anarchronistic by the faceless representatives of the International Monetary Fund. Solidarity-style democracy had become a burden. The sea change was captured in a contemporary headline in the *New York Times*, which a short time earlier had hailed the "triumph" of democracy: "East Eu-

1. For a more extended discussion, see my *Constitutional Order, Revolutionary Violence, and Modern Power*, Politics: Occasional Papers (North York: York University, Department of Political Science, 1990), 1–21.

2. Cited in Jean-Clause Lamberti, *Tocqueville et les deux démocraties* (Paris: Presses Universitaires de France, 1983), 180.

3. For a further discussion of constitutionalism, see my "Tending and Intending a Constitution: Bicentennial Misgivings," in *The Presence of the Past: Essays on the State and the Constitution* (Baltimore: Johns Hopkins University Press, 1989), 82–99.

rope's Next Test: To Survive Democracy." And so too in Asia, where immediately after the electoral victory of Thailand "prodemocratic forces" over the military, their leader remarked, "The Cold War is over. Now is the era of the economic leading the political."[4]

Nonetheless, it is probably true that insofar as the modern political consciousness favors any universal political form, it is constitutional democracy; and insofar as it has an image of "normal" democracy, it is of democracy housed within a constitution.

I

> We must, I think, regard it as fairly certain that the other institutions as well [as class distinctions] have been in the course of the ages discovered many times over, or rather infinitely often. . . . So we should accept it as fact that the same process takes place in the case of constitutional features too. . . . Thus we ought to make full use of what has already been discovered while endeavoring to find what has not.
>
> ARISTOTLE, *Politics*

In the estimation of virtually all the canonical political theorists from Plato to Jean Bodin, democracy was rated either the worst of all forms of government, save for tyranny, or the least objectionable of the worst forms.[5] As most of these writers had Athenian democracy in mind, it is hardly surprising that it stood in equally bad odor. The recurrent charge has been that, by nature, democracy is prone to bouts of extreme lawlessness. "The vice engendered by it and inseparable from it," according to Polybius, was "the savage rule of violence."[6] The impression left by these accounts was of a natural incompatibility, a lack of proper fit between democracy and the sort of law-defined, institutionally constrained political structure represented by a constitution.

4. Quoted in *San Francisco Chronicle*, September 15, 1992, A7.

5. Spinoza was an exception; see *Tractatus Politicus* 11. See also Alexandre Matheron, *Individu et communauté chez Spinoza* (Paris: Minuit, 1988), 420–24, 493–94.

6. Polybius *The Histories*, trans. W. R. Paton, Loeb ed. (Cambridge: Harvard University Press, 1923), 6.10.4–5. See also Thucydides' description of the popular leader, Cleon, as "the most violent man at Athens," *History of the Peloponnesian War* 3.36.

In contrast, American democracy appears to have succeeded precisely where Athenian democracy failed. When Tocqueville asserted that in nineteenth-century New England he had discovered "a democracy more perfect than antiquity had dared to dream of," he meant that Americans had resolved the tension between democracy and constitutionalism, between liberty and law, majority rule and legal limitations on power. Not coincidentally, Tocqueville also attributed the stability of American democracy to the fact that democracy was not the product of a great revolutionary upheaval.[7] Tocqueville's judgment seems thrice vindicated: the United States is the world's oldest democracy combined with the world's oldest continuous written constitution and the beneficiary of a revolution whose genius was its nonrevolutionary character.

That facile formula leaves unanswered, however, a question that, curiously, is rarely raised: How is it that a political society that had been deliberately constituted as an antidote to democracy is able to identify its collective self with the type of system that its founders set out to check? My purpose in this essay is to explore the political implications of understanding democracy in constitutional and institutional terms. I attempt to show that "constitutional democracy" is not a seamless web of two complementary notions but an ideological construction designed not to realize democracy but to reconstitute it and, as a consequence, repress it. I also want to show that the ancient theory of democracy as well as the practices of Athenian democracy have figured importantly in the texts constructed by modern and contemporary theorists in their efforts to set democracy within a constitutional frame.

James Madison's contribution to the *Federalist Papers* is the crucial link connecting ancient democracy to the democracy of his day and both of them to the democracy of ours. Madison's essays are significant both for what they defend, a theory of national government as yet untested by practice, and for what he chose to attack, the theory and practice of democracy. An essential part of Madison's strategy was to deflect the criticism that the proposed constitution was insufficiently democratic in comparison with democracy being practiced by the American states and localities. It would have been impolitic for him to attack local democracy, so he did the next best thing. He attacked the ancient democracy of Athens, hoping that by indicting the

7. Alexis de Tocqueville, *Démocratie en Amérique*, in *Oeuvres complètes*, ed. J.-P. Mayer et al. (Paris: Gallimard, 1961–), 1(1):34. "The great advantage of Americans is to have arrived at democracy without the ordeal of democratic revolutions and to have been born equal instead of becoming equal" (1[2]:108).

weaknesses of the latter, he would be indirectly exposing those of the former. His critique was summed up in a single sentence: "Had every Athenian citizen been a Socrates every Athenian assembly would still have been a mob."[8]

The ghost of Athenian democracy still haunts the thinking of Madison's heirs and none more than the doyen of American political scientists, Robert Dahl. "The theory and practice of democracy," he writes, "had to burst the narrow bounds of the polis."[9] Dahl's life work has been to join the theory of American democracy with its practice, and that has meant explicitly building a political science upon "Madisonian democracy" and critically engaging the meaning of Athenian democracy.

Why should a rupture between ancient and modern conceptions of democracy be considered a necessary condition for modern democracy to come into being? The familiar answer, and one that Dahl develops at length, is that the huge physical dimensions, large populations, and social complexity of modern societies render the politics of a tiny polis anachronistic. Accordingly, modern democracy is said to consist of two principal elements: a constitution that establishes representative government and so enables a large, scattered citizenry to "participate"; and a pluralistic politics that is generated by free competition between highly organized economic and social interests. These are the means by which democracy is adapted to modern conditions.

If the stakes involved merely quantitative differences, it is difficult to see why the memory of Athens should continue to nag, unless Athenian democracy stands as a judgment. If representative government constitutes the form of modern democracy and interest group politics its content, these may not be merely the means by which democracy has been enlarged; they may also be the means by which it has been diminished in order to smooth the way for a third element, the effective organization of the power to govern. The third element was clearly uppermost in the minds of the framers of the American Constitution, and it is taken for granted by Dahl. A central government that stands as the culminating point of national power and which includes not only a representative legislature but such nonrepresentative institutions as bureaucracy, the courts, and the armed forces, reveals how democracy has been suppressed: at its height, Athenian democracy extended to all institutions, not only those now designated

8. Alexander Hamilton, John Jay, and James Madison, *The Federalist*, ed. Jacob E. Cooke (Middletown, Conn.: Wesleyan University Press, 1961), no. 55, 374.

9. Robert A. Dahl, *Democracy and Its Critics* (New Haven: Yale University Press, 1989), 23.

"representative" but those that clearly are not and one, the presidency, which is representative only in the most tortuous sense. The exclusion of the practice of democracy from the center suggests other stakes than practical necessities.

II

Is it that the moderns have broken with the ancient practice of democracy while preserving continuity with both the ancient theory critical of democracy and its project of constitutionalizing democracy? If it is the persistence of ancient suspicions rather than their disappearance that is defining of modern democracies, then the reason may be the persistence of certain "dangerous" tendencies of democracy which ancient theory could name but modern constitutional theory and practice represses.

The attacks on Athenian democracy have owed much to the consistently hostile portrait of democracy drawn by Greek political theorists, such as Plato, Aristotle, Thucydides, and Polybius. Although it has become commonplace today to write of the Greek invention of the idea of political theory, of democracy, and of politics,[10] it is rarely noted that the Greeks also invented the theory of constitutionalism.[11] Over the centuries, that theory has furnished a large part of the basic grammar of political theorists discussing constitutions. The notions that a constitution enshrines certain ideals (see the Preamble to the U.S. Constitution); that it is the "foundation" of government; that it represents the rule of law rather than caprice; and that it expresses "a way of life" are examples of Greek influences. Before the nineteenth century, a politically well-read person would have been familiar with the typology invented by Greek theorists to classify and distinguish three good or rightly ordered constitutions (monarchy, aristocracy, and some "mixed" system) from three bad or perverted ones (tyranny, oligrachy, and democracy). The underlying assumption of the scheme was that politics occurred only within a determinate form and that the function of a form was to order politics so that it served the "ends" distinctive to that form.

Ancient Greek theorists were the first to conceive the idea of codify-

10. Sheldon S. Wolin, "Political Theory," *International Encyclopedia of the Social Sciences* (New York: Collier-Macmillan, 1968); Moses I. Finley, *Politics in the Ancient World* (Cambridge: Cambridge University Press, 1983), 53; Cynthia Farrar, *The Origins of Democratic Thinking: The Invention of Politics in Classical Athens* (Cambridge: Cambridge University Press, 1988), 1.

11. Still useful as a general discussion: Charles H. McIlwain, *Constitutionalism Ancient and Modern* (Ithaca: Cornell University Press, 1940).

ing both the practices of ruling and the competing claims to rule
while, at the same time, enclosing the dynamics of politics within a
determinate structure and designated political space. Their achievement was to create nothing less than a theory of structure by concep-
tualizing various institutions, such as kingship or assemblies, *normaliz-
ing* their operation,[12] diagnosing their maladies, and relating different
institutions in space and projecting them over time. The purpose they
all inscribed in structure was the establishment of stability through the
containment of the demos.[13] Greek theorists developed a critique of
democracy and then constructed a conception of a constitution as a
means of demonstrating how democracy might be domesticated, rendered stable, orderly, and just. Constitutionalism might be defined as
the theory of how best to restrain the politics of democracy while ensuring the predominance of the social groups and classes represented
by the "best men."

Athenian democracy was not founded or established by a singular
act. A long string of events, which included reverses as well as gains,
brought a new political way of life into existence. Traditionally, its
beginnings are identified with the archonship of Solon (594 or 593
B.C.). Modern historians continue to dispute the significance, even the
substance, of such Solonian reforms as the cancellation of debts, the
elimination of debt bondage for citizens, the division of citizens into
four distinct classes according to wealth, allowing the least wealthy of
the four access to the Assembly, and establishing a people's court.
Most historians agree that Solon was no democrat and his reforms did
not establish a democratic constitution. Yet, as an incident related by
Plutarch reveals, there were moments when democracy was created by
citizens in a way that overflowed the institutions introduced by Solon.
After enacting his reforms, Solon was besieged by citizens who sought
him out to deliver their opinions of his laws, to ask for detailed explanations and clarifications, and to urge revisions. Plutarch recounts Solon's reaction: "He saw that to do this was out of the question, and
that not to do it would bring odium upon him, and wishing to be
wholly rid of these perplexities and to escape from the captiousness
and censoriousness of the citizens . . . [he] set sail after obtaining from
the Athenians leave of absence for ten years." Plutarch concludes by

---

12. Aristotle *Politics* 1313a34ff.

13. The relationship between democracy and constitutionalism is discussed in my forthcoming "Equality, Transgression, and Voice," in the forthcoming *Democracy, Ancient and Modern*, edited by Charles Hedrick and Josiah Ober.

recording the firm faith of the institutionalizer: Solon hoped that during his absence the citizens "would be accustomed to his laws."[14]

Athenian democracy of the fifth century was shaped by class conflicts, rivalries between the rich and the well-born, the ambitions of politicians, and the struggle for empire. It developed as the demos became a self-conscious actor. Democracy began as a demand for a "share" of power in the institutions for making and interpreting the laws and deciding questions of diplomacy and warfare. It culminated in popular control over most of the main political institutions at Athens. Democracy's triumphal occupation of those institutions was, however, the beginning of its transformation.

Institutionalization brings not only settled practices regarding such matters as authority, jurisdiction, accountability, procedures, and processes but routinization, professionalization, and the loss of spontaneity and of those improvisatory skills that Thucydides singled out as an Athenian trademark.[15] Institutionalization depends on the ritualization of the behavior of both rulers and ruled to enable the formal functions of the state—coercion, revenue collection, policy, mobilization of the population for war, law making, punishment, and enforcement of the laws—to be conducted on a continuing basis. It tends to produce internal hierarchies, to restrict experience, to associate political experience with institutional experience, and to inject an esoteric element into politics.

III

Modern political discourse, especially in its social science version, has largely abandoned the ancient vocabulary of "form" but not the idea. The modern variant is the concept of "organization" or its equivalents "bureaucracy," "administration," or "management."[16] The idea of organization is comparable to the idea of form in specifying a set of integrated conditions for the production of power. Among the conditions are a hierarchical system of authority; centralization of decision making; division of labor and specialization, especially in the form of professional politicians; and increasing reliance on expert knowledge.

The institutionalization I associate with the transformation of democracy into a constitution is viewed differently in the writings of

14. Plutarch *Solon* 25; see also *Constitution of Athens* [= *Athēnaiōn Politeia*] 11.
15. Thuc. *History* 1.70.
16. On organization theory, see my discussion in *Politics and Vision: Continuity and Innovation in Western Political Thought* (Boston: Little, Brown, 1960), chap. 10.

some classical scholars, who see it as the stablization of democracy.[17] One striking feature of this scholarship is the self-conscious attempt to draw on the methods and concepts of twentieth-century sociology; another is an unselfconscious acceptance of organizational values. Thus one historian describes his work as concerned with "how the evolving relationship between mass and elite was institutionalized and how constitutional development in turn contributed to changes or encouraged stability in the political sociology of Athens."[18] A main concern here is to defend Athenian democracy against the charges of lawlessness, incompetence, and leveling by showing that during the fourth century B.C., Athenian democracy did not discriminate unduly against the wealthy, nor expropriate their wealth, nor show disrespect for law but, rather, that the demos imposed limitations on its own powers. Thus one scholar says of restrictions on the Assembly that these "protected democracy, but an orderly and constitutional democracy, not an undisciplined one."[19] In arguing that Athenian democracy eventually purged itself of the tendencies toward excess which ancient critics had insisted were natural to democracy, modern revisionistss are tacitly claiming the same curative properties for constitutionalism as the ancient writers.

Instead of a conception of democracy as indistinguishable from its constitution, I propose accepting the familiar charges that democracy is inherently unstable, inclined toward anarchy, and identified with revolution and using these traits as the basis for a different, *a*constitutional conception of democracy. Instead of assuming that the "natural" direction, the telos, of the democratic encounter with the political is toward greater institutional organization and that the problem is to adapt democracy to the requirements of organization, we might think of democracy as resistant to the rationalizing conceptions of power and its organization which for centuries have dominated western thinking and have developed constitutionalism and their legitimating rationale. This democracy might be summed up as the idea and practice of rational disorganization. The claims of the demos and its kind of power appear to ancient critics and modern democrats as both inefficient and disruptive because the demos has been keyed to values

17. Josiah Ober, *Mass and Elite in Democratic Athens: Rhetoric, Ideology, and the Power of the People* (Princeton: Princeton University Press, 1989); Barry S. Strauss, "On Aristotle's Critique of Athenian Democracy," in *Essays on the Foundations of Aristotelian Political Science*, ed. Carnes Lord and David K. O'Connor (Berkeley and Los Angeles: University of California Press, 1991), 212–33.
18. Ober, *Mass and Elite*, 52.
19. B. Strauss, "On Aristotle's Critique," 220, 221. See also Peter J. Rhodes, "Athenian Democracy after 403 B.C.," *Classical Journal* 75 (1980): 305–23.

38   SHELDON S. WOLIN

other than the economy of power suggested by Max Weber and Robert Michels and championed by a long succession of priests, philosophers, warrior chiefs, and kings who have presented variations on the
same theme: that ruling should be organized by some representatives
of "the best," of those who truly know how to organize, exercise, sac-
ralize, and exploit power.

One of the shrewdest analyses of why the demos should be distrustful of the best was written by an enemy of Athenian democracy who is
known to us only as the "Old Oligarch." In his *Constitution of the Athenians* (ca. 412 B.C.), he imagines a situation in which some disreputable
demagogue persuades the Assembly to adopt a proposal that is to the
advantage of the common people as well as to himself. Then the Old
Oligarch asks the question that the "better" sort of citizen would raise:
Why would the people prefer to follow the advice of a bad man rather
than "a respectable man of virtue and wisdom"? The answer is that
the people know that the bad man is well disposed toward the people
whereas the good man is not. The demos thus has a very different
understanding of what is politically best, one that is not comprehended by ruling elites and philosophers: "Such practices do not produce the best city, but they are the best way of preserving democracy.
For the common people do not wish to be deprived of their rights in
an admirably governed city, but to be free and to rule the city. . . .
[T]he common people get their strength and freedom from what you
define as inferior laws."[20]

IV

A hint of the antagonism between democracy and institutionalized
politics is in the paradoxical status democracy occupies in contemporary political discourse. Democracy is, on the one hand, widely ac-
claimed to be the universal criterion of legitimacy for political systems
and, on the other, almost universally dismissed as an impractical
scheme of government and condemned as a bad one. The contemporary euphemism for "bad" or "perverted" democracy is "populism."

Perhaps the most compelling testimony to the paradox is that although very few publicly deny the claims of democratic legitimacy
periodically made by the official spokesmen for each of the so-called
advanced, industrialized democracies, fewer still dare to argue that
"the people" actually rule in any of them. What is being measured by

20. "Old Oligarch" [Pseudo-Xenophon] *Constitution of the Athenians*, trans. J. M. Moore, ed.,
Aristotle and Xenophon on Democracy and Oligarchy (Berkeley and Los Angeles: University of
California Press, 1975), 7–8.

their claim to democratic legitimacy is, therefore, not the vitality of democracy in those nations but the degree to which democracy is attenuated so that it may serve other ends. The most fundamental of these ends—which more than any other could be safely called "the original intent of the framers of the American Constitution"—is the establishment of political conditions favorable to the development of the modernizing state. This suggests that the contemporary "problem of democracy" is not, as Dahl and others have asserted, that the ancient conception of democracy is incompatible with the size and scale of modern political societies. Rather, it is that any conception of democracy centered on the citizen-as-actor and politics-as-episodic-activity is incompatible with the modern choice of the state as the fixed center of political life and the corollary conception of politics as organizational activity aimed at a single, dominating objective, control of the state apparatus.

In what follows I use "constitutional democracy" and "democratic constitutionalism" to signify alternatives rather than similars. The first term refers to a situation in which constitutionalization has priority over democracy; the second, to a situation in which democratization has dictated the form of constitution. The first involves the selective addition of democratic elements to a constitution that previously was not democratic and, despite the addition, remains such. Thus we might claim that the Reform Act of 1832 was a first small step in the democratizing of the British constitution, but it was absorbed into a political system in which all the other major political institutions—the monarchy, the two houses of Parliament, administration, courts, and the military—remained highly undemocratic in recruitment, structure, and operation. Democracy was incorporated on terms set by the constitution, that is, by the social and political powers that had shaped the constitution to their needs and preferences. A broader social and political constitution or hegemony was defined which conceded a measure of democracy while simultaneously marginalizing and repressing the larger movement. At the same time, and often reluctantly and without fully appreciating the consequences, the dominant groups redefined themselves.

The second term, *democratic constitutionalism,* can mean the domination of democracy over constitution: that has been, historically and contemporaneously, the view of critics of democracy. In the words of Apollodorus, "The Athenian demos has supreme authority over all things in the polis and it is in its power to do whatever it wishes" (*Against Neaera* 88). I try here to account for the mostly abortive afforts at democratic constitutionalism and for the stubborn reemergence of democratic movements by proposing a theory in which dem-

ocratic constitutionalism is representative of a moment rather than
a teleologically completed form.

V

> Solon realized that the city was often split by factional dis-
> putes but some citizens were content because of idleness to
> accept whatever the outcome might be; he therefore pro-
> duced a specific law against them, laying down that anyone
> who did not choose one side or the other in such a dispute
> should lose his citizen rights.
>
> *Constitution of Athens*

The common assumption of both defenders and critics of democracy is that the extent and degree of democratization, present or absent, in any given society, whether "real" or "ideal," corresponds to, or
is a function of, the extent to which democracy has been embodied in
the "core" political institutions of that society.[21] That assumption encourages the view that the history of democracy is a search for its
proper form, as suggested, for example, in the very Aristotelian title
of Martin Ostwald's magistral study of Athenian democracy, *From
Popular Sovereignty to the Sovereignty of Law*. Ostwald writes, "The end
of the fifth century B.C." was "the time [when] the principle of the
sovereignty of law was given official primacy over the principle of
popular sovereignty."[22]

Ostwald's formulation suggests that before the end of the fifth century, Athenian democracy was defined by popular sovereignty rather
than the rule of law—that, in effect, there were two Athenian democracies. In my formulation, first there was Athenian democratic
constitutionalism, and then there was Athenian constitutional democracy, or what Ostwald describes as "a new kind of democracy, which
subordinated the will of the people to the regulating hand of the law."[23]

21. See in particular Martin Ostwald, *From Popular Sovereignty to the Sovereignty of Law: Law,
Society, and Politics in Fifth-Century Athens* (Berkeley and Los Angeles: University of California
Press, 1986), and Christian Meier, *The Greek Discovery of Politics*, trans. David McLintock (Cambridge: Harvard University Press, 1990), esp. chap. 4, "Cleisthenes and Institutionalizing the
Civic Presence." See also Bruce Ackerman, *The Future of Liberal Revolution* (New Haven: Yale
University Press, 1992), and Jon Elster and Rune Slagstad, eds., *Constitutionalism and Democracy: Studies in Rationality and Social Change* (Cambridge: Cambridge University Press, 1988).
22. Ostwald, *Sovereignty*, xx.
23. Ibid., xi.

A hypothetical line separating the two democracies might be located in two counterrevolutions—one by the Four Hundred in 411 B.C. and the other by the Thirty in 404—which overthrew democracy and attempted to replace it by oligarchy. In 403, democracy was restored and continued until the Macedonian conquest of 322.

Concerning the restoration of 403, the Aristotelian author of the *Constitution of Athens* wrote, "It was just that the people should take control because they had secured their return by their own efforts. This was the eleventh change of constitution."[24] Thus 403 might be taken as the dividing line between what one historian has called "the radical democracy" of the fifth century and what another has called "the constitutional democracy" of the fourth.[25]

What makes this division suggestive for the problem of the institutionalization of democracy and for the distinction between constitutional democracy and democratic constitutionalism is that, by and large, the same political institutions of "radical democracy" were revived and continued to function down to 322. The demos was not disenfranchised, nor were its powers formally curtailed. Yet the political life of the two democracies presented a contrast between the active democratization of political life and the virtually total institutionalization of it.

VI

The fifth-century democratization of the Athenian constitution was the work of the demos. It was not established by a single document or one heroic act of founding but by a series of struggles that ended (ca. 403–399) with the provision that those who attended the Assembly were to be paid. The politics of the demos was disorderly and often rebellious, defined by its opposition to existing arrangements rather than by them. Its hegemony was achieved by repeatedly challenging regimes dominated by the men of wealth and noble birth. To be sure, many of the democratic reforms of the century were associated with notable leaders, such as Solon, Cleisthenes, Ephialtes, and Pericles, but the evidence suggests that the demos was an active force in all the reforms, exerting pressure, siding with one leader rather than another, and gradually extending its power by gaining access to existing institutions or by establishing new ones. Often its leaders were dema-

24. *Constitution of Athens* 61.1–2.
25. Charles Hignett, *A History of the Athenian Constitution to the End of the Fifth Century B.C.* (Oxford: Oxford University Press, Clarendon, 1952), chap. 9; B. Strauss, "On Aristotle's Critique," 229.

gogues and tyrants, that is, men who owed their legitimacy not to institutional authority but to popular support and who became the means of breaking through existing forms to extend the power of the demos.[26]

The author of the *Constitution of Athens* summarized the results by saying that the demos "had made themselves supreme in all fields" (41.2). By any standard of civism, the intensity and varieties of participation, as well as the sheer number of participants, was impressive. Concretely, by 400, there ceased to be property qualifications for citizenship; the Assembly of citizens was the principal legislative body; the boards of lawmakers (*nomothetai*) and the juries were chosen by lot from the citizen body; the Council, which prepared the agenda for the Assembly, was chosen annually by lot from the citizenry; the decisions of the Assembly were subject to review only by the people's courts; most of the offices were open to all citizens and were filled annually by lot; the magistrates' actions were subject to legal audits by the people's courts.[27] Citizens deliberated and took decisions in the Assembly, the Council, and the courts. They chose leaders, made decisions about foreign policy and war, judged the credentials of officeholders, issued decrees, and much more.[28] Nor was the political culture limited to the central institutions of Athens. There was a flourishing system of local institutions in the demes, where citizens acquired experience and joined in nominating local men to serve in the central institutions.[29] Athens was, in effect, a complete democracy insofar as that democracy defined its identity against an alternative of antidemocratic regimes.

The great achievement of self-government was to transform politics in sight and speech; power was made visible; decision making was opened so that citizens could see its workings; ordinary men personified power, spoke to it unservilely, and held themselves answerable. The most crucial and revealing element in Athenian democracy was the system of annual rotation in office, the lot, and the public subsidization of citizen participation.

26. For general background and still useful: Antony Andrewes, *The Greek Tyrants* (London: Hutchinson University Library, 1956).

27. I have borrowed Ober's summary, *Mass and Elite*, 54–55. For estimates of how many Athenian citizens participated during the fourth century and how often, see Mogens H. Hansen, *The Athenian Democracy in the Age of Demosthenes: Structure, Principles, and Ideology* (Oxford: Blackwell, 1991).

28. For details, see R. K. Sinclair, *Democracy and Participation in Athens* (Cambridge: Cambridge University Press, 1988), 65–134, and David Stockton, *The Classical Athenian Democracy* (Oxford: Oxford University Press, 1990), 65–116.

29. Stockton, *Classical Athenian Democracy*, 57–67; David Whitehead, *The Demes of Attica: 508/7–ca. 250 B.C.* (Princeton: Princeton University Press, 1986), esp. pt. 3.

Rotation and lot both function to limit the effects of institutionaliza-tion: they are, paradoxically, institutions that subvert institutionaliza-tion. When a legislature, a council, or an administrator enjoys secure and lengthy tenure, the tendency is to develop the traits associated with the ideology of organization: offices tend to become the perma-nent property of a political class; distance is quickly established be-tween knowledgeable professionals and ignorant citizens; and that distance becomes real rather than symbolic. The contrast is between experience based on continuous practice and reactive impressions grounded in passivity. Rotation and lot, together with pay for the citi-zen, sharply reduce the contrast. The disruption in continuity of per-sonnel injected an element of rational disorganization.

Before its fourth-century institutionalization, Athenian democracy was less a constitution in the Aristotelian sense of a fixed form than a dynamic and developing political culture, a culture not only of partici-pation but of frequent rebellion. For Athenian democracy to continue to democratize, it would have had to confront itself rather than its enemies. The crucial moment occurred in 403 or 402 B.C. when the restored democracy rejected a proposal to limit the franchise to prop-erty owners, thereby preserving its egalitarian conception of citizen-ship. At the same time, however, it refused to extend citizenship to those slaves who had assisted in the revolution against the Thirty.[30] Each of the proposals, from opposite directions, struck at the Athe-nian conception of democracy; one would contract it, the other en-large it. The double rejection was symptomatic not simply of a deter-mination to defend democracy against oligarchy—which it was—but of a conservative temper indicating that democracy had "settled down" and found its constitutional form, its ne plus ultra.

In the fourth century, however, subtle changes took place. In the words of one scholar sympathetic to those changes, certain restrictions placed on the Assembly "protected democracy" and produced "an or-derly and constitutional democracy, not an undisciplined one." He goes on to note that "other developments . . . did restrict the direct and immediate power of the people" and that "Athens took a number of steps in the direction of governmental efficiency and specialization, sometimes at the expense of democracy." This "constitutional democ-racy" was one in which "the wealthy were overrepresented."[31] The phenomenon of institutionalization, none of it offensively antidemo-cratic to twentieth-century sensitivities, become pronounced. A dis-

30. Ober, *Mass and Elite*, 97.
31. B. Strauss, "On Aristotle's Critique," 228, 229; see also Hansen, *Athenian Democracy*, 65, 94–95.

tinction emerged between what one scholar has called the "expert politician" and the ordinary citizen.[32] At the same time, certain inhibiting devices assumed greater importance in the fourth century: the *graphē paranomōn* (indictment for proposing a law contrary to existing law) and *eisanglia* (political impeachment) posed grave risks for a citizen (not holding an official position) if found guilty of having proposed an unlawful decree to the Assembly or, among other things, of having been bribed to speak against the public interest.[33]

Modern scholars who have defended fourth-century democracy against Aristotle's criticism of it as "extreme democracy" have been less concerned to defend fifth-century democracy, thus tacitly implying that Aristotle may have been correct about fifth-century democracy but wrong about fourth.[34] It is argued that experts became "necessary" because of the inhibitions of the *graphē paranomōn* and *eisanglia*; that without the experts "there would be few bold and original policy initiatives";[35] that "consensus" had been "lost" in the polarization of the fifth-century, and "the question" for fourth-century Athens "was how effective leadership and decision-making could be achieved within the context of egalitarian direct democracy."[36] The twentieth-century image of the "constitutional democracy" of the fourth century bears a striking resemblance to Madisonian democracy.

VII

It is curious that in the abundant literature produced in the greatest democracy in Greece there survives no statement of democratic political theory.

A. H. M. JONES, *Athenian Democracy*

Greek political theory developed a political science that was notable for its rule-centeredness.[37] Its preoccupations were with who should

32. Ober, *Mass and Elite*, 111.
33. R. Sinclair, *Democracy and Participation in Athens*, 52–60; Stockton, *Classical Athenian Democracy*, 45–46, 78–82, 101–2.
34. See B. Strauss, "On Aristotle's Critique," 213–14.
35. Ober, *Mass and Elite*, 112.
36. Ibid., 99–100.
37. Examples would be Plato's *Republic* where the political arrangement turns entirely on the governing class and his *Laws* with its Nocturnal Council; Aristotle's definition of the citi-

rule and how rule by the best or better sort might be assured. In defining and working out those concerns, Greek writers succeeded in establishing a stable vocabulary in which constructs such as "the many" or the "few," "the people" and "the best" were assigned attributes and behavioral regularities that were then connected to what was asserted to be the nature of "rule" so that what would or should be done was made in accord with the "nature" of some social groups (e.g., the highest military offices require certain skills or experience that only aristocrats are likely to possess) and to be incongruous with the nature of others (the demos was said to lack the experience, knowledge, and temperament necessary to command). According to the Old Oligarch, "Throughout the world the aristocrats are opposed to democracy, for they are naturally least liable to loss of self control and injustice and most meticulous in their regard for what is respectable, whereas the masses display extreme ignorance, indiscipline and wickedness, for poverty gives them a tendency towards the ignoble, and in some cases lack of money leads to their being uneducated and ignorant."[38]

Generally speaking, Greek political theory understood "rule" to mean the exercise of power by some over others. Its major thinkers mostly recognized this relationship as potentially, possibly inherently, debasing. Plato and Aristotle, for example, tried repeatedly to distinguish right rule from forms of rule which were not right, but the distinction kept breaking down, as in Aristotle's attempt to moderate tyranny without transforming it or in Plato's attempt to etherealize oligarchic rule by denying his guardians money or property yet subsidizing their lives by the labors of workers, farmers, and slaves.[39] Rule was understood to be inherently exploitative. In Aristotle's words: "But whenever one thing is a means and another an end, there can be no other thing in common between them than this—that the one acts, the other is acted upon."[40]

Aristotle did seek to modify the harshness of this principle by stipulating that in a politeia in which citizenship was restricted to true equals, the citizen should know how to rule and be ruled.[41] But that dictum applied primarily to oligarchies, aristocracies, and the "polity" of middle-class property owners and did not significantly qualify his

---

zen in terms of ruling and being ruled and his emphasis on the ruling group (*politeuma*) as defining the nature of a politeia.

38. Old Oligarch *Constitution of the Athenians* 5 (trans. slightly altered).

39. Plato *Republic* 3.416d–e; Aristotle. *Pol.* 1313a18– 1315b10.

40. Aristot. *Pol.*, trans. T. A. Sinclair, rev. Trevor J. Saunders (Harmondsworth: Penguin, 1981), 1328a28–30.

41. Ibid., 1277a13–15.

belief that the virtue or function of a ruler lay in knowing how to use others. The virtue of the ruled, he noted, is "like a flute-maker while the ruler is like the flute player, the user [of what the other makes]."[42]

Theoretical justifications, such as appeals to a principle of "natural" hierarchy (higher and lower) or to a right of the superior to rule over inferiors, merely restated the exploitative relationship without altering it. The movement toward democracy in fifth-century Athens, and its ideology of equality (*isonomia*), can be seen as a protest by the demos against that conception of rule. The democratic practices of rotation, lot, and ostracism, by emphasizing "taking turns" in office or banishing those whose power or prestige seemed to threaten democracy, struck directly at the debasing effects of rule conceived as a superior-inferior relationship. Perhaps nothing symbolizes more strikingly the divergence between the politics legitimated by constitutional theory and the assertive politics of democracy than the mute silence of the demos—the lack of its own voice—in the pages of Plato and Aristotle and the contrasting explosion of demotic speech once the people won *isēgoria*, the right of speaking freely in the Assembly.[43]

The push toward democracy during the fifth century was not, as it was and still is represented to be, a simple demand for "equality before the law."[44] It was an attempt to redefine the terms of ruling and being ruled by insisting on a share of power. That demand issued not from a leveling impulse but from a realization by the demos that the power of the polis was, in large measure, their power. No one recognized that brute fact more squarely than the Old Oligarch: "[I]t is right that the poor and ordinary people [in Athens] should have more power than the noble and rich, because it is the ordinary people who man the fleet and bring the city her power; they provide the helmsmen, the boatswains, the junior officers, the lookouts and the shipwrights; it is these people who make the city powerful much more than the hoplites and the noble and respectable citizens."[45]

In response, the theorists of constitutionalism qualified the questions of who should rule and how they should rule, by inventing the question of *what* should rule. That led to treating a constitution as the

42. Aristot. *Pol.*, trans. Carnes Lord (Chicago: University of Chicago Press, 1984), 1277b29–30. See also 1279a33–35.

43. See Kurt A. Raaflaub, "Democracy, Oligarchy, and the Concept of the 'Free Citizen' in Late Fifth-Century Athens," *Political Theory* 11(1983):517–44.

44. Gregory Vlastos, "Isonomia," *American Journal of Philology* 74 (1953):337–66, and "Isonomia Politikē," in *Platonic Studies* (Princeton: Princeton University Press, 1973), 164–203. And see W. Robert Connor's note in *The New Politicians of Fifth-Century Athens* (Princeton: Princeton University Press, 1971), 202–6.

45. Old Oligarch *Constitution of the Athenians* 2.

means of stabilizing a way of life according to certain principles, such as justice, goodness, and manly action, whose function was to serve as metaprinciples, superior to other principles. They were ruling principles, a (syn)*tactical* representation of the axiom of Greek constitutional theory that a constitution was essentially about ruling and being ruled.

The objective status of those principles was contrasted with the flux, uncertainty, and subjectivism attributed to politics and, most important, to the forced entry into politics of social strata previously excluded. The essence of the contrast, which became, as well, the essence of constitutionalism, was between depersonalized principles and partisan politics. The freer, more accessible politics came to be, the more threatening it appeared. The principal means for ensuring and representing depersonalization, and for containing the perpetual challenge to established power potentially present in politics, was the law. Aristotle's famous characterization of law distilled all these elements of depersonalization and objectivism: "He who commands that law should rule may thus be regarded as commanding that God and reason alone should rule; he who commands that a man should rule adds the character of the beast. . . . Law may thus be defined as 'Reason free from all passion.'"[46]

It was but a small theoretical step to compare democracy's transgressive disrespect for limits and boundaries with tyranny and to claim that both displayed an innate impulse toward lawlessness.[47] This step prepared the way for the project, first undertaken by Aristotle, of devising mechanisms that would force the politics of democracy to be law abiding or, more precisely, to express itself structurally. Together with objective normativity and depersonalization, legalism formed the center of a project that I call "the constitutionalizing of surplus democracy." What is the nature of the surplus in democracy such that it is seen to require confinement within a constitution?

A clue to an answer is in the contrast Aristotle constructed between the unchanging character of law and the changing character of political practice. He explains that, as one of the arts, politics share in the claim made on behalf of other arts, such as medicine, that beneficial changes have resulted from abandoning traditional notions. But, Aristotle then insists, "To change the practice of an art is not the same as to change the operation of a law." Law depends on the habits of obedience which have been fostered over time. A disposition to change the laws, which is one of the most persistent charges leveled against

46. Aristot. *Pol.*, trans. Ernest Barker (Oxford: Oxford University Press, Clarendon Press, 1946), 1287a28–32.
47. Ibid., 1292a15–24.

democracy from ancient to modern times, allegedly undermines the power of law and the habits of obedience to government.[48]

The reified status Aristotle wanted to assign law in theory appears as special pleading in the context of the continuous struggle of the demos to equalize its economic and social condition by changing the practice of the political art. That struggle was to redefine politics from being a "civilized" version of warrior politics in which elites compete for honors and office to being the means of reversing the universal tendency of institutionalized systems of power to advantage the few and exploit the many. The political challenge of the demos inevitably overflowed the customary and institutional boundaries within which elites were attempting to fix politics. Consequently, democratic politics appeared as revolutionary and excessive, irregular and spasmodic. The response of Greek constitutional theory was to attempt to suppress the eruptive character of demotic politics but, if necessary, to incorporate it selectively as a preliminary to reconceptualizing the "problem" of politics as a contest involving competing claims to rule and conflicting views of equality. The solution was "contained" in the pivotal notion of "form."[49]

VIII

Determinatio negatio est.
BENEDICT SPINOZA, *Correspondence*

Since antiquity the idea of a form has often served as a metaphor of control signifying mastery, hence superiority, over "content." Implicit in the metaphor were political questions such as Who designed the form? Who had knowledge of the design? What or who was destined to be content, and were they naturally receptive to the impress of that form? How were the limits of a form established, and what was excluded in the process?

Adapted by Plato and Aristotle to political discourse, form was made into a justification for various distinctions, each of which im-

48. Ibid., 1268a14–28. On Aristotle's association of "extreme democracy" with the superiority of decrees over the established laws, see B. Strauss, "On Aristotle's Critique," 215–19.

49. On the idea of form, especially in its uses by Plato, see William K. C. Guthrie, *A History of Greek Philosophy* (Cambridge: Cambridge University Press, 1978), 5:147–54, (1981), 6:100–105, 243–46.

plied subordination: the distinctions between ruling (applying the form) and being ruled (accepting the form), between acting and being acted upon, between authority and submission, and inevitably, between the best or better men and the common or base people, such as workers, women, and slaves. Accordingly, a form symbolized a structure that contained the distinctions allowing the actions of the few to direct the activities of the many.

From there it was but another short step to employing form as a synonym for "constitution" and for constitution to mean a "preform," and a priori shape, the articulation prior to content and defining of it. The form was assigned a monopoly over the political and became the locus of legitimate politics. It reconstitutes politics as identity. A form supplied a distinctive character, structure, order, and boundaries, and a mode of ruling in which power was sublimated into presiding over and preserving the identity of that form. A constitutional form signified a structure to which politics should con*form* and become the kind of politics expressive of that constitution. Whatever did not conform was extraconstitutional, improper, illegal, and non- or antipolitical. Form might be described as constitutional theory's answer to ostracism.

That conception of form allowed an Aristotle to assert that a democracy manipulated by demagogues (i.e., leaders of the demos) who bring all matters before the people and persuade them to rule by decree was not a constitution at all.[50] To exist, democracy had to satisfy or to contradict the criteria that would qualify it as a form. Those requirements were merely another way of asserting the primacy of a philosophically based political science, of saying that democracy must be in*formed* or mis*informed*, that is, so constituted that it could be treated discursively as a theoretical object.[51]

IX

Democracy's political surplus, the unwillingness of the demos to remain contented with a simple "share" in the major political institutions, produced perplexities about how to account for democracy as a form, a politeia. This was true even for Plato, the master theorist of

50. Aristot. *Pol.* 1292a5–35.
51. On the various usages connected with democracy, see R. Sinclair, *Democracy and Participation*, 13–17; Raphael Sealey, "The Origins of Demokratia," *California Studies in Classical Antiquity* 6 (1973): 253–95; and particularly helpful, Charles W. Fornara and Loren J. Samons II, *Athens from Cleisthenes to Pericles* (Berkeley and Los Angeles: University of California Press, 1991), chap. 2.

forms. Beneath his sardonic descriptions of democracy in the *Republic* (whose Greek title was *Politeia*, or "constitution") was an uncertainty about what democracy "is." He did not describe it as rule by the people, nor did he dwell on democracy's scandal of equality (although he did mention it).[52] Instead he produces a paradox of a distinct life-form that he associates—significantly for our notion of democracy's surplus politics—with absolute freedom, that is, with a total disrespect for form. Democracy is not primarily a set of political institutions but a cultural practice that extends to striking changes in the behavior of women, children, and slaves. Democratic freedom and equality signify the radical denial that social deference and hierarchy are "natural." Democracy permits all manner of dress, behavior, and belief: it is in-*formal*, indifferent to *form*alities. Democracy is as careless about obeying the law as it is about respecting distinctions of age or social status. Its citizens, according to Plato, do not observe any constitution in the strict sense (8.557e–558a). They finally pay no heed even to the laws written or unwritten so resolved are they to have no master over them" (563d–e). Thus democracy is wayward, inchoate, unable to rule yet unwilling to be ruled. It does not naturally con*form*. It is inherently formless.

But Plato then makes a remark about democracy and constitutions which introduces a somewhat different note. Because of the diverse human types it breeds, democracy is worth examining if one is looking for any sort of constitution: "Anyone who wishes to organize a state . . . must find his way to a democratic city and select the model that pleases him, as if in a bazar of constitutions" (8.557d). Although its intention was satiric, the passage preserves a suggestive point that democracy, far from evoking images intimative of monochromatic, mass society, is diverse and colorful. Democracy is unique in being related to all constitutions; it is not so much amorphous as polymorphous.[53]

In the *Laws*, Plato appears more appreciative of democracy, even borrowing, with suitable modifications, many of the practices of Athe-

52. Plato *Rep.* 8.557A.

53. In *Politicus*, Plato still treats democracy at arm's length. He concedes that it is a kind of constitution but only barely. Unlike monarchy and aristocracy, which can be perverted into tyranny and oligarchy, democracy remains democracy, whether it is lawless or law abiding (291e–292a). Only toward the end of that dialogue does he concede that if the choice were between the three lawless types—tyranny, oligarchy, and democracy—it is better to live under democracy (303a–b). Thus Plato could be summarized: Democracy is the worst of the best forms and the best of the worst.

nian democracy.[54] He describes it, along with monarchy, as one of the two generative principles of all constitutions (3.693d). Its distinctive quality is the friendly feeling that liberty and equality promote among citizens. Yet when Plato lists seven distinct claims to rule, democracy is not among them (690a–c).[55]

These theoretical gyrations were the consequence of the dilemma emerging from a growing recognition that the demos was the necessary basis of any constitution, that to exclude the masses was not only, as Aristotle put it, to place a constitution under siege but to contradict the kind of comprehensiveness which distinguished a polity from other groupings.[56] Aristotle could recommend a constitution as one that allows most men to participate and as suitable to most cities; yet it would exclude the poor and the skilled craftsmen because they were akin to slaves in their lack of autonomy and consequent deficiency in reasoning ability.[57]

As Greek thinkers came to conceive of a constitution as an object requiring a "ground" or a "base," they began to realize that exclusion of the demos was not so much morally wrong as politically incoherent.[58] If, as Aristotle argued, a constitution should serve the common good, how can that good be common when it is identified with virtues whose excellence is that they are uncommon? How could an exclusionary conception of the political, one that explicitly withholds citizenship from those whose labors are acknowledged to be "necessary" to the existence of the polis, be reconciled with a vision of the polis as an association of shared advantages?[59]

The incoherence attending political theory's vision of the political produced the guilty knowledge that all political forms are prone to favor some group. Again, the Old Oligarch, whose commentary was

54. For details, see Glenn Morrow, *Plato's Cretan City: A Historical Interpretation of "The Laws"* (Princeton: Princeton University Press, 1960), esp. 229–33.

55. Leo Strauss asserted, with scant evidence, that Plato's account of rule by the strongest was an allusion to democracy; see his *Argument and Action of Plato's "Laws"* (Chicago: University of Chicago Press, 1975), 47. See also, R. F. Stalley, *An Introduction to Plato's "Laws"* (Indianapolis: Hackett, 1983), 73.

56. See Plato *Rep.* 4.420b–c, where Socrates insists that the aim of a politeia is not the happiness of one class but of the whole.

57. Aristot. *Pol.* 1295a25–33, 1277b33–1278a12.

58. Thus in the course of Aristotle's several stipulations about what a constitution is, he remarks that in every constitution the citizen body (*politeuma*) is sovereign and that the politeuma is the politeia; then he applies those formulas to oligarchies and democracies while silently passing over monarchy, even though monarchy is included among the rightly ordered constitutions. Obviously it is awkward to find a place for an Aristotelian politeuma in a monarchy.

59. Aristot. *Pol.* 1278a1–13, 1280b32–1281a8.

not remarkable for its subtlety, testifies to the point. After noting that the people prefer a faulty constitution that preserves their power to a better one that does not, he remarks, "If you are looking for an admirable code of laws, first you will find that the ablest draw them up in their own interest; secondly, the respectable will punish the masses and will plan the city's affairs and will not allow men who are mad to take part in planning or discussion or even sit in the Ekklesia. As a result of this excellent system the common people would very soon lose all their political rights."[60]

Aristotle virtually conceded that point by acknowledging that a *politeuma*, or ruling group, whether one, few, or many, was the politeia, or constitution.[61] The admission that all constitutions were one-sided made the realization of distributive justice—equal rewards, honors, and offices for the equal, unequal ones for the unequal—appear as a confession that built-in political tendencies toward partiality could be overcome only under ideal conditions. "It so happens," Aristotle remarks in the course of arguing that happiness is the end of the state, "that some can get a share of happiness while others can get little or none" (1328a38–40).[62] Accordingly, Aristotle's rightly ordered constitutions seem less the realization of justice than a balancing act intended to enable one set of biases to "correct" another (e.g., democracy should allocate some offices to the wealthy). Although Aristotle also suggested that nondemocratic regimes could achieve stability by granting some political concessions to the demos, his political science was not evenhanded. Monarchy and aristocracy, even tyranny—but not democracy—were treated as capable of surmounting their biases if rulers and elites were properly educated. Not so for the demos. Democracy and education were viewed as contradictory notions. Instead of offering to teach the demos how to rule in the interests of all, Greek theorists showed how democracy could be controlled by constitutional reforms that would reserve offices for the other social classes.

It is revealing of the perplexities of Greek theory when confronting the political abundance of Greek democracy that the two forms of acceptable democracy proposed by Aristotle, one agrarian and the other pastoral, both separate democracy from the city and thereby deny the heterogeneity of the political and identify its value with its scarcity. Aristotle's best democracy consisted of farmers who would, of necessity, be so busy tending their land that they would have "no time for attending the assembly." Such people, Aristotle observed, prefer

60. Old Oligarch *Constitution of the Athenians* 9.
61. Aristot. *Pol.* 1278b10–11.
62. T. Sinclair trans.

work to politics, money to honor—except of course when some profit
was to be made from office (1318b9–16).

X

The tensions were compounded by a further admission that nagged
virtually all constitutional thinking: that while all forms were biased,
not all were biased to the same degree or in the same way. Although a
democracy might be biased in favor of the people, that "perversion"
appeared to be a closer approximation to the ideal of a polis than the
perverted constitutions that favored one or the few. In Herodotus's
famous "Persian" debate about political forms, the defense of democracy closes with the claim that in a democracy, polity and people are
the same.[63] This view was echoed by Thucydides, who, however, was
careful not to put the sentiment in the mouth of an Athenian: "The
word demos, or people, includes the whole state, oligarchy only a
part.[64] Precisely because the demos was a fuller representation of the
polis and its different kinds of ordinariness, democracy appeared to
be closer in spirit to the principle that most theorists insisted on, that
the distinctive mark of all "right" constitutions was that rule served
the well-being of all. In other words, the more general or inclusive the
criterion of the political, the more persuasive the case for democracy
as being the most political of constitutions.[65]

Greek constitutional theorists tried to ward off the claims of democracy to be the true representation of the political by a strategy of
transforming political practices into fixed structures or "arrangements." The theoretization of structure depended on the ability to
envision discrete institutions as forming a whole—a constitution—
made up of interrelated parts or functions and then to combine this
imaginary with the logically separate notion that the interrelationship
provides a nexus wherein the meaning of the whole constitution allegedly inheres.[66] At the same time, theoretization of structure also
included another principle that seemed to contradict the emphasis on
the wholeness of a constitution by suggesting that the parts of a constitution need not be homogeneous. Both Plato and Aristotle adopt
the notion that though a constitution consists of interconnected parts,
those parts are potentially replaceable by a part or parts from an en-

63. Herodotus *Histories* 3.80.
64. Thuc. *History* 6.39.
65. One of the best formulations of this point is in Cicero, *De re publica* 1.31–32.
66. Aristot. *Pol.* 1252a17–24.

tirely different, even "opposed" constitution; or, stated the other way round, that a part of one constitution, or, more precisely, the idea represented by that part's place in another form, could be transplanted along with the part to an entirely different constitution, where it would modify the "natural" tendencies of that constitution. Thus the requirement of a property qualification for office, which was the normal practice of an oligarchical constitution, could be inserted into an otherwise democratic constitution and thereby not only modify democracy but institutionalize within it the political claims of wealth.

XI

If any democracy has ever flourished, it has been at its peak for only a brief period, so long as the people were neither numerous enough nor strong enough to cause insolence because of their good fortune, or jealousy because of their ambition.

· Dio Cassius, *History of Rome*

I have been attempting to retrieve aspects of democracy that are in tension with the organizational impulses of ancient and modern constitutionalism. A reflection of that tension is the fact that democracy has no continuous history after the absorption of Athens into the Macedonian empire. From 322 B.C. to the political experiments launched by the American and French revolutions of the eighteenth century, there were examples of city-state republics in which the "people" sometimes had a small share, but the evidence overwhelmingly indicates that these were oligarchies dominated by the rich and wellborn. That hiatus ends in the destruction of democratic hopes by the failure of modern revolutions and in the creation, instead, of the modern misrepresentation of democracy, the nation-state organization.

Democracy in the late modern world cannot be a complete political system, and given the awesome potentialities of modern forms of power and what they exact of the social and natural world, it ought not to be hoped or striven for. Democracy needs to be reconceived as something other than a form of government: as a mode of being conditioned by bitter experience, doomed to succeed only temporarily, but a recurrent possibility as long as the memory of the political survives. The experience of which democracy is the witness is the realization that the political mode of existence is such that it can be, and is, periodically lost.

As I have noted, ancient democratic politics never possessed its own voice. From the fifth century B.C. to the end of the eighteenth century, democratic theory's sole spokesmen were the English Levellers of the seventeenth century and Tom Paine in the eighteenth. The idea of democracy comes to us, therefore, primarily through hostile interpreters. But because of the meaning of the "people" overlaps that of "the political," making it virtually impossible to discuss the latter without including the former, the politics of the demos has not been lost to memory but is preserved though half-buried in the political theories of democracy's critics.

The idea of the political and the democratic experience of its loss can be found in the myth recounted in Plato's *Protagoras* (320c–323a). The notions are also preserved by Polybius, in his theory of cycles, and in early modern times by Locke in particular. In a few paragraphs largely overlooked by commentators who have concentrated on Locke's myth of the state of nature, is another myth that serves to explain why there *was* a state of nature, not in the first place but in the second. Locke's "original myth" describes a golden age that came to an end when the people "forgot" what men might do when naïvely entrusted with absolute power.[67]

The lesson embedded in Polybius's cyclic myth and in Locke's myth of an original contract and right of revolution, is that, historically, it falls to democracy to have to reinvent the political periodically, perhaps even continually. Democracy does not complete its task by establishing a form and then being fitted into it. A political constitution is not the fulfillment of democracy but its transfiguration into a "regime" and hence a stultified and partial reification. Democracy, Polybius remarks, lapses "in the course of time."[68] Democracy is a political moment, perhaps *the* political moment, when the political is remembered and recreated.

Here we might recall that in the classical theories of cycles of political forms, democracy typically followed after aristocracy or oligarchy or monarchy.[69] According to most cyclic accounts, democracy

67. John Locke, *Two Treatises of Government*, 2.107, 110, 111.
68. Polybius *Histories* 6.9.4–5.
69. See G. W. Trompf, *The Idea of Historical Recurrence in Western Thought* (Berkeley and Los Angeles: University of California Press, 1979).

emerged from the trauma of misgovernment and the exhaustion of alternatives represented by the other forms. In most of the classical versions, each form, whether monarchy or aristocracy, begins by being "political"; that is, those who rule are, for the moment, public spirited, genuinely concerned with the common good. Each is supported by the people. Yet each, according to its own nature, betrays that trust and perverts the political.

Polybius, no friend of democracy, describes a situation in which rule by aristocracy has degenerated into a corrupt and rapacious oligarchy:

> When the common people have killed some of the oligarchs and driven the rest into exile, they neither dare to make a king their ruler, since they still think with terror of the wickedness of the kings of former times, nor do they have the courage to entrust the state to a selected group, since they have the results of their former mistakes before their eyes. Thus they naturally turn to the only hope that has not yet been disappointed, namely the hope that they place in themselves. This is why the people turn from oligarchy to democracy and take the administration and the trust of public affairs upon themselves.[70]

Democracy, historically, has not just been about oppositions, however. It has been about the abuse and misuse of one's powers by others. As the Polybian passage suggests, democracy is a rebellious moment. It involves the taking back of one's powers, not just the revocation of legitimacy. When powers are taken back, when the "flow" of power from people to ruler (or "trust") is interrupted, what was being depicted by political theorists was a kind of cautionary fable about political consciousness. Among modern political theorists, Locke recorded just such a fable when he tried to explain why monarchy seemed to be the oldest and most natural form of government. He attributed its origins to "the Innocence and Sincerity of that poor but vertuous Age" when, in addition to their powers, men naïvely transferred to one man the natural affection they felt toward their fathers.[71]

Such fables register a moment when the people realize that all forms of governance have built into them a principle of partiality that promotes the exploitation of the powers of the many by the few. Aristocracy confines rule to those of noble birth and uses power for pur-

<hr>

70. Poly. *Histories* 6.9.1–4, trans. Kurt von Fritz, *The Theory of the Mixed Constitution in Antiquity* (New York: Columbia University Press, 1954), 363.
71. Locke, *Two Treatises of Government*, 2.110.

poses associated with aristocracy, most notably, for war. Hereditary monarchy does the same, whereas nonhereditary monarchy wants to rest its case on sheer ability or virtue. Oligarchy elevates wealth as the principle governing access to public offices and wants to organize society into a machine for the production of wealth, to make wealth the measure of achievements as well as the principle governing access to public office (this can be done indirectly by allowing wealth to dominate formally democratic elections). Tyranny proclaims the intention of the stronger to use the powers of others to satisfy the tyrant's ambitions or desires.

The taking back of one's powers is the crucial move. In the history of political theory, it was expressed through the concept of the state of nature. State-of-nature theorists who were not themselves democrats nonetheless preserved an archaic remnant of a democratic experience. When governments fail or, in Locke's formulation, when they violate the principles according to which they were constituted, power reverts either to a natural "community" or to individuals. Then follows the truly "democratic moment" and the crucial political moment, the moment when power is to be renewed democratically (2.243). Locke's theory stipulates that each individual must consent to the terms on which power is to be reconstituted and a political condition resumed. Underlying Locke's thinking was the assumption that the political is a condition subject to failure and hence requiring healing and renewal. The sole source of renewal is democracy (2.132, 149, 155).

XII

> But were the whole frame here,
> It is of such a spacious, lofty pitch,
> Your roof were not sufficient to contain it.
>
> SHAKESPEARE, *Henry VI*

It is no longer fashionable to appeal to cycles of government or to states of nature. Yet it might be argued that a belief in the restorative power of democracy is still part of the American political consciousness. Certain events illustrate that belief: the recurrent experience of constituting political societies and political practices, beginning with

colonial times and extending through the Revolution and beyond to
the westward migrations, where new settlements and towns were
founded by the hundreds; the movement to abolish slavery and the
abortive effort at reconstructing American life on the basis of racial
equality; the populist and agrarian revolts of the nineteenth century;
the struggle for autonomous trade unions and for women's rights; the
civil rights movement of the 1960s and the antiwar, antinuclear, and
ecological movements.

Just what constitutes a restorative moment is a matter for contesta-
tion. Ancient historians claimed that the hegemony Athens established over Greece as a result of her leadership in the war against
Persia was due to the energies and talents encouraged by democracy.
In the most recent "Persian War," American leaders hailed the triumph of American arms as a new restorative moment. "Desert Storm"
was represented not as the restoration of democracy, nor as the taking
back of power by the people, but as a certain kind of healing, one that
meant "kicking the Vietnam syndrome" and thus restoring the national unity deemed essential to remaining the world's only superpower. That understanding of the restorative moment represents a
perfect inversion in which the state of war, rather than the state of
nature, serves as the condition of renewal.

Desert Storm, or postmodern democracy's "Persian War," demonstrates the futility of seeking democratic renewal by relying on the
powers of the modern state. The possibility of renewal draws on a
simple fact: that ordinary individuals are capable of creating new cultural patterns of commonality at any moment. Individuals who concert their powers for low-income housing, worker ownership of facto-
ries, better schools, better health care, safer water, controls over toxic
waste disposals, and a thousand other common concerns of ordinary
lives are experiencing a democratic moment and contributing to the
discovery, care, and tending of a commonality of shared concerns.
Without necessarily intending it, they are renewing the political by
contesting the forms of unequal power which democratic liberty and
equality have made possible.

ELLEN MEIKSINS WOOD

2 *Democracy: An Idea of Ambiguous Ancestry*

"The Glorious Revolution," said Margaret Thatcher, opening Parliament's tricentenary celebration of that ambiguous event in 1988, "established the enduring qualities of democracy—tolerance, respect for the law, for the impartial administration of justice." These are all admirable qualities. It would have been a good thing if the Settlement of 1688 had indeed established them, as it would have been a distinct improvement on Thatcher's regime if her government had indeed been committed to them.[1] But they have little specifically to do with *democracy*. Conspicuously absent from this catalog of democratic characteristics is the very quality that gives democracy its specific and literal meaning: rule by the demos. It remained for the left wing of the

My thanks to Peter Euben and Neal Wood for their comments on an earlier draft of this essay.

1. The "tolerance" of the Settlement was, of course, strictly limited, excluding Catholics from the monarchy, and indeed all non-Anglicans from public office and the established universities. As for "respect for the law," it was unambiguously the law of the dominant propertied class, embodied in a Parliament that embarked on a spree of self-interested legislation, multiplying the number of capital crimes to protect private property, undertaking a series of parliamentary enclosures, and so on. The "impartial administration of justice" is a quaint way of describing the justice of the gentry as administered by the landed class itself, notably in the persons of justices of the peace. But then, this unqualified praise for the Glorious Revolution came from a prime minister who presided over the most sustained attack on both popular power *and* civil liberties in Britain since the advent of universal suffrage—in the form of security laws, destruction of local authorities, profoundly restrictive trade union legislation, and so forth.

If anything, 1688 represented a regression of democratic power, not only relative to the more radical period of the English Civil War but in some respects even in comparison to the restored monarchy, with, for example, the ascendant Whigs becoming more rather than less inclined to narrow the franchise. In fact, the franchise was more restricted in the eighteenth century than it had been for much of the seventeenth.

Labour party, in the person of Tony Benn, to point out in his own
response to these parliamentary festivities that there was little democracy in a "revolution" that did nothing to promote popular power, as
it excluded women and propertyless people, while firmly consolidat-
ing the rule of the dominant class.

It is instructive to contrast Thatcher's definition with that of an ancient antidemocrat, Aristotle, who was no more keen than Margaret
Thatcher on rule by the demos but who (if we make allowances for
the Athenian exclusion of women and slaves) knew rather better what
the word democracy meant: "The proper application of the term 'democracy' is to a constitution in which the free-born and poor control
the government—being at the same time a majority." (*Politics* 1290b)
The diametric opposite of this rule by the poor majority was oligarchy, "a constitution in which the rich and better-born control the government—being at the same time a minority"—a remarkably apt description, one might think, of Thatcher's own British "democracy."
Aristotle qualifies this definition by pointing out that even if the poor
were a minority, their rule would constitute a democracy. The true
difference between democracy and oligarchy is the difference between poverty and wealth (1279b). The philosopher's criteria, then,
have to do not primarily with institutional forms or procedures, nor
even only with numbers, but above all with the distribution of class
power. They are social criteria as well as political.

Athenian democracy was certainly exclusive, so much so that it may
seem odd to call it a democracy at all. The majority of the population—women, slaves, and resident aliens (metics)—did not enjoy the
privileges of citizenship. But the necessity of working for a living and
even the lack of property were not grounds for exclusion from full
political rights. Indeed, the inclusion of banausic classes, those engaged in "base" and "menial" occupations, was the hallmark of the
democracy. In this respect, Athens exceeded the criteria of all but the
most visionary democrats for many centuries thereafter. Early modern republicans, for example, never looked beyond a community of
propertied citizens. Nor is it self-evident that even the most democratic polity today confers on its propertyless and working classes
powers equal to those enjoyed by banausic citizens in Athens. Modern
democracy has become more inclusive, finally abolishing slavery and
granting citizenship to working men as well as to women. It has also
gained much from the absorption of "liberal" principles, respect for
civil liberties and "human rights." But the progress of modern democracy has been far from unambiguous; for as political rights have become less exclusive, they have also lost much of their power; and the

word *democracy* itself has been domesticated and diluted, emptied of its social content, its reference to the distribution of class power.

The redefinition of democracy exemplified by Thatcher's usage is no Tory monopoly. The identification of democracy with the formal and procedural principles of "toleration," the rule of law, civil liberties, constitutionalism, "limited" or "responsible" government, representation, "pluralism," and so on—*in place of* its essential association with popular power—has, if anything, become dominant. Indeed, a reconceptualization of democracy is one of the most notable features of modern western cultural history, encapsulating political and economic developments in the capitalist world since the eighteenth century. It certainly is, and has been for some time, a common feature of the ruling ideologies, from "conservative" to "liberal"; and even on the Left, the tradition that identifies democracy with rule by the demos and a redistribution of social power has tended to be submerged in the doctrine of "formal democracy."[2]

THE TRANSFORMATION

As late as the last quarter of the eighteenth century, the predominant meaning of "democracy," in the vocabulary of both advocates and detractors, was essentially the meaning intended by the Greeks who invented the word: rule by the *dēmos*, the "people." The social content of "democracy" was conveyed by the dual meaning of *dēmos*, which typically encompassed the "people" not only as a civic status, like the Roman *populus* or the American "people" ("We the people . . ." of the Preamble to the Constitution), but also the "people" as *plebs*, the common people as a social category, or even the poor. This accounts for the widespread and unapologetic denigration of democracy by the dominant classes, even, indeed especially, by the most distinguished founders of the American republic—a republic whose dominant ideology in the ensuing centuries would designate these unabashed antidemocrats as the "founding fathers" of the world's most perfect democracy. In the interim, the concept had undergone a transformation that allowed its erstwhile enemies to embrace it, indeed often to make it the highest expression of praise in their political vocabulary.

The American experience was decisive. At least, a critical moment

2. A distinction is sometimes made between "formal" democracy, referring to electoral and representative procedures, civil liberties, and the institutional checks and balances of the modern "liberal democratic" state, and "substantive" definitions of democracy that refer not only to political procedures and institutions but also to their social context, the distribution of class power within society.

in the process of redefinition can be situated at the point of transition
from the open rejection of democracy voiced by Federalist leaders like
James Madison, to the characterization of the proposed antidemocratic federation as a new political type, what Alexander Hamilton
called "representative democracy." We have become so accustomed to
this formulation that we tend to forget the novelty of the American
idea. In its Federalist form, at any rate, it meant that something hitherto perceived as the antithesis of democratic self-government was
now not only compatible with but constitutive of democracy: not the
exercise of political power but its relinquishment, its transfer to
others, its alienation.

The alienation of political power was so foreign to the Greek conception of democracy that even election could be regarded as an oligarchic practice, one democracies might adopt for certain specific
purposes but which did not belong to the essence of the democratic
constitution. Thus Aristotle, outlining how a "mixed" constitution
might be constructed out of elements from the main constitutional
types, such as oligarchy and democracy, suggests the inclusion of election as an oligarchic feature. Election was understood to favor the
gnōrimoi, the notables; men of property and good birth. Athenians,
for example, might elect their military leaders (like Pericles), but they
did so on the basis of a distinction between offices requiring a narrowly technical expertise and the general political functions for which
the appropriate qualification was the kind of civic wisdom that all citizens could be assumed to possess. The quintessentially democratic
method was selection by lot, a practice that, while acknowledging the
practical constraints imposed by the size of a state and the number of
its citizens, embodies a criterion of selection in principle opposed to
the alienation of citizenship and to the assumption that the demos is
politically incompetent.

The American republic firmly established a definition of democracy
in which the transfer of power to "representatives of the people" constituted not just a necessary concession to size and complexity but
rather the very essence of democracy itself. It is worth remembering
that the Federalist argument—at a time when other options were still
in contention and many anti-Federalists were opposing the proposed
constitution precisely on the grounds that it alienated power from the
people—was not that representative democracy was expedient in a
large republic but, on the contrary, that a large republic was desirable
because it necessitated representation. It is also worth remembering
that other, more democratic conceptions of representative democracy
were possible, as conceived, for example, by Tom Paine. For the Federalists, the virtue of their federation, as against the existing Confed-

eration or any other system that preserved too much local autonomy and manageable units of self-government, was precisely that it precluded democracy in the traditional sense. Indeed, argued Madison, the larger the republic the better, because the ratio of representatives to represented would thereby be reduced. Nor, of course, was the Federalist definition of democracy incompatible with the assumption that the mass of ordinary people would be represented by their social superiors.[3]

The Americans, then, though they did not invent representation, can be credited with establishing an essential constitutive idea of modern democracy: its identification with the alienation of power. There was, however, more to the process of redefinition, and it would take more than another century to complete. In the United States and Europe, the essential question of the social composition and inclusiveness of the "people" who had the right to choose their representatives had not yet been resolved, and it continued to be a fiercely contested terrain until well into the twentieth century. It took a long time, for example, for the Americans to improve on the ancient Greek exclusion of women and slaves, and the laboring classes cannot be said to have won full inclusion until the last property qualifications were abolished (and even then, there remained a wealth of devices for excluding the poor, especially blacks). But already in the second half of the nineteenth century, it had become sufficiently clear that the issue was being decided in favor of "mass democracy"; and the ideological advantages of redefining democracy became increasingly obvious as the era of mass mobilization progressed.

The imperatives and constraints imposed on the ruling classes of Europe by an inevitably growing democratization have been very effectively described by Eric Hobsbawm:

> Unfortunately for the historian, these problems [posed for governments and ruling classes by mass mobilization] disappear from the scene of open political discussion in Europe, as the growing democratization made it impossible to debate them publicly with any degree of frankness. What candidate wanted to tell his voters that he considered them too stupid and ignorant to know what was best in

3. Federalist attitudes to democracy in its original sense, together with a conception of representation that distances the ordinary citizen from political power, is particularly well illustrated by Federalist no. 10, written by James Madison. Madison does not here refer to the Federalist republic as a democracy, but his colleague, Alexander Hamilton, describes it elsewhere as a "representative democracy" and also makes it clear in Federalist no. 35 that lower-class citizens will generally be represented by their social betters. For an illuminating discussion of the Federalists in the context of the debates leading up to and surrounding the Constitution, see Gordon Wood, *The Creation of the American Republic, 1776–1787* (Chapel Hill: University of North Carolina Press, 1969).

politics, and that their demands were as absurd as they were dangerous to the future of the country? What statesman, surrounded by reporters carrying his words to the remotest corner tavern, would actually say what he meant? . . . Bismarck had probably never addressed other than an elite audience. Gladstone introduced mass electioneering to Britain (and perhaps to Europe) in the campaign of 1879. No longer would the expected implications of democracy be discussed, except by political outsiders, with the frankness and realism of the debates which had surrounded the British Reform Act of 1867. . . . The age of democratization thus turned into the era of public political hypocrisy, or rather duplicity, and hence also into that of political satire.[4]

In earlier times, democracy had meant what it said. At the same time, its critics showed no hesitation in denouncing the stupidity, ignorance, and unreliability of the "common herd." Adam Ferguson was speaking in the eighteenth century for a long and unembarrassed tradition of antidemocrats when he asked, "How can he who has confined his views to his own subsistence or preservation, be intrusted with the conduct of nations? Such men, when admitted to deliberate on matters of state, bring to its councils confusion and tumult, or servility and corruption; and seldom suffer it to repose from ruinous factions, or the effects of resolutions ill formed and ill conducted."[5]

Such views were not confined to the academic speculations of elite intellectuals but could be openly declared by politicians. This kind of *glasnost'* was no longer possible in the late nineteenth century. Just as the ruling classes sought various ways to limit mass democracy in practice, they adopted ideological strategies to place limits on democracy in theory. And just as they—for example, French, American, and even English ruling classes[6]—"domesticated" revolutionary theories, so too, it can be argued, they appropriated and naturalized democracy, assimilating its meaning to whatever political goods their particular interests could tolerate. The reconceptualization of democracy belongs, it might be said, to the new climate of political hypocrisy and duplicity.

In an age of mass mobilization, then, the concept of democracy was subjected to new ideological pressures from dominant classes, demanding not only the alienation of "democratic" power but a clear

4. Eric Hobsbawm, *The Age of Empire, 1875–1914* (London: Weidenfeld and Nicolson, 1987), 87–88.
5. Adam Ferguson, *An Essay on the History of Civil Society*, ed. Duncan Forbes (Edinburgh: Edinburgh University Press Paperbacks, 1978), 187.
6. Hobsbawm, *Age of Empire*, 93–94.

dissociation of "democracy" from the demos—or at least a decisive shift away from popular power as the principle criterion of democratic values. The moment of this transvaluation is more difficult to isolate, associated as it was with protracted and arduous political and ideological struggles. But hints can be found in the unresolved tensions and contradictions in the theory and practice of nineteenth-century liberalism. The principal actors here are those liberals and "radicals" torn between a distaste for democracy and a recognition of its inevitability, perhaps even its necessity and justice, who acknowledged the advantages of mass mobilization in promoting their programs of reform or at least conceded the wisdom of domesticating the "many-headed hydra," the turbulent multitude, by drawing it into the civic community.

John Stuart Mill is perhaps only the most extreme example of the contradictions that constituted nineteenth-century liberalism. On the one hand, there was his strong distaste for the "levelling" tendencies and "collective mediocrity" of mass democracy (nowhere more than in the locus classicus of modern liberalism, his essay "On Liberty"), his Platonism, his elitism, and his imperialist conviction that colonial peoples would benefit from a period of tutelage under the rule of their colonial masters. On the other hand, he advocated the rights of women and universal suffrage (which he thought could be made compatible with a kind of class tutelage by maintaining weighted voting, as he proposed in *Considerations on Representative Government*), and he flirted with socialist ideas (always on the condition that capitalism be preserved until "better minds" had lifted the multitude out of its need for "coarse stimuli," the motivations of material gain, and subjection to the lower appetites). Mill never resolved this systematic ambivalence toward democracy, but we can perhaps find some hint of a possible resolution in a rather curious place, in his judgment on the original democracy of ancient Athens.

In the late eighteenth century, and increasingly in the nineteenth, the history of classical Greece became a vehicle for conducting controversies about contemporary political issues.[7] These debates began with ferocious attacks on Athenian democracy by enemies of political reform, in Britain notably Tory opponents of parliamentary reform like William Mitford, author of an influential political history of Greece, who made no attempt to disguise his antidemocratic message to his contemporaries. It then became a matter of policy for liberals and

7. These historiographic issues are discussed at length in my *Peasant-Citizen and Slave: The Foundations of Athenian Democracy* (London: Verso, 1988), chap. 1.

radicals, such as Mill and his friend, George Grote, author of a distinguished history of ancient Greece, to defend the ancient democracy against its Tory critics on behalf of their own projects of political reform.

It is in these liberal interventions that a subtle change in the meaning of democracy can be detected. What is striking about them is their identification of Athenian democracy with its encouragement of variety and individuality, in contrast to the narrow and stultifying conservatism of the Spartans—whom Mill, in his review of Grote's history, even called the Tories of Greece. This characterization of ancient Athens contrasts sharply, of course, with Mill's account of modern democracy and the threat he perceives in it to individuality and excellence. The very different assessment of democracy in its ancient form was, however, made possible only by the most conspicuous evasiveness about the one literally democratic feature of Athenian democracy, its extension of citizenship to laboring, "base," and "mechanic" classes. The liberal defenders of Athenian democracy remained studiously vague about the political economy of the democracy and the position of producing classes in it, not only to evade the embarrassment of slavery but perhaps also to avoid acknowledging the central role of the laboring multitude. Even those who, like Mill, advocated a (qualified) extension of the suffrage to the multitude evinced a notable lack of enthusiasm for rule by the demos and were not inclined to dwell on its role in the ancient democracy. Far better to invoke the liberal values of classical Athens—and here lay a possible solution to the liberal-democratic conundrum: a simple redefinition of democracy which identifies it not with popular power but with the values of liberalism.

The concept of democracy has now become wonderfully elastic, permitting liberals to confine it to parliamentary representation and civil liberties, or perhaps even to the "alternation of elites" (according to a formula beloved by some modern "pluralists"), leaving intact the gross disparities of class power, while neoliberals and conservatives can identify it with the market. What all these flexible definitions of democracy have in common is the eclipse of its literal meaning.

Rewriting History: Democracy and Lordship

As these changes in the meaning of "democracy" were being effected, democracy acquired a new pedigree, a different historical lineage, bearing little relation to the origins of the idea in ancient

Greece. The ancient concept of democracy had grown out of a historical experience that had conferred a unique civic status on subordinate
classes, creating in particular that unprecedented formation, the peasant-citizen. In all—or at least a great deal—but name, the modern
concept belongs to a different historical trajectory, most vividly exemplified in the Anglo-American tradition. The landmarks along the
road to the ancient democracy, such as the reforms of Solon and
Cleisthenes, represent pivotal moments in the elevation of the demos
to citizenship. In the other history, originating not in Athenian democracy but in European feudalism and culminating in liberal capitalism, the major milestones, like the Magna Carta and 1688, mark the
ascent of the propertied classes. In this history, it was not peasants
liberating themselves from the political domination of their overlords
but lords themselves asserting their independent powers against the
claims of monarchy. This is the origin of modern constitutional principles, ideas of limited government, the separation of powers, and so
on—principles that have displaced the social content of rule by the
demos as the central criterion of democracy. If the peasant-citizen is
the most representative figure of the first historical drama, in the second it is the feudal baron and the Whig aristocrat.

If citizenship is the constitutive concept of ancient democracy, the
founding principle of the other variety is, perhaps, lordship. The
Athenian citizen claimed to be masterless, a servant to no mortal man.
He owed no service or deference to any lord, nor did he waste his
labor to enrich a tyrant by his toil.[8] The *eleutheria* entailed by his citizenship was the freedom of the demos *from* lordship. The Magna
Carta, in contrast, was a charter not of a masterless demos but of
masters themselves, asserting feudal privileges and the freedom *of*
lordship against both Crown and popular multitude, just as the "liberty" of 1688 represented the privilege of propertied gentlemen, their
freedom to dispose of their property and servants at will.

Certainly, the assertion of aristocratic privilege against encroaching
monarchies produced the tradition of "popular sovereignty" from
which the modern conception of democracy derives; yet the "people"
in question was not the demos but a privileged stratum constituting an
exclusive political nation situated in a public realm between the monarch and the multitude. Whereas Athenian democracy had the effect
of breaking down the age-old opposition between rulers and producers by turning peasants into citizens, the division between ruling
landlords and subject peasants was a constitutive condition of "popu-

8. These points are discussed in greater detail in ibid., 126–37.

lar sovereignty" as it emerged in early modern Europe. On the one hand, the fragmentation of sovereignty and the power of lordship that constituted European feudalism, the check on monarchy and state centralization exercised by these feudal principles, were to be the basis of a new kind of "limited" state power, the source of what were later to be called democratic principles, such as constitutionalism, representation, and civil liberties. On the other hand, the obverse side of feudal lordship was a dependent peasantry, while the "political nation" that grew out of the community of feudal lords retained its exclusiveness and the political subordination of producing classes.

In England, the exclusive political nation found its embodiment in Parliament, which, as Sir Thomas Smith had written in the 1560s, "hath the power of the whole realme both the head and the bodie. For everie Englishman is entended to bee there present, either in person or by procuration and attornies, of what preheminence, state dignitie, or qualitie soever he be, from the Prince (be he King or Queene) to the lowest person of England. And the consent of the Parliament is taken to be everie man's consent."[9] It is worth noting that a man was deemed to be "present" in Parliament even if he had no right to vote for his representative. Smith, like others before and after him, took it for granted that a propertied minority would stand for the population as a whole. But there is more to this conception of parliamentary supremacy than its restriction of the active political nation to a relatively small community of property holders. Indeed, its implications for modern concepts of democracy have become more apparent as the political nation, the "people," has grown to include the "popular multitude."

In Britain today, for example, politics is the special preserve of a sovereign Parliament. Parliament may be ultimately accountable to its electorate, and (in the more radical Lockean parliamentarianism) the "people" (however defined) may, in extremis, even have the right of rebellion. In this sense, power "derives" from the people. But they are not truly sovereign. For all intents and purposes, there is no politics—or at least no legitimate politics—outside Parliament. There have, of course, existed other political arenas, such as municipal and regional government; but the degree to which even these have existed merely on the sufferance of Parliament—or, more precisely, of its governing party and cabinet, or even the prime minister—was demonstrated in the most dramatic way by the Thatcher government. Whole layers of

9. Thomas Smith, *De Republica Anglorum*, ed. Mary Dewar (Cambridge: Cambridge University Press, 1982), 79.

local and regional government were abolished with ease, while the remaining institutions were drastically restricted, if not disabled, particularly in response to democratic initiatives by the Greater London Council. Indeed, the more inclusive the "people" has become, the more the dominant political ideologies—from Conservative to mainstream Labour—have insisted on depoliticizing the world outside Parliament and delegitimating "extraparliamentary" politics. Running parallel with this process has been a growing centralization of parliamentary power itself in the executive, producing something very much like cabinet, or even prime ministerial, sovereignty.

There did emerge, in early modern England, a body of political thought—especially in the work of James Harrington, Algernon Sidney, and Henry Neville—which, on the face of it, appears to run counter to this dominant parliamentary tradition. This school of political theory, which has come to be known as classical republicanism, had, or seemed to have, as its central organizing principle a concept of citizenship, implying not simply the passive enjoyment of individual rights we have come to associate with "liberal democracy" but a community of active citizens in pursuit of a common good. Yet there is one fundamental point on which early modern republicans like James Harrington agreed with their "liberal" contemporaries: the exclusivity of the political nation.[10] Active citizenship was to be reserved for men of property and must exclude not only women but also those men who lacked, as Harrington put it, the "wherewithal to live of themselves," that is, those whose livelihood depended on working for others. This conception of citizenship had at its core a division between propertied elite and laboring multitude. It is not surprising that republicans of this variety, when seeking models in antiquity, chose the aristocratic ("mixed") constitutions of Sparta or Rome instead of democratic Athens.

Indeed, such a division between propertied elite and laboring multitude may have belonged to the essence of English classical republicanism even more absolutely and irreducibly than to, say, Lockean liberalism. When Harrington set out to construct political principles appropriate to a society where feudal lordship no longer prevailed, he did not altogether jettison the principles of feudalism. It is even possible to say that his conception of citizenship was modelled in certain important respects on feudal principles. On the one hand, there was no longer to be a category of dependent property, a juridical and

10. The practical differences between republicans and Whigs, or at least the more radical wing, in the politics of the seventeenth century were not always clear.

political division between different forms of landed property, as there had been between feudal lords and their dependents. All landed property was to be juridically and politically privileged. On the other hand, property itself was still defined as a political and military status; it was, in other words, still characterized by the inextricable unity of economic and political-military power which had constituted feudal lordship.

In this conception of citizenship, classical republicanism was already an anachronism at the moment of its conception. Landed property in England was already assuming a capitalist form, in which economic power was no longer inextricably bound up with juridical, political, and military status, and wealth depended increasingly on "improvement" or the productive use of property subject to the imperatives of a competitive market. Here, John Locke's conception of property and agricultural "improvement" was more in keeping with current realities.[11] And while Locke himself was no democrat, it is arguable that a conception of property such as his was ultimately more amenable to relaxing the restrictions on membership in the political nation.[12] To put it simply, once the economic power of the propertied classes no longer depended on extraeconomic status, a monopoly on politics was no longer indispensable to the elite. By contrast, within a framework dominated by an essentially precapitalist conception of property, with all its juridical and political "embellishments" (as Marx once called them), the "formal" equality made possible by the capitalist separation of the "economic" and the "political" was not even thinkable (literally), let alone desirable.

CAPITALISM AND DEMOCRACY

Capitalism, by shifting the locus of power from lordship to property, made civic status less salient, as the benefits of political privilege gave way to purely "economic" advantage. This shift eventually made possible a new form of democracy. Whereas classical republicanism had solved the problem of propertied elite and laboring multitude by restricting the extent of the citizen body, capitalist or liberal democ-

11. See Neal Wood, *John Locke and Agrarian Capitalism* (Berkeley and Los Angeles: University of California Press, 1984).

12. For a powerful critique of attempts to portray Locke as a democrat, see David McNally, "Locke, Levellers and Liberty: Property and Democracy in the Thought of the First Whigs," *History of Political Thought* (Spring 1989): 17–40. See also my "Locke against Democracy," *History of Political Thought* (Winter 1992): 657–89; and "Radicalism, Capitalism, and Historical Contexts," forthcoming in *History of Political Thought*.

racy would permit the extension of citizenship by restricting its powers. Whereas one proposed an active but exclusive citizen body, in which the propertied classes ruled the laboring multitude, the other could—eventually—envisage an inclusive but largely passive citizen body, embracing both elite and multitude, but whose citizenship would be limited in scope.

Capitalism transformed the political sphere in other ways too. The relation between capital and labor presupposes formally free and equal individuals, without prescriptive rights or obligations, juridical privileges, or disabilities. The detachment of the individual from corporate institutions and identities began very early in England. It is, for example, reflected in Smith's definition of a commonwealth as "a societie or common doing of a multitude of free men collected together and united by common accords and covenauntes among themselves"[13] and in the individualistic psychologism that runs through the tradition of English social thought from Hobbes and Locke to Hume and beyond. The rise of capitalism was marked by the increasing detachment of the individual (not to mention individual property) from customary, corporate, prescriptive and communal identities and obligations.

The emergence of this isolated individual did, needless to say, have its positive side, the emancipatory implications of which are emphasized by liberal doctrine, with its constitutive concept (myth?) of the sovereign individual. But there was also another side. In a sense, the creation of the sovereign individual was the price paid by the laboring multitude for entry into the political community; or to be more precise, the historical process that gave rise to capitalism, and to the modern "free and equal" wage laborer who would eventually join the body of citizens, was the same process in which the peasant was dispossessed and deracinated, detached from both his property and his community, together with its common and customary rights.

Let us consider briefly what this means. The peasant in precapitalist societies, unlike the modern wage laborer, remained in possession of property, in this case land, the means of labor and subsistence. This meant that the capacity of landlord or state to appropriate labor from him depended on a superior coercive power, in the form of juridical, political, and military status. The principal modes of surplus extrac-

13. Smith, *De Republica Anglorum*, 57. It is interesting in this connection to compare Smith's definition with that of his contemporary, Jean Bodin, who, in his *Six Books of the Commonwealth*, treats "families, colleges, or corporate bodies," not individual free men, as the constituent units of the commonwealth, reflecting the realities of France, where corporate institutions and identities continued to play a prominent role in political life.

tion to which peasants were subject—rent and tax—typically took the form of various kinds of juridical and political dependence: debt bondage, serfdom, tributary relations, obligations to perform corvée labor, and so on. By the same token, the capacity of peasants to resist or limit their exploitation by landlords and states depended in great measure on the strength of their own political organization, notably the village community. To the extent that peasants were able to achieve a degree of political independence by extending the jurisdiction of the village community—for example, imposing their local charters or replacing landlord representatives with their own local magistrates—they also extended their economic powers of appropriation and resistance to exploitation. But however strong the village community became from time to time, there generally remained one insurmountable barrier to peasant autonomy: the state. The peasant village almost universally remained, as it were, outside the state and subject to its alien power, as the peasant was excluded from the community of citizens.

It is here that Athenian democracy represents a radically unique exception. Only here was the barrier between state and village breached, as the village effectively became the constitutive unit of the state, and peasants became citizens. The Athenian citizen acquired his civic status by virtue of his membership in a deme, a geographic unit generally based on existing villages. The establishment by Cleisthenes of the deme as the constituent unit of the polis was in a critical sense the foundation of the democracy. It created a civic identity abstracted from differences of birth, an identity common to aristocracy and demos, symbolized by the adoption by Athenian citizens of a *dēmotikon*, a deme-name, as distinct from (though in practice never replacing, especially in the case of the aristocracy) the patronymic. But even more fundamentally, Cleisthenes' reforms "politicised the Attic countryside and rooted political identity there."[14] They represented, in other words, the incorporation of the village into the state, the peasant into the civic community. The economic corollary of this political status was an exceptional degree of freedom for the peasant from extraeconomic exactions in the form of rent or tax.[15]

The medieval peasant, in contrast, remained firmly excluded from the state and correspondingly more subject to extraeconomic surplus extraction. The institutions and solidarities of the village community

14. Robin Osborne, *Dēmos: The Discovery of Classical Attika* (Cambridge: Cambridge University Press, 1985), 189.

15. For more on these points, see my *Peasant-Citizen and Slave*, 101–7, and "Capitalism and Human Emancipation," *New Left Review* 167 (1988): 9–12.

could afford him some protection against landlords and states (though it could also serve as a medium of lordly controls, as for example, in manorial courts), but the state itself was alien, the exclusive preserve of feudal lords. And as the feudal parcellation of sovereignty gave way to more centralized states, the exclusivity of this political sphere survived in the privileged political nation.[16]

Finally, as feudal relations gave way to capitalism, specifically in England, even the mediation of the village community, which had stood between peasant and landlord, was lost. The individual and his property were detached from the community, as production increasingly fell outside communal regulation, whether by manorial courts or village community (the most obvious example of this process is the replacement of the English open-field system by enclosure). Customary tenures became economic leaseholds subject to the impersonal competitive pressures of the market. Smallholders lost their customary use-rights to common land; increasingly, they were dispossessed, whether by coercive eviction or the economic pressures of competition. Eventually, as landholding became increasingly concentrated, the peasantry gave way to large landholders, on the one hand, and propertyless wage laborers on the other. In the end, the "liberation" of the individual was complete, as capitalism, with its indifference to the extraeconomic identities of the laboring multitude, dissipated prescriptive attributes and extraeconomic differences in the solvent of the labor market, where individuals become interchangeable units of labor abstracted from any specific personal or social identity.

It is as an aggregate of such isolated individuals, without property and abstracted from communal solidarities, that the laboring multitude finally entered the community of citizens. Of course the dissolution of traditional prescriptive identities and juridical inequalities represented an advance for these now "free and equal" individuals; and the acquisition of citizenship conferred on them new powers, rights, and entitlements. But we cannot take the measure of their gains and losses without remembering that the historical presupposition of their citizenship was the devaluation of the political sphere, the new relation between the "economic" and the "political" which had reduced the salience of citizenship and transferred some of its formerly exclusive powers to the purely economic domain of private property and the

16. For a discussion of the relations among peasants, lords, and the state in medieval and early modern Europe, see Robert Brenner, "The Agrarian Roots of European Capitalism," in *The Brenner Debate: Agrarian Class Structure and Economic Development in Pre-Industrial Europe*, ed. T. H. Aston and C. H. E. Philpin (Cambridge: Cambridge University Press, 1985), 213–327.

market, where purely economic advantage takes the place of juridical privilege and political monopoly. The devaluation of citizenship entailed by capitalist social relations is an essential attribute of modern democracy. For that reason it is inexcusably one-sided for liberal doctrine to represent the historical developments that produced formal citizenship as nothing other than an enhancement of individual liberty, the freeing of the individual from an arbitrary state as well as from the constraints of tradition and prescriptive hierarchies, from communal repressions or the demands of civic virtue.

Nor can we assess the ideological effects of the modern relation between individual citizen and civic community or nation without considering the degree to which that "imagined community" is a fiction, a mythical abstraction, in conflict with the experience of the citizen's daily life.[17] The nation can certainly be real enough to inspire individuals to die for their country; but we must consider the extent to which this abstraction is also capable of serving as an ideological device to deny or disguise the more immediate experience of individuals, to disaggregate and delegitimate, or at least to depoliticize, the solidarities that stand between the levels of individual and nation, such as those forged in the workplace, the local community, or a common class experience. When the political nation was privileged and exclusive, the "commonwealth" in large part corresponded to a real community of interest among the landed aristocracy. In modern democracies, where the civic community unites extremes of social inequality and conflicting interests, the "common good" shared by citizens must be a much more tenuously abstract notion.

Here, again, the contrast with ancient democracy is striking. Constructed on the foundation of the deme, the democratic polis was built on what Aristotle in the *Nicomachean Ethics* called a "natural koinonia." That this "real community" had real political implications is suggested by the tangible consequences of peasant citizenship. Nor was the contradiction between civic community and the realities of social life as great in Athenian democracy as in the modern democratic state. Modern liberal democracy has in common with the ancient Greek version a dissociation of civic identity from socioeconomic status which permits the coexistence of formal political equality with class inequality. But this similarity disguises a deeper difference between the two forms, reflecting radically different relations between "political" and "social" or "economic" planes in the two cases. In ancient Athenian

17. On the nation as an "imagined community," see Benedict Anderson, *Imagined Communities* (London: Verso, 1983).

democracy, the right to citizenship was not determined by socio-economic status; but the power of appropriation, and relations between classes, were directly affected by democratic citizenship. The most obvious instance is the juridical division between citizens and slaves, but there were other ways in which citizenship in the democracy determined economic relations.

One need only consider democratic Athens against the background of other precapitalist societies: say, the poet Hesiod's Boeotia, where "gift-devouring" lords, as he describes them, used their jurisdictional powers to milk the peasants (even, it would appear, a prosperous and slave-owning peasant like Hesiod himself); or Sparta, where the ruling community appropriated the labor of Helots by means of what amounted to a military occupation; or medieval Europe, where the juridical and military status of feudal lords allowed them to appropriate the labor of dependent peasants; or European absolutism, where office holders used the state as a means of private appropriation through the taxation of a subject peasantry.

In Athens, by contrast, democratic citizenship meant that small producers, and peasants in particular, were to a great extent free of such extraeconomic exactions. Their political participation—in the assembly, in the courts, and in the street—limited their economic exploitation. At the same time, unlike workers in capitalism, they were still not subject to the purely economic compulsions of propertylessness. Political and economic freedom were inseparable—the dual freedom of the demos in its simultaneous meaning as a political status and a social class. Political equality did not simply coexist with, but substantially modified, socioeconomic inequality. In this sense, democracy in Athens was not formal but substantive.

In capitalist democracy, the separation between civic status and class position operates in both directions. Socioeconomic position does not determine the right to citizenship, and that is what is democratic in capitalist democracy. But neither does civic equality directly affect or significantly modify class inequality, and that is what limits democracy in capitalism. The power of the capitalist to appropriate the surplus labor of the worker, for instance, does not depend on a privileged juridical or civic status. The division between capitalist property and the propertylessness of workers is sufficient to produce an economic compulsion that obliges workers to exchange their labor power for a wage, simply in order to gain access to the means of labor and subsistence.

In ancient Athens, the granting of citizenship to peasants and craftsmen had substantial consequences for class relations and modes of appropriation; and the extension of civic rights to slaves or women would, of course, have transformed the society entirely. In feudalism, too, juridical privilege and political rights were scarce resources that could not have been widely distributed without completely undermining the prevailing social order. In capitalism, class relations between capital and labor can survive even with juridical equality and universal suffrage. In that sense, political equality in capitalist democracy not only coexists with socioeconomic inequality but leaves it fundamentally intact.

THE AMERICAN EXPERIENCE

Capitalism, then, made it possible to conceive of formal democracy, a form of civic equality that could coexist with social inequality and leave economic relations between the "elite" and the laboring multitude in place. Needless to say, however, the conceptual possibility of formal democracy did not make it a historical actuality. There were to be many long and arduous struggles before the "people" grew to encompass the laboring multitude, let alone women. It is a curious fact, however, that in the dominant ideologies of Anglo-American political culture, these struggles have not achieved the status of principal milestones in the history of democracy. In the canons of English-speaking liberalism, the main road to modern democracy runs through Rome, the Magna Carta, the Petition of Rights, and the Glorious Revolution, not through Athens, the Levellers, the Diggers, and Chartism. Nor is it simply that the historical record belongs to the victors; for if 1688, not Levellers and Diggers, represents the winners, should not history record that democracy was on the losing side?

It is here that the American experience was decisive. English Whiggery could have long remained content to celebrate the forward march of Parliament without proclaiming it a victory for democracy. The Americans had no such option. Despite the fact that in the struggle to determine the shape of the new republic it was the anti-democrats who won, even at the moment of foundation, the impulse toward mass democracy was already too strong for the victory to be complete. Here, too, the dominant ideology divided governing elite from governed multitude; and the Federalists might have wished, had it been possible, to create an exclusive political nation on the model of oligarchic republicanism, an aristocracy of propertied citizens in which property—and specifically landed property—remained a privileged juridical-political-military status. But economic and political realities

in the colonies had already foreclosed that option. Property had irre-
vocably discarded its extraeconomic embellishments, in an economy
based on commodity exchange and purely economic modes of appropriation, which undermined the neat division between politically privileged property holders and the disenfranchised laboring multitude.
Moreover, the colonial experience culminating in revolution had created a politically active populace. The Federalists thus faced the unprecedented task of preserving what they could of the division between mass and elite in the context of an increasingly democratic
franchise and an increasingly active citizenry.

The framers of the Constitution embarked on the first experiment
in designing a set of political institutions that would embody, and at
the same time curtail, popular power, in a situation where it was no
longer possible to maintain an exclusive citizen body. With the option
of an active but exclusive citizenry unavailable, it was necessary to create an inclusive but passive citizen body with limited scope for its political powers. Many commentators on the Constitution have noted the
deliberately antidemocratic intentions that informed some of the most
characteristic U.S. institutions: the creation of a large federal republic,
instead of a confederation of smaller and more autonomous entities,
which would reduce the ratio of representatives to represented; the
strengthening of the federal government at the expense of local autonomy, and the executive at the expense of the legislative power; the
powerful, almost monarchical, executive presidency; the indirect election of the president and (originally) the Senate; and so on. Even the
system of checks and balances, generally regarded as the principal
safeguard of American liberties, including the power of the Supreme
Court, can be interpreted as a means of limiting the power of representative bodies accountable to the electorate.[18]

The Federalist ideal may have been to create an aristocracy combin-
ing wealth with republican virtue (an ideal that would inevitably give
way to the dominance of wealth alone); but their practical task was to
sustain a propertied oligarchy with the electoral support of a popular
multitude. This task also required the Federalists to produce an ideology, and specifically a redefinition of democracy, which would disguise the ambiguities in their oligarchic project. It is not surprising
that, like the classical republicans, the founders sought ideological
support for this delicate balancing act not in Athens but in Rome. The
Roman "mixed constitution," the "oligarchic democracy" of the Ro-

18. For a discussion of some democratic criticisms of the Constitution, see C. W. Barrow,
"Historical Criticism of the US Constitution in Populist-Progressive Political Theory," *History
of Political Thought* (Spring 1988): 111–28.

man republic, the peculiar combination of aristocracy and popular politics summed up in the Roman formula SPQR (the senate and the people of Rome), provided just the right ideological mix to give the Federalist experiment a historical pedigree. So the founding fathers, conceiving of themselves as latter-day Catos, a natural aristocracy of republican virtue, adopted Roman pseudonyms, called their upper house a Senate, and set the Roman eagle to watch over their "representative democracy."

If American political institutions have not been imitated everywhere, there is nevertheless another sense in which the American experiment has become the universal model of democracy.[19] It was the antidemocratic victors in United States who gave the modern world its definition of democracy, a definition in which the alienation of popular power is an essential ingredient. With that new definition came a new sustaining ideology, in which the winner's account of history played a critical role. It was the American experience that made it possible—and necessary—to track the history of democracy not through advances in popular power but through progress in the evolution of representative institutions and the liberty of property, irrespective of their consequences for the power of the demos.

Where We Are Now

Democracy, in common usage, has at best become synonymous with liberalism, and the tradition of democracy in its literal sense has been more or less submerged in the mainstream of western political culture. To say this is not to deny that liberal values (civil liberties, individual rights, the protection of a "civil society" against intrusion by the state, the establishment of institutions to check alienated power, and so on) are vital to any functioning democracy or that in respect to these values, modern formal democracy represents significant progress. The point is, rather, that the dominant ideologies in modern capitalist states have tended to dilute the democratic idea, to dissolve it altogether into the concept of liberalism, to offer liberalism not as a complement to, but as a substitute for, democracy as popular power; and in the process, much of value has been lost.

The first premise of ancient Athenian democracy was that the demos, and specifically people who were obliged to labor for their livelihood, even the banausic classes, were competent to make political

19. On this model and its implications, see Peter Manicas, "The Foreclosure of Democracy in America," *History of Political Thought* (Spring 1988): 137–60.

judgments, not just to elect their governors but to decide matters of substance. This principle is, for example, the central point at issue between Socrates and Protagoras in Plato's dialogue, *Protagoras*, where the debate concerns the Athenian practice of permitting any shoe-maker or smith to render political judgments even though in other domains, such as shipbuilding, they naturally look to specialists and experts.

Modern concepts of representative democracy operate on an assumption very different from the ancient democratic idea, namely, that though our governors must be ultimately accountable to the electorate, the demos must alienate its political power and its right to make substantive judgments. It is instructive to contrast the principles underlying political representation with those that inform the one modern institution that still bears the mark of ancient democracy: the jury. It is worth considering, too, the difference between the often mindless behavior of citizens each time they alienate their sovereignty in the election of representatives (when they bother to vote at all), and their intelligent good sense in jury deliberations on complex and substantive judgments for which they bear direct responsibility.[20]

It is not here simply a matter of distinguishing between "direct" and "representative" democracies. Representation is undoubtedly essential and desirable in any complex democracy, and there is no doubt much to be said for the liberal recognition that freedom may include the right *not* to participate in politics. The issue is rather the assumption underlying the principle of representation itself. Hamilton and Madison recommended a "representative democracy" not on the grounds that representation was a necessary expedient in a large and complex society, nor even because individuals must have the freedom to be apathetic, but on the grounds that it was desirable to increase the distance between the popular multitude and the process of political decision. The smaller the ratio of representatives to represented, for instance, the better. Nor was it simply a matter of numbers, because the Federalists took it for granted that the small representative elite would reflect the social hierarchy: merchants, for instance, would be the natural representatives of craftsmen and laborers. Like Smith's "lowest person of England," Hamilton's laborer could be deemed to

20. Consider too the role of this democratic institution in protecting liberal values: e.g., in the Mapplethorpe obscenity trial, in which a jury composed of largely working-class men and women in Cincinnati delivered a particularly enlightened verdict, defending the freedom of artistic expression; or the Clive Ponting case in Britain, where a jury defied clear instructions from the judge in order to acquit a civil servant of breaching security by revealing state secrets, on the grounds that his action was in the public interest. Recent changes in the British legal system have closed this loophole, eliminating the "public interest" defense.

be "present" in representative assemblies in the person of his natural superior.

No doubt the founding fathers, who had little use for government by the people (much preferring their own government *for* the people), did respect the liberal values of constitutional government, the rule of law, and civil liberties. Whether it is strictly accurate to describe their achievements in this respect as advances in *democracy*, inasmuch as these principles have less to do with the disalienation of power than with the control of alienated power, there can be little doubt that they represent a major advance. Yet we must also take note of what is missing in the modern idea of liberal democracy. The difference in spirit between the ancient democratic idea and modern liberal values might be summed up in the distinction between the modern concept of free speech and the ancient idea of *isēgoria*, something more like equality of speech, the principle that peasants and craftsmen are as much entitled to speak as gentlemen, philosophers, and specialists in the art of politics. If modern liberalism, with its freedom of expression, at least in principle precludes the silencing of such demotic voices, it has no positive commitment to their equality of speech. The fact that the modern liberal idea represents a great achievement does not mean that the suppression of the old democratic one has not been a substantial loss.

There is, however, a more difficult question. The devaluation of democracy has not been just a matter of deliberate ideological choice. Capitalist social relations, as we have seen, place structural limits on the value of citizenship. Something more than reform of representative institutions would be required in modern democracies to reproduce anything approaching the effects citizenship would have had for the laboring multitude in precapitalist societies. If capitalism has replaced political privilege with the powers of economic coercion, how could citizenship recover its former salience? What would it mean to extend citizenship—and this means not just a greater equality of "opportunity," or the passive entitlements of welfare provision, but democratic accountability or active self-government—into the economic sphere? It is at this point that the concept of democracy begins to challenge the very foundations of capitalism itself.

JENNIFER ROBERTS

3 *The Creation of a Legacy:*
A Manufactured Crisis in
Eighteenth-Century Thought

Curiosity about the possible relevance of the Athenian experiment in democracy to American realities has waxed and waned across
the centuries and among different decades of the same century. Anxiety about the state of popular involvement in government, moreover,
and about the withdrawal of energies from the body politic has promoted many American thinkers in the last decade of the twentieth
century to reopen the study of Athenian democracy and to ask once
again whether the experiences of the Athenians might contain valuable lessons and might, mutatis mutandis, provide a positive model in
at least some areas. This belief contrasts strikingly with the conviction
of America's founders that what little Athens had to teach was entirely
of the negative variety.

It was in 1967 that the American historian Bernard Bailyn outraged
the sentiments of classicists and patriots alike by his suggestion that
Greek and Roman tags were "illustrative, not determinative" of the
thinking of America's founders.[1] In Bailyn's formulation, classical allusions provided the founders with effective rhetorical weapons, but

Much of the wording and substance of this essay is derived from my book *Athens on
Trial: The Antidemocratic Tradition in Western Thought* (Princeton: Princeton University Press,
1994), and I thank Princeton University Press for permission to use this material here.

Several friends and colleagues read the essay at various stages of its development. I particularly thank Peter Euben, Carl Richard, and my husband, Robert Lejeune, all of whom read
all or part of it with more frequency than anyone has a right to expect. I also owe a great debt
to the late Michael Shute for discussing these questions with me at length.

1. Bernard Bailyn, *The Ideological Origins of the American Revolution* (Cambridge: Harvard
University Press, Belknap, 1967), 23–26.

the thought of the ancients did not in fact play a key role in their intellectual development. Bailyn's assertion has provoked an intense and tremendously creative debate among classicists and historians—the latter comfortable with the possibility that he might be right, the former anxious about losing the classics' claim to have molded modern republicanism.

One cannot help wondering what it was like to live in the eighteenth-century equivalent of a space installation on another planet, surrounded by a wilderness that seemed to promise alternatively a brave new world and the kingdom of darkness. Clearly one of the central questions that faced the colonists would have to be their relationship to the culture from which they had sprung, and we know from their writings that this was so. The need of Americans to define their relationship to their European heritage became still more pressing once separation from England became first a prospect and then a reality. Part of this heritage involved more and less recent texts by men such as Locke, Hume, and Montesquieu, and the republican agitation of the English civil wars; but another important element lay in the history of the classical world (a history often discussed by Hume, Montesquieu, and seventeenth-century British republicans, though not by Locke). Inevitably the study of classical history brought the founders into contact with the earliest experiment in self-government, that of the ancient Athenians. The use the founding fathers made of what they read about Athenian democracy provides one forum in which to examine how they interacted with the classical past—or more precisely, with what they thought they knew about that past. For the founders' view of the classical world was ultimately a product of three only partially separable ideologies: the ideology of the ancient sources, that of the corpus of writings they inherited from early modern Europe, and their own ideology as eighteenth-century men of property. The Athens against which they sought to define their new nation was not Athens of the fifth and fourth centuries B.C. but rather the Athens of eighteenth-century Europe and America.

America's founders were the heirs to a long tradition about Athenian democracy and to a rather shorter tradition about popular government in general. What they had gleaned from their youthful study differed dramatically from what adolescents are taught in American schools today. Everyone today claims to be a democrat: American capitalists, Third World dictators, and erstwhile Soviet communists alike now announce themselves to be the true democrats of the twentieth century. The semantics of democracy have dissolved into pablum. Consider the following advertisement for democracy: "The meaning of democracy is precisely that the people, from time to time, should be called upon to judge the achievements and acts of a government, to judge whether the program of the government is of any use or whether the men are of any use who take it upon themselves to execute that program." Consider the author: Adolf Hitler.[2] As the political scientist John Dunn has put it, "Democratic theory is the moral Esperanto of the present nation-state system, the language in which all Nations are truly united."[3] But it was not always so. Just as jarring to our sentimental twentieth-century ears as Hitler's formulation is the contention of Leibniz some three hundred years ago that "today there is no prince so bad that it would not be better to live under him than in a democracy," or for that matter, the 1767 Christmas homily in which the future Pope Pius VII tried nervously to convince his diocese that democracy was not necessarily incompatible with Christianity.[4] "Democrat" was a word one used of one's enemies, never of oneself; no eighteenth-century thinker would identify himself or herself as a democrat any more that white civil rights activists would refer to themselves as "nigger-lovers" or feminists introduce themselves as "libbers."

Though democracy was first developed in Greece, moreover, no one would have been more astonished than the average classical Greek by the current competition to be more democratic than thou. Most Greeks, indeed, brought back to life to overhear the fervid democratic rhetoric of the twentieth century, would be not only astonished but appalled. Greeks were intensely concerned with differences among individuals—differences between humans and animals, between males and females, between free people and slaves, between men who owned property and men who did not, and of course, between Greeks and non-Greeks. Under these circumstances, it would be surprising if most Greek states had become happily democratic, according equal privilege to the rich and low-born alike. The truth is that few Greek states practiced democracy, and many of those that did had adopted this egalitarian form of government under pressure from imperial Athens, which preferred that the states that belonged to its alliance employ democratic constitutions.

2. Adolf Hitler, *Speeches* (London, 1942), 1:254, cited in Arne Naess et al., eds., *Democracy, Ideology and Objectivity: Studies in the Semantics and Cognitive Analysis of Ideological Controversy* (Oslo: University Press for the Norwegian Research Council for Science and the Humanities, 1956), no. 193.

3. John Dunn, *Western Political Theory in the Face of the Future* (Cambridge: Cambridge University Press, 1979), 2.

4. These and other valuable citations about the early uses of the words *democracy* and *democrat* are collected in Dunn, *Western Political Theory*, chap. 1; R. R. Palmer, "Notes on the Use of the Word 'Democracy,' 1789–1799," *Political Science Quarterly* 68 (1953): 203–26, and more broadly, *The Age of the Democratic Revolution*, 2 vols. (Princeton: Princeton University Press, 1959); and Naess et al., *Democracy, Ideology and Objectivity*, 95–131.

Even in Athens, members of prominent families resented the dilution of their power and prestige under democracy and, like Thucydides and Plato, developed elaborate constructs to demonstrate why
democracy was an unacceptable form of government. The contemporary sources for Athenian democracy are almost entirely derogatory;
to Thucydides and Plato we must add Aristotle, Xenophon, and the
anonymous author known as the "Old Oligarch," whose brief tract on
Athenian government was ascribed for many centuries to Xenophon.
(In reality, both Thucydides and Plato has some positive things to say
about democracy as well, but as a rule it was their strictures on popular government that were remembered—Thucydides' stress on the
volatility of the masses and Plato's condemnation of amateur government. Similarly the negative was commonly extracted from Aristotle's
mixed picture.) By the time of the Macedonian conquest in 338, all
the fundamentals of the anti-Athenian tradition had been established.
Athenian democracy, it was maintained, was mob rule and constituted
the tyranny of the poor over the rich. It disregarded the critical principle that awarded privilege in accord with property. The Athenian
demos was ungrateful, unstable, and fickle, and the phenomenon of
ostracism illustrated the prominent role given to emotion and irrationality in the Athenian state. The situation worsened markedly after
the death of Pericles—who had corrupted the citizens by offering
them state pay for state service—and came to be run by self-interested
demagogues. Athens was perceived as offering a shining example of
what could happen if the inherent inequalities among men were disregarded and government built on a specious egalitarianism.

It is a curious fact that those who were captivated by the democratic
ethos did not leave behind them texts celebrating the Athenian
achievement. Athenian democracy was on the whole a spoken, not
written, phenomenon. The give and take of debate in the assembly
survives only in the sanitized version that appears in the works of
cultivated historians like Thucydides and Xenophon; of the daily conversations that filled the agora we have only the reconstructed
snatches that suited the agenda of Aristophanes. Whereas the Platonic
dialogue became the chief vehicle for antidemocratic ideology, the
ideology of the democracy was conveyed chiefly through tragedy, en-
coded in a way that has made it hard to recover and hidden away
where, until recently, political theorists did not think to look for it.
The Athenian democratic ethos entailed a dialectical and communitarian way of life that involved drama, festivals, meetings of the
neighborhoods and wards known as demes, and constant disagreement and debate in the noisy marketplace. It was never captured in

the sober prose of historians and political theorists (although, ironically, for all Plato's antidemocratic pronouncements, the verbal spar-
ring on which his dialogues were based was firmly grounded in the
dialectic of democracy.) Had it been, egalitarian thinkers of the nineteenth and twentieth centuries would not have had to probe beneath
the elitist overlay to uncover a very different picture of Athens—an
Athens resilient in peace and in war, cradle of the arts, nurse of the
intellect, managed by a citizenry better informed about affairs foreign
and domestic than any citizenry before or since, dedicated to the principle of trial by jury, and so committed to responsible government
that between the Persian Wars and the Macedonian conquest, the democracy was overthrown only twice. Each coup, inspired by treason,
lasted just a few months, the second ultimately judged so appallingly
un-Greek that even the king of Sparta assisted the democrats in restoring their government. This, however, was not the image that appeared in the writings of disaffected intellectuals of aristocratic lean-
ings.

If Anthenian intellectuals had themselves so little use for democracy, Roman thinkers had still less. Cicero in his speeches portrayed
Athenian democracy as a form of mob rule from which it was advis-
able for Romans to depart as much as possible. Among the Greco-
Roman historians, Polybius carried forward Aristotle's advocacy of a
"mixed government" and concomitant condemnation of pure democracy, and Plutarch was fond of decrying the volatile nature of the
untutored mob. The revulsion of staid Romans from Athenian democracy is easier to understand than the parallel revulsion of the
Romans' heirs, the thinkers of Renaissance Italy. One might imagine
that the Florentines in particular would have sought to emulate the
dynamic creativity of the Athenians and have rejected the static anti-
intellectualism of the Spartans. In actuality, however, Florentine political thinkers like Machiavelli, Francesco Guicciardini, and Donato Gian-
notti uniformly rejected Athens in favor of Sparta. For so strong was
the fear of instability among the city-states of Renaissance Italy that
even the Florentines blinded themselves to the weaknesses of Sparta
and set it up as their model. In part this may be traced to the Renaissance worship of Plutarch.

The anti-Athenian tradition traveled happily northward along with
the rest of the cultural movement that was the Renaissance. Predictably, the monarchists Jean Bodin and Robert Filmer had no use for
Athenian democracy; Hobbes condemned it roundly; and even the
seventeenth-century utopian James Harrington, who incorporated
several features of Athenian government into his ideal state, had

many unkind things to say about Athens. Amid the civil strife of Harrington's era, however, Athens did find some defenders. The republican martyr Algernon Sydney, who went to the scaffold in 1683, defended the Athenians' exile of so many of their prominent politicians
as an important part of the political process, and Marchamont Nedham, whose political convictions seem to have regrouped themselves
with remarkable facility to suit the convenience of the hour, maintained in one of his republican phases that the so-called sins of the
Athenian people were in fact provoked by sinister politicians for their
own ends. Like Sydney, Nedham defended the Athenians' exile of so
many of their leaders as illustrating an important principle of accountability. Solon, Nedham argued, had left the only pattern of a free
state available for all the world (i.e., Britain) to follow.

A hostile tradition about Athens dominated in France, which produced one of the most popular ancient histories of the eighteenth
century, the virulently antidemocratic *Ancient History* of Charles Rollin, as well as Montesquieu's disquisition on the joys of mixed government; and Rousseau was seized by a fervid passion for the Spartans
which led him to deploy the Athenians as a foil to their legendary
virtues. The sententious treatises of the Abbé Mably portrayed classical Athens as decadent beyond redemption. In Britain, Oliver Gold-
smith, Temple Stanyan, and John Gillies echoed the sentiments of
Rollin in their own histories of Greece, and Hume was hard on the
Athenians. Altogether, the eighteenth century wisdom about Athens
was composed largely of "warning literature" wherein the ultimate
collapse of polished, commercial Athens was adduced as irrefutable
evidence of the connection between democracy and decadence. The
most dramatic example of the genre was the *Reflections on the Rise and
Fall of the Ancient Republics Adapted to the Present State of Great Britain*,
published in 1749 and generally attributed to the eccentric Edward
Wortley Montagu, whose more famous mother Lady Mary Wortley
Montagu (the celebrated letter writer) thought so well of him that she
left him in her will the sum of one guinea. There, readers could learn
that Athens "has left us some instructions highly useful for our present conduct," because "warned by her fate, we may learn . . . [that]
luxury, and a prevailing fondness for publick diversions are the
never-failing fore-runners of universal idleness, effeminacy and corruption."[5] In France, Rousseau decried the purported decadence of
the Athenians and denied that virtue could develop in a civilization
where a self-indulgent overeducation was the rule of the day, so dif-

5. Edward Wortley Montagu, *Reflections*, 3d ed. (1769), 144.

ferent from the virtuous training offered to Spartan youth. It was this mixed but fundamentally hostile tradition that was inherited by eighteenth-century Americans—mixed, but dominated by a heady draught of the antidemocratic Plutarch, whose writings have been found in more colonial homes than any works beside the Holy Scriptures. Though, on the whole, die-hard monarchists like Bodin and Filmer were neglected in America, Machiavelli, Rollin, and Hobbes were regularly found in colonial libraries.

Not all Americans saw merit in studying the classical past. Some believed classical learning conduced to un-Christian values; in 1769, John Wilson resigned his position at the Friends Academy in Philadelphia because of his belief that the reading of classical authors promoted "Ignorance, Lewdness and Profanity" in America's youth.[6] Others rejected the study of antiquity on grounds of irrelevance: Benjamin Franklin, for example, censured the lack of self-confidence that led his fellows to turn to the ancients for political wisdom and condemned the study of ancient history on the grounds that the ancient republics had failed to endure and hence offered no model to Americans.[7] Others, like William Vans Murray, cited the differences between American and classical states to demonstrate the irrelevance of ancient history.[8] Hamilton and other authors of *The Federalist* were persuaded that a new "science of politics" had developed which made the experiments of the ancients obsolete.[9] On other occasions, however, ancient history appeared in a different light. Participants in the Federal Convention plainly expected that references to antiquity would lend authority to their arguments. Classical exempla, however, were as likely to be negative as positive. The eventual collapse of all the ancient states, particularly in Greece, and still more particularly in Athens, was frequently counted against them. On the whole, Athens served as an object lesson in how not to structure a state.

To be sure, some eighteenth-century Americans had a kind word or two for Athenian government. The anonymous T. Q. and J., writing in 1763, stressed the need for a check on excessive power in the hands of one man, and the Athenians are presumably meant when the au-

6. Cited by Meyer Reinhold, *Classica Americana: The Greek and Roman Heritage in the United States* (Detroit: Wayne State University Press, 1984), 157–58.

7. In Max Farrand, ed., *The Records of the Federal Convention of 1787* (New Haven: Yale University Press, 1937), 1:457.

8. William Vans Murray, *Political Sketches* (London, 1787), also in *American Museum* 2 (September 1787): 228–35.

9. See, e.g., Hamilton in Federalist no. 9, in Clinton Rossiter, ed., *The Federalist Papers* (New York: New American Library, Mentor, 1961), 72; Madison and Hamilton, in no. 18, 126; Madison, in no. 37, 228–29; and Hamilton, in no. 66, 402.

thors praise "the Greeks" for keeping "their good men from growing formidably great."[10] All governments, the authors go on, would do well in this particular to imitate the Greek example. Predictably, the most dramatic defense of Athens appears in the anonymous 1776 New Hampshire pamphlet entitled "The People the Best Governors," in which the author applauds the example of Athens, where the legislature was composed of "tent makers, cobblers, and common tradesmen."[11] It did not go without saying, however, that the model of ancient Athens was applicable to modern America. Already in 1645 the New England divine John Cotton had written that "a democratical government might do well in Athens, a city fruitful of pregnant wits, but will soon degenerate into an *Anarchia* . . . amongst rude common people."[12] In the eighteenth century, Athenian democracy was rarely considered suitable even for Athens, and by and large the Athenian example was one from which the founding fathers were eager to dissociate themselves. Thus for instance in Federalist no. 14, Madison made a point of distinguishing the American republics from "the turbulent democracies of ancient Greece and modern Italy." This allusion to the instability of Renaissance governments makes plain the continuing role of Florence in thinking about the Athenian past. In the representative principle he saw the remedy for this turbulence, which he considered inherent to democracy. "In all very numerous assemblies," he maintains, "of whatever characters composed, passion never fails to wrest the sceptor from reason. Had every Athenian citizen been a Socrates, every Athenian assembly would still have been a mob."[13] It was probably also Madison who in Federalist no. 63 appealed to his audience to recognize the need for a "well-constructed Senate" to protect the people at moments when, "stimulated by some irregular passion, or some illicit advantage, or misled by the artful misrepresentations of interested men," they "may call for measures which they themselves will afterwards be the most ready to lament and condemn," and he cites Athens once more as a negative example, asking "What bitter anguish would not the people of Athens have often escaped if their government had contained so provident a safeguard against the tyranny of their own passions? Popular liberty might then have escaped the indelible reproach of decreeing to the

10. In Charles Hyneman and Donald Lutz, eds., *American Political Writing during the Founding Era, 1760–1805* (Indianapolis: Liberty, 1983), 21.

11. Ibid., 397.

12. John Cotton, *The Way of the Churches of Christ in New England* (1645), cited by Richard Gummere, "Church, State, and Classics: The Cotton-Williams Debate," *Classical Journal* 54 (1959): 175–83.

13. Rossiter, *Federalist Papers*, 100, 342.

same citizens the hemlock on one day and statues on the next."[14] Similar arguments were put forward by Hamilton. Like Madison, he coupled the chaos of ancient Greece with that of Renaissance Italy. In both the Continentalist no. 1 of 1781 and the later Federalist no. 9, he compared the bright future of an America that had discovered the virtue of checks and balances and representation with the history of the Greek states (except Sparta), a history that "no friend to order or to rational liberty can read without pain and disgust." He found it impossible, he reported, "to read the history of the petty republics of Greece and Italy without feeling sensations of horror and disgust . . . at the rapid succession of revolutions by which they were kept in a state of perpetual vibration between the extremes of tyranny and anarchy."[15] Writing in 1794, Samuel Williams of New England pointed out that the representative system distinguished America from the deficient democracies of antiquity.[16]

The French Revolution further intensified the revulsion of many Americans from notions of direct democracy, and in a letter to Joseph Priestley, Noah Webster distinguished the direct democracy of Athens from the republican system of America, contending that "the word *Democrat* has been used as synonymous with the word *Jacobin* in France; and by an additional idea, which arose from the attempt to control our government by private popular associations, the word has come to signify a person who attempts an undue opposition to or influence over government by means of private clubs, secret intrigues, or by public popular meetings which are extraneous to the constitution."[17] Russell Hanson, who cites Webster's observation, also connects the revolution in France with the Federalist hostility to the Democratic-Republican Societies that had grown up in the new American nation. Attacks on the Kentucky Democratic Society, Hanson has argued, are reminiscent of the virulent antidemocratic literature of eighteenth-century Britain, one especially virulent opponent labeling the society a "hateful synagogue of anarchy,—that odious conclave of tumult,—that frightful cathedral of discord,—that poisonous garden

14. Ibid., 384.
15. Alexander Hamilton, *Papers*, ed. Harold Syrett, vol. 2 (New York: Columbia University Press, 1961), 657, and Rossiter, *Federalist Papers*, 71.
16. Samuel Williams, "The Natural and Civil History of Vermont" (1794), chap. 15, in Hyneman and Lutz, *American Political Writing*, 963.
17. H. R. Warfel, ed., *The Letters of Noah Webster* (New York: Library Publishers, 1953), 208.

of conspiracy,—that hellish school of rebellion and opposition to all regular and well-balanced authority."[18]

It is not actually true that ancient republics failed to develop any system of representation; at Athens alone one could cite the Boule. Still, the topos of the superiority of American government in regard to representation was dear to the founders' hearts, and it is a theme to which John Adams recurs with some frequency. The aversion of the founding fathers to Athenian democracy is articulated nowhere more fully than in Adams's writings, which repeat Madison's charge of the "turbulence of democracy" in Athens. Adams's works make plain that Adams had a large amount of enthusiasm for a small amount of democracy. If there is one lesson that leaped from the pages of history, Adams claimed, it was the necessity for a separation of powers. Adams considered democratic governments to be the most factious and unstable of all unmixed constitutions, and he viewed the reforms of Solon—about which he made several factual errors—to be the first step in the destruction of Athens. Solon, Adams wrote, "put all power into hands the least capable of properly using it; and, accordingly, these, by uniting, altered the constitution at their pleasure, and brought on the ruin of the nation."[19] Though Solon meant well and instituted the Boule and the Council of the Areopagus as checks on the democracy, nonetheless "factious demagogues" often encouraged the dēmos to headstrong self-assertion, and the subsequent instability of the government of Athens led Adams to inquire, in a sentence that stands alone as a paragraph, "Is this government, or the waves of the sea?"[20] Adams dismissed Cleisthenes as a man of "no great abilities," and Aristides was even worse; for in throwing open the archonship to the poor, he was "giving way to the furious ambition of the people." Adams had no use for ostracism, claiming, "History nowhere furnished so frank a confession of the people themselves of their own infirmities and unfitness for managing the executive branch of government, or an unbalanced share of the legislature, as this institution." Adams's most forceful indictment of the Athenian state appears in his discussion of the bloody oligarchy of the Thirty Tyrants that ruled postwar Athens under the aegis of Sparta. There he argued

18. In Philip Foner, *The Democratic-Republican Societies, 1790–1800: A Documentary Sourcebook of Constitutions, Declarations, Addresses, Resolutions, and Toasts* (Westport, Conn.: Greenwood, 1976), 27, cited in Russell Hanson, *The Democratic Imagination in America: Conversations with Our Past* (Princeton: Princeton University Press, 1985), 86; on democracy, republicanism, and the Federalists, see Hanson's chapter "Republican Rhetoric in the Founding Period," 54–91.
19. Charles Francis Adams, ed., *The Works of John Adams, Second President of the United States* (Boston: Little, Brown, 1850–56), 4:285.
20. Ibid., 4:480–485.

that what undid the Thirty was the quintessentially Athenian nature of their power, which was unchecked. While modern historians have tended to contrast the bloodthirstiness of the Thirty with the comparative moderation of the democrats, Adams saw in their murderous oligarchy not a lurid contrast with the democracy but rather its natural outgrowth. It was in fact their experience of the tyranny of the assembly, Adams claimed, that had inspired the Thirty. "Every body of men," Adams concluded, "every unchecked assembly in Athens, had invariably behaved in this manner: the four hundred formerly chosen; now the thirty; and afterwards the ten." Historians are dead wrong, he argues, to be surprised at the "never-failing passion for tyranny, possessing republicans born in the air of liberty"; what is really astonishing, he claims is "that there is one sensible man left in the world who can still entertain . . . any other sentiment than abhorrence, for a government in a single assembly."[21]

Most of all, Adams saw in popular sovereignty an alarming threat to the sanctity of property and argued that majority rule was to be rejected, as it would entail "the eight or nine millions who have no property . . . usurping over the rights of the one or two millions who have." Debts, Adams feared, "would be abolished first; taxes laid heavy on the rich, and not at all on the others; and at last a downright equal division of every thing be demanded, and voted."[22] Adams was convinced that Solon had not in fact canceled debts. The records of the Federal Convention of 1787 make clear the primacy of property for most framers of the Constitution. Madison argued that "the primary objects of civil society are the security of property and public safety"; three delegates, Gouverneur Morris, John Rutledge, and Rufus King, gave the preservation of property primacy over liberty as the principal object of society; and James Wilson set himself conspicuously apart from the others in arguing that the primary function of government was not the protection of property but rather the cultivation and improvement of the human mind.[23]

Like many of his contemporaries, Adams was more conversant with Greek political theory than with Greek history, and like Aristotle, he believed that Greek democrats habitually violated the sanctity of property. In fact, the evidence suggests that this did not happen in Athens, the Greek democracy about which by far the most is known. But the class prejudices of classical writers led them to see things differently, and as we have seen, the anti-Athenian tradition had a long pedigree.

21. Ibid., 4:486, 3:101, 4:490, 3:102.
22. Ibid., 6:9.
23. These citations have been assembled in Forrest McDonald, *Novus Ordo Seclorum: The Intellectual Origins of the Constitution* (Lawrence: University Press of Kansas, 1985), 3–4.

Adams's habit of holding up Athens as a negative example of the sanctity of property was hardly unique to America. Analogous concerns can be extracted from the virulently anti-Athenian literature that appeared in England around the same time. This literature was influenced in part by the revolution in France, but the preoccupation with property was also evident in some prerevolutionary work as well. It appears most dramatically in the apoplectically antidemocratic *History of Greece* composed throughout the 1780s and 1790s by William Mitford, who did know a good deal about Greek history and was in a position to know that Athenian democrats respected private property. Mitford was convinced, however, that property was insecure under democratic governments. "The satisfaction . . . of an Englishman," he wrote, "in considering his house and his field more securely his own, under the protection of the law, than a castle defended by its own garrison, or a kingdom by its armies, was unknown in Attica," where, after the overthrow of the Solonic constitution, "soverein power became absolute in the hands of those without property." In time, Mitford complained, the nobility were forced to "cringe" to the rabble in order to protect their property under the Athenian democracy, where "property, liberty and life itself were incomparably less secure" than "under the mild firmness of our mixed government." And not only this; Mitford also made invidious comparisons between the government of the Athenians and that of Macedonia, where, he maintained, that exemplary monarch Philip ruled so well that not even his enemies imputed to him the slightest "injury to the civil rights of the Macedonian people."[24] (I expect that anyone alive today who happens to know where the bill of Macedonian civil rights may be found can look forward to a distinguished career.) Though Adams was a staunch republican and Mitford a committed monarchist, the two men were united in their conviction that the best form of government was a mixed state in which power followed property. While Adams and Mitford disagreed as to the ideal proportions of the recipe for the mixed state, they shared an unflinching opposition to the preponderance of any one branch of government, and democracy was the branch they feared most—Mitford because of his loathing for the lower classes, and Adams because democracy seemed a more imminent danger in America than monarchy.

It would be possible to temper the founders' rejection of Athenian democracy by mentioning their admiration for the Greek colonial system, which granted complete political autonomy to newly founded city-states, or by dredging up the enthusiasm some expressed for the

24. William Mitford, *History of Greece* (1822 ed.), 5:31, 34, 219; 3:4.

Amphictyonic League, which seemed to offer an example of the possibilities of federation (though Hamilton was quick to throw cold water on this surge, pointing out that the Amphictyony had been a dismal failure in discouraging intercity warfare and promoting concord). All in all, however, the founders were inclined to view Greece in general as a hotbed of divisiveness and disorder—things they greatly feared would sap the vitality of their bold new venture. Besides, the prevalence of a hostile orientation to Athens was probably itself a factor in their need to distance their new nation from the Athenian experiment and to cleanse their own brand of republicanism from any taint of democracy. And yet to suggest that their rejection of Athenian democracy was the most significant element in the founders' response to Greek government would be to miss the point. For the very fact that the founders' generation was so exercised about the relevance of classical government (as they believed it to have been) tells us a great deal. Like many other critics of Athens—Plato, perhaps, most conspicuously—the founders do, it seems, protest too much. There seems to be something seductive in the simplicity of this egalitarianism they are to eager to deplore; and the earnestness with which the detractors of the classics plead their case is in part a testimonial to the hold the Greeks and Romans exercised on people's souls. We now use the expression "New World"—as in "New World archaeology"—with little or any of the sense of wonder that the notion must have occasioned in the seventeenth and eighteenth centuries. Inevitably, Americans striking out into uncharted waters asked searching questions about the relevance of the ancient past, and in fact the references to classical history in their writings reveal a powerful ambivalence about antiquity. Tom Paine, for example, was bound and determined that Americans should stride boldly into the future with no backward glances, creating a new world out of new materials, and Hamilton decried his countrymen's lack of originality in questing insecurely after classical models. But the very existence of such complaints makes plain that anxious regression to the legitimating authority of the classical past was the rule and not the exception; Hamilton often recurred to the Athenian model as a counterexample for his own arguments, and even Franklin in a mellower mood insisted that the study of Greek and Roman history would tend "to fix in the minds of youth deep impressions of the beauty and usefulness of virtue of all kinds."[25] In 1772, John Adams expressed the wish that Americans emulate the mixed governments of antiquity; in 1780, Jonathan Mason advocated

25. Benjamin Franklin, "Proposals relating to the Education of Youth in Pennsylvania," in Thomas Woody, *The Educational Views of Benjamin Franklin* (New York: McGraw-Hill, 1931), 167.

the study of Greece and Rome to teach the lesson that the waning of patriotic virtue would ruin a state, and Charles Lee, writing in 1782, maintained that it was natural for "a young person whose chief companions are the Greek and Roman Historians and Orators to be dazzled with the splendid picture."[26] Certainly the participants in the Federal Convention expected that references to antiquity would lend weight and dignity to their arguments.

And weight and dignity were tremendously important to the founders. In thinking about just how daring the revolutions in America and France really were, it may be helpful to think back to a far earlier day, to the dawning, in fact, of democracy in Greece. It is important to remember that one reason the Athenians were so elated at their victory over the Persians on the plain of Marathon was that it soothed their apprehensions that the gods simply would not allow the overthrow of aristocracy—of a government controlled by men whose ancestry ultimately might be traced to divine origins. Probably one explanation for the use of the lot in selecting Athenian officeholders was that this system permitted the gods to play a role in what seemed to many people a most ungodly state. The Athenians, in short, had no precedent for what they were doing, and this made them enormously nervous. The Americans, however, did have at least a little in the way of precedent, and inevitably this afforded them a tremendous amount of comfort, while at the same time it compelled them to define the government they were proposing in contradistinction to vaguely similar constitutions that had gone before. For this reason, I see no reason to doubt—though we can never know for certain—that the classical allusions of America's founders were heartfelt. For men—and sometimes women—cut loose from the mother ship on a strange new continent, such allusions offered vital grounding in a past that bound the colonists not only to heroes and heroines long dead but to generations before, both in America and in England, who had agonized over the same texts as they themselves were growing up.

The founders did not live in a vacuum. At much the same time as they were framing the structure of the new nation, thinkers in France and England were wrestling with similar ideas. Like their American counterparts, the French revolutionaries read classical authors. They may indeed have read them a good deal more than their fellow republicans across the ocean; for the circumstances of life in Europe afforded more leisure than did those in the colonies. The republican heroes of antiquity afforded genuinely compelling models to the

26. Cited in Reinhold, *Classica Americana*, 41, 49.

French revolutionaries, though their desire to set in motion the forces of revolution had surely been sparked by conditions in eighteenth-century France far more than by childhood reading in Plutarch, whatever Madame Roland may have said about its galvanizing effect on her conscience. The debate about the merits of Solon and Lycurgus was engaged with real sophistication, and the martyrdoms of Phocion and Cato had an intense afterlife in the lonely cells of imprisoned Girondists. There was certainly something comical in the flurry of classical names that marked the revolutionary generation, and the debate over the comparative virtues of Spartan and Athenian institutions and the adoption of ancient modes of dress in revolutionary France often appears positively childlike to twentieth-century eyes. But though the Americans carried off their classical heritage with more dignity, the spectacle of classical affectation in the revolution across the Atlantic affords a salutary reminder of how very important it was for eighteenth-century republicans to ground their bold new experiment in hallowed tradition.

It is in this context that I think we must view the frequent allusions to the sins of the Athenians among men who sincerely believed that the same new "science of politics" that would make it possible to govern a large territory by republican institutions also made the direct democracies of Greece irrelevant. And this they plainly believed; Montesquieu had warned against it, but the authors of the *Federalist* insisted that it could be done. As Sheldon Wolin has pointed out, Madison managed to present the dynamics of representative government in "abstract, quasi-scientific language" that managed to elevate his views about federal government "to an objective plane where *The Federalist*'s teaching about them could appear axiomatic rather than contestable."[27]

The same abstraction and pretention to science were evident in the most influential detractors of ancient democracy, Plato and Aristotle, who discussed democracy in the abstract while living in the most vibrant democracy the world had ever seen. For all Plato's sniping at the "democratic man" in Book 8 of the *Republic* and his complaints that in a democracy even the animals refuse to yield the right of way to humans while walking down the street, the truth is that his work made no attempt to capture the flavor of the democracy in which he lived. Nor did Aristotle offer any living examples—not in his discussion of how collective wisdom might produce a good decision or in his

27. Sheldon S. Wolin, *The Presence of the Past: Essays on the State and the Constitution* (Baltimore: Johns Hopkins University Press, 1989), 97.

contention that people who did unpleasant physical labor could not make prudent political choices. And in all this high-sounding science, what was lost was art. The Athenians had, after all, produced painting and sculpture and drama that has received the almost universal approbation of posterity. Aristotle in his *Poetics* had not stressed the democratic roots of tragedy or its role in fostering community and dialogue of a high caliber; his discussion of education in Book 8 of the *Politics* advocated two different kinds of *mousikē* (the Greek equivalent of both literature and music), a challenging one for the class of serious political men and one for the lower orders of society which was merely entertaining and not designed to inculcate growth.

It was in part the rediscovery of the visual arts in Greece and the Hellenic aesthetic ideal that made possible the new valuation of Athens that began in the nineteenth century. The celebrated art historian Johann Winckelmann himself had called attention to the connection between Athens's democratic institutions and the flourishing of the plastic arts there. Hölderlin and Schiller and Herder and Hegel all took delight in the fullness of life in Athens, and not long afterward the English liberals put forward a new argument in favor of the Athenians: whereas Samuel Johnson and Mitford had cringed at the thought of the ignorance of a democratic decision-making body, Macaulay and John Stuart Mill and George Grote saw the great strength of the Athenian democracy in the high level of cultivation that citizens enjoyed and called for improvements in the educational system of Britain that would make possible a shared civic consciousness parallel to that achieved by the ancient Athenians. Celebrating the Greek victory over Persia which made the growth of the Athenian democracy possible, Mill proclaimed, "The battle of Marathon, even as an event in English History, is more important than the battle of Hastings."[28] The London banker Grote for his part produced a multivolume history of Greece that would change the shape of the debate about Athens down to our own time. As the classicist Arnaldo Momigliano wrote in a famous essay on the historiography of Greece, after the appearance of Grote's work, all writing about Greece was "for or against Grote."[29] Citing Johnson's insistence that the orator Demosthenes must have addressed an audience of ignorant brutes, as they

28. John Stuart Mill, "Grote's History of Greece [I]," reprinted in Mill, *Dissertations and Discussions*, in *Essays on Philosophy and the Classics*, vol. 11 of his *Collected Works* (Toronto: University of Toronto Press, 1978), 273.

29. Arnaldo Momigliano, "George Grote and the Study of Greek History" (Paper delivered at University College, London, 1952); reprinted in Momigliano, *Studies in Historiography* (New York: Harper and Row, 1966), 65.

did not appear to read books, Macaulay contended that in fact "the Athenian populace far surpassed the lower orders of any community that has ever existed. Books were, indeed, few; but they were excellent; and they were accurately known." In the end, however, it was not books (or indeed any kind of formal education) so much as the energizing nature of public life in the city itself that educated and edified the Athenian citizen—conversation about philosophy in "the public space," and the production of tragedies. "I know of no modern university," Macaulay concluded, "which has so excellent a system of education."[30] The happiest society, Macaulay maintained in his review of Mitford's *History*, "is that in which supreme power resides in the whole body of a well-informed people," and he proclaims that "he alone deserves the name of a great statesman whose principle it is to extend the power of the people in proportion to the extent of their knowledge, and to give them every facility for obtaining such a degree of knowledge as may render it safe to trust them with absolute power."[31]

The American founders simply asked different questions from those posed by the British reformers. The founders worried how their state might achieve endurance, stability, and freedom from faction; and their anxiety led them, as has often been pointed out, to don the coroner's coat when they examined an ancient state: What had they died of, and had modern science found a cure? The questions that exercised liberal thinkers in early nineteenth-century Britain were different: How had the Athenians achieved such a cohesive community and one that produced such astonishing works of art? It is not that Americans of the late eighteenth century were indifferent to education. Americans took pride in the fact that literacy was high among whites in the American colonies at the time of the revolution—perhaps as high in some areas as 90 percent among adult males—and writers such as Franklin, Webster, Jefferson, and Benjamin Rush were all committed to education as one of the bulwarks of the new nation. Its connection with free political institutions was not ignored. Webster proclaimed that "while *property* is considered as the *basis* of the freedom of the American yeomanry, there are other auxiliary supports; among which is the *information of the people*. In no country is education so general—in no country, have the body of the people such a knowledge of the rights of man and of the principles of gov-

30. Thomas Babington Macaulay, "On the Athenian Orators," in *Complete Works of Lord Macaulay*, ed. Lady Trevelyan (London [1866]), 8:153–55.

31. Thomas Babington Macaulay, "On Mitford's History of Greece," *Knight's Quarterly*, November 1824, in Trevelyan, *Works*, 188.

ernment. This knowledge," he declared, "joined with a keen sense of liberty and a watchful jealousy, will guard our institutions."[32] But the leap to understanding just what had made Athens work was not made; and it could be argued too that "knowledge" is something quite different from what participation in the assemblies and the theatrical festivals gave the Athenians. Much can be learned about late eighteenth-century American thinking about education from Samuel Knox's 1799 prize-winning essay on education for Americans. Presumably because of its reputation for cultivation and its role as a university city in the Hellenistic and Roman periods, Knox inferred that Athens provided public education to its citizens, something the evidence suggests is not true. What Athens did provide was an extraordinarily active civic life that included attendance at extremely demanding tragic dramas that examined the most difficult questions facing humans. But Knox dismissed tragedy in his treatise on education; after encouraging the reading of Rollin's insipid *Ancient History* and the uninspired *Antiquities* of Bishop Potter—both common items in early American libraries—and of some Virgil, Theocritus, Hesiod, Anacreon, Pindar, and Horace, he suggests, "In order also to be acquainted with the state of dramatic poetry among the ancients, one or two of the most celebrated performances in each language might be read, but it does not appear that a long attention to that species of composition would be either proper or improving."[33]

In 1991, Basic Books published a book by Eli Sagan of the New School in New York City entitled *The Honey and the Hemlock: Democracy and Paranoia in Ancient Athens and Modern America*. Sagan's central thesis concerns the conflict between a healthy decency and openness in people's hearts on the one hand and, on the other, anxious elements that stand in the way of an optimistic and inclusive view of the human race. By examining this conflict in Athens, he hopes to offer Americans a chance to choose what was most open and reject what was most anxious. I submit that the circumstances of life in late eighteenth-century America disposed the founders more in the direction of anxiety, whereas the circumstances of life in nineteenth-century Britain opened the door to a greater relaxation and openness about the possibilities of a state that enjoyed not only stability and tranquility but also a remarkable level of cultural achievement. That the Athe-

32. Noah Webster, "Leading Principles of the Federal Constitution, etc.," in *Pamphlets on the Constitution of the United States Published during Its Discussion by the People, 1787–1788*, ed. P. L. Ford (1888; reprint, New York: Da Capo, 1968), 57–58.
33. Samuel Knox, "An Essay on the Best System of Liberal Education, Adapted to the Genius of the Government of the United States," in Ford, *Pamphlets*, 304, 342.

nian state was in fact stable and tranquil is believed by Sagan, as it is believed by most scholars of the late twentieth century. It was also believed by Mill, whose assessment of Athenian democracy in his review of Grote's work contended that no other Greek state enjoyed "the unimpeded authority of law, and freedom from factious violence, which were quite as characteristic of Athens as either her liberty or her genius; and which, making life and property more secure than in any other part of the Grecian world, afforded the mental tranquility which is also one of the conditions of high intellectual or imaginative achievement."[34] It is noteworthy that Mill's assessment includes praise of the security of life and property in Athens, something Mitford and Adams, with their particular anxieties, could not believe. The relaxation of tensions in the nineteenth century was, in fact, perceptible on both sides of the Atlantic. In America, where anxiety about the stability of a nonmonarchic government had been assuaged by decades of success, "democracy"—and along with it "Athens"—lost many of its frightening connotations. Already in 1792, Paine felt comfortable boasting that what "Athens was in miniature, America will be in magnitude," announcing that "the one was the wonder of the ancient world; the other is becoming the admiration, the model of the present."[35] Jefferson proclaimed in 1816, "We in America are constitutionally and conscientiously democrats."[36] When Grote's work was received, its merit was instantly recognized. The edition of John Adams's works published in Boston in 1856 with notes by Adams's grandson Charles Francis Adams reflected this new perspective and included numerous corrective footnotes to Adams's discussion of Athens. These on the whole were derived from Grote's *History*, to which they contain several references. One particularly poignant note on John Adams's discussion of Solon (who, he insisted in the face of the evidence, had not really canceled debts) observes tactfully that "the better opinion is, that the statement in this text is below the truth."[37]

The founders' uncritical incorporation of the elitist anti-Athenian tradition into western thought was a profoundly political statement. Working with precisely the same sources, Victorian critics were soon to come to radically different conclusions. Many of the founders were

34. Mill, "Grote's History of Greece, II," in Mill, *Collected Works*, 316.
35. Thomas Paine, *The Rights of Man, Part II* (1792; reprint, London, 1915), 176.
36. Thomas Jefferson to Dupont de Nemours, April 24, in *The Correspondence of Jefferson and Du Pont de Nemours*, ed. Gilbert Chinard (Baltimore: Johns Hopkins University Press, 1931), 256. On the growing acceptability of the words *democrat* and *democracy*, see Hanson, *Democratic Imagination*, 82–88.
37. Adams, *Works* 4:477.

still alive when the ground was laid for an entirely different valuation of Athens by British writers like Macaulay and Grote in the essays they wrote responding to Mitford; they were dead by the time Grote's epoch-making volume on Athens appeared at the middle of the nineteenth century. Thinkers of the later twentieth century, in contrast, are likely to censure the Athenians not from the right but from the left, viewing the equality of citizens as dependent on the denigration of outgroups such as women, slaves, and subjects of the Athenians' overseas tribute-paying empire. Feminists and Marxists have generally taken the lead in arguing, like Sarah Pomeroy of Hunter College, that when the class stratification of earlier days had given way to an "ideal of equality among male citizens," this "intolerable" state of affairs prompted the denigration of all outsiders, something modern egalitarians do not associate with a democratic ethos. "The will to dominate," Pomeroy contends, was such that Athenian men "then had to separate themselves as a group and claim to be superior to all nonmembers: foreigners, slaves, and women."[38] Sagan's book is an excellent example of the ambivalence of the late twentieth century about classical Athens—a work of passion and mission that alternates celebration of the Athenians' development of democratic ideals with indictment of their failures.

One of the most significant developments in the shaping of western political thought has been the way in which Athenian democracy articulated itself through life as it was lived and not in self-conscious political treatises or works of history. A richer picture of Athenian life might reveal a government that stressed accountability of officials, encouragement of the arts, trial by jury, and intense engagement in civic life on the part of a singularly well-informed citizenry. This was not, however, the Athens that emerged from written texts; the founders' reading in both ancient and modern writings encouraged them to think of Athens as a chaotic state in which the masses of the poor wrested dignity and power from the propertied classes and then, having gathered the government into their own incompetent hands, showed that they had neither the integrity nor the intellect to frame a stable polity. Like the men and women of the Renaissance, the founders were haunted by the specter of instability, and when this was compounded by a fear for the sanctity of property congruent with the anxieties of propertied writers throughout the western tradition, little hope remained for a positive valuation of Athens. The prestige of classical antiquity, then, coupled with the popularity of "warning liter-

38. Sarah Pomeroy, *Goddesses, Whores, Wives, and Slaves: Women in Classical Antiquity* (New York: Schocken, 1975), 78.

ature," made it appear helpful to drag in the Athenians as an admonitory counterexample in efforts to caution readers and listeners about the dangers of democracy and as a rhetorical device by which the more complex American representative system might be defended as republican in distinction to democratic. Americans of the founding era did not ask how best they might emulate the civilization that had produced the plays of Sophocles or Phidias's statue of Zeus, because the intensity of their fears stood in the way of their seeing a dynamic connection between Athenian democracy and Athenian creativity; they did not read the history of Greece by Lysias or Demosthenes' essays on government; for no such texts had been written. What they found in their reading was a composite picture, built up over the centuries, into which little critical or creative thought had been put; and the end product rendered by this tedious process taught the vices of Greek democracy alongside the virtues of a certain bland, generic republicanism. To this republican heritage, John Adams paid tribute in a letter he wrote to Lafayette proclaiming that nearly "every thing that is estimable in civil life has originated under [republican] governments" and that "two republican powers, Athens and Rome, have done more honor to our species than all the rest of it."[39] But these sentiments existed side by side with a horror of what Adams believed had actually gone on in Athens, a society in which power did not follow property.

Only in the twentieth century with the professionalization of historical writing did Greek history come to be studied in the new nation on its own merits and for its own sake, rather than as a compendium of cautionary tales. America's founders could not enjoy or analyze classical history in isolation from the pressing demands of their own circumstances, and so it came to be that daring men, whom the formidable army of King George III had not been able to deter from a risky revolution, found themselves quaking at the picture of mob rule painted by Plato and Aristotle, Rollin and Montagu. It would be many generations before Americans could examine classical history in a context at least partially set apart from the challenges of their own day; perhaps the only early American statesman truly to engage with the Athenians as a culture in their own right was the South Carolinian Hugh Swinton Legaré, attorney general, acting secretary of state, and editor of the *Southern Review*. The long monograph on ancient governments penned by James Monroe (after his presidency) focused obsessively on the superiority of the Constitution of the United States to those of the classical republics, and the Greek portions of Thomas

39. May 21, 1782, in Adams, *Works* 7:593.

Dew's 1853 *Digest of the Laws, Customs, Manners, and Institutions of the Ancient and Modern Nations* frequently took the form of object lessons for modern Americans. Ironically, indeed, the most positive reaction to classical Athens in America made its appearance in an exceedingly presentist context: the greatest excitement generated by the history of Athens in America before the twentieth century came when Dew joined others like John Calhoun, George Frederick Holmes, and George Fitzhugh in adducing the Athenian example in support of the merits of slavery.

The response of America's founders to Athenian democracy illuminates, I think, the extreme complexity of the Bailyn problem. Were the man and women who lived during the age of revolution made republicans, rather than monarchists, primarily by their classical reading? Of course not; it was their experience of monarchy that sparked this response. Were they turned against Greek democracy by the ideas their reading had formed about the two objects "Greece" and "democracy"? Now that is a more troublesome question.

It was a famous contention of Hobbes in *Leviathan* (2:21) that nothing was more conducive to seditious republicanism than the study of the classics. This allegation is undermined, of course, by the fact that Hobbes himself was an eager student of antiquity and the translator of Thucydides. Nor did the study of antiquity make republicans of Jean Bodin or Robert Filmer. In truth, there seem to be no attested cases of erstwhile monarchists who were converted to republicanism by classical reading—or indeed by any other reading. Because of the founders' pressing need for a historical context for their own experience, a neat distinction between the illustrative and formative roles of classical models is ultimately a fantasy. Nor was the model of ancient Greece the founders saw before them a truly classical one; rather, it had evolved for many years as one era after another recreated its own anxious Athens. As Fredric Jameson observes in the preface to his book *The Political Unconscious*, "texts come before us as the always-already-read"; for "we apprehend them through sedimented layers of previous interpretations."[40] Although the founders' classical references arose from a profound need to ground their thinking in a historical framework and were plainly more than rhetorical window dressing, the classical world to which the founders appealed in their argumentation was to a considerable degree a world created by a long series of thinkers ultimately alienated from life in democratic Athens itself.

40. Fredric Jameson, *The Political Unconscious: Narrative as a Socially Symbolic Act* (Ithaca: Cornell University Press, 1981), 9.

KURT A. RAAFLAUB

4 Democracy, Power, and Imperialism in Fifth-Century Athens

To Zvi Yavetz

"It is difficult to say," wrote Alexis de Tocqueville, "what place is taken up in the life of an inhabitant of the United States by his concern for politics. To take a hand in the regulation of society and to discuss it is his biggest concern and, so to speak, the only pleasure an American knows. . . . [I]f an American were condemned to confine his activity to his own affairs, he would be robbed of one half of his existence; he would feel an immense void in the life which he is accustomed to lead, and his wretchedness would be unbearable."[1]

Tocqueville's observation concerns political life and customs in nineteenth-century American democracy. Like much else in the sec-

I dedicate this paper to Zvi Yavetz (as a supplement to his festschrift, *Leaders and Masses in the Roman World* [Leiden: Brill, 1993]) in friendship, gratitude, and respect for his lifelong dedication to the truth, on the occasion of his retirement from the University of Tel Aviv, of which he was one of the founders in 1953. I thank Deborah Boedeker, Alan Boegehold, Charles Fornara, Karl-Joachim Hölkeskamp, Loren J, Samons II, Mark Toher, Robert Wallace, and the editors for helpful criticism and suggestions, and Gregory Bucher for assistance beyond the call of duty.

I have used the following translations (often with slight modifications): Herodotus, *The History*, trans. David Grene (Chicago: University of Chicago Press, 1987), and *The Persian Wars*, trans. George Rawlinson (New York: Random House, Modern Library, 1942); Thucydides, *History of the Peloponnesian War*, trans. Rex Warner (Harmondsworth: Penguin, 1954), and *History*, bk. 2, ed. and trans. with commentary Peter J. Rhodes (Warminster: Aris and Phillips, 1988); J. M. Moore, *Aristotle and Xenophon on Democracy and Oligarchy* (Berkeley and Los Angeles: University of California Press, 1975); Plato, *Gorgias*, ed. Walter Hamilton (Harmondsworth: Penguin, 1960), *Gorgias*, trans. W. C. Helmbold (New York: Liberal Arts Press, 1952), and *The Laws*, trans. Trevor J. Saunders (Harmondsworth: Penguin, 1970).

1. Alexis de Tocqueville, *Democracy in America*, trans. Henry Reeve, rev. Francis Bowen, ed. Phillips Bradley (New York: Knopf, 1945), 250.

tion from which this passage is taken, it reminds us forcefully of ideals
and realities described by Thucydides and other authors of late fifth-
century Athens. Similar analogies might in fact extend beyond the
realm of domestic politics into the sphere of foreign policy and relations. In this essay, I demonstrate that there existed in democratic
Athens a close connection between an interventionist and imperialist
foreign policy on the one hand and, on the other, a politically active
and involved citizen body, and I explain why. Such a connection between democracy and imperialism may well be more frequent and
typical of democracy—or of certain forms of democracy—than we are
used to think. Students of modern democracy, not least that of the
United States, as it developed in the nineteenth century, may even
tend to assume that this connection is self-evident. Any conclusion of
this kind, however, would only be possible on the basis of a comprehensive comparative examination of ancient and modern democracies—an examination that would make the connection between democracy and imperialism explicit and explain it in each case. This task
obviously lies beyond the scope of this essay, but by focusing on the
case of ancient Athens and analyzing at least part of this wide complex of problems, I hope to stimulate our thinking and make us more
aware of possible modern parallels worth our attention.[2]

POWER AND THE ATHENIANS' COLLECTIVE
CHARACTER

In 432 B.C., delegates of several Peloponnesian cities met in Sparta
to discuss their grievances against Athens and urge Sparta to take a
firm stand in defending its allies' interests. Tensions between the
Athenian and Spartan power blocs had been mounting for some time;
particularly Corinth felt directly threatened by recent Athenian actions, which it perceived as interfering with its own sphere of influence. According to Thucydides, the Corinthians were the most vig-

2. For pertinent observations on comparative aspects, see, e.g., Moses I. Finley, *Democracy
Ancient and Modern* (New Brunswick: Rutgers University Press, 1973), and "Colonies—an Attempt at a Typology," *Transactions of the Royal Historical Society*, ser. 5, 26 (1976): 167–88; and
Peter A. Brunt, "British and Roman Imperialism," *Comparative Studies in Society and History* 7
(1965): 267–88. Throughout this essay, I use "imperialism" in an elementary and non-
theoretical way to denote the interventionist and expansionist foreign policy pursued by the
Athenians in connection with their empire in the fifth century. Most of what I say, especially
concerning the close connection between democracy and imperialism in the fifth century,
applies only to Athens. I am well aware of the big differences between Athens and other
Greek democracies; see, e.g., Wolfgang Schuller, "Zur Entstehung der griechischen Demokratie ausserhalb Athens," in *Auf den Weg gebracht: Festschrift Kurt Georg Kiesinger*, ed. Horst
Sund and Manfred Timmermann (Konstanz: Universitätsverlag Konstanz, 1979), 433–47.

orous opponents of Sparta's cautious policy of avoiding war as long as possible. In a speech, which he attributes to them at the meeting in Sparta, he lets them assess the "enormous difference" between Spartans and Athenians. The latter he describes as follows:

> An Athenian is always an innovator, quick to form a resolution and quick at carrying it out. . . . Athenian daring will outrun its own resources; they will take risks against their better judgement, and still, in the midst of danger, remain confident. . . . They never hesitate. . . . They are always abroad; for they think that the farther they go the more they will get. . . . As for their bodies, they regard them as expendable for their city's sake, as though they were not their own; but each man cultivates his own intelligence, again with a view to doing something notable for his city. . . . And so they go on working away in hardship and danger all the days of their lives, seldom enjoying their possessions because they are always adding to them. Their view of a holiday is to do what needs doing; they prefer hardship and activity to peace and quiet. In a word, they are by nature incapable of either living a quiet life themselves or of allowing anyone else to do so. (Thucydides *History of the Peloponnesian Wars* 1.70, trans. Warner)

This is the famous character portrait of the Athenians, as seen (or presented as being seen) from the outside and focusing on their activities toward the outside, in foreign policy and war. Several elements of this portrait recur in the more general description of the Athenian citizens' characteristic qualities in Pericles' Funeral Oration; the picture is substantiated in Thucydides' sketch of the development of Athenian power in the fifty years between the Persian and Peloponnesian wars and reiterated throughout the work both in speeches and in Thucydides' own authorial statements.[3] Frequent parallels in contemporary Athenian literature confirm that this was not just Thucydides' own assessment but one widely shared in Athens, if not in Greece, at the time. In fact, much of Thucydides' portrait is anticipated in Sophocles' *Oedipus the King* (performed soon after 430) and Euripides' *Suppliants* (performed between 424 and 420), a play that emphasizes, directly and indirectly, the Athenians' tendency to let anger, pride, or hope influence important decisions, to neglect the safety of their own persons, to subordinate the interest of the family to that of the state, to sacrifice peace and prudence in rash decisions, to interfere in matters that are not their own (476–510). They toil incessantly for their

3. On Pericles' Funeral Oration, see Thuc. 2.35–46, esp. 2.40 with 36.4; on the fifty years, see 1.89–117; see also 8.96.4f. and, generally, W. Robert Connor, *Thucydides* (Princeton: Princeton University Press, 1984), 36–47 and passim (see index s.v. "tropoi").

happiness (576f.), but they are unable to enjoy it because every victory induces them to reach for the stars and because hope to gain all makes them despise a partial success (728–30, 736–44).[4]

But what is the purpose of, and the reward for, such restless labor? The answer is given most forcefully in Pericles' last speech. Its historic date is 430, after the breakdown of Athenian morale that was caused by the plague and the devastation of Attica during the first two years of war. Pericles says about his policy:

> It is a policy which entails suffering, and each one of you already knows what this suffering is; but its ultimate benefits are still far away and not yet clear for all to see. . . . Yet you must remember that you are citizens of a great city and that you were brought up in a way of life suited to her greatness; you must therefore be willing to face the greatest disasters and be determined never to sacrifice the glory that is yours. . . . Remember, too, that the reason why Athens has the greatest name in all the world is because she has never given in to adversity, but has spent more life and labor in warfare than any other state, thus winning the greatest power that has ever existed in history, such a power that will be remembered forever by posterity . . . [namely] that of all Hellenic powers we held the widest sway over the Hellenes, that we stood firm in the greatest wars against their combined forces and against individual states, that we lived in a city which had been perfectly equipped in every direction and which was the greatest in Hellas. (Thuc. 2.61.2, 4; 64.3, trans. Warner)

The Athenians' incessant striving "to acquire" (*ktasthai*), as observed by the Corinthians (1.70.4, 7, 8) thus serves the primary purpose of preserving and increasing their city's power, rule and empire.[5]

The concept of power in Thucydides is a rich, fascinating, even overwhelming subject.[6] I am concerned here not with this concept as

4. On *Oedipus*, see Bernard M. W. Knox, *Word and Action: Essays on the Ancient Theater* (Baltimore: Johns Hopkins University Press, 1979), 91–93; on the *Suppliants*, see Kurt A. Raaflaub, "Contemporary Perceptions of Democracy in Fifth-Century Athens," *Classica et Mediaevalia* 40 (1989): 50–52, reprinted in W. Robert Connor et al., *Aspects of Athenian Democracy* (Copenhagen: Museum Tusculanum, 1990), 50–52. See also William Arrowsmith, "Aristophanes' *Birds*: The Fantasy Politics of Eros," *Arion*, n.s. 1 (1973): 126–30 and passim on analogies in Aristophanes' *Birds*.

5. For *ktasthai* in the context of the creation or expansion of the Athenian empire, see, e.g., Thuc. 1.73.1; 1.93.3; 2.36.2, 4; and see text below, after n. 11.

6. See, among others, Jacqueline de Romilly, *Thucydides and Athenian Imperialism* (Oxford: Blackwell and Mott, 1963); Arthur G. Woodhead, *Thucydides on the Nature of Power* (Cambridge: Harvard University Press, 1970); Edmond Lévy, *Athènes devant la défaite de 404: Histoire d'une crise idéologique* (Paris: Boccard, 1976); Virginia Hunter, *Past and Process in Herodotus*

such, however, but rather with the problem of what such power meant to the Athenians themselves; what role it played in their political life, thought, and attitudes; and why it was a democratic polis for which "power" became so important. To grasp more specifically the nature of this problem, I begin by emphasizing a few particularly important aspects in the passages just cited.

First, the quality that underlies the Athenians' power and, in the Corinthians' assessment, explains their inability to enjoy peace and let others enjoy theirs, is their activism, their willingness to be involved, constantly to "do something" (*dran ti, prassein ti*). In the Athenians' own, positive presentation, such activism is directed domestically toward contributing whatever service each citizen can offer the community, and externally toward preserving the city's safety and liberty, enhancing its greatness, and helping those in need of support.[7] Those who dislike such attitudes distinguish between the wish "to acquire more" (*pleon echein, pleonexia*), which is considered a natural human desire and thus understandable and acceptable, though not neces-

---

and *Thucydides* (Princeton: Princeton University Press, 1982), chap. 1 and passim (see index s.v. power, *dynamis*); Antonios Rengakos, *Form und Wandel des Machtdenkens der Athener bei Thukydides* (Stuttgart: Steiner, 1984), with a survey of scholarship, 13–22; June W. Allison, *Power and Preparedness in Thucydides* (Baltimore: Johns Hopkins University Press, 1989); Karl Reinhardt, "Thukydides und Macchiavelli," in *Vermächtnis der Antike* (Göttingen: Vandenhoeck und Ruprecht, 1960), 184–218; Franz Kiechle, "Ursprung und Wirkung der machtpolitischen Theorien im Geschichtswerk des Thukydides," *Gymnasium* 70 (1963): 289–311; Joseph Vogt and Gerhard Ritter, "Dämonie der Macht und Weisheit der Antike," in *Thukydides*, ed. Hans Herter (Darmstadt: Wissenschaftliche Buchgesellschaft, 1968), 282–308, 309–16; Henry Immerwahr, "Pathology of Power and the Speeches of Thucydides," in *The Speeches of Thucydides*, ed. Philip Stadter (Chapel Hill: University of North Carolina Press, 1973), 16–31; Herwig Görgemanns, "Macht und Moral: Thukydides und die Psychologie der Macht," in *Spielarten der Macht*, ed. Eckart Olshausen (Stuttgart: Historisches Institut der Universität, 1977), 64–93; Alfred French, "Thucydides and the Power Syndrome," *Greece and Rome* 26/27 (1979/80): 22–30; and Steven Forde, "Thucydides on the Causes of Athenian Imperialism," *American Political Science Review* 80 (1986): 433–48. Christian Meier, "Macht, Gewalt," in *Geschichtliche Grundbegriffe: Historisches Lexikon zur politisch-sozialen Sprache in Deutschland*, ed. Otto Brunner, Werner Conze, and Reinhart Koselleck, vol. 3 (Stuttgart: Klett, 1986), 820–30, provides a brief sketch of the development of the Greek concept and terminology of power, which, however, still awaits an in-depth treatment.

7. See esp. Thuc. 1.70.6 (cf. 8); 2.37.1, 40.4; 2.63.3, 64.4; furthermore, 6.87 and esp. 6.18. For more complete references, see Victor Ehrenberg, "Polypragmosyne: A Study in Greek Politics," *Journal of Hellenic Studies* 67 (1947): 46–67 = idem, *Polis und Imperium* (Zurich: Artemis, 1965), 466–501; Arthur W. H. Adkins. "*Polypragmosyne* and 'Minding One's Own Business': A Study in Greek Social and Political Values," *Classical Philology* 71 (1976): 301–27; June W. Allison, "Thucydides and *Polypragmosyne*," *American Journal of Ancient History* 4 (1979): 10–22, with "Additional Note," ibid., 157–58 (but see n. 9 below); and Phillip Harding, "In Search of a Polypragmatist," in *Classical Contributions: Studies in Honour of Malcolm F. McGregor*, ed. Gordon S. Shrimpton and David J. McCargar (Locust Valley, N.Y.: Augustin, 1981), 41–50.

sarily welcome,[8] and the Athenian brand of "activism," which they really see as hyperactivism, "doing a lot, doing too much" (*polla prassein*), with the connotation of being a busybody (*polypragmōn*), meddling in other people's affairs, or stepping beyond one's station. "You and your city are used to busying yourself with too much," complains a foreigner in Euripides' *Suppliants;* the Athenian leader responds, "But by toiling a lot she enjoys great success and happiness" (576f.).

This attitude of interventionist hyperactivism is labeled *polypragmosynē* only once in Thucydides (6.87.3), but familiarity with this term is firmly assumed in other authors in the 420s; thus it is perfectly legitimate to use it to describe this Athenian attitude.[9] Its opposite is expressed by "being not active" (*apragmōn*, hence *apragmosynē*) and "holding one's peace, being quiet" (*hēsychian echein*). Both these terms are often closely associated with *sōphrosynē* (prudence, moderation); they are thus applauded in some aristocratic circles and typical of Sparta's conservative policies but rejected by Athenian politicians who support democracy and activism in foreign policy.[10] All this is widely confirmed in other sources of the time and thus is certainly not a Thucydidean idiosyncrasy.[11]

Second, as is clear from the specific emphasis given it by various

8. Ehrenberg, "Polypragmosyne," 49–50 = *Polis und Imperium*, 471–73. On *pleonexia*, see H. O. Weber, *Die Bedeutung und Bewertung der Pleonexia von Homer bis Isokrates* (Diss., Bonn, 1967).

9. *Contra:* Allison, "Thucydides and *Polypragmosyne*," esp. 16 and 19. For references in Aristophanes, see Ehrenberg, "Polypragmosyne," 54–55 = *Polis und Imperium*, 480–81. See esp. Pseudo-Xenophon *Athēnaiōn Politeia* [= *Constitution of the Athenians*] 2.18, the obscure use of *polypragmosynē* in Aristophanes *Acharnians* 833, and its parody in 382 (*molynopragmonoumenos:* "get into dirty quarrels" [LSJ]), which is usually overlooked (I thank Alan Boegehold for the reference). All this weakens Allison's argument.

10. On *apragmosynē*, see the titles listed in n. 7 above and also Wilhelm Nestle, "*Apragmosynē*," *Philologus* 81 (1925): 129–40; Gustav Grossmann, *Politische Schlagwörter aus der Zeit des Peloponnesischen Krieges* (Zurich: Leemann, 1950), 126–37; Donald Lateiner, "'The Man Who Does Not Meddle in Politics': A *Topos* in Lysias," *Classical World* 76 (1982): 1–12; Laurence B. Carter, *The Quiet Athenian* (Oxford: Oxford University Press, 1986); and Lowell Edmunds, *Cleon, Knights, and Aristophanes' Politics* (Lanham, Md.: University Press of America, 1987), 17–20, with more lit., 19 n. 10. On the connection with aristocratic values, see Grossmann, *Politische Schlagwörter*, 126–37; Ehrenberg, "Polypragmosyne," 47 = *Polis und Imperium*, 467–68; and Adkins, "Polypragmosyne." On *sōphrosynē*, see Helen North, *Sophrosyne* (Ithaca: Cornell University Press, 1966); see also John Wilson, "Sophrosyne in Thucydides," *Ancient History Bulletin* 4 (1990): 51–57. On *hēsychia*, see Edmunds, *Cleon, Knights, and Aristophanes' Politics*, 17–37. On repudiation by democratic leaders, see Thuc. 2.40.2; 2.63.2f., 64.4; 6.18.6, 7; 6.87.3f.; cf. 1.70.8. Harding, "In Search of a Polypragmatist," 41–44, 47–48, rightly warns of sweeping generalizations.

11. See Ehrenberg, "Polypragmosyne," 53–56 = *Polis und Imperium*, 478–83; John H. Finley, "Euripides and Thucydides," *Harvard Studies in Classical Philology* 49 (1938): 45–46 = idem, *Three Essays on Thucydides* (Cambridge: Harvard University Press, 1967), 27–28 (for parallels in Euripides); Kurt A. Raaflaub, "Herodotus, Political Thought, and the Meaning of History," in *Herodotus and the Invention of History*, ed. Deborah Boedeker and John Peradotto, *Arethusa* 20 (1987): 227–28; and Arrowsmith, "Aristophanes' *Birds*," 126–29.

speakers early in Thucydides' *History*, the Athenian concept of power is dynamic and expansionist. In the Corinthians' presentation, the Athenians hustle not to preserve or solidify their power but "to always acquire more" (*aiei ktasthai:* 1.70.8). In another speech they describe this attitude as daring expansionism ("the will to have more through [at the cost of] dangers") rather than security based on justice (1.42.4). Pericles praises the men of his own generation because they have "enlarged" (*auxanein*) the empire "acquired" by their fathers (2.36.2f.).[12] This dynamic concept of power is developed further in later stages of the war and culminates in Alcibiades' assertion before the Sicilian expedition: "It is not possible for us to calculate, like housekeepers, exactly how much empire we want to have. The fact is that we have reached a stage where we are forced to plan new conquests and forced to hold on to what we have got, because there is a danger that we ourselves may fall under the power of others unless others are in our power" (6.18.3; cf. 6.87; trans. Warner).

Third, such activism involves risk (*kindynos*) and requires labor and exertion (*ponos*). The Athenians, say the Corinthians, are willing to submit to such constant toil, even enjoy it in an almost perverse equation of hardship and duty with pleasure (1.70.8). In the Funeral Oration, Pericles corrects this view by emphasizing his fellow citizens' ability to enjoy pleasures, to fully develop their individual qualities, and to achieve with ease and voluntary commitment what others—notably the Spartans—toil for under the oppression of a harsh law and strict regimen (2.35.1, 39.4, 40.1, 41.1); but he too insists here—and even more in his last speech—on their willingness to accept hardship for the common good and on the decisive contribution of this very factor to the city's rise to power (2.36.2, 41.5; cf. 2.60.2–4, 61.2, 62.1 and 3, 64.3 and 6). Once again, there is no lack of confirmation by other authors for this specific character trait and the Athenians' pride in it.[13]

Fourth, this concept of *ponos* had a long aristocratic tradition. Ever since the Homeric epics, *ponos* was seen as exertion worthy of glory,

12. On *auxanein* as an expression of progress, see the discussion of "*auxanein*-consciousness" in Christian Meier, "An Ancient Equivalent of the Concept of Progress: The Fifth-Century Consciousness of Ability," in *The Greek Discovery of Politics*, trans. David McLintock (Cambridge: Harvard University Press, 1990), 191–204.

13. See Nicole Loraux, "Sur quelques difficultés de la peine comme nom du travail," in *Annali del Seminario di studi del mondo classico, Napoli, Archeologia e storia antica* 4 (1982): 171–92; Alan L. Boegehold, "A Dissent at Athens, ca 424–421 B.C.," *Greek, Roman and Byzantine Studies* 23 (1982): 154–55; and H. Alan Shapiro, "*Ponos* and *Aponia*," ibid., 25 (1984): 107–11; furthermore, J. Finley, "Euripides and Thucydides," 45–46 = *Three Essays on Thucydides*, 27–28; and Romilly, *Thucydides and Athenian Imperialism*. For the historical application of this concept, see Herodotus *History* 6.11–12 with Thuc. 6.82.3–4; 1.99.1. For Pericles on pleasures and *charites* of the Athenians, see Christian Meier, *Politik und Anmut* (Berlin: Siedler, 1985), 17–23 and passim.

"the price of greatness" primarily in fighting, the noblest sphere of aristocratic activity. Accordingly, "characterized by its exploits in war, which equally are exploits of labor, the city of Athens, in the texts of the fifth-century authors, assumes the stature of the hero-city."[14] Not surprisingly, we hear Pericles boast in the Funeral Oration, "We do not need the praises of a Homer, or of anyone else," because the mighty marks and monuments of empire established by the Athenians and the everlasting memorials left everywhere "of good done to our friends or suffering inflicted on our enemies" will speak for themselves (2.41.4). Even more directly, Pericles' last speech extols the empire as the Athenians' claim to eternal glory: their power "will be remembered forever by posterity!" (2.64.3). "All who have taken it upon themselves to rule over others have incurred hatred and unpopularity for a time; but if one has a great aim to pursue, this burden of envy must be accepted. . . . Hatred does not last for long; but the brilliance (*lamprotēs*) of the present is the glory (*doxa*) of the future stored up forever in the memory of man. It is for you to safeguard that future glory and to do nothing now that is dishonourable" (2.64.5, trans. Warner).

Lamprotēs and *doxa*, words of high individual distinction and praise, equivalent to *timē* (honor) and *kydos* (glory) in Homer, here serve as collective incentives to motivate all Athenian citizens in their decision between the activist's ("doer," *drastēr*) acceptance of hardship, risk, and suffering for the sake of greatness and the nonactivist's (*apragmōn*) life of peace and safety—which, however, is possible only in a subject ("slave") city (2.63.3, cf. 64.4; 6.18.6f.). This choice is comparable to those of Achilles or Heracles and elevates the Athenian demos to the same heroic level.[15] Already in the seventh century the poet Tyrtaeus extended the heroic concept of *aretē* (virtue, achievement) to the citizens fighting in the hoplite phalanx; now, in democratic Athens, Pericles applies it to *all* citizens who fight and die for their polis.[16] "When I have lauded the city, it has been for qualities

14. Loraux, "Quelques difficultés," 174; the earlier citation is from Boegehold, "Dissent at Athens," 148. See also Gregory Nagy, *Pindar's Homer: The Lyric Possession of an Epic Past* (Baltimore: Johns Hopkins University Press, 1990), 138–39, 151–52.

15. See Loraux, "Quelques difficultés," 183–92; Jacqueline de Romilly, "Le thème du prestige dans l'oeuvre de Thucydide," *Ancient Society* 4 (1973): 39–58; and Carter, *Quiet Athenian*, chap. 1.

16. On Tyrtaeus, see Werner Jaeger, "Tyrtaeus on True *Aretē*," in *Five Essays* (Montreal: Casalini, 1966), 103–42; and Elke Stein-Hölkeskamp, *Adelskultur und Polisgesellschaft* (Stuttgart: Steiner, 1989), 123–25. On Athens, see Carter, *Quiet Athenian*, 8–10, citing the funeral epigram for those fallen at Potidaea in 431; see also Lowell Edmunds, *Chance and Intelligence in Thucydides* (Cambridge: Harvard University Press, 1975), 47–53; Nicole Loraux, "Mourir devant Troie, tomber pour Athènes: De la gloire du héros à l'idée de la cité," in *La mort, les*

bestowed on it by the virtues (*aretai*) of these men and of men like them. . . . I believe that the way in which these men have died is a proof of their *aretē*" (2.42.2, trans. Rhodes).

Fifth, in their speech at the second congress in Sparta, the Corinthians call for decisive action against the tyrant city (*polis tyrannos*) that has established itself in Greece (1.122.3, 124.3). Pericles picks this up in his last speech (and Cleon will echo him more forcefully in the Mytilenian debate: 3.37.2): "You now possess the empire like a tyranny, and, though it may be considered unjust to have acquired it, to renounce it would be dangerous" (2.63.2, trans. Rhodes). Again, the terminology is not Thucydides' own.[17] Although Pericles emphasizes its negative connotations, the term *tyrannos* in fact is ambivalent. In many ways the tyrant epitomizes the ambitions shared by most nobles in the archaic period and beyond: he succeeds in surpassing all his rivals, in monopolizing power, and in leading a rich and splendid life. Around 600 B.C., Solon was criticized by some of his peers for not seizing the tyranny when he had the opportunity to do so.[18] The same ambivalence is reflected in the last third of the fifth century, both on the individual and collective levels, particularly in the tension between increasing self-centeredness and aspiration to power among unscrupulous politicians and fear of conspiracy and tyranny, and in that between the same fear and the joys experienced by the Athenian demos

morts dans les sociétés anciennes, ed. Gherardo Gnoli and Jean-Pierre Vernant (Paris: Maison des Sciences de l'Homme, 1982), 27–43, and *The Invention of Athens: The Funeral Oration in the Classical City*, trans. Alan Sheridan (Cambridge: Harvard University Press, 1986), 98–118; and Jeffrey Rusten, "Structure, Style, and Sense in Interpreting Thucydides: The Soldier's Choice (Thuc. 2.42.4)," *Harvard Studies in Classical Philology* 90 (1986): 46–76, esp. 71–76 on 2.42.4.

17. Rhodes, 239; cf. Romilly, *Thucydides and Athenian Imperialism*, 125–26, and Bernard M. W. Knox, *Oedipus at Thebes* (New Haven: Yale University Press, 1957), 60–66. On the concept of *polis tyrannos*, see W. Robert Connor, "Tyrannis Polis," in *Ancient and Modern: Essays in Honor of Gerald F. Else*, ed. John H. D'Arms and John W. Eadie (Ann Arbor: Center for Coordination of Ancient and Modern Studies, 1977), 95–109; Wolfgang Schuller, *Die Stadt als Tyrann: Athens Herrschaft über seine Bundesgenossen*, Konstanzer Universitätsreden 101 (Konstanz: Universitätsverlag Konstanz, 1978); Kurt A. Raaflaub, "Polis Tyrannos: Zur Entstehung einer politischen Metapher," in *Arktouros: Hellenic Studies Presented to Bernard M. W. Knox*, ed. Glen W. Bowersock, Walter Burkert, and Michael C. J. Putnam (Berlin: Gruyter, 1979), 237–52, "Athens 'Ideologie der Macht' und die Freiheit des Tyrannen," in *Studien zum Attischen Seebund*, ed. Wolfgang Schuller (Konstanz: Universitätsverlag Konstanz, 1984), 73–76, and *Die Entdeckung der Freiheit: Zur historischen Semantik und Gesellschaftsgeschichte eines politischen Grundbegriffes der Griechen*, Vestigia 37 (Munich: C. H. Beck, 1985), 181–84; and Christopher Tuplin, "Imperial Tyranny: Some Reflections on a Classical Greek Metaphor," in *Crux: Essays in Greek History Presented to Geoffrey E. M. de Ste. Croix*, ed. Paul A. Cartledge and F. David Harvey (London: Imprint Editions, Imprint Academic, 1985), 348–75.

18. Solon frag. 33 West (*Iambi et Elegi Graeci Ante Alexandrum Cantati*, ed. M. L. West, vol. 2 [Oxford: Oxford University Press, 1972]); cf. Connor, "Tyrannis Polis," 98–101, and Leo Strauss, *On Tyranny* (New York: Free Press, 1948), 20.

in their collective rule. These feelings are most clearly expressed in Aristophanes' *Knights*, performed only six years after Pericles' last speech. Thus once again the citizens of Athens collectively are elevated to a status previously accessible only to the very elite.

Sixth, in the Funeral Oration the Athenian achievement is explicitly connected with the city's political system (politeia) as well as its communal character and habits (2.36.4 with 37). Democracy and imperial greatness are thus linked; so, throughout the speech, are democracy and the specific characteristics of its citizens. The same connection is, of course, implied in the speech of the Corinthians (1.70). It is made explicit in a famous chapter of Herodotus (*Histories* 5.78: below, after n. 105) and in Euripides' *Suppliants* (above, at n. 4), where the Athenians' typical traits are registered in their full ambivalence and linked closely with a critical analysis of democracy. The authors of the late fifth century thus were fully aware that democracy—which, like all forms of government, was considered not merely a "constitution" in the sense of a set of norms or laws but an integrated social and political system, a specific way of life—created and required a specific type of citizen who typically promoted a specific type of foreign policy.[19] In other words, at least in the perception of the late 430s and 420s, power politics and imperialism were typically Athenian and typically democratic.

Finally, the Athenians' character portrait is especially remarkable for its exclusive focus on devotion and service to the city and the common good. According to Pericles, the arete of the Athenian citizens consists of subordinating their own interests to the needs and demands of their city and accepting the common good as an absolute priority (Thuc. 2.60.2–4); in doing so, they act as "lovers (*erastai*) of their city" (2.43.1; cf. 60.5). This lofty ideal of the heroic city, especially as it is projected in Pericles' last speech, however, contrasts sharply with the dire reality surrounding this speech. For the audience addressed by Pericles is not a group of heroes, shining in splendid armor and in the beauty poured over them by their divine protectors; it is an assembly of disgruntled and unhappy citizens, many of them poor and homeless, most of them demoralized by hardships and losses of war and plague.

The authenticity of the content of Thucydides' speeches is a much-discussed problem.[20] Not least because of the close parallels in many

19. For this comprehensive concept of politeia, see Aristotle *Politics* 1295a40–41. This is the basis of Plato's parallel sketches of constitutions and corresponding citizens in *Republic* 8 and 9.

20. See, e.g., Geoffrey E. M. de Ste. Croix, *The Origins of the Peloponnesian War* (London:

contemporary sources, however, we are justified in assuming that the issues considered here essentially could have been, and were in fact, raised in political debates at these or similar occasions around the time concerned. If so, the remarkable emphasis laid in Pericles' speeches and in the Athenians' collective character portrait on activism, imperialism, and the intimate connection of both with democracy raises important questions. Why could Pericles, at a critical juncture for his city and his own career, expect that these particular arguments would effectively boost the morale of the discouraged and angry assembly? What did such concepts mean to the men sitting in front of him? What did they associate with them, particularly when other arguments used in the same speech, such as survival, safety, and liberty, may have seemed much more directly important? More generally, why could power and imperialism with their activist and aggressive connotations assume such priority in Athenian thought and motivation and even become widely recognized as crucial factors in shaping the Athenians' collective character? In other words, why would the Athenians be willing to toil and fight continually and to accept hardships and suffering for this particular purpose? Furthermore, why was it possible to construct a character portrait that inseparably linked "the Athenian" to a specific brand of aggressive foreign policy just as it linked him to democracy and specific attitudes in domestic politics? Why, that is, were power politics and imperialism typical of democratic Athens and the democratic citizen? What role did "power" play in the city's political life and in the thinking or "mentality" of its citizens?

In this essay, I focus especially on the set of problems indicated by the last questions, particularly the connection between power and democracy, the function of power in fifth-century thought and politics, and its role in the motivation of the democratic citizen. To set our questions in perspective, I begin by briefly discussing some fundamental changes in the experience and perception of "power" during the fifth century, and the pervasiveness of "power," resulting from such changes, in Athenian politics and political thought. I then explain in what ways the attitudes connected with Athenian "activism" differed from traditional Greek attitudes, and finally, I analyze the motives that made "activism" such a dominant Athenian character

---

Duckworth, 1972), 7–16; Stadter, *Speeches of Thucydides* (with bibliog., 124–61); Charles W. Fornara, *The Nature of History in Ancient Greece and Rome* (Berkeley and Los Angeles: University of California Press, 1983), chap. 4; Anthony Woodman, *Rhetoric in Classical Historiography: Four Studies* (London: Croom Helm, 1988), 10–15; and Jeffrey Rusten, *Thucydides: The Peloponnesian War*, bk. 2 (Cambridge: Cambridge University Press, 1989), 7–17.

trait and caused the Athenians to pursue relentlessly their imperialist policies.

POWER AS A NOVEL EXPERIENCE

Two points need clarification at the outset. First, Athenian imperialism has often been explained as a result of Athenian *polypragmosynē*, or to put it the other way round, *polypragmosynē* is usually seen as the psychological basis of Athenian imperialism.[21] Imperialism, however, could only be caused by Athenian "activism" if the latter was an innate characteristic of Athens or if it was at least clearly in evidence before the emergence of Athenian imperialism. Neither was the case. In fact, despite earlier indications of changing attitudes and policies,[22] the roots of both lie in the overwhelming and defining experience of the Persian Wars and their immediate aftermath. Thus, I suggest, imperialism and the mental attitudes supporting it developed in close interaction with each other, so that activism was as much a consequence as a basis of imperialism.

Second, the linkage, mentioned above (at n. 19), among "nationality," constitution, policies, and collective character, was observed and formulated by Greek thinkers in the late fifth century. Thucydides and Euripides provide the earliest evidence we have for it.[23] Probably the Spartans served as its prime example, and ethnography developed the model for it; but the very possibility of distinguishing—on an explicitly political rather than general ethnic, social, or cultural level—"national characters" within the Greek world presupposes, I think, the emergence of sharp *political* contrasts such as that between Athens as the model of a democratic polis and Sparta as exemplary of an aristocratic or oligarchic one, or that between Athens as an aggressive, expanding power and Sparta as a cautious, defensive one. The

---

21. Thus, e.g., Ehrenberg, "Polypragmosyne," 47 = *Polis und Imperium*, 469; Edouard Will, *Le monde grec et l'orient*, vol. 1 (Paris: Presses Universitaires de France, 1972), 173; Wolfgang Schuller, *Die Herrschaft der Athener im Ersten Attischen Seebund* (Berlin: Gruyter, 1974), 191; and Timothy J. Galpin, "The Democratic Roots of Athenian Imperialism in the Fifth Century B.C.," *Classical Journal* 79 (1983–84): 108.

22. Konrad H. Kinzl, "Athens: Between Tyranny and Democracy," in *Greece and the Eastern Mediterranean in Ancient History and Prehistory: Studies Presented to Fritz Schachermeyr*, ed. idem (Berlin: Gruyter, 1977), 215 n. 90; Charles W. Fornara and Loren J. Samons II, *Athens from Cleisthenes to Pericles* (Berkeley and Los Angeles: University of California Press, 1991), 102–3; Christian Meier, "Die Rolle des Krieges im klassischen Athen," *Historische Zeitschrift* 251 (1990): 580–81. See also the discussion by Thomas J. Figueira, *Athens and Aigina in the Age of Imperial Colonization* (Baltimore: Johns Hopkins University Press, 1991), chap. 5.

23. It was systematized in the fourth century: e.g., Isocrates *Areopagiticus* 13–14 and *Panathenaicus* 138; Plato *Menexenus* 238c and often in *Rep.* Cf. Rusten, *Thucydides*, 2.19, 151.

sources available to us for the period between the Persian and Peloponnesian wars do not allow us to determine with any precision when such contrasts became firmly fixed in public perception—probably in the late 460s and 450s, perhaps as late as the 440s. At any rate, an Athenian character portrait, such as we read it in Thucydides, probably could not have been conceived of more than about twenty years before the date of its historical setting.

For both democracy and the phenomenon of imperial power had fully emerged in the world of Greek poleis only in recent decades. True, important institutional changes had been introduced by Cleisthenes already in 507, resulting in what might perhaps best be called a "protodemocracy." But our earliest evidence for the term *dēmokratia* dates to soon after circa 470; and in 463, Aeschylus staged in the *Suppliants* a vivid show of "democracy in action." In 462 the demos, the entire citizen body including the lowest census class (*thētes*), assumed full power of making decisions, supervising their execution, and controlling the holders of public office. By roughly the middle of the century, supplementary measures were in place that defined the citizen body precisely and narrowly and made it possible for all Athenians to participate at public expense in all aspects of their government. Even so, it may have taken some more time before most citizens were fully used to their new role and prepared to take advantage of it. In short, by 432 the full impact of democracy in the specific Athenian sense of the word had been visible for as little as ten to fifteen or as long as thirty years, depending on how we assess the early stages of democratic development.[24]

24. On Cleisthenes and the development of democracy, see Charles Hignett, *A History of the Athenian Constitution to the End of the Fifth Century B.C.* (Oxford: Oxford University Press, Clarendon, 1952); William G. Forrest, *The Emergence of Greek Democracy* (New York: McGraw-Hill, 1966); Will, *Le monde grec*, 63–76; Jochen Martin, "Von Kleisthenes zu Ephialtes: Zur Entstehung der athenischen Demokratie," *Chiron* 4 (1974): 5–42; Jochen Bleicken, *Die athenische Demokratie* (Paderborn: Schöningh, 1985), chap. 1; Martin Ostwald, *From Popular Sovereignty to the Sovereignty of Law: Laws, Society, and Politics in Fifth-Century Athens* (Berkeley and Los Angeles: University of California Press, 1986), and "The Reform of the Athenian State by Cleisthenes," in *Cambridge Ancient History*, 2d ed., vol. 4 (1988), 303–ND36,025; Meier, *Greek Discovery of Politics*, 53–81; Fornara and Samons, *Athens from Cleisthenes to Pericles*, chap. 2; Josiah Ober, *Mass and Elite in Democratic Athens: Rhetoric, Ideology, and the Power of the People* (Princeton: Princeton University Press, 1989), chap. 2; Peter J. Rhodes, "The Athenian Revolution," *Cambridge Ancient History*, 2d ed., vol. 5 (1992), 62–95; and Kurt A. Raaflaub, "Kleisthenes, Ephialtes und die Begründung der Demokratie," in *Dēmokratia: Der Weg der Griechen zur Demokratie*, ed. Konrad H. Kinzl (Darmstadt: Wissenschaftliche Buchgesellschaft, forthcoming). The term *dēmokratia* is not attested before Herodotus (6.43.3; 6.131.1; cf. also 4.137.2) and Ps. Xen. (e.g., *Ath. Pol.* 1.4–5, 8), but see Mogens H. Hansen, "The Origin of the Term *Dēmokratia*," *Liverpool Classical Monthly* 11, no. 3 (1986): 35–36 for Demokrates, born ca. 470 B.C.; this clearly is a "political name," suggesting that *dēmokratia* existed by then (but see Raaflaub, "Kleisthenes," sec. 5), which confirms the obser-

"Power," of course, had always been exercised and experienced. For the longest time, however, it had been out of reach, and thus beyond the active interest, of most citizens. In the archaic period it was a privilege, almost a property, of the noble families, who competed for it in fierce rivalries, occasionally saw it monopolized by an individual (tyrant) or group of families, eventually succeeded in bringing it back "into the middle," but basically took it for granted. What gave cause for discussion thus was not power per se but its loss and abuse.[25] Similarly, in interstate politics, power had obviously been a factor in wars among poleis (often resulting in territorial expansion) and in efforts to establish control over adjacent communities or hegemonic leadership in a system of alliances. Thus variations of superiority and dependence existed among the Greek poleis, some of which acquired large territories and considerable power and influence; but military subjection with the purpose or effect of outright rule of one polis over others was unknown in archaic Greece.[26] Moreover, until the very end of the sixth century, despite the large size of its territory and population, Athens lacked both power and influence; in prestige and leadership capacity it was not at all comparable to Sparta.[27]

---

vation of Victor Ehrenberg, "Origins of Democracy," *Historia* 1 (1950): 520–22 = idem, *Polis und Imperium,* 270–71, that *dēmokratia* is paraphrased in Aeschylus's *Suppliants* (esp. 604), plausibly dated to 463. On the politics of this play, see Christian Meier, "Der Umbruch zur Demokratie in Athen (462/1 v. Chr.)," in *Epochenschwelle und Epochenbewusstsein,* ed. Reinhart Herzog and Reinhart Koselleck (Munich: W. Fink, 1987), 353–80, and *The Political Art of Greek Tragedy* (Baltimore: Johns Hopkins University Press, 1993), 84–97; and Kurt A. Raaflaub, "Politisches Denken im Zeitalter Athens," in *Pipers Handbuch der politischen Ideen,* ed. Iring Fetscher and Herfried Münkler, vol. 1 (Munich: Piper, 1988), 286–88.

25. E.g., Solon frag. 4 West for abuse of power and Alcaeus frags. 70, 130B, and 141 Campbell (*Greek Lyric,* ed. David A. Campbell, vol. 1 [Cambridge: Harvard University Press, 1982]) for loss of power. On archaic tyranny in general, see Antony Andrewes, *The Greek Tyrants* (London: Hutchinson University Library, 1956); Helmut Berve, *Die Tyrannis bei den Griechen,* 2 vols. (Munich: C. H. Beck, 1967); Harry W. Pleket, "The Archaic Tyrannis," *Talanta* 1 (1969): 19–61; Andrew Lintott, *Violence, Civil Strife and Revolution in the Classical City* (Baltimore: Johns Hopkins University Press, 1982), chap. 2; and James McGlew, *Tyranny and Political Culture in Ancient Greece* (Ithaca: Cornell University Press, 1993). On archaic aristocrats and tyrants, esp. in Athens, see Stein-Hölkeskamp, *Adelskultur und Polisgesellschaft,* and Michael Stahl, *Aristokraten und Tyrannen im archaischen Athen* (Stuttgart: Steiner, 1987). On "to put in the middle" (*es meson tithenai*) in this context, see Her. 3.142.3; see also Marcel Detienne, "En Grèce archaïque: Géométrie, politique et société," *Annales: ESC* 20 (1965): 425–41.

26. Kurt A. Raaflaub, "Expansion und Machtbildung in frühen Polis-Systemen," in *Staat und Staatlichkeit in der frühen römischen Republik,* ed. Walter Eder (Stuttgart: Steiner, 1990), 511–45 with bibliog., and *Entdeckung der Freiheit,* 82–96.

27. See Her. 1.59.1, 65.1, 68.6–69; 5.78, 91–92. On Sparta's leadership in Greece before the Persian Wars, see Hans Schaefer, *Staatsform und Politik* (Leipzig: Dieterich, 1932), 196–272; William G. Forrest, *A History of Sparta, 950–192 B.C.* (London: Hutchinson, 1968), chaps. 7 and 8; and Paul A. Cartledge, *Sparta and Lakonia: A Regional History, 1300–362 B.C.* (London: Routledge and Kegan Paul, 1979), chap. 9. On Athens in the sixth century, see

This picture changed dramatically in the confrontation of the Greeks with the expanding Persian Empire. For the first time, the Greek poleis were threatened by, and in part suffered, subjection and foreign rule. They experienced dimensions and applications of power hitherto unfamiliar to them, and they came to recognize power as a crucial political factor and liberty as a central political value.[28] During the war and in its aftermath, Athens emerged as a leading power, contributing decisively to the Greek victories, claiming recognition and leadership, and displaying a remarkable commitment to the "Greek cause" and much skill in exploiting political opportunities. The conversion of the Delian League into an Athenian empire permanently established imperial power as a decisive phenomenon in the Greek world. Probably by the late 460s, certainly by the late 450s, the Athenians as well as the other Greeks were fully conscious of Athens' imperial rule, which was expressed in a differentiated terminology and became the object of thought and debate.[29]

To emphasize, this was the first time that a Greek polis assumed the role of a "world power" and created a large, permanent, and well-organized empire, which extended over a vast number of poleis and directly or indirectly affected all other Greeks and many non-Greek neighbors. And for the first time, such rule was exercised not by a monarch and his noble vassals but by the entire citizen body of a democratic polis. The Athenian people thus were actively involved, controlled power, and ruled at home and abroad, in their own community, over the empire, and beyond. This is the context in which the political contrast between Athens and Sparta took on its sharp contours; this is the background for the Athenian character portrait as we read it in Thucydides and other authors; and on this basis the Athenians developed their own "ideology of power," culminating in their concept of "the greatest and freest city," which stands behind the

Karl-Wilhelm Welwei, *Die griechische Polis* (Stuttgart: Kohlhammer, 1983), 150–68, and *Athen: Vom neolithischen Siedlungsplatz zur archaischen Grosspolis* (Darmstadt: Wissenschaftliche Buchgesellschaft, 1992), chap. 3; Frank Frost, "The Athenian Military before Cleisthenes," *Historia* 33 (1984): 283–94; Figueira, *Athens and Aigina*, 131–60; and the chapters by Antony Andrewes, David M. Lewis, and Martin Ostwald in *Cambridge Ancient History*, 2d ed., vols. 3.3 (1982) and 4 (1988).

28. Raaflaub, *Entdeckung der Freiheit*, chap. 3.

29. For the development of the Athenian empire, see Russell Meiggs, *The Athenian Empire* (Oxford: Oxford University Press, 1972); Will, *Le monde grec*, 171–79; Schuller, *Herrschaft der Athener*, pt. 2; Michael Steinbrecher, *Der Delisch-Attische Seebund und die athenisch-spartanischen Beziehungen in der kimonischen Ära, ca. 478/7– 462/1* (Stuttgart: Steiner, 1985); Anton Powell, *Athens and Sparta: Constructing Greek Political and Social History from 478 B.C.* (London: Routledge, 1988), chaps. 1–3; Fornara and Samons, *Athens from Cleisthenes to Pericles*, chap. 3; and Peter J. Rhodes, "The Delian League to 449 B.C.," *Cambridge Ancient History*, 2d ed., 5: 34–61. On the changes in terminology, see Raaflaub, *Entdeckung der Freiheit*, 162–84.

speeches of Pericles and other Athenians in Thucydides (see below, at
n. 49).

As a result of these developments, it is not exaggerated to say that
"power" stood in the center of the life, experiences, and expectations
of the Athenians. The acquisition, preservation, and organization, the
exploitation and justification of such power, both in the polis and in
the empire, increasingly determined thoughts and actions of the
leaders and the entire citizen body. As firmly as it seemed established,
though, such power was not uncontested in either sphere. Athens'
imperial rule and the rule of the demos in Athens in all their aspects
and consequences were so new and unusual, and violated so many
traditional norms, attitudes, and interests, that criticism and conflicts
were inevitable.

THE PERVASIVENESS OF "POWER" IN POLITICS AND POLITICAL THOUGHT

Very little evidence survives for political life and thought in Athens
in the 450s to early 430s B.C. But from what we know of Athens'
involvement in wars and other activities abroad, it is clear that questions pertaining to the city's position of power must have provided the
majority of issues on the agenda of Council and Assembly. In fact, it is
likely that it was precisely the enormous increase of decisions to be
made by the Assembly as a result of Athens' multiple interests abroad
that gave the Assembly the decisive role in politics.[30] At any rate, in
their capacities as citizens listening to reports of ambassadors or magistrates and to debates in Council and Assembly, as jurors deciding
trials that often involved foreigners or issues connected with foreign
policy, and as soldiers or sailors fighting the city's wars and patrolling
its sphere of influence all over the eastern Mediterranean, the Athenians inevitably acquired a strong sense of their own and their city's
power and its many implications.

In varying but generally remarkably high intensity, large segments
of all imperial societies are affected by the burdens and advantages of
their country's imperial rule; the Roman, Dutch, and British empires
provide good examples.[31] This was true in Athens as well, but probably to an even higher degree. In any given year, many thousands of

30. Schuller, *Herrschaft der Athener*, 177–82, and "Wirkungen des Ersten Attischen See-
bundes auf die Herausbildung der athenischen Demokratie," in idem, *Studien zum Attischen
Seebund*, 87–101.

31. Cf. Brunt, "British and Roman Imperialism."

citizens—close to half of the adult male citizen population—were active at least part time in paid functions for their city. The city's power and empire were constantly present in monuments, communal events, and celebrations, in daily life as experienced in market and streets, and in people's minds and private lives, not least because of the frequent absence of large numbers of men and the heavy losses suffered in many wars. Thus politics pervaded all aspects of private and communal life; the community was politicized to an extent that we can hardly imagine. And an exceptionally large share of Athenian politics dealt with power and empire.[32]

The lives, occupations, social roles, and identities of the Athenian citizens were profoundly transformed in little more than one generation after the Persian Wars.[33] Tensions and conflicts were inevitable, both in the political sphere and in that of private lives and mentalities. Even our fragmented evidence permits us to perceive some of these conflicts.[34] In the early and middle 440s, Pericles radically and comprehensively reoriented Athenian policies: he ceased hostilities with Persia, concluded peace with Sparta, yielded control on the mainland over most areas outside of Attica, and concentrated all efforts on the preservation of the thalassocracy and suppression of revolts of major allies; domestically, citizenship was redefined, the citizen roll revised, and an ambitious building program started.[35] It is clear that some of

32. On the latter, see Schuller (as cited in n. 30). On the citizens' participation in politics, see Arnold W. Gomme, "The Working of the Athenian Democracy," in *More Essays in Greek History and Literature* (Oxford: Oxford University Press, 1962), 177–93; A. H. M. Jones, *Athenian Democracy* (Oxford: Blackwell and Mott, 1957; reprint, Baltimore: Johns Hopkins University Press, 1986), 99–133; Bleicken, *Athenische Demokratie*, 102–58; R. K. Sinclair, *Democracy and Participation in Athens* (Cambridge: Cambridge University Press, 1988), and Meier, *Greek Discovery of Politics*, 140–54. On paid functions, see below, n. 67 and text. On celebrations and festivals, see Meiggs, *Athenian Empire*, chap. 16; Schuller, *Herrschaft der Athener*, 112–18; and Simon Goldhill, "The Great Dionysia and Civic Ideology," *Journal of Hellenic Studies* 107 (1987): 58–76, rev. in *Nothing to Do with Dionysos? Athenian Drama in Its Social Context*, ed. John J. Winkler and Froma I. Zeitlin (Princeton: Princeton University Press, 1990), 97–129. On monuments as symbols of power, see C. J. Herington, *Athena Parthenos and Athena Polias* (Manchester: Manchester University Press, 1955); Russell Meiggs, "The Political Implications of the Parthenon," *Greece and Rome* 10 suppl. (1963): 36–45, and *Athenian Empire*, chap. 15; Peter Berger, ed., *Parthenon-Kongress Basel* (1982), 2 vols. (Mainz: Zabern, 1984), pt. 1; and Tonio Hölscher, "The City of Athens: Space, Symbol, Structure," in *Athens and Rome, Florence and Venice: City-States in Classical Antiquity and Medieval Italy*, ed. Anthony Molho, Kurt A. Raaflaub, and Julia Emlen (Ann Arbor: University of Michigan Press, 1991), 368–75.

33. See, e.g., Frank J. Frost, "Tribal Politics and the Civic State," *American Journal of Ancient History* 1 (1976): 66–75, esp. 70–72, and Sarah C. Humphreys, "Economy and Society in Classical Athens," in *Anthropology and the Greeks* (London: Routledge and Kegan Paul, 1978), 143–57. On changes in identity, see Meier, *Greek Discovery of Politics*, 140–54.

34. For those connected with the reforms of Ephialtes in 462, see Ostwald, *Sovereignty*, 47–83, and Meier, "Umbruch zur Demokratie," and *Greek Discovery of Politics*, chap. 5.

35. On foreign policy, see the lit. cited in n. 29, esp. Meiggs, *Athenian Empire*, 129–85, and

these changes caused (or, perhaps, also were caused by) a long and bitter conflict between Pericles and his opponents led by Thucydides, son of Melesias. According to Plutarch, such opposition focused mostly on the use of tribute money to finance the building program. Probably much more was at stake. At least the citizenship law seems to have contained a marked anti-aristocratic component, and Thucydides' ostracism in 443 sealed the defeat of open and organized opposition to Pericles and the latter's ascendance to a position of exceptionally strong and durable personal leadership. This too caused vivid reactions and criticism.[36]

Thus on the political level the 440s were the period when the democratic methods of organizing power and leadership were firmly established. To borrow a phrase from Herodotus, Pericles succeeded in making the demos his *hetaireia*, that is, he extended, in such a way, the circle of friends and supporters (*hetairoi*) traditionally maintained by aristocratic leaders that it encompassed, on a fairly stable basis, the majority of citizens.[37] Accordingly, in decisions on crucial issues, proposals coming out of Pericles' circle and supported by this majority, would tend to prevail over others. A pattern emerged: there were certain policies that were likely to be proposed by Pericles and his friends, to be opposed by Thucydides and his supporters, and to be

Fornara and Samons, *Athens from Cleisthenes to Pericles*, 88–113. On the citizenship law of 451–50 and related measures, see Peter J. Rhodes, *A Commentary on the Aristotelian Athēnaion Politeia* (Oxford: Oxford University Press, 1981), 331–35, and "Athenian Revolution," 75–77; Cynthia B. Patterson, *Pericles' Citizenship Law of 451–50 B.C.* (New York: Arno, 1981); and Fornara and Samons, *Athens from Cleisthenes to Pericles*, 74–75; see also David Whitehead, "Norms of Citizenship in Ancient Greece," in Molho, Raaflaub, and Emlen, *Athens and Rome, Florence and Venice*, 135–54, esp. 141–51. On the building program, see Johannes Boersma, *Athenian Building Policy from 561/0 to 504/3 B.C.* (Groningen: Wolters-Noordhoff, 1970), 65–81; Meiggs, *Athenian Empire*, chap. 15; and the lit. cited in Philip Stadter, *A Commentary on Plutarch's Pericles* (Chapel Hill: University of North Carolina Press, 1989), 144.

36. On Plutarch *Pericles* 12 and 14.1, see Stein-Hölkeskamp, *Adelskultur und Polisgesellschaft*, 226 and bibliog. in nn. 74, 76; Stadter, *Commentary on Plutarch's Pericles*, ad loc.; and Fornara and Samons, *Athens from Cleisthenes to Pericles*, 29–35. On the use of imperial revenues to finance building programs, see E. Kluwe, "Die athenische Geldwirtschaft im 5. Jahrhundert und die Finanzierungsweise des Parthenon," in Berger, *Parthenon-Kongress*, 11–14; Lisa Kallet-Marx, "Did Tribute Fund the Parthenon?" *Classical Antiquity* 20 (1989): 252–66; and Loren J. Samons II, "Athenian Finance and the Treasury of Athena," *Historia* 42 (1993): 129–38. On criticism of Pericles' power, see Victor Ehrenberg, *Sophocles and Pericles* (Oxford: Blackwell and Mott, 1954), chap. 4, esp. 84–91, and Joachim Schwarze, *Die Beurteilung des Perikles durch die attische Komödie und ihre historische und historiographische Bedeutung* (Munich: C. H. Beck, 1971), 11–12, 170–71.

37. Her. 5.66.2 (I consider it possible that Herodotus took Pericles as his model for the description of Cleisthenes' success in the late sixth century). On the *hetaireiai*, see W. Robert Connor, *The New Politicians of Fifth-Century Athens* (Princeton: Princeton University Press, 1971), 25–29; Bleicken, *Athenische Demokratie*, 387 and 419 (bibliog.); and Ostwald, *Sovereignty*, 354–58. On Pericles' refusal to cultivate traditional aristocratic *hetaireiai*, n. 63 below.

accepted by a majority in the assembly. Although both democracy and the empire seem to have been largely uncontested, there still were many possibilities for radical disagreement. In particular, many of the policies favored by the "Periclean camp" were designed to reinforce the city's tight control over the empire, to exploit opportunities to further expand the Athenian sphere of influence, to enhance generally the security and power as well as the beauty and glory of Athens, and to focus the citizens' attention entirely on the interests of their city. Conversely, that group tended to ignore or even disdain the interests and relationships of the aristocracy, which traditionally reached far beyond their own polis.[38] Certain policies, "power politics" foremost among them, thus became the hallmark of democracy; they could easily be contrasted with the noninterventionist policies of Sparta and its aristocratic allies, who favored preservation of the status quo. It seems possible, therefore, that the idea of a collective Athenian character portrait linking imperialism and democracy emerged only during the Periclean era, not long before its first attestation in situations described by Thucydides.[39]

On the intellectual level, the emergence of full-fledged imperialism and democracy, with the corresponding political methods and attitudes, provided an immense stimulus for political thought. Aeschylus, Sophocles, and the poets of Old Comedy paid much attention to these issues and dramatized some of the resulting tensions, both before and during the Periclean era. Especially Sophocles and Herodotus were passionately interested in the manifold aspects of "power," which they interpreted through myth and history, using these in their full topical potential to analyze questions of great importance to their audiences.[40]

38. See Sarah C. Humphreys, "The Nothoi of Kynosarges," *Journal of Hellenic Studies* 94 (1974): 93–94; Wilfried Nippel, *Mischverfassungstheorie und Verfassungsrealität in Antike und früher Neuzeit* (Stuttgart: Klett-Cotta, 1980), 66; Stein-Hölkeskamp, *Adelskultur und Polisgesellschaft*, 224–28; and the bibliog. cited in n. 60 below.

39. To clarify, aggressive, interventionist, and expansionist policies were typical of Athens already in the 460s and 450s; it is their combination with the fully developed democracy of the Periclean type that dates to the 440s.

40. On Aeschylus and Sophocles, see Ehrenberg, *Sophocles and Pericles*; Knox, *Word and Action*, 87–95; Meier, *Political Art of Greek Tragedy*, and *Greek Discovery of Politics*, 82–139; and Raaflaub, "Politisches Denken im Zeitalter Athens," 281–301; on comedy, see Ehrenberg, *Sophocles and Pericles*, and Schwarze, *Beurteilung des Perikles*. On Herodotus, see Hermann Strasburger, "Herodot und das perikleische Athen," *Historia* 4 (1955): 1–25 = idem, *Studien zur Alten Geschichte*, vol. 2 (Hildesheim: Georg Olms, 1982), 592–626 = W. Marg, ed., *Herodot*, 2d ed. (Darmstadt: Wissenschaftliche Buchgesellschaft, 1965), 574–608; Jutus Cobet, *Herodots Exkurse und die Frage der Einheit seines Werkes* (Wiesbaden: Steiner, 1971), 111–15, 158 and passim; Michael Stahl, "Tyrannis und das Problem der Macht," *Hermes* 111 (1983): 202–20; Walter Nicolai, *Versuch über Herodots Geschichtsphilosophie* (Heidelberg: Carl Winter, 1986), esp. 20–26; and Raaflaub, "Herodotus," and "Politisches Denken im Zeitalter Athens," 307–14.

Both these authors were associated with Pericles, who also maintained a close relationship with Protagoras and other leading intellectuals of the time. Protagoras was the most distinguished of the early Sophists who flocked to Athens to take advantage of the new opportunities offered them by democracy. The ideas Plato attributes to him (*Prot.* 320e–322d) suggest that he made a serious effort to provide a theoretical foundation for democracy. The main focus of his activity, however—one he shared with most Sophists—was to teach "political skills or excellence" (*politikē technē* or *politikē aretē*) and "good counsel" (*euboulia*), that is, the methods by which a politician could succeed in politics—which necessarily included the ability to gain and maintain power.[41]

In particular, "power" seems to have played a prominent role in two much-debated contexts. One was the function of oratory and persuasion in democratic politics. In his dialogue *Gorgias*, Plato lets the famous orator define his art "in truth as the greatest good" because it "is the source, not only of personal freedom for individuals, but also of mastery (*archein*) over others in one's own city. . . . I mean the ability to persuade with words the judges in a law court, councillors in the Council, assemblymen in the Assembly and men in any other meeting of citizens whatever it may be" (*Gorg.* 452d–e, trans. Helmbold, modified). By virtue of this power (*dynamis*) of persuasion, the orator will have total control over everybody as of his slaves, and there is no issue on which the skilled orator will not be able to speak more persuasively than any specialist (456d). While Gorgias himself emphasizes that such rhetorical power is to be used only for just purposes and those who violate this principle deserve severe punishment (457a–c), later in the dialogue Callicles has to admit that the speakers in the assembly generally "strive to gratify their fellow-citizens and, in seeking their own private interest, neglect the common good, dealing with public assemblies as though the constituents were children" (502d–e).[42] Protagoras was the first to teach how "to make the weaker cause the stronger." Thus the art of rhetoric became an indispensable

41. See, generally, William K. C. Guthrie, *A History of Greek Philosophy*, vol. 3 (Cambridge: Cambridge University Press, 1969), pt. 1; George B. Kerferd, *The Sophistic Movement* (Cambridge: Cambridge University Press, 1981); Bleicken, *Athenische Demokratie*, 268–79 with 387–90 and 419–20; Ostwald, *Sovereignty*, 229–50; and Cynthia Farrar, *The Origins of Democratic Thinking: The Invention of Politics in Classical Athens* (Cambridge: Cambridge University Press, 1988). On Pericles, see now Philip A. Stadter, "Pericles among the Intellectuals," *Illinois Classical Studies* 16 (1991): 111–24.

42. On all this, see the comments by Eric R. Dodds in *Plato's Gorgias*, rev. with intro. and comm. Eric R. Dodds (Oxford: Oxford University Press, 1959), henceforth Dodds, *Gorgias*; Ostwald, *Sovereignty*, 243–47.

prerequisite for success in politics and for political power. Thucydides, Euripides, and their contemporaries were well aware of the negative and dangerous aspects of this development.[43]

The other context providing for a heated debate about power was the discrepancy perceived by some Sophists between the law of nature (physis) and man-made laws or conventions (*nomoi*). This discrepancy seemed particularly noticeable in the clash between the strong individual's natural claim to unrestrained power and the restrictions imposed on him by the community's norms. Greek thought perceived a correlation not only between the microcosm of the individual and the cosmos of the community but also between the latter and the macrocosm of poleis and states (and the even bigger one of the world or cosmos at large).[44] Thus patterns of behavior observed outside the polis, that is, in spheres of life not controlled by laws and thus unaffected by "artificial" human conventions, were used to construct the norms of nature or natural laws, which were then opposed to the conventions of the polis. Again Plato's *Gorgias* offers a good example:

> By convention (*nomos*) an attempt to gain an advantage (*pleon echein*) over the majority is said to be wrong and base, and men call it criminal; nature (*physis*), on the other hand, herself demonstrates that it is right that the better man should prevail (*pleon echein*) over the worse and the stronger over the weaker. The truth of this can be seen in a variety of examples, drawn both from the animal world and from the complex communities and races of human beings; right consists

43. Protagoras (no. 80) frag. B6b Diels-Kranz (*Die Fragmente der Vorsokratiker*, ed. Hermann Diels, rev. Walther Kranz, vol. 1, 10th ed. [Berlin: Weidmann, 1961]). See, e.g., Thuc. 2.65; 3.37–38, 42–43; 6.8–24; and Eur. *Suppl.* 232–47, 412–25, and *Orestes* 884–945. See, generally, George Kennedy, *The Art of Persuasion in Greece* (Princeton: Princeton University Press, 1963); Jochen Martin, "Zur Entstehung der Sophistik," *Saeculum* 27 (1976): 143–64; R. G. A. Buxton, *Persuasion in Greek Tragedy: A Study of Peitho* (Cambridge: Cambridge University Press, 1982); and bibliog. cited in nn. 41 above and 81 and 107 below.

44. For the former correlation, see above at n. 23; for the principle of the latter, see Kenneth J. Dover, *Greek Popular Morality in the Time of Plato and Aristotle* (Berkeley and Los Angeles: University of California Press, 1974), 310–11. An example is provided by the principle of *isonomia* (equal distribution), which is applied on three levels: (a) the cosmos, as implied by Anaximander (no. 12) frag. B1 Diels-Kranz (see Guthrie, *History of Greek Philosophy*, vol. 1 [1962], 72–89, and Gregory Vlastos, "Isonomia," *American Journal of Philology* 74 [1953]: 361–63); (b) the citizen body and polis (see Raaflaub, *Entdeckung der Freiheit*, 115–18; Vincent J. Rosivach, "The Tyrant in Athenian Democracy," *Quaderni Urbinati di cultura classica*, n.s. 30 [1988]: 49–51; and Fornara and Samons, *Athens from Cleisthenes to Pericles*, 166–67); and (c) the human body (Alkmaion [no. 24] frag. B4 Diels-Kranz; cf. Vlastos, "Isonomia," 344–47, and Charlotte Triebel-Schubert, "Der Begriff der Isonomie bei Alkmaion," *Klio* 66 [1984]: 40–55).

in the superior ruling over the inferior and having the upper hand
(*archein kai pleon echein*).[45]

These consequences were applied to both domestic and foreign politics—and challenged in both. Thus we find the same arguments in
debates opposing aristocratic or individual power to democratic equality in the polis and, on the international level, the imperial rule of one
polis over others to equality between two or more powers. A prime
example of the former is the discussion concerning power and equality between Eteocles and Iocasta in Euripides' *Phoenician Women* (499–
585); of the latter, Thucydides' "Melian Dialogue" (5.84–113). Both
within the polis and outside of it, "freedom and power over others"
provided the magic formula for the "greatest good."[46]
   It is certain, however, that the Sophists' analyses and theories dealt
much more broadly and systematically with power politics in interstate
relations and with problems of imperial rule. Our main evidence lies
in the application of such theories in Thucydides' work; stringent parallels in other authors prove once again that such ideas were widely
familiar at the time.[47] Thus they were likely to be used in actual political debates as well. They focused both on the specifics of the application of power (the theory of seapower, reflected in Thucydides and
Pseudo-Xenophon, provides a good example) and, more generally, on
the nature of power and its function in human society.[48] For our pres-

45. Plato *Gorg.* 483c–d (trans. Hamilton) with the parallels cited by Dodds, *Gorgias,* at
483d2. Generally on the *nomos-physis* debate, see Felix Heinimann, *Nomos und Physis* (Basel:
Reinhardt, 1945; reprint, Darmstadt: Wissenschaftliche Buchgesellschaft, 1972); Guthrie,
History of Greek Philosophy, vol. 3, chap. 4; Kerferd, *Sophistic Movement,* 111–130; and Ostwald,
Sovereignty, 250–73. See Her. 3.38 on the difference between the *nomoi* of various peoples.
   46. Plato, *Gorg.* 452d; Thuc. 3.45.6.
   47. On Thucydides, see Wilhelm Nestle, "Thukydides und die Sophistik," *Neue Jahrbücher
für das klassische Altertum* 33 (1914): 649–85; Fritz Taeger, *Thukydides* (Stuttgart: Kohlhammer,
1925), 74–119; John H. Finley, *Thucydides* (Cambridge: Harvard University Press, 1942), 36–
73; Kiechle, "Ursprung und Wirkung"; Romilly, *Thucydides and Athenian Imperialism,* pt. 2
passim; Lévy, *Athènes,* chaps. 3–6; and Guthrie, *History of Greek Philosophy* 3: 84–88. For parallels, see J. Finley, "Euripides and Thucydides," and Hartwig Frisch, *The Constitution of the
Athenians: A Philological-Historical Analysis of Pseudo-Xenophon's Treatise De re publica Athenien-
sium* (Copenhagen: Gyldendal, 1942), 79–87.
   48. On seapower, see Arnaldo Momigliano, "Sea-Power in Greek Thought," *Classical Review* 58 (1944): 2–3 = idem, *Secondo Contributo alla storia degli studi classici e del mondo antico*
(Rome: Storia e Letteratura, 1960), 58–61; Frisch, *Constitution of the Athenians,* 63–87; and
Chester G. Starr, "Thucydides on Sea Power," *Mnemosyne* 31 (1979): 343–50. For Herodotus
on sea-power, see Binyamin Shimron, *Politics and Belief in Herodotus* (Stuttgart: Steiner, 1989),
89–92; see also Cobet, *Herodots Exkurse,* esp. 172–76. More generally, see Romilly, *Thucydides
and Athenian Imperialism,* and *The Rise and Fall of States according to Greek Authors* (Ann Arbor:
University of Michigan Press, 1977); Lévy, *Athènes,* esp. 88–109; and Meier, *Greek Discovery of
Politics,* chap. 8. We should keep in mind that no one source gives us a systematic analysis or
summary of such theories and that they changed considerably over time and became more
radical, particularly under the impact of the Peloponnesian War.

ent purposes it is especially important that such theories postulated a link between power and liberty that was seen as operating both inside the polis and outside of it. Just as the polis was capable of maintaining its liberty only by being powerful and, preferably, ruling over others, so within the community the demos could be free only by controlling power and participating in government. Democracy as institutionalized rule by the people thus guaranteed the liberty of all citizens.[49] In Athens the two aspects of this concept eventually were conflated: the two-sided rule of the demos in the polis and over the empire was linked with its two-sided freedom to form a new and superior type of "liberty through power"—a privileged status that was available only to the members of the imperial democracy at the height of its domination. We grasp this concept in Thucydides' comment on the oligarchic coup of 411: "It was no easy matter about 100 years after the expulsion of the tyrants to deprive the Athenian people of its liberty—a people not only unused to subjection itself, but, for more than half of this time, accustomed to exercise power over others" (8.68.4; cf. 71.1, trans. Warner). Furthermore, after his flight to Sparta, Alcibiades justifies his earlier prodemocratic stance by pointing out that his family had always supported the traditional form of government, "under which the city was greatest and freest" (6.89.6: *megistē polis kai eleutherotatē;* see also 7.69.2). The slogan of Athens, "the greatest and freest city," expresses the proud self-assertion of a community that is aware of its unique accomplishment, and it probably represents, around the outbreak of the war, the imperial city's determined refutation of its enemies' war cry demanding the liberation of the Greeks from the tyrant city's oppression.[50]

Thus in the late 430s the connection between democracy and imperialism was well established and taken for granted. It is interesting that no ancient source provides an analysis of the cause and development of this connection. Rather, if Herodotus is representative, the assumption seems to have been that the two went together from the very beginning of democracy in the days of Cleisthenes.[51] As we have

49. Ps.-Xen. *Ath. Pol.* 1.8–9; Eur. *Suppl.* 352–53, 403–7, 438–41.

50. For details, see Raaflaub, "Ideologie der Macht"; and *Entdeckung der Freiheit*, 233–46; on the *polis tyrannos*, see n. 17 above. The concept fits in well with the superlatives used to emphasize the same point in Pericles' last two speeches: 2.36.3, 64.3; on the latter, see Rusten, *Thucydides* 2: 205, and generally, Romilly, *Thucydides and Athenian Imperialism*, 80.

51. Her. 5.66.1 and 78 (see below after n. 105); cf. 6.109.3, 6. Both passages seem to me anachronistic retrojections, reflecting the sentiments of the time of the work's composition. Cf. Konrad H. Kinzl, "Herodotos-Interpretationen," *Rheinisches Museum* 118 (1975): 200, on the latter passage; and Frank J. Frost, *Plutarch's Themistocles: A Historical Commentary* (Princeton: Princeton University Press, 1980), 177–79, on similar retrojections in Plut. *Them.* 20.1–2 and *Aristides* 22.3–4 (with Diodorus *Historical Library* 11.42). For the established connection in the 420s, see Ps.-Xen. *Ath. Pol.* 1.2 (quoted below, after n. 82).

seen, despite some early indications of changing attitudes, this is unlikely to be correct. Democracy and imperialism, and even more so
the possibility of linking the two and explaining one through the
other, were more recent phenomena. Equally, and contrary to widespread perceptions in Thucydides' time, neither were the corresponding attitudes typical of the Athenians a part of their nature nor had
they been typical of them for a very long time. Rather, these attitudes
were acquired, the result of a unique historical constellation and, I
suggest, of a massive effort of collective political reorientation if not
reeducation. In fact, most elements of this character sketch represent
a break with traditional Greek ways.

NONTRADITIONAL ELEMENTS IN ATHENIAN ATTITUDES

Certainly, Athenian democracy in several respects offered to all citizens the opportunities previously open only to the noble and wealthy;
the extended but closed citizen group adopted many of the views and
attitudes of the social elite. To some extent, therefore, democracy not
only "democratized" the aristocracy but "aristocratized" the demos.[52]
All citizens now shared the responsibility for the security of the community, and all claimed—and were institutionally enabled to claim—
an equal share in the activities, hardships, privileges, and honors connected with political life and full citizen status. But in other respects
the involvement expected of them took on forms that contrasted
sharply with the traditional aristocratic way of life and politics. This is
an issue that needs detailed investigation; here a few examples will
suffice.

First, naval warfare had not been a very important, let alone predominant, type of warfare in mainland Greece before the Athenians
developed it to unprecedented levels in the wake of the Persian Wars
and in pursuit of their hegemony in the Delian League. It required
exceptional resources and manpower and it changed the experience
of fighting drastically: much larger numbers of citizens were engaged
for much longer periods of time, but they served much more anony-
mously; their individual contributions were absorbed entirely by the

---

52. Cf. Bleicken, *Athenische Demokratie*, 193–95; Meier, *Greek Discovery of Politics*, 145 (with
n. 19 on p. 272); Stein-Hölkeskamp, *Adelskultur und Polisgesellschaft*, 205–30; and Ober, *Mass
and Elite*, 290–91.

collective effort of their ship's crew and the entire fleet. This difference had significant consequences, to which I shall return.[53]

Second, opinions that may have been common toward the end of the fifth century and later, are formulated by Plato as follows: "What most men call 'peace' is really only a fiction (*onoma*), and in cold fact all states are by nature (*kata physin*) fighting an undeclared war against every other state" (*Laws* 626a2–5). Xenophon describes war, like agriculture, as being among those most necessary human activities that are carried out in the open air (*Memorabilia* 2.1.6). Although neither author states that wars are in fact fought all the time, this is the interpretation that has been widely accepted by modern scholars,[54] who tend to overlook that such statements are based on experiences of a recent past (Athenian imperialism, the Peloponnesian War, and the wars of the early fourth century) and that the nature and frequency of wars changed dramatically in the course of Greek history. Certainly war had always been a reality, but hardly ever-present: not the state of war, but the danger of it, was permanent. However frequent, in the archaic age it was mostly limited to neighborhood conflicts for land and booty and to freebooting and raiding expeditions, and it was often a formalized, even ritualized affair.[55] But then the expansion of

53. See below at n. 83. Resources required: 36,000 on 180 Athenian ships at Salamis (Moshe Amit, *Athens and the Sea: A Study in Athenian Sea-Power* [Brussels: Latomus, 1965], 20 with sources—who, however, prefers the alternative tradition of 100–110 Athenian ships), compared with 9,000 Athenian hoplites at Marathon. For the development of Athenian naval strength, see Amit, 18–27; of naval warfare in general, see Yvon Garlan, *La guerre dans l'antiquité* (Paris: F. Nathan, 1972), 140–41; Chester G. Starr, *The Influence of Sea Power on Ancient History* (Oxford: Oxford University Press, 1989), chaps. 2 and 3; and H. T. Wallinga, *Ships and Sea-Power before the Great Persian War: The Ancestry of the Ancient Trireme* (Leiden: Brill, 1993).

54. Arnaldo Momigliano, "On Causes of War in Ancient Historiography," *Studies in Historiography* (London: Weidenfeld and Nicolson, 1966), 120; Jean-Pierre Vernant, "City-State Warfare," in *Myth and Society in Ancient Greece* (New York: Zone, 1990), 47; cf. Yvon Garlan, *War in the Ancient World* (London: Chatto and Windus, 1975), 15–18, and Moses I. Finley, "War and Empire," in *Ancient History: Evidence and Models* (New York: Viking, 1986), 67–69.

55. See, e.g., Angelo Brelich, *Guerre, agoni e culti nella Grecia arcaica* (Bonn: Habelt, 1961); Peter T. Manicas, "War, Stasis and Greek Political Thought," *Comparative Studies in Society and History* 24 (1982): 673–88; Frost, "Athenian Military before Cleisthenes"; Raaflaub, *Entdeckung der Freiheit*, 82–92, and "Expansion," 516–31; Hans-Joachim Gehrke, *Jenseits von Athen und Sparta: Das dritte Griechenland und seine Staatenwelt* (Munich: C. H. Beck, 1986), 50–55; W. Robert Connor, "Early Greek Land Warfare as Symbolic Expression," *Past and Present* 119 (1988): 3–29; and Meier, "Rolle des Krieges," esp. 556–63 with n. 5. Control of contested land continued to be a frequent issue in wars of the fifth century, *pace* M. Finley's criticism ("War and Empire," 78–79) of Ste. Croix, *Origins of the Peloponnesian War*, 218–20. On the nature of hoplite warfare, see in addition Jacqueline de Romilly, "Guerre et paix entre cités," in Vernant, *Problèmes de la guerre*, 207–20; John K. Anderson, *Military Theory and Practice in the Age of Xenophon* (Berkeley and Los Angeles: University of California Press, 1970); W. Kendrick Pritchett, *The Greek State at War*, vol. 4 (Berkeley and Los Angeles: University of California Press, 1985), 1–93; and Victor D. Hanson, *Warfare and Agriculture in Classical Greece*

eastern empires to and across the Aegean resulted in great wars of conquest and liberation, and the Athenian empire made this new type of warfare a familiar feature within the world of Greek poleis as well. Thus the short and limited military involvement typically required by hoplite warfare among independent cities was replaced by a type of military service that was much more frequent and lasted much longer and thus put much higher demands on the individual. At the same time, it was paid service, thus semiprofessional, and highly technical, which contrasted starkly with aristocratic ideals (see text below, at n. 87). In addition, it served purposes very different from those traditionally pursued by war: with the new, more abstract goals, individuals could identify only through collective ideals or ideologies; thus Pericles' effort in his last speech to play down the traditional motives of individual safety and survival and to emphasize instead the new ones of collective greatness and glory. Whereas hoplite warfare was designed primarily to defend the city's territory, Pericles convinced the Athenians to sacrifice their territory and to fight the war as if Athens were a fortified island, that is essentially, to entrust their fortune to an abstract theory of naval warfare.[56]

Third, the main component of the Athenians' collective character, their activism (*polypragmosynē*), was not a feature of archaic Greek society. The aristocrat fought for tangible, not abstract, goals or ideals. His arete and his desire for glory focused on purposes of immediate and personal significance to himself and to those important to him. The same perspective determined his willingness to endure toil and hardship. *Ponos* indeed was a heroic and thus aristocratic concept, but its purpose was to secure honor, wealth, and influence (or power). It was a necessary evil, not a purpose in itself. The same is true for the athlete's *ponos*, celebrated in Pindar's *Odes*,[57] although this form of *ponos*, extended and repeated over long periods of time, may seem closer to the Athenian case. Still, the Athenian tendency, as formulated by the Corinthians, to toil always, to enjoy hardship as if it were a festival, and to labor primarily not for one's personal glory and advantage but for those of a collective entity, really almost was a caricature of this aristocratic concept. Consequently, we should expect that the introduction of this "Athenian version" of *ponos* did not meet with

(Pisa: Giardini, 1983), *The Western Way of War: Infantry Battle in Classical Greece* (Oxford: Oxford University Press, 1990); and idem, ed., *Hoplites: The Classical Greek Battle Experience* (London: Routledge, 1991).

56. Thuc. 1.141–43, 2.62. For more abstract goals, see, e.g., the Mytilenian or Sicilian debates in Thucydides (3.36–50, 6.8–26); for theories, see n. 48 above.

57. See Loraux, "Quelques difficultés," 177 n. 28, and Nagy, *Pindar's Homer*, 138–42, 151–52.

utter enthusiasm. Confirmation is perhaps found in the resistance among allies to the extended naval operations initiated by the Delian League: "They soon became tired of foreign expeditions, for they felt they no longer needed to fight, and only wanted to live in peace and till their lands." Initially, this attitude may have applied to many Athenians as well. Their propensity to spend long periods on military duty away from home was an acquired virtue, not a natural one.[58]

Finally, few archaic aristocrats would have gone so far as to call themselves "lovers of their polis."[59] Of course leadership and service to the community traditionally were among the foundations of the aristocrats' privileged position. As even the powerful individual was unable to be completely self-sufficient and independent, some devotion to the community's well-being was expected and necessary. In some cases, for example that of Solon, such devotion took on strong and pronounced forms, and criticism of traditional aristocratic values and priorities increased markedly during the seventh and sixth centuries. Still, the aristocrats' connections and commitments reached far beyond the polis. In their thoughts and actions, there was a constant tension between personal and communal obligations—a tension that was frequently resolved in favor of the former and caused the community much harm. Such attitudes were as much alive in the fifth century as they had been in the archaic age.[60] Thus by demanding

58. Thuc. 1.70.4: *apodēmētai*. On allies, see Plut. *Cimon* 11.1 (cited in Ian Scott-Kilvert's trans. [Harmondsworth: Penguin, 1960]); cf. Thuc. 1.99.3. See also Her. 6.11–12 on the Ionian revolt.

59. See above, after n. 19. *Philopolis* occurs in Aeschylus *Seven against Thebes* 176 and Pindar *Olympian* 4.18 in connection with deities. Applied to a politician who loves his polis and is devoted to it, it is typical of the last third of the fifth century: Thuc. 2.60.5 (Pericles); 6.92.2, 4 (Alcibiades); see also Aristophanes *Lysistrata* 541–48, which echoes many traits of the (male) Athenians' character portrait. For other echoes and variations in Aristophanes, see Aristophanes *Lysistrata*, ed. with intro. and comm. Jeffrey Henderson (Oxford: Oxford University Press, 1987), 138 at *Lys.* 547; cf. Arnold W. Gomme, *A Historical Commentary on Thucydides*, vol. 2 (Oxford: Oxford University Press, 1956), 168 at Thuc. 2.60.5, and vol. 4 (1970), 366 at 6.92.4. The political use of *erastēs* (of the polis in Thuc. 2.43.1, of tyranny in Her. 3.53.4) is stronger and mocked by Aristophanes as well (see Gomme, 2: 136). See Nathan M. Pusey, "Alcibiades and *to philopoli*," *Harvard Studies in Classical Philology* 51 (1940): 215–31 and lit. cited in n. 61 below.

60. See esp. Hermann Strasburger, "Der Einzelne und die Gemeinschaft im Denken der Griechen," *Historische Zeitschrift* 177 (1954): 227–48 = idem, *Studien*, 1 (1982): 423–48 = F. Gschnitzer, ed., *Zur griechischen Staatskunde* (Darmstadt: Wissenschaftliche Buchgesellschaft, 1969), 97–122; Arthur W. H. Adkins, *Merit and Responsibility: A Study in Greek Values* (London: Oxford University Press, 1960), and *Moral Values and Political Behaviour in Ancient Greece* (New York: Norton, 1972); J. Creed, "Moral Values in the Age of Thucydides," *Classical Quarterly* 23 (1973): 213–31; Gabriel Herman, *Ritualised Friendship and the Greek City* (Cambridge: Cambridge University Press, 1987); and Mary W. Blundell, *Helping Friends and Harming Enemies: A Study in Sophocles and Greek Ethics* (Cambridge: Cambridge University Press, 1989). For communal obligations, see, e.g., James Redfield, *Nature and Culture in the Iliad: The Tragedy of*

that the citizens subordinate their personal interests completely to those of the polis, love their polis, and like true lovers, find satisfaction primarily in service to the beloved polis even at the cost of their lives, the democrats intended not an extension but a repudiation of widespread aristocratic attitudes and values.[61]

We find here a new concept of civic–mindedness that consciously exploits the powerful connotations of erotic language. True, the use of such language in political contexts was not invented by the democrats. But usually it was applied either generally to love for one's country or specifically to the individual's quest for power, particularly tyranny. Moreover, philia had always been a central concept in aristocratic social and political life.[62] Accordingly, the maxim of being the city's (or, for a politician, the demos') lover implied a commitment to renounce the traditional aristocratic habit of seeking personal power even at the expense of communal welfare. It is certainly significant, therefore, that both Pericles and Cleon openly renounced other typically aristocratic habits as well, while at least Cleon embarked on a veritable crusade against would-be tyrants and oligarchic conspirators among his rivals.[63] In sum, the insistence on being "a lover of the polis" is perhaps the most conspicuous example of the reorientation of values and reeducation of the citizens attempted by democracy.

POWER AND THE CITIZENS' MOTIVES

If, then, what Thucydides' contemporaries perceived as the character typical of "democratic imperialists" was neither natural nor really traditional to the Athenians, what was it that made them acquire these

---

Hector (Chicago: University of Chicago Press, 1975), chap. 3; on criticism of traditional aristocratic values (in Tyrtaeus, Xenophanes, and others), see Walter Donlan, "The Tradition of Anti-Aristocratic Thought in Early Greek Poetry," *Historia* 22 (1973): 145–54, and *The Aristocratic Ideal in Ancient Greece* (Lawrence: University of Kansas Press, 1980), chaps. 2 and 3; and Stein-Hölkeskamp, *Adelskultur und Polisgesellschaft*, esp. 125–33.

61. Connor, *New Politicians*, 96–108; Kenneth S. Rothwell, Jr., *Politics and Persuasion in Aristophanes' Ecclesiazusae* (Leiden: Brill, 1990), 26–43, esp. 37–43.

62. On philia, see Connor, *New Politicians*, chap. 2; Horst Hutter, *Politics as Friendship: The Origins of Classical Notions of Politics in the Theory and Practice of Friendship* (Waterloo, Can.: Wilfred Laurier University Press, 1978); David Konstan, "*Philia* in Euripides' *Electra*," *Philologus* 129 (1985): 176–85; and Blundell, *Helping Friends and Harming Enemies*, esp. 31–49. On erotic language, see Rothwell, *Politics and Persuasion*, 37–39 with bibliog.; see also Arrowsmith, "Aristophanes' *Birds*," esp. 129–35 and passim, on the Athenians' collective eros for power. See further n. 107 below.

63. See Plut. *Per.* 7.5ff. Connor, *New Politicians*, 91–94, 121–31; Stein-Hölkeskamp, *Adelskultur und Polisgesellschaft*, 224–25. On Cleon's crusade, see Lévy, *Athènes*, 137–42; Eberhard Ruschenbusch, *Athenische Innenpolitik im 5. Jahrhundert v. Chr. Ideologie oder Pragmatismus?* (Bamberg: Aku, 1979), 37–40; and Lintott, *Violence*, 129–31.

characteristics in the first place, and why did they continue to display
them even when their polis had reached the pinnacle of power in
Greece? If their activism is not itself the answer, what was the driving
force behind it? Especially, how convincing were the political and
ideological arguments used by Thucydidean speakers?

Fear, Honor, Self-Interest The Athenian ambassadors in Sparta give
a concise summary of their city's motives: "It was the actual course of
events which first compelled us to increase our *archē* to its present
extent, mostly because of fear, then also for honor, and later also for
self-interest." Thus, as in Pericles' last speech, fear and honor appear
as the primary concerns.[64]

At first sight, all these concerns seem inherently plausible. The Delian League had been forged against the Persians, and fighting against
the Persians continued, though in varied intensity, for almost thirty
years. In the same period, the league was transformed into an Athenian empire, the first revolts were suppressed, and the *polis tyrannos*
began to reveal its ugly face. When the hostilities with the Persians
ended in the middle of the century, a whole generation of Athenians
had become used to their city's hegemonic and imperial role—and to
constant fighting. Once the big revolts of the 460s and especially the
440s had been brutally put down, a new fear, of the subjects' hatred
and revenge, may indeed have made the loosening of imperial control
seem inopportune. In addition, Athens' relationship with Sparta was
mostly troubled and competitive from the time of Cleisthenes; tensions were frequent, outright hostility almost the rule since 462—
which made it imperative for Athens to control an amount of power
that was at least equal to that of Sparta and its Peloponnesian allies.
Thus we need not doubt that the factor of fear or security, which
probably was conjured up consistently by Athenian leaders, had a
powerful impact on the citizens' collective thinking. After all, our own
century is familiar enough with the effects of comparable political
rhetoric on various peoples' willingness to support decisions for war.
The same is true for the aspect of honor (*timē*). Thucydides and Aristophanes attest to the pride the Athenians felt about their city's power
and the glory and honor that came with it.[65] Collective pride is a powerful force; again, there is no lack of modern parallels.

64. Thuc. 1.75.3 (*malista men hypo deous, epeita kai timēs, hysteron kai ōphelias*); cf. 1.76.2
(honor and fear and self-interest); 2.60–64 (honor and security); cf. 6.82–87 (security). See
de Romilly, *Thucydides and Athenian Imperialism*, 251–54, "Le thème du prestige," and "La
crainte dans l'oeuvre de Thucydide," *Classica et Mediaevalia* 17 (1956): 119–27. See also the
general remarks by M. Finley, "War and Empire," 75–77.
65. See Meiggs, *Athenian Empire*, chap. 21, esp. 384, and Victor Ehrenberg, *The People of*

So much for fear and honor. What about self-interest? The modern historian typically looks first for economic motives. This question has been investigated as thoroughly as the meager evidence permits—for wars in general and for the Athenian empire in particular.[66] No doubt, generally speaking, the Greeks did not ignore the fact that victorious wars could be and often were very profitable; Athens as a community and all Athenians, citizens and noncitizens, even slaves, profited in many ways from the empire and the opportunities connected with it.

To list only the most important categories of such profits, the operation and maintenance of the fleet provided many jobs for citizens and noncitizens, even in peacetime; so did the extensive public building programs. Citizens, of course, had exclusive access to many compensated functions; Aristotle counts more than eleven thousand peacetime jobs, though not all full time or fully paid: offices and magistracies in Athens and abroad, the council and the juries, and many military functions—not counting the sixty ships on constant patrol for eight months of the year.[67] Thousands of lower-class citizens acquired land, mostly in colonies and cleruchies and mostly on allied

Aristophanes: A Sociology of Old Attic Comedy, 2d ed. (Cambridge: Harvard University Press, 1951), 157.

66. E.g., for the Athenian empire, see Jones, *Athenian Democracy*, 3–20; Alfred French, *The Growth of the Athenian Economy* (London: Routledge and Kegan Paul, 1964); Meiggs, *Athenian Empire*, 255–72; Will, *Le monde grec*, 201–11; Schuller, *Herrschaft der Athener*, 71–74, 184–89; Moses I. Finley, "The Fifth-Century Athenian Empire: A Balance-Sheet," in *Imperialism in the Ancient World*, ed. Peter D. A. Garnsey and C. R. Whittaker (Cambridge: Cambridge University Press, 1978), 103–26 with 306–10 = Finley, *Economy and Society in Ancient Greece* (New York: Viking, 1981), 41–61; Winfried Schmitz, *Wirtschaftliche Prosperität, soziale Integration und die Seebundpolitik Athens* (Munich: Tuduv, 1988), pt. 1; and Lisa Kallet-Marx, *Money, Expense, and Naval Power in Thucydides' History 1–5.24* (Berkeley and Los Angeles: University of California Press, 1993). For war in general, see André Aymard, "Le partage des profits de la guerre dans les traités d'alliance antiques," *Revue des études grecques* 81 (1957): 236 = idem, *Etudes d'histoire ancienne* (Paris: Presses Universitaires de France, 1967), 502; Pierre Ducrey, "L'armée, facteur de profits," in *Armées et fiscalité dans le monde antique*, Collection CNRS 936 (Paris: CNRS, 1977), 421–32; Yvon Garlan, "Le partage entre alliées des dépenses et des profits de guerre," ibid., 149–64, esp. 159–62, and idem, *Guerre et économie en Grèce ancienne* (Paris: Découverte, 1989); and William K. Pritchett, *Ancient Greek Military Practices* (Berkeley and Los Angeles: University of California Press, 1971), chap. 3. All these publications give detailed references to sources and bibliography. See also n. 107 below.

67. Aristotle *Athēnaiōn Politeia* [= *Constitution of Athens*] 24.3 (counting only the peace-time jobs); the sixty patrol ships (Plut. *Per.* 11.4) would have employed another twelve thousand (the number of sixty is debated: Meiggs, *Athenian Empire*, 427). For details, see Rhodes, *Commentary*, and Mortimer Chambers, *Aristoteles, Staat der Athener, übersetzt und erläutert* (Berlin: Akademie, 1990), ad loc.; Mogens Herman Hansen, "Seven Hundred Archai in Classical Athens," *Greek, Roman and Byzantine Studies* 21 (1980): 151–73; and M. Finley, "Fifth-Century Athenian Empire," 122–24 = *Economy and Society*, 57–60. For the building program, see the lit. listed in n. 35 above. On the juries and jury pay, see Ps.-Xen. *Ath. Pol.* 3.1–8; Minor M. Markle III, "Jury Pay and Assembly Pay at Athens," in Cartledge and Harvey, *Crux*, 265–97; and Stephen Todd, "Lady Chatterley's Lover and the Attic Orators: The Social Composition of the Athenian Jury," *Journal of Hellenic Studies* 110 (1990): 146–73.

territory; an estimated ten thousand of these thereby reached hoplite status. In addition, the supply of grain from the Black Sea area, on which Athens depended, was guaranteed, and the Piraeus became the center of trade in the Aegean and far beyond; accordingly, there were countless opportunities for indirect profits in trade, production, and the "hotel and entertainment industry."[68] The upper classes obviously shared in these profits—according to a pointed statement in Thucydides (8.48.5–6) they even profited most—but details are not easy to determine: acquisition of land in allied territory, booty, interest from loans, fees for representing foreigners, even bribes counted for much; and the large amount of public revenues relieved the tax pressure on the wealthy.[69] Finally, the empire made democracy possible by initiating the indispensable social changes and mental adaptations and by providing the necessary impulses and the financial resources, without which such an unprecedented system could not have been realized.[70]

All this, though often uncertain in detail, is undeniable and significant. Some ancient observers, critical of "radical democracy," took it for granted that the Athenian demos relied on these material benefits and was highly motivated by them—if not outright venal.[71] Most important, Thucydides explains the vote for the Sicilian expedition in 415 (among other reasons) with the fact that the "mass of the people, including those in the army, [were seduced by] the prospect of getting pay for the time being and of adding to the empire so as to secure permanent paid employment in the future" (6.24.3, trans. Warner).

68. Ps.-Xen. *Ath. Pol.* 1.16–17, 2.7; Thuc. 2.38.2; Hermippos frag. 43; cf. Meiggs, *Athenian Empire*, 266–71. Romilly, *Thucydides and Athenian Imperialism*, 253, stresses food supplies. On land, see Jones, *Athenian Democracy*, 7, 167–77 with detailed discussion.

69. Jones, *Athenian Democracy*, 7; M. Finley, "Fifth-Century Athenian Empire," 123–24 = *Economy and Society*, 59. On landed property abroad, see Meiggs, *Athenian Empire*, 262; Schuller, *Herrschaft der Athener*, 73–74; M. Finley, "Fifth-Century Athenian Empire," 115–17 = *Economy and Society*, 51–53; and Antony Andrewes, in Gomme, *Historical Commentary on Thucydides*, vol. 5 (1985), 111–12. On bribes and other forms of corruption, see Shalom Perlman, "On Bribing Athenian Ambassadors," *Greek, Roman and Byzantine Studies* 17 (1976): 223–33; Hermann Wankel, "Die Korruption in der rednerischen Topik und in der Realität des klassischen Athen," in *Korruption im Altertum*, ed. Wolfgang Schuller (Munich: Oldenbourg, 1982), 29–47; Jennifer Roberts, *Accountability in Athenian Government* (Madison: University of Wisconsin Press, 1982), index s.v. "bribery"; F. David Harvey, "Dona ferentes: Some Aspects of Bribery in Greek Politics," in Cartledge and Harvey, *Crux*, 76–117; and Barry S. Strauss, "The Cultural Significance of Bribery and Embezzlement in Athenian Politics: The Evidence of the Period 403–386 B.C.," *Ancient World* 11 (1985): 67–74.

70. Despite democracy's later ability to continue without such revenues: thus see M. Finley, "Fifth-Century Athenian Empire," 122–23 = *Economy and Society*, 58; and Galpin, "Democratic Roots," 107–8; *contra:* Jones, *Athenian Democracy*, 5–6, 19. For the social and mental adaptations, see above, n. 33.

71. E.g., Ps.-Xen. *Ath. Pol.* 1.3, 13, 15, 16–18; Aristophanes *Knights* and *Wasps* 707–11; and Plato *Gorg.* 515e, 517b–19a. See Anton Meder, *Der athenische Demos zur Zeit des Peloponnesischen Krieges im Lichte zeitgenössischer Quellen* (Diss., Munich, 1938), 51–82, 172–79, 203–4, and, more generally, Ehrenberg, *People of Aristophanes*, chap. 12.

This is a unique and surprising statement, particularly because there is no comparable remark in Thucydides' earlier books or in the debates preceding it in Book 6 and because it attributes to the citizen masses a motive that is otherwise assumed only of the leaders and especially of Alcibiades.[72] Thus it raises urgently the question of whether such material considerations indeed provided primary and sufficient motivation for the Athenian masses to support continually their city's aggressive and expansionist policies.

Scholars who have examined the related question of whether there was a conscious and official policy of "economic imperialism" have concluded that Athenian imperialism, as much as it was expected to support the material interests of the community, was conceived of primarily as a means to power and that the driving force behind it was the will to dominate. The economic advantages of empire should thus be seen not as goals in themselves but as means toward, and consequences of, primarily political goals. As Moses I. Finley states categorically, "There were no commercial or commercially inspired wars . . . at any time in antiquity." Accordingly, there was no economic imperialism.[73]

This conclusion is of direct importance to our present inquiry. Particularly in a direct democracy of the Athenian type, we should not expect the sum of individual priorities to be completely at odds with official communal policies. Thus if Thucydides' comment on the motives of the masses in 415 were generally applicable, we should expect the factor of private and communal economic gain to be emphasized more often, directly and naturally, both in Thucydides and in other authors. This is not the case, the testimonia mentioned above (n. 71) notwithstanding. Instead, what is stressed primarily and consistently is acceptance of toil and risk for the sake of enhancing the power, safety, and glory of the polis. We have to conclude, therefore, that

72. On 6.24.3, see the comments by Kenneth J. Dover, in Gomme, *Historical Commentary on Thucydides*, vol. 4, ad loc.; M. Finley, "War and Empire," 77, 82; and Connor, *Thucydides*, 168 n. 24. On Alcibiades, see Thuc. 6.12.2, 15.2. See generally 2.65.7f. and the accusation made in 3.38.3 (and echoed in 6.39.2) that the gains go to the wealthy and the risks to the masses. More generally, on profiteering by politicians, see, e.g., Eur. *Suppl.* 232ff., esp. 236; Aristoph. *Knights* and *Hellenica Oxyrhynchia* 7.2 (p. 8 in the ed. by Vittorio Bartoletti [Leipzig: Teubner, 1959]), with Lysias, or. 27.9–10.

73. Moses I. Finley, *The Ancient Economy* (Berkeley and Los Angeles: University of California Press, 1973), 158. See generally Will, *Le monde grec*, 201–11; Ste. Croix, *Origins of the Peloponnesian War*, 214–20; M. Finley, *Ancient Economy*, chap. 6, "Fifth-Century Athenian Empire," 117–21 = *Economy and Society*, 53–57, and "War and Empire," 75–77; Schuller, *Herrschaft der Athener*, 74–80; and Paul Rahe, "The Primacy of Politics in Classical Greece," *American Historical Review* 89 (1984): 265–93, and *Republics Ancient and Modern* (Chapel Hill: University of North Carolina Press, 1992), 28–54.

economic motives played an important but probably not primary role; they certainly seem to have been less dominant than we moderns tend to expect on the basis of more recent experiences.[74]

Moreover, the heroization of *ponos* for the greater glory of the community should not blind us to the realities of death and suffering brought upon the Athenians even by victorious warfare.[75] Despite all the opportunities mentioned before, even for the lower classes the gains might not have been that overwhelming; and for the farmers— according to Thucydides (2.14.2, 16.1) still the majority before the war—the losses were painful and certainly by far outweighed the gains. Nevertheless, they too, except for the crisis of 430, seem to have supported the official "hardline" policies, and until late in the war no major political split is visible in this respect between farmers and lower classes.[76]

All in all, the triad of motives emphasized by the Athenian ambassadors in Thucydides—fear, pride, and self-interest—no doubt goes a long way toward explaining the emergence of activism in the pursuit of power and glory as a constituent part of the Athenian collective character. In public debate the arguments supporting such motives, though potentially very emotional, were backed, as all effective ideology is, by shared experiences, a certain amount of factual plausibility, and often highly rational, even theoretical, reasoning. The politicians increasingly were skilled orators who, by instinct or training, were sensitive to mass psychology. They must have used the arguments they considered most effective—which in turn justifies our assumption that these reflected powerful motives. Thus as long as Athens generally was successful, the citizens will have found sufficient

74. Thus too Schuller, *Herrschaft der Athener*, 184–89; *contra:* M. Finley, "Fifth-Century Athenian Empire," 124 = *Economy and Society*, 59–60; but see Meier, "Rolle des Krieges," 590 n. 107. Generally, see bibliog. cited in nn. 66 and 73. It is useful to compare the treatment of economic motive in the ancient sources on Roman imperialism; see William V. Harris, *War and Imperialism in Republican Rome, 327–70 B.C.* (Oxford: Oxford University Press, 1979), esp. 57.

75. On casualties, see Johannes Mälzer, *Verluste und Verlustlisten im griechischen Altertum bis auf die Zeit Alexanders des Grossen* (Diss., Jena, 1912); Peter Krentz, "Casualties in Hoplite Battles," *Greek, Roman and Byzantine Studies* 26 (1958): 13–20; Barry S. Strauss, *Athens after the Peloponnesian War* (Ithaca: Cornell University Press, 1986), 70–86, 173, 179–82; and Nicholas G. L. Hammond, "Casualties and Reinforcements of Citizen Soldiers in Greece and Macedonia," *Journal of Hellenic Studies* 109 (1989): 56–68. Furthermore, widespread emphasis on the blessings of peace is attested throughout fifth-century literature: see Meier, "Rolle des Krieges," 589–90 with n. 105.

76. Ehrenberg, *People of Aristophanes*, chap. 11; Arrowsmith, "Aristophanes' *Birds*," 120–26; Nippel, *Mischverfassungstheorie*, 68–71. On the crisis of 430, see Thuc. 2.59. On the gains of the lower classes, see, e.g., French, *Growth of the Athenian Economy*, 172–74, and the discussion by Todd, "Lady Chatterley's Lover."

strength in their collective enthusiasm, "national" pride, and shared concern for the safety and glory of their polis to support continually the policies that had carried it to the pinnacle of power and greatness. Both these policies and collective attitudes would tend to develop their own dynamics, reinforce each other, get ever more deeply ingrained, and become practically irreversible. Even the more skeptical and distant would be swept along by such collective sentiments—and by the will not to miss out on good opportunities; but they would be the first to back out in situations of failure and crisis.[77]

Thus the motives stressed by Thucydides appear compelling. But are they sufficient? After all, except in rare crisis constellations, how realistic did the Persian danger appear after the early 460s, how serious the threat from vengeful allies before the later part of the Peloponnesian War?[78] Were the Spartans not indeed, as the Corinthians emphasize in Thucydides (1.69–71), known to refrain from decisive action and massive commitments beyond their sphere of influence? And how long could the Athenian citizens' enthusiasm last, how much *ponos* could they be expected to tolerate primarily for the reward of pride in the glory of their city? We cannot know the answers to such questions. Unless we accept Thucydides' assessment as complete or believe that the Athenians simply internalized the arguments used by their leaders to justify their policy of continuing aggressive imperialism, however, we might be well advised to look for additional motives to explain the citizens' support of such policies. I suggest one other factor which, though not appearing directly in our sources, is likely to have affected strongly both the leaders and the masses of citizens. This factor is democracy itself.

The Leaders: Opportunities for Distinction   I begin with the leaders. Although their backgrounds and outlooks differed and they may have disagreed vehemently on individual policies or decisions and the modalities or intensity of Athens' imperial rule, they all seem to have supported this rule at least in principle. Such agreement had good reasons. In the average Greek polis the political agenda was limited: the domestic sphere was politically undeveloped and offered few opportunities for political initiatives; and interstate politics were increasingly dominated by the interests of the big powers and their alliances.

77. As happened in 415, before the Sicilian expedition (Thuc. 6.24.3–4), and in 413–411, after its disastrous end (see Lintott, *Violence*, chap. 4; and Ostwald, *Sovereignty*, chaps. 6 and 7). Unfortunately, nothing is known about the impact on Athenian domestic politics of the Egyptian disaster in the 450s.

78. On the latter, see the debate about the "popularity of the Athenian empire," summarized in Raaflaub, *Entdeckung der Freiheit*, 207–14, with bibliog.

Thus, normally, few important decisions needed to be made, and the potential for political competition or distinction was restricted. By contrast, when Athens assumed the role of a "superpower" and became involved in countless military, diplomatic, and administrative activities, the political agenda multiplied rapidly. This expanded agenda was not only a crucial precondition for the full realization of democracy; it also created new conditions for politics, competition, and distinction. Within the framework of the generally accepted pursuit of imperial power, there were many opportunities for disagreement, alternative plans, "better" proposals, particularly in times of war.[79]

For a long time, however, the resulting and potentially fierce competition for leadership and power was, with few exceptions, contained by the authority of exceptionally strong and capable personalities: Cimon and Pericles, one the architect of the empire, the other of democracy. But after Pericles' death and under the divisive impact of a long and difficult war, as Thucydides recognized so well, no politician was able to reach the same level of stable influence and authority.[80] The rivalry—deeply rooted in aristocratic traditions—for the first rank among leaders was intense and fought without restraints, particularly since many of the "new politicians" were trained by the Sophists in political skills and rhetoric. These struggles were fought in the arena of foreign policy and war strategy. Decisions concerning the empire and the war thus became tools in Athens' domestic power struggle. Inevitably, the prevailing tendency called for activist policies, new involvement, and further expansion because it was such policies, not those of caution and restraint, that offered their sponsors the opportunity to gain success, glory, wealth, and personal power.[81]

Thus, to satisfy their ambition, many of the politicians bred by and

79. On all these issues, see Eberhard Ruschenbusch, *Untersuchungen zu Staat und Politik in Griechenland vom 7.–4.Jh. v. Chr.* (Bamberg: Aku, 1978), 68–71, and *Innenpolitik*, 15–17; Schuller, "Wirkungen," esp. 94–97; and Stein-Hölkeskamp, *Adelskultur und Polisgesellschaft*, 205–30.

80. Thuc. 2.65.10–13, on which see the comments by Gomme, *Historical Commentary on Thucydides*, vol. 2; Rhodes, in *Thucydides*, bk. 2; and Rusten, in *Thucydides*, bk. 2, with bibliog. on 213.

81. See, e.g., the Mytilenian Debate (esp. Thuc. 3.37–38 and 42–43) and the Sicilian Debate (6.8–23). On the problems of Athenian leadership, see Moses I. Finley, "Athenian Demagogues," *Past and Present* 21 (1962): 1–25 = idem, ed., *Studies in Ancient Society* (London: Routledge and Kegan Paul, 1974), 1–25; Connor, *New Politicians*; Welwei, *Die griechische Polis*, 214–18; Sinclair, *Democracy and Participation in Athens*, esp. chaps. 6 and 7; Ober, *Mass and Elite*; Stein-Hölkeskamp, *Adelskultur und Polisgesellschaft*, 182–87, 202 and passim in pt. 4; Walter Eder, "Who Rules? Power and Participation in Athens and Rome," in Molho, Raaflaub, and Emlen, *Athens and Rome, Florence and Venice*, 169–96; Harvey Yunis, "How Do the People Decide? Thucydides on Periclean Rhetoric and Civic Instruction," *American Journal of Philology* 112 (1991): 179–200; and the titles listed in n. 32 above.

adapted to the political conditions of the fully developed democracy needed the empire, imperialism, and war; for them, the activism that had become typical of Athenian politics was almost indispensable. To some extent, this is true already for Pericles, who, despite the restraint he displayed in crucial situations, certainly was one of the most ambitious and aggressive imperialists Athens ever had; it is even more true, under the conditions of war, for Cleon and many others, and especially for Alcibiades, whose motives for advocating the Sicilian expedition Thucydides describes as "his desire to hold the command and his hopes that it would be through him that Sicily and Carthage would be conquered—successes which would at the same time bring him personally both wealth and honor" (6.15.2, trans. Warner).

The leaders, however, could not have exploited these opportunities so intensely if their fellow citizens had not been willing to go along. Beyond the aspects of collective ideology and material advantages I have discussed, what was at stake for them? To find an answer, I examine more closely the political situation and psychology of the lower-class citizens.

The Masses: Legitimacy through Success   Before the Thirty Years' Peace with Sparta in 446, the hoplite army played an important role in Athens' power politics. By then, however, Athens' territorial possessions on the mainland were mostly lost. The city and Piraeus had been transformed into an impregnable fortress. Henceforth, Athens relied entirely on naval warfare, which in turn depended almost exclusively on the military involvement of the *thētes* and relegated the hoplites to an inferior and subsidiary role. Thus it was the lower classes who bore the brunt of the actual fighting, suffered the heaviest losses, and contributed most to the power, glory, and wealth of their city. But did they receive the lion's share of recognition and benefits as well? I have discussed the latter; what about the former?

They were included, of course, in the praise of the Athenian citizens' unique achievements and collective glory. Pride in the splendid fleet and its efficient and disciplined crews is expressed vividly in Aristophanes and elsewhere.[82] Yet specific acknowledgment of their

82. Ehrenberg, *People of Aristophanes*, 300–301, and generally in the chapter titled "War and Peace." See esp. Aristophanes *Acharnians* 162–63, *Knights* 1365–72, and *Wasps* 1092–97; furthermore, Aeschylus *Persians* 391–405; Thuc. 2.88.1–2, 89.3 (cf. for contrast 84.3); and Xenophon *Memorabilia Socratis* 3.5.18–19 (I thank Barry Strauss for some of these references). On Timotheus of Miletus' *Persians*, which shortly after the restoration of democracy in 410 revived the glorious memory of Salamis, see Tjitte Janssen, *Timotheus, Persae: A Commentary* (Amsterdam: Hakkert, 1984), who argues for a date near Euripides' *Orestes* (13–22). Cf. also Sophocles *Oedipus at Colonus* 707–19, performed posthumously after the fall of the Thirty in 401.

crucial contribution is rare; paradoxically, it is formulated most explicitly by Pseudo-Xenophon, the resentful admirer of democracy's effectiveness: "My first point is that it is right that the poor and the ordinary people there should have more power than the noble and the rich, because it is the ordinary people who man the fleet and . . . make the city powerful much more than the hoplites and the noble and respectable citizens" (*Ath. Pol.* 1.2). Yet it was the hoplites who inherited the ethics and enjoyed the prestige of heroic man-to-man combat—despite the stress on collective discipline and the increased anonymity brought about by the phalanx. The rowers fought in faceless masses, hidden in the bellies of their ships and thus mostly invisible and unable even to see their enemies.[83] Plato offers a sharp rebuttal to Pseudo-Xenophon's statement: "When a state which owes its power to its navy wins a victory, the bravest soldiers never get the credit for it because the battle is won thanks to the skill of steersman, boatswain and rower, and the efforts of a motley crowd of ragamuffins, which means that it is impossible to honor each individual in the way he deserves. Rob a state of its power to do that, and you condemn it to failure" (*Laws* 4.707a–b).[84] Elsewhere, Plato harshly contrasts the "shame of Salamis" with the "glory of Marathon and Plataea"—which may be extreme but was not unique and had its predecessors in the fifth century in the glorification of Marathon and its heroes (the "Marathonomachoi"), highlighted for us in the monuments of Cimon's time and in Aristophanes' comedies.[85]

In 411, the supporters of an oligarchic regime proposed to restrict full citizenship to those who "would best be able to contribute materially and personally" (literally: "with money and bodies"). This formula refers exclusively to men of hoplite status and above; it obviously implies that only those fighting in open land battle (as hoplites or horsemen) properly used their bodies to benefit their community. Thus it directly challenges the view, reflected in the Corinthian summary of the Athenian character portrait and vigorously espoused by

83. For details, see John S. Morrison and John F. Coates, *The Athenian Trireme* (Cambridge: Cambridge University Press, 1986).

84. Plato was thinking of a fleet manned largely by mercenaries, occasionally even by slaves. Before the Peloponnesian War, this would have been different, but aristocratic critics of democracy would probably have passed the same judgment.

85. Plato *Laws* 4.707b–d; see also *Gorg.* 519a; for a more balanced judgment, see *Menex.* 241a, and *Laws* 3.692d. For Cimon, see Pierre Vidal-Naquet, "The Tradition of the Athenian Hoplite," in *The Black Hunter: Forms of Thought and Forms of Society in the Greek World* (Baltimore: Johns Hopkins University Press, 1986), 90–91, and "An Enigma at Delphi," ibid., 302–24, esp. 310–14; see also Charles W. Fornara, "The Hoplite Achievement at Psyttaleia," *Journal of Hellenic Studies* 86 (1966): 51–54. For Aristophanes and the Marathonomachoi, see Ehrenberg, *People of Aristophanes*, 298–300. See further Nicole Loraux, "'Marathon' ou l'histoire idéologique," *Revue des études anciennes* 75 (1973): 24–25, and *Invention of Athens*, 161–62.

the democrats, that *all* Athenians used their bodies to best serve their polis.[86] This aristocratic concept is related to another that emphasizes fighting and tilling the land as the only occupations truly worthy of the free and noble man. In fact, it is precisely the techne involved in naval warfare that equates it to all the base occupations, which were characterized by technical skills and professionalism and thus disqualified as "unfree" or "unnoble" (*aneleutheron*). All such concepts had a long aristocratic tradition and combined to exclude the despised members of the lower classes.[87]

In light of all this, a few puzzling inequalities that are still much debated, and cannot be discussed here in detail, should at least be mentioned briefly.[88] First, there existed a central register of cavalry and, according to the predominant view, "a catalogue of hoplites that informed the city about the number of men it could call on to form its regiments of heavy infantry," but there certainly was no corresponding register of *nautai* (sailors).[89] Second, some form of *ephēbeia* (the

86. Thuc. 1.70.6; 2.42 (esp. 4). See also 2.39.3. The oligarchic formula is in Thuc. 8.65.3; cf. Aristot. *Ath. Pol.* 29.5 and the parallels for the formula cited by Rhodes, *Commentary*, 382–83, esp. Xenophon *Hipparchikos* 1.9.

87. See Jean-Pierre Vernant, "Travail et nature dans la Grèce ancienne," in *Mythe et pensée chez les Grecs*, vol. 2 (Paris: Maspero, 1965), 16–36; André Aymard, "Hiérarchie du travail et autarcie individuelle dans la Grèce archaïque," in *Etudes d'histoire ancienne*, 316–33; Christian Meier, "Arbeit, Politik, Identität: Neue Fragen im alten Athen?" *Chronik der Ludwig-Maximilians-Universität München* (1983/4): 69–95; Raymond Descat, *L'acte et l'effort: Une idéologie du travail en Grèce ancienne* (Paris: Belles Lettres, 1986); and Stanislav Mrozek, *Lohnarbeit im klassischen Altertum* (Bonn: Habelt, 1989). For techne in naval warfare, see Vidal-Naquet, "Tradition of the Athenian Hoplite," 93 with sources, esp. Isocr. *Panath.* 116. To attain such techne, constant training was required: Amit, *Athens and the Sea*, 49–50; Borimir Jordan, *The Athenian Navy in the Classical Period* (Berkeley and Los Angeles: University of California Press, 1975), 103–6; Garlan, *War in the Ancient World*, 130. For *analeutheroi technai*, see Kurt A. Raaflaub, "Zum Freiheitsbegriff der Griechen," in *Soziale Typenbegriffe im alten Griechenland und ihr Fortleben in den Sprachen der Welt*, ed. Elisabeth C. Welskopf, vol. 4 (Berlin: Akademie, 1981), 305–13, and "Democracy, Oligarchy, and the Concept of the 'Free Citizen' in Late Fifth-Century Athens," *Political Theory* 11 (1983): 531–32. See also Xenophon *Oeconomicus* 4.2–4.

88. For a more detailed discussion, see Kurt A. Raaflaub, "Equalities and Inequalities in Athenian Democracy," in *Democracy Ancient and Modern*, ed. Josiah Ober and Charles Hedrick (forthcoming).

89. For the register of cavalry, see Glenn R. Bugh, *The Horsemen of Athens* (Princeton: Princeton University Press, 1983), 52–55. For that of the hoplites, see Vidal-Naquet, "Tradition of the Athenian Hoplite," 87–88 (with the citation); Jones, *Athenian Democracy*, 163; Dover, in Gomme, *Historical Commentary on Thucydides* 4: 264; and Antony Andrewes, "The Hoplite *Katalogos*," in Shrimpton and McCargar, *Classical Contributions*, 3–5. *Contra:* see Mogens H. Hansen, "The Number of Athenian Hoplites in 431 B.C." *Symbolae Osloenses* 56 (1981): 24–29. For the *thētes* conscripted to serve on the fleet, see Jordan, *Athenian Navy*, 101–3; and Mogens H. Hansen, *Demography and Democracy: The Number of Athenian Citizens in the Fourth Century B.C.* (Herning, Denmark: Systime, 1986), 22–23. Vincent J. Rosivach, "Manning the Athenian Fleet, 433–426 B.C.," *American Journal of Ancient History* 10 (1985 [publ. 1993]): 41–66, suggests that the *thētes* were mostly volunteers. See n. 107 below.

training of the young citizens for their obligations as soldiers and citizens), well-known from the fourth century, most probably existed already in the fifth century. Whatever its exact nature, however, it certainly was not compulsory for all young male citizens. Moreover, in its military aspects the *ephēbeia* was exclusively a preparation for hoplite service. Thus, as long as the *thētes* did not regularly serve as hoplites, they were a priori excluded from the rituals that prepared the Athenian men for their function as citizens and from the prestige and recognition that went with participation in those rituals and public festivals.[90] Third, for similar reasons, we might also wonder whether in the fifth century the war orphans who received the panoply at the Great Dionysia after having been raised at public expense, really included, as is always assumed, all citizens reaching adulthood and not perhaps only those of hoplite descent and above.[91] Fourth, on various occasions Thucydides gives precise figures for deaths of hoplites but is vague about those of members of the lower classes.[92] Fifth, it seems far from impossible that the *thētes* were not—or not always—recorded by name in the Athenian casualty lists[93] and that still in the second half of the fifth century not all *thētes* were registered in the list of citizens kept by the demes (the *lēxiarchika grammateia*).[94] All these questions are

90. For discussion of various aspects, see Chrysis Pélékidis, *Histoire de l'éphébie attique des origines à 31 av. J.-C.* (Paris: Boccard, 1962); Oscar Reinmuth, *The Ephebic Inscriptions of the Fourth Century B.C.* (Leiden: Brill, 1971); Reinhold Merkelbach, "Der Theseus des Bakchylides (Gedicht für ein attisches Ephenbenfest)," *Zeitschrift für Papyrologie und Epigraphik* 12 (1973): 56–62; Peter Siewert, "The Ephebic Oath in Fifth-Century Athens," *Journal of Hellenic Studies* 97 (1977): 102–11; Rhodes, *Commentary*, 493–510; John J. Winkler, "The Ephebes' Song: *Tragoidia* and *Polis*," *Representations* 11 (1985): 26–62, rev. in Winkler and Zeitlin, *Nothing to Do with Dionysos?* 20–62; and Pierre Vidal-Naquet, "The Black Hunter and the Origin of the Athenian *Ephebeia*," in *Black Hunter*, 106–28, and "Sophocles' *Philoctetes* and the *Ephebeia*," in *Myth and Tragedy in Ancient Greece*, ed. Jean-Pierre Vernant and Pierre Vidal-Naquet (New York: Zone, 1990), 161–79. On noncompulsory participation before the late fourth century, see Philippe Gauthier, *Un commentaire historique des Poroi de Xénophon* (Geneva: Droz, 1976), 190–95.

91. For details, see Arthur Pickard-Cambridge, *The Dramatic Festivals of Athens*, 2d ed. (Oxford: Oxford University Press, 1968), 59 with nn. 1–2; Ronald Stroud, "Greek Inscriptions: Theozotides and the Athenian Orphans," *Hesperia* 40 (1971): 288–90; Loraux, *Invention of Athens*, 26–27; and Goldhill, "Great Dionysia and Civic Ideology," 63–68 and 105–14, respectively.

92. Thuc. 3.87.3; 4.101.2. See Loraux, *Invention of Athens*, 361 n. 127; and Patterson, *Pericles' Citizenship Law of 451–50 B.C.*, 47.

93. Thus, e.g., Anthony Raubitschek, "Greek Inscriptions," *Hesperia* 12 (1943): 48 n. 102; Harold Mattingly, "Athenian Imperialism and the Foundation of Brea," *Classical Quarterly* 16 (1966): 191; *contra*: Donald Bradeen, "Athenian Casualty Lists," *Hesperia* 33 (1964): 25 n. 15, and "The Athenian Casualty Lists," *Classical Quarterly* 19 (1969): 153–54, followed by Vidal-Naquet, "Tradition of the Athenian Hoplite," 88, and Loraux, *Invention of Athens*, 34.

94. For discussion, see Hignett, *History of the Athenian Constitution*, 132–42; Christian Habicht, "Falsche Urkunden zur Geschichte Athens im Zeitalter der Perserkriege," *Hermes* 89 (1961): 5–6; Michael Jameson, "The Provisions for Mobilization in the Decree of Themisto-

far from settled but, cumulatively, the uncertainties they reveal support much other evidence suggesting that both in life and in death the hoplites were considered much more noble and important and taken far more seriously than those citizens who served as archers or oarsmen. As Nicole Loraux comments, "Could it be that someone was less of an Athenian if he specialized in nonhoplite warfare? Some Athenians thought so, and, without really taking back with one hand what it was giving with the other, the community was concerned to make the distinction."[95]

Thus, as far as their military role was concerned, not all citizens were equal: whatever the merits of the *nautai*, their prestige trailed far behind that of the hoplites and horsemen. This discrepancy was even more marked in the political sphere. There was no lack of voices that considered sea power incompatible with decent government.[96] Institutionally, with a few sensible exceptions, all Athenian citizens were supposed to be equal. Democratic ideology continually emphasized this principle—aristocratic critics repudiated such numerical equality and set against it their own ideal of proportional or socially differentiated equality. The democrats praised the freedom their system provided for all citizens and the city as a whole—the opponents ridiculed such liberty and developed their own definition of the truly free citizen.[97] The democrats were proud of their constitution, which allowed all citizens to exert themselves for their own *and* their community's interests at the same time and encouraged them to contribute whatever they could and to bring out their best qualities for the common good. The opponents' reaction was cold contempt: how good could a system be, in which the rabble, crazy men, all who were base, poor, unedu-

cles," *Historia* 12 (1963): 399–400, expanded in "Apollo Lykeios in Athens," *Archaiognosia* 1, no. 2 (1980): 213–23, esp. 222 with 223 n. 1; Henri van Effenterre, "Clisthène et les mesures de mobilisation," *Revue des études grecques* 89 (1976): 7–15; Patterson, *Pericles' Citizenship Law of 451–50 B.C.*, 8–28, esp. 27; Robin Osborne, *Demos: The Discovery of Classical Attika* (Cambridge: Cambridge University Press, 1985), 72–73; David Whitehead, *The Demes of Attica, 508/7–ca. 250 B.C.* (Princeton: Princeton University Press, 1986), 34–35; and Bugh, *Horsemen of Athens*, 55 n. 64.

95. Loraux, *Invention of Athens*, 34, cf. 361 n. 126; cf. also Garlan, *War in the Ancient World*, 130. The political aftermath of the battle at Arginusae in 406 provides an obvious exception: Nicholas G. L. Hammond, *A History of Greece to 322 B.C.*, 2d ed. (Oxford: Oxford University Press, 1967), 414–16 with sources.

96. Momigliano, "Sea-Power in Greek Thought," 2 and 58–59 respectively, singles out Pseudo-Xenophon and Stesimbrotus of Thasos's pamphlet, *On Themistocles, Thucydides and Pericles* (no. 107 in F. Jacoby, *Die Fragmente der griechischen Historiker [FGrHist]*, pt. 2, vol. B [Leiden: Brill, 1962]), written after 430; but see Frost, *Plutarch's Themistocles*, 85–87, in part against Jacoby's commentary at *FGrHist* no. 107 F2.

97. On equality, see F. David Harvey, "Two Kinds of Equality," *Classica et Mediaevalia* 26 (1965): 101–46; on freedom, see Raaflaub, "Concept of the 'Free Citizen,'" and *Entdeckung der Freiheit*, 304–11.

cated, and undisciplined, were allowed to speak and make decisions? Where the demos was in charge, they claimed, evil could not fail to creep in, and things inevitably turned out badly. The masses simply lacked the qualities needed to participate competently and responsibly in politics.[98] As one of the participants in Herodotus's "Constitutional Debate" says about the hubris of the demos, "There is nothing stupider, nothing more given to outrage, than a useless mob. . . . There is no insight in the demos. How can men know anything when they have never been taught what is fine, nor have they any innate sense of it? They rush into things and push them this way and that without intelligent purpose, like a river in winter spate" (3.81.1f., trans. Grene, modified).

Such criticism was frequent and well known; it has left its traces all over the literature of the time.[99] How would it affect those attacked by it? We do not really know; our sources do not address such issues directly, but they give us some indications from which we can form an impression.[100] The masses were liable to flattery; they hated criticism, accepted it only from those they considered their true friends and sponsors; they tried to appear competent, refined, knowledgeable.[101] Like some of the other components of their "collective character," such reactions seem typical of men with little—or mostly artificial—self-confidence.

In his appearance and dress, we hear, the lower-class Athenian was hardly distinguishable from a slave. Socially and economically, he was worse off than many metics. Thus what remained to distinguish him from all the others, foreigners and unfree alike, was the political sphere. There, despite the criticism and contempt he felt on the part of the upper classes, he belonged not to the "have-nots" but to the "haves," he was equal and had to be taken seriously; there, the rich and the powerful, whether Athenians or foreigners, had to respect him and seek his approval.[102] For the average Athenian, therefore,

98. See Her. 5.78, and Thuc. 2.37, 41, for the positive view; for the negative, Her. 3.82.4; cf. Eur. *Suppl.* 417–22; and Ps.-Xen. *Ath. Pol.* 1.1–9.

99. Jakob A. O. Larsen, "The Judgment of Antiquity on Democracy," *Classical Philology* 49 (1954): 1–14; Jones, *Athenian Democracy*, 41–72; and, focusing on the fifth century only, Raaflaub, "Contemporary Perceptions of Democracy."

100. The following comments are preliminary and somewhat speculative. The whole issue needs a thorough reexamination. For fuller documentation, see, on Aristophanes and Pseudo-Xenophon, Meder, "Der Athenische Demos"; on Euripides, Wilhelm Nestle, *Euripides: Der Dichter der griechischen Aufklärung* (Stuttgart: Kohlhammer, 1901; reprint, Aalen: Scientia, 1969), chaps. 6 and 7. See also Sinclair, *Democracy and Participation in Athens*, and Ober, *Mass and Elite.*

101. See, e.g., Aristoph. *Knights*, and Thuc. 2.65.8–9; 3.37–38, 42–43.

102. Ps.-Xen. *Ath. Pol.* 1.6–9, 18; Aristoph. *Knights* and *Wasps.* On appearance, see Ps.-

who otherwise lacked distinction and identity, his political status and function became exceedingly important. He developed, in Christian Meier's words, a strong and, in many cases, primary "political identity."[103] This identity, however, was precarious, and the status on which it rested was unprecedented in the Greek world and under constant challenge; accordingly, it constantly needed to be reaffirmed. In other words, precisely those citizens who supported democracy most vigorously and profited most from it were under constant pressure to justify the political status they had achieved and the political role they played.

Now the Greek polis was not an abstract political or social entity; it was a community of citizens. Democracy was not the result of theoretical speculation but of a necessary political adjustment to changes in the military sphere. Thus efforts to justify democracy abstractly (institutionally or theoretically), though by no means lacking already in the fifth century, remained insufficient unless due emphasis was given to the human factor: the citizen's responsibility for the community.[104]

Ultimately, the only truly compelling and generally acceptable—though not always happily accepted—justification of democracy and the status it accorded the lower-class citizens was the indispensable role played and achievements attained in the past and present for the community by these citizens and, through them, by the system as a whole.[105] This is what Pseudo-Xenophon admits (*Ath. Pol.* 1.2, cited above, at n. 82) and the Thucydidean Alcibiades concedes: democracy essentially is crazy and absurd, but it is difficult not to support the system under which one's city has become the greatest and freest of all (6.89.6). This too is the gist of Herodotus's comment on the rise of

Xen. *Ath. Pol.* 1.10–12. See Ehrenberg, *People of Aristophanes*, chaps. 6 and 7; Michael M. Austin and Pierre Vidal-Naquet, *Economic and Social History of Ancient Greece: An Introduction* (Berkeley and Los Angeles: University of California Press, 1977), 99–106; and Siegfried Lauffer, "Die Bedeutung des Standesunterschieds im klassischen Athen," *Historische Zeitschrift* 185 (1958): 497–514.

103. Meier, *Greek Discovery of Politics*, 140–54; cf. idem, "Die politische Identität der Griechen," in *Identität*, ed. Odo Marquard and Karlheinz Stierle (Munich: Wilhelm Fink, 1979), 371–406, "Bürgeridentität und Demokratie," in Christian Meier and Paul Veyne, *Kannten die Griechen die Demokratie?* (Berlin: Klaus Wagenbach, 1988), 47–95; and Humphreys, "Economy and Society."

104. For justifications of democracy, see Raaflaub, "Contemporary Perceptions of Democracy"; for an impressive application of the criterion of the citizens' responsibility, see Aesch. *Suppl.* (esp. 365–69) and the bibliog. cited in n. 24 above.

105. Although here too counterclaims were lodged early on; see, e.g., the efforts in the Cimonian era to challenge the attribution of Athenian successes primarily to the navy and *thêtes* by emphasizing the hoplites' contribution to Athenian victories: Fornara, "Hoplite Achievement at Psyttaleia," and Vidal-Naquet, "Tradition of the Athenian Hoplite," 90–91, and "Enigma at Delphi," 310–14.

Athens after the fall of tyranny—a comment that clearly seems informed by thoughts of the author's own time:

> Thus did the Athenians increase in strength. And it is plain enough
> . . . that "democracy" [*isēgorie:* equality of speech] is an excellent
> thing; since even the Athenians, who, while they continued under
> the rule of tyrants, were not a whit more valiant than any of their
> neighbours, no sooner shook off the yoke than they became de-
> cidedly the first of all. These things show that, while undergoing
> oppression, they let themselves be beaten, since then they worked
> for a master; but so soon as they got their freedom, each man was
> eager to do the best he could for himself. (5.78, trans. Rawlinson,
> modified)

Thus success provided democracy with legitimacy and was crucial to
both justifying the political equality and supporting the political identity of the lower-class citizens. Such success could only be achieved
through war and ongoing expansion. Imperialism in its relentlessly
activist form typical of Athens, therefore, provided the citizens with
the opportunities they needed to prove themselves, to renew their
legitimation, and to keep it alive through continuing success.[106]

Whether or not the Athenians themselves were fully aware of this
factor, it played, I suggest, an important role in their motivation. It
helps to explain their willingness to accept the ideology of power and
glory presented to them by their leaders, to identify with the policies
that seemed necessary to support this ideology, and to become toiling
and self-sacrificing enthusiasts of their city's imperial greatness. It
helps us understand their readiness continually to be active and involved both politically and militarily, in remarkable intensity and con-

---

106. This conclusion, which substantiates earlier suggestions (see Kurt A. Raaflaub, "City-
State, Territory and Empire in Classical Antiquity," in Molho, Raaflaub, and Emlen, *Athens
and Rome, Florence and Venice*, 581–82), converges with that of Meier, "Rolle des Krieges," esp.
586–605. For another aspect of this need to prove oneself, see ibid., 593–94. The factor of
social and political psychology is emphasized ibid., 594–600. Welwei, *Die griechische Polis*, 219–
32, treats the same problem ("Demokratie und Machtpolitik") from a different perspective
and reaches different conclusions; Martin, "Von Kleisthenes zu Ephialtes," 38–39, emphasizes the continuing influence of archaic aristocratic ethics on democratic attitudes and policies; Galpin, "Democratic Roots," 100–109, examines, rather superficially, the question of
compatibility between imperialism and democratic values. Finally, as Detlev Lotze, "Ent-
wicklungslinien der Athenischen Demokratie im 5. Jh. v. Chr.," *Oikumene* 4 (1983): 23–24,
and many others (see the discussion in Meiggs, *Athenian Empire*, chap. 21) have pointed out,
the empire and, to some extent, imperialism basically were supported by all classes of Athenians; thus elite criticism of the political role of the lower classes did not necessarily imply
opposition to imperialism. I agree but think that the issue needs more differentiated analysis;
my purpose here is to explain why, in the fully developed democracy of the fifth century, for
both the leaders and the lower-class citizens, imperialism was almost indispensable.

stancy, without slackening, over an extraordinary period of time. All this is quite astounding—unique in world history. It made power a crucial element in democratic politics, and activism for power a central component in the democratic citizens' "collective character"; it turned the Athenian citizens not only into true "political beings" but also into true "lovers of their city."[107]

107. Addenda: in n. 43: Ian Worthington, ed., *Persuasion: Rhetoric in Action* (London: Routledge, 1994); in n. 62: see also Aeschylus *Eumenides* 851–52, and David Konstan, *Friendship in the Classical World* (forthcoming); in n. 66: Paul Millett, "Warfare, Economy, and Democracy in Classical Athens," in *War and Society in the Greek World*, ed. John Rich and Graham Shipley (London: Routledge, 1993) 177–96; in n. 89: Vincent Gabrielsen, *Financing the Athenian Fleet: Public Taxation and Social Relations* (Baltimore: Johns Hopkins University Press, 1994), 105–10.

II

CRITICAL
DISCOURSE
IN ATHENIAN
DEMOCRACY

JOSIAH OBER

5   How to Criticize Democracy in Late Fifth- and Fourth-Century Athens

Some twenty-five hundred years after the revolution that made it possible, democracy is widely regarded as the most attractive form of practical (as opposed to utopian) political organization yet devised. Among democracy's virtues is revisability—the potential of the political regime to rethink and to reform itself while remaining committed to its core values of justice, equality, dignity, and freedom. How is this highly desirable flexibility achieved in practice? The *willingness* to contemplate change may be regarded as an innate characteristic of democratic political culture, and the *capacity* for nondestructive political change can be institutionalized in a democratic constitution. But I maintain that actual revisions generally require interventions from critics, and major revisions require critics who stand, in some sense, outside the dominant political culture. Because actualizing a democratic regime's latent capacity for major revision is predicated on the identification of structural problems by cultural critics, the regime that is to maintain its flexibility must allow social space exterior to itself: if a political system could ever encompass the whole of society and the whole field of discourse, it would lose its capacity for internally generated change; no one would be able to point out that "the

This essay is a preliminary introduction to a book in progress tentatively entitled "Athenian Critics of Popular Rule." Fellowships at the Center for Hellenic Studies (Washington D.C.) and the University of New England (Armidale, Australia) provided time for research and writing. The essay was presented in a somewhat different form at a May 1992 Cambridge University colloquium, The Greek Revolution. I am indebted for constructive criticism to many scholars, notably John Dunne (my Cambridge respondent), Quentin Skinner, Paul Cartledge, Peter Euben, John Wallach, and Adrienne Mayor.

Emperor is naked" or that "2 plus 2 does *not* equal 5." While this degree of encompassing may be impossible except in the realm of dystopian fiction, the claim that revisibility is among democracy's attractions and strengths suggests that it is actually in the self-interest of a democracy (unlike brittle, nonrevisable authoritarian regimes) to defend and even to seek to enlarge space for criticism. Moreover, a democratic regime must allow the cultural critic to maintain his or her distance, to remain a partial outsider, if it is to remain truly democratic and avoid the totalizing tendencies inherent in every value-based system of social organization. In a direct democracy on the Athenian model, therefore, not only is freedom of speech a good idea but the power of the people exists in a symbiotic relationship with resistance to that selfsame power.[1]

If, in late fifth- and fourth-century Athens, *dēmokratia* meant "the political power of the ordinary people" and if power includes control over the development and deployment of systems of meaning (including popular ideology and the rhetoric of public communication), then, for Athenians, criticism of the language of democratic government and of the assumptions of popular ideology could be a means of resisting political power.[2] It seems probable that critics of the status quo existed at every level of Athenian society; it is not hard to imagine that in each village and neighborhood of the polis there were men and women who could be counted on to interrogate, humorously or angrily, various aspects of the current order of things. The voices of these "local critics" are now lost, and we cannot say to what extent they were able to (or desired to) get outside that order. But a number of Athenian intellectuals committed pungent and profoundly critical opinions to writing, and in the process they contributed to the construction of what we might well call an "outside." Studying classical Athenian literature critical of the democratic regime thus offers access to one very important fragment of what was probably much more diverse and widespread resistance to political power. We may regret

1. On the impossibility of complete suppression of resistance, see David Large, ed., *Contending with Hitler: Varieties of German Resistance in the Third Reich* (Cambridge: Cambridge University Press, 1992). On the need for an "outside," see Andrei Codrescu, *The Disappearance of the Outside: A Manifesto for Escape* (Reading, Mass.: Addison Wesley, 1990). On revisability and cultural criticism, see Cornel West, *The American Evasion of Philosophy: A Genealogy of Pragmatism* (Madison: University of Wisconsin Press, 1989).

2. I emphasize that the texts I address here (with the exception of Pseudo-Xenophon, sometimes dated as early as ca. 440 B.C.) were completed after the end of the Peloponnesian War (431–404 B.C.)—that acid test of democratic practice. This is a deliberate choice, made because my approach to criticism of democracy requires the prior establishment of the ideological context through analysis of public speech, and the surviving corpus of Attic oratory is overwhelmingly postwar. The relationship between democracy and "political" texts may have been rather different during the floruit of Attic tragedy in the fifth century; see, e.g., J. Peter Euben, *The Tragedy of Political Theory: The Road Not Taken* (Princeton: Princeton University Press, 1990).

the loss of nonliterary forms of criticism. But if we hope to gain even a partial understanding of the link between Athenian democratic politics and unease with how the people's political power was manifested and deployed, we must come to grips with the texts we have.

Exploring the symbiosis of democracy and criticism should be significant for intellectual historians and political theorists alike. For historians, it promises to furnish part of the deep context for some of the works of Pseudo-Xenophon, Thucydides, Aristophanes, Plato, Isocrates, and Aristotle, among others. For the political theorist, looking at how classical democracy was criticized offers an alternative to the long-dominant but increasingly problematic paradigms of state socialism and individual rights/civil society—oriented liberalism. The history of political criticism in late fifth- and fourth-century B.C. Athens helps to explain how an attractive (in at least certain respects), revisable system of popular authority that was neither truly liberal nor truly socialistic could be sustained, and how such a system might be resisted. Given the differences between ancient and modern styles of politics, studying Athenian democracy and its critics certainly will not offer the late twentieth century an off-the-shelf technique for reconstructing a theory of politics. But if the complex relationship among justice, political power, and resistance to power no longer seems adequately explained by paradigms of liberalism and socialism (either alone or in combination), then trying to understand politics in classical Athens may be worth our while.

There is, of course, nothing particularly original in studying "the critics of Athenian democracy," and the ancient texts that lend themselves to such a study are well known. Some forty years ago, A. H. M. Jones pointed out the two key issues:[3] First, although we have a good many classical texts in various genres that are critical of democracy, we have no surviving texts written with the explicit intention of explaining the principles on which Athenian democracy was predicated. Second, in the absence of theoretical defenses of democracy, understanding the "positive" argument an Athenian would make for democracy depends on a close reading of Athenian public rhetoric. While deeply impressed by Jones' fundamental insights, I find his approach to "criticizing democracy" problematic. Jones argued that Athenian democracy was stable because it was dominated by "bourgeois" or "middle-class" citizens.[4] I view *dēmokratia* rather as a dynamic

---

3. A. H. M. Jones, *Athenian Democracy* (Oxford: Blackwell and Mott, 1957), 41–72, originally pub. in *Cambridge Historical Journal* 11 (1953): 1–26.

4. See Minor M. Markle, "Jury Pay and Assembly Pay at Athens," in *Crux: Essays in Greek History Presented to Geoffrey E. M. de Ste. Croix*, ed. Paul A. Cartledge and F. David Harvey (London: Imprint Editions, Imprint Academic, 1985), 265–297, for a detailed criticism.

system through which the mass of ordinary citizens (*hoi polloi, to plēthos, hoi penētes*) (a) maintained personal dignity and political equality; (b) restrained the privileges and power of elites (*hoi oligoi, hoi chrēstoi, hoi plousioi*); and (c) thereby protected themselves from certain forms of socioeconomic exploitation and political dependency.

Furthermore, Jones saw the debate over ancient democracy primarily in instrumental terms. For him, democracy was criticized and should be defended on the grounds of whether it allowed for rational decision making about issues of state policy and whether it provided a secure environment in which civil society could flourish and in which private goods (especially material prosperity) could be enjoyed by individuals. Jones argued persuasively that democratic equality and freedom neither led necessarily to poor policy nor threatened civil society and, thus, that the ancient critics were wrong to cast aspersions on the democratic government. But classical Athenian political life cannot be explained by a model of political behavior that assumes either a neat subdivision of the political realm into discrete categories of state, citizenry, and government, or a hierarchical differentiation between the (primary) private and (secondary) public spheres.[5] The Athenian did not engage in political activity solely as a functional means to gain the end of guarding against threats to his property or to his private pursuit of happiness. Rather, the values of equality and freedom that he gained by the possession and exercise of citizenship were substantive, central to his identity, and provided a measure of meaning to his life.[6]

It was this noninstrumental aspect of Greek political life that attracted the attention of Hannah Arendt, who provides a noteworthy example of a modern theorist looking to classical Greece to construct a political theory that was neither traditionally liberal nor socialist. For Arendt, the polis provided an ideal and explicitly public/political sphere for free human action and speech, for the "appearance" of human individuality through extraordinary deeds, and for the creation and collective maintenance of historical memory.[7] To focus on

5. I have explored this issue in more detail in "The *Polis* as a Society: Aristotle, John Rawls, and the Athenian Social Contract," in *The Ancient Greek City-State*, ed. Mogens H. Hansen (Copenhagen: Royal Danish Academy, 1993), 129–60.

6. On identity, see, e.g., Charles Taylor, *Sources of the Self: The Making of the Modern Identity* (Cambridge: Harvard University Press, 1989); Euben, *Tragedy of Political Theory*; and Philip Brook Manville, *The Origins of Citizenship in Ancient Athens* (Princeton: Princeton University Press, 1990).

7. See Hannah Arendt, *The Human Condition* (Garden City N.Y.: Doubleday, Anchor, 1959), *On Revolution* (New York: Viking, 1963), and *Between Past and Future*, enlarged ed. (Baltimore: Penguin, 1968). See George Kateb, *Hannah Arendt: Politics, Conscience, Evil*

the role of public action in creating the identity of the free and equal
citizen, and on public speech as a form of political action, is both historically defensible and theoretically useful.[8] But Arendt's Greek
model cannot be adopted wholesale by the intellectual historian or by
the political theorist interested in an empirical test of alternative
models of politics. Arendt's polis, strictly divided between the private
realm of necessity and economics and the public realm of freedom,
action, and politics, had no place for social interaction that blurred
the distinction between the citizen-warrior and the laborer-house-
holder. Arendt's polis was an ahistorical ideal, based in large part on
her own reading of Aristotle's *Politics*. Arendt's access to the polis was
through ancient texts both critical of democracy and written in the
context of the democratic regime. But, in common with many other
readers before and since, Arendt largely ignored the context and accepted the criticism as a description of reality.[9]

If there is anything new in my approach to Athenian criticism of
democracy, it is a concentration on the context in which critical texts
were produced: Athens' dominant political ideology and sociopolitical
practices. I attempted to delineate that ideology and those practices in
Mass and Elite in Democratic Athens (1989). There I was concerned with
how the ordinary citizens of Athens gained and held power through a
form of ideological hegemony that constrained the public and private
behavior of the elite (the wealthy, highly educated, and well born).
Here I am concerned with how a few elite Athenians opposed democratic ideology through critical discourse. I hope that this meditation
on the problem of "how to criticize," which is intended to prepare the
way for a much more detailed assessment of the substance of individual ancient works of criticism, will hold some interest both for intellectual historians and for political theorists concerned with the "founding generations" of the western political tradition. To focus on the
critical force of works by Thucydides, Plato, and others as resistance
to a socially constructed regime of power and discourse—rather than
as instrumental critiques of how and why democratic governmental

---

(Totowa, N.J.: Rowman and Allanheld, 1983), esp. 1–51, for discussion of Arendt's view of
Greece and why it is disquieting and even threatening from the liberal point of view. See also
Gabriel Masooane Tlaba, *Politics and Freedom: Human Will and Action in the Thought of Hannah
Arendt* (Lanham, Md.: University Press of America, 1987), ix–x, 1–35, 38–42, and Stephen T.
Holmes, "Aristippus in and out of Athens," *American Political Science Review* 73 (1979): 113–
28.

8. Cf., from their different perspectives, Jean-Pierre Vernant, *The Origins of Greek Thought*
(Ithaca: Cornell University Press, 1982), and Christian Meier, *The Greek Discovery of Politics*,
trans. David McLintock (Cambridge: Harvard University Press, 1990).

9. There is some question whether Arendt actually believed in the polis she presents; see
Tlaba, *Politics and Freedom*, 41–42.

institutions malfunctioned—is to suggest that western political theory
first emerged in the context of a fruitful and relatively nonviolent
struggle over the means of the production of political knowledge.

CONTEXT

Athenian political texts (e.g., Thucydides, Plato's *Republic*, Aristotle's *Politics*) provided foundations for what was to become the dominant western tradition of political philosophy. Origins are necessarily
discovered (or invented) only in retrospect.[10] Yet as a result of their
retroactive designation as foundational, Athenian political texts are
typically read backwards: from the perspective of the philosophical
tradition that eventually grew up from and around them, rather than
against the political context in which they were written. Teleology is
fatal to the enterprise of the intellectual historian, but the study of
Athenian political texts (at least qua political texts) has long been the
preserve of theorists and philosophers with a disciplinary tendency to
be disinterested in original context. When it is noticed, the historical
context for Athenian political writers is extrapolated from these selfsame authors. Thus the cockeyed picture that Thucydides, Plato, and
Aristotle offer of Athenian democracy as an inherently foolish system
gone wrong is sometimes taken at face value and read as an "objective" description of Athenian practice.

While "historicist" readings are often frowned on in literary and
theoretical circles, the primacy of context is a point of convergence
for several analytic traditions. The so-called Cambridge school of intellectual history focuses on how political terminology is used and revised by writers in arguments with their literary predecessors and contemporaries. Even the most innovative writers appropriate preexisting
vocabulary for discussing problems, but they often deploy that vocabulary in self-consciously innovative ways. In some periods (e.g., the
eighteenth century A.D. and the fifth century B.C.), the ways in which
terms are used in arguments change very rapidly. But even a text
produced during a revolution can and should be situated in its own
proximate context. Political writing thus becomes historically mean-

10. By "Athenian political text" I mean a text that was written by an author who spent
formative years in Athens and so wrote within a context defined in part by Athenian political
discourse. Thus Aristotle (though not an Athenian) and Thucydides (though he did not necessarily write his history in Athens) both qualify as authors of Athenian political texts. For a
critical assessment of the concept of foundations, see Benjamin Barber, *The Conquest of Politics*
(Princeton: Princeton University Press, 1988). For origins as retroactively constructed, see
Edward W. Said, *Beginnings: Intention and Method* (New York: Basic Books, 1975).

ingful when read against the backdrop of terms, assumptions, and ideas hammered out in earlier and contemporary discussions. That backdrop is typically best illuminated by the writings of lesser (because less innovative and original) intellectual lights.[11] A "Cambridge school" reading of Athenian political texts would require a reconstruction of the fifth- and fourth-century intellectual context: the conceptual apparatus available for modification by the authors of our surviving texts. This sort of contextualist approach to political thought is not entirely foreign to classical scholarship; something like it is, for example, employed by the "Begriffsgeschichte" school of Christian Meier.[12] But an approach that presupposes that the context for surviving texts was defined primarily by *literary* discourse cannot fully explain Athenian political texts if it ignores the role played by the Athenian dēmos.

An exclusive emphasis on the elite literary context (or, alternatively, on "intertextuality") will make it difficult for historians to link ideas with practices and events. It may lead them to fall into the habit of supposing that more or less fully worked out political theories must precede political practices. In the Athenian case, democratic practices were established well before any (surviving) text discussed democracy in abstract terms. A second consequence is that historical crises may come to be defined by elite perception: when the historian can show that contemporary intellectuals agreed that a crisis was occurring, are we then to assume that a real and general crisis pertained? Fourth-century B.C. Athens was long seen as beset by decline and disorder at least in part because writers such as Plato and Isocrates described it that way. The hypothesis that fourth-century Athens was characterized by a pervasive malaise is much harder to sustain if we look beyond the opinions of the literary elite to the social and political conditions of Athenian citizen society as a whole.[13]

The "climate of intellectual opinion" approach is doubly problematic in the Athenian case. First, we possess few "lesser light" texts of

11. See Quentin Skinner et al., *Meaning and Context: Quentin Skinner and His Critics*, ed. James Tully (Princeton: Princeton University Press, 1988).

12. Cf. Christian Meier, *Introduction à l'anthropologie politique de l'antiquité classique*, trans., from the German, P. Blanchaud (Paris: Presses Universitaires de France, 1984), focusing on the revolution of the conceptual universe in the fifth century and the comparison with the eighteenth century. Christian Meier, *Entstehung des Begriffs 'Demokratie'* (Frankfort on Main: Suhrkamp, 1970), and Kurt A. Raaflaub, *Die Entdeckung der Freiheit: Zur historischen Semantik und Gesellschaftsgeschichte eines politischen Grundbegriffes der Griechen*, Vestigia 37 (Munich: C. H. Beck, 1985), are good examples of the genre.

13. C. Mossé, *La fin de la démocratie athénienne: Aspects sociaux et politiques du déclin de la cité grecque au IVe siècle avant* J.C. (Paris: Presses Universitaires de France, 1962), a book that remains fundamentally important, nonetheless tends to focus on decline and fall. The issue of Athens' "decline" is not, one might point out, identical to that of the "crisis of the polis."

the sort that have allowed students of early modern political thought
to define in detail the context of the major luminaries of the Renaissance. Moreover, as Jones pointed out, we have several important
classical texts critical of democracy but no surviving texts that sympa-
thetically enunciate the theory on which Athenian democracy was
predicated. If we accept that in order to comprehend how political
vocabulary was employed in classical Athens, we must read our surviving political texts contextually, as interventions in an ongoing debate
about politics, the question necessarily arises: Who defined the other
side of the dialogue? If Thucydides, Plato, and Aristotle can be characterized as critics of democracy, with whom were they arguing? The
absence of formal democratic theory in the text record has long both-
ered classical historians of ideas and has led to inventive efforts (e.g.,
by Eric A. Havelock and Cynthia Farrar) to find expressions of democratic theory lurking in extant elite texts. Though interesting as theoretical exercises, these efforts are unsatisfactory as intellectual history.[14] The simplest hypothesis is that there are no surviving texts to
explain democratic theory because few such texts ever existed. And
the reason for this lacuna is not far to seek: in Athens, democratic
ideology so dominated the political landscape that formal democratic
theory was otiose.[15] The climate of opinion to which the authors of
critical political texts were responding was defined less by the reasoned positions of prodemocracy elite intellectuals than by democratic
popular ideology and public rhetoric.

   To understand Athenian political literature we must extend our
contextual scope beyond the circle of Athens' intellectual elite to explore the linkages between public discourse, knowledge, and power.
The idea that texts can fruitfully be read as products of complex ma-
trices of social relations which are in turn formed through the play of
power[16] helps to define the relationship between Athenian political

14. Eric A. Havelock, *The Liberal Temper in Greek Politics* (New Haven: Yale University
Press, 1957); Cynthia Farrar, *The Origins of Democratic Thinking: The Invention of Politics in
Classical Athens* (Cambridge: Cambridge University Press, 1988). See my comments in "The
Athenians and Their Democracy," *Echos du monde classique/Classical Views*, n.s. 10 (1991): 81–
96.

15. Although it *is* worth noting that Athenian dicanic (courtroom) rhetoric may actually be
more "theoretical" than often realized and may have functioned as a way of discussing democratic values in abstract as well as pragmatic terms. I hope to pursue this notion in future
studies.

16. This approach to power is particularly associated with Michel Foucault; see his *Disci-
pline and Punish: The Birth of the Prison*, trans. Alan Sheridan (New York: Random House,
Vintage, 1979), *The History of Sexuality*, trans. Robert Hurley, vol. 1, *An Introduction* (New
York: Random House, Vintage, 1980), and the essays collected in *Power/Knowledge: Selected
Interviews and Other Writings, 1972–1977*, ed. Colin Gordon, trans. Colin Gordon et al. (New

texts on the one hand and, on the other, the modes of discourse and the social practices typical of Athenian political society. In short, the historian cannot hope to understand Athenian political texts outside the context of their production, nor can he or she grasp the context without a prior analysis of late fifth- through late fourth-century Athenian social practices, political ideology, and public speech.

IDEOLOGY, POLITICAL KNOWLEDGE, SPEECH ACTS

In *Mass and Elite*, I argued that Athenian political ideology and significant aspects of Athenian social practice were formulated through, maintained by, and revealed in the processes of public speech. Because Assembly and lawcourt debates were particularly important forums, a careful reading of Athenian symbouleutic (Assembly) and dicanic (court room) rhetoric allows us to reconstitute in some detail the tenets of the popular political ideology of the very late fifth and fourth centuries B.C. In brief summary, among the central holdings of that ideology were:

1. A belief in the autochthonous nature of the Athenians, their innate intellectual superiority compared with all other peoples, and the necessity of maintaining the exclusivity of the citizenry
2. An assumption that the ideal of political equality could be achieved and maintained in the face of existing and legitimate social inequality
3. A conviction that both consensus and freedom of public speech were desirable
4. A belief in the superior wisdom of decisions made collectively by large bodies of citizens
5. A presumption that elites were simultaneously a danger to democracy and indispensable to the political decision-making process.

The general acceptance by most Athenians of these ideological premises allowed democratic Athens to work in practice, as a society and as a state. Ideology mediated between the reality of social inequality and

York: Pantheon, 1980). It is worth noting, however, that in his own late work on Greek society, *The History of Sexuality*, trans. Robert Hurley, vol. 2, *The Use of Pleasure* (New York: Random House, Vintage, 1986), which focuses on how prescriptive philosophical and medical texts "problematized" sexuality, Foucault made what Edward W. Said, "Michel Foucault, 1926–1984," in *After Foucault: Humanistic Knowledges and Postmodern Challenges*, ed. Jean Arac (New Brunswick: Rutgers University Press, 1988), 1–11, has called a "particular and over-determined shift from the political to the personal" (8).

the goal of political equality and thereby arbitrated class tensions that elsewhere in Greece led to protracted and destructive civil wars. It provided a role for elite leadership within a political system that was based on frequent, public expressions of the collective will. But it also required elite leaders to remain closely attuned to popular concerns and prevented the formation of a cohesive ruling elite within the citizen body.

In democratic Athens there was no very meaningful separation between the realms of politics, political society (citizenry), and government. In the Athenian democracy, major government decision making (by Boule, Assembly, lawcourts, and boards of *nomothetai* ["lawmakers"]) was legitimate specifically because it *was* political. And thus there was no meaningful separation between supposedly objective and scientific truths of the sort used (so we are told) by modern political rulers when making "serious" decisions, and the subjective political truths of the sort modern politicians find it expedient to present to the citizenry during elections and occasional plebiscites. In Athens, the general understanding held by the citizenry regarding the nature of society was the same understanding employed by decision-making bodies in formulating government policy for deployment in the real world. For most Athenians, the shocking "postmodern" conclusion that all knowledge is political (i.e., implicated in relations of power) was simply a truism; neither the possibility nor the normative desirability of apolitical forms of knowledge about society or its members ever entered the ordinary Athenian's head.[17]

In the decades after the Peloponnesian War, this relationship between ideology and political power provided the grounds for a remarkably stable sociopolitical order. Athenian democracy was not founded on a formal constitution or on a set of metaphysical/ontological/epistemological certainties but rather was undergirded by a socially and politically constructed "regime of truth" (i.e., an integrated set of assumptions about what is right, proper, and true).[18] I propose calling that regime "democratic knowledge." The existence and practical

17. For the definition of *postmodern*, see David Couzens Hoy, "Foucault: Modern or Postmodern," in Arac, *After Foucault*, 12–41. The modern horror at the politicization of knowledge is perhaps still best summed up in George Orwell, *Nineteen Eighty-Four* (New York: Harcourt, Brace, 1949); note that in Orwell's dystopia there remains a distinction between ideology (2 + 2 = 5) and brute reality (2 + 2 = 4), a distinction that is recognized by the rulers of society.

18. See Foucault, *Power/Knowledge*, 131: "Each society has its régime of truth, its 'general politics' of truth: that is, the types of discourse which it accepts and makes function as true; the mechanisms and instances which enable one to distinguish true and false statements, the means by which each is sanctioned; the techniques and procedures accorded value in the acquisition of truth; the status of those who are charged with saying what counts as true."

functioning of democratic knowledge depended on the implicit willingness of most citizens to accept the political verities they lived by as
"constative" (by which I mean that political and social "truths" were
brought into being by felicitously performed speech acts) rather than
as absolutes denoted by a transcendent natural or divine order. The
authority of the demos was legitimated neither by "divine right" nor
by "natural right"—which distinguishes it from the dominant early-
modern and Enlightenment European explanations of sovereignty.

The Athenian political order was grounded in democratic knowledge. And democratic knowledge was predicated, in the language of
J. L. Austin's speech-act theory, on the "conventional effect of a conventional procedure" rather than on an objective, metaphysical, or
"natural" view of social reality; it was created and re-created through
collective practices of public communication, not given by an external
authority or discovered through intellectual effort. In the terminology
of semiotics, democratic knowledge did not need to suppose that signifiers attached directly, permanently, or naturally to referents, only
that signifiers pointed to commonly accepted codes and socially constituted meanings. This democratic and (in modern philosophical
terms) pragmatic position allowed the Athenians to avoid the epistemological traps (and the political ugliness they can entail) of value-
free relativism, on the one hand, and positivist absolutism on the
other.

Athenian political culture was specifically based on collective opinion, rather than on objectively verifiable, scientific truths. By this I do
not mean that the Athenians supposed that their collective opinion
could cause the sun to rise in the west or alter other "brute" physical
facts. But they regarded social facts as conventional and political, not
homologous to the brute facts of nature.[19] The expression *edoxe tōi
dēmōi*—"it appeared right to the Citizenry" that such and such should
be the case—defines the democratic approach to the relationship between social knowledge, decision, and action. A politics based on common opinion can be built from the bottom up and potentially allows
for the integration of "local knowledges" (e.g., the specific practices of
village, cult, or family life) into the broader community of the polity.
As a result of the complex structure of Athenian political institutions,
there was a constant give and take between center and periphery, between specific local understandings, local critics, and the generalized

19. On brute vs. social facts, see John R. Searle, *Speech Acts: An Essay in the Philosophy of
Language* (Cambridge: Cambridge University Press, 1969), 50–53, with the comments of
Sandy Petrey, *Speech Acts and Literary Theory* (New York: Routledge, Chapman and Hall,
1990), 59–69.

poliswide democratic ideology.[20] This "system" (keeping in mind that it was not designed by any single authority, nor entirely rational in its workings) integrated Athenian processes of discussion and decision into a public way of knowing about society that was simultaneously a way of being a citizen, doing politics, and making policy.

The Athenian sociopolitical order was relatively stable because of the integrative tendencies and relative conservatism of popular ideology. Ideological conservatism allowed the Athenians the luxury of a degree of epistemic continuity adequate to provide a basis for collective decision making—Assemblymen and jurors employed as the premises of their deliberations opinions that were generally accepted as valid by the citizenry as a whole. Yet, in practice, the democracy was flexible, dialectical, and revisable. The frequent meetings of Assembly and people's courts allowed (even required) contrasting, critical views to be aired publicly, and this process in turn periodically forced constative meanings (the assumptions used in decision making) to change in response to changing external circumstances. Thus democratic knowledge evolved over time (sometimes very rapidly) without precipitating a political revolution. Meanwhile, democratic ideology and institutional procedure allowed for practical decisiveness: reasonably intelligent, binding (although open to legal challenge at the initiative of any individual citizen) decisions on internal matters and foreign policy were made in the Assembly by the Athenian demos in the absence of ruling elites, genuine consensus, or complete and objectively verifiable scientific knowledge about details of political affairs.[21]

The complex relationships among democratic knowledge, social practice, and critical political writing are, I believe, clarified by Austinian speech-act theory. Austin argued that speech is not only descriptive but performative. To the linguistic categories of locution (speech itself) and perlocution (the effect of speech on an audience), Austin added "illocution"—the intended force of speech that enables speakers to do things in the world. Austin showed that in ordinary language, description and enactment are not easily separated. The constative role of speech (to state what is so) is in practice inseparable

20. On local knowledge (as a possible source of criticism and resistance), see Foucault, *Power/Knowledge*, 80–85. On the complexity of the "grammar" of Athenian institutions, see Mogens H. Hansen, "On the Importance of Institutions in an Analysis of Athenian Democracy," *Classica et Mediaevalia* 40 (1989): 108–13.

21. The sheer volume of political business done in this manner is staggering. Mogens H. Hansen, *The Athenian Democracy in the Age of Demosthenes: Structure, Principles, and Ideology* (Oxford: Blackwell, 1991), 156, suggests that some thirty thousand decrees of the Assembly were passed in the period 403 to 322.

from and a product of speech's illocutionary, performative function (to make something happen). If description is a subcategory of performance, then the production of meaning and "truth" is a social process, accomplished by "felicitous" speech performances that are necessarily carried out in the context of accepted social and linguistic conventions. Sandy Petrey, who applies Austinian theory to the study of literature, points out that these conventions are revisable: to the degree that they are politically determined, conventions can be contested, or even overthrown by revolutionary action. But once again, even in the midst of a revolution, people do communicate. For speech to act, for human communication to be possible, conventions of some sort must pertain.[22] Returning to Athens, we can now see how the citizens enacted social, legal, and political realities when they voted in the Assembly and lawcourts: that which *edoxe tōi dēmōi* was constituted as true, for all social and political intents and purposes, through felicitously performed acts of collective decision and proclamation. When the Assembly votes for war with Sparta, a state of war is caused to come into existence by the Assembly's proclamation; when the jury votes that Socrates is guilty, he is constituted a guilty man.

In speech-act theory, as in intellectual history, context takes center stage. The successful performance of a speech act depends on existing social, political, and linguistic protocols: a courting couple would not be made man and wife by a child's proclamation that they were so; a judge's statement does things that a child's does not do because it is performed in the context of a set of conventions that are accepted as valid by the participants.[23] The felicity of the speech act is proved by perlocutionary effects: the subsequent behavior of the relevant

22. J. L. Austin, *How to Do Things with Words*, ed. J. O. Urmson and Marina Sbisà, 2d ed. (Cambridge: Harvard University Press, 1975). Exactly how speech-act theory deals with reference has been the subject of an ongoing debate, notably between Jacques Derrida, *Limited Inc.*, ed. Gerald Graff and trans. Jeffrey Mehlmann and Samuel Weber (Evanston: Northwestern University Press, 1988), and John R. Searle, "Reiterating the Differences: A Reply to Derrida," *Glyph* 2 (1977): 198–208, both of whom owe much to Austin's work and criticize certain aspects of it. The interpretation of Austin that I advance here is very close to that enunciated by Sandy Petrey, *Realism and Revolution: Balzac, Stendahl, Zola, and the Performances of History* (Ithaca: Cornell University Press, 1988), and *Speech Acts and Literary Theory*. Petrey emphasizes the breakdown of the distinction between constative and performative but also points out that Austin tended to underestimate the role of politics in the construction of the conventions that permit speech acts to perform felicitously.

23. This is explained by Austin's Rules A.1 and A.2 (*How to Do Things*, 13–14, 26–35): A.1: [In order for a speech act to be felicitously performed], "there must exist an accepted conventional procedure having a certain conventional effect, the procedure to include the uttering of certain words by certain persons in certain circumstances." A.2: "The particular persons and circumstances in a given case must be appropriate for the invocation of the particular procedure invoked."

members of society. If, after the ceremony, our hypothetical couple acts like a married couple and is treated as a married couple by their society, we may say that the act of the judge who said "I pronounce you man and wife" was felicitous. And likewise in the case of a declaration of war by the Athenian Assembly or the conviction of Socrates. Thus the felicity of an illocutionary speech act is context dependent and sociopolitically determined.

But what of the situation in which a speech act is felicitous within a local subcommunity but infelicitous in the larger community (e.g., the case of a homosexual couple who enact a marriage ceremony)?[24] This potential conflict between "local" and "national" spheres was not discussed by Austin, but it is important for the historical analysis of critical discourse as resistance. The act of performing a speech act that the speaker knows will be infelicitous within the larger community can be read as an intentional act of resistance.[25] The act brings the conventions valid within the local community into overt conflict with the conventions of the larger society and thus exposes the partial and socially constructed nature of the broader context. This exposure is dangerous (and thus meaningful as an act of resistance) because it challenges the tendency of the larger society to equate convention with human nature (in Greek terms: *nomos* with *phusis*), to see social facts as brute facts. Likewise, the promulgation of a system of knowing about society that a thinker recognizes will not be accepted by most within his or her community can be read as resistance to the dominant system of power and knowledge.[26]

An "Austinian" analysis of politics may help us to understand why traditional Marxist theory, with its essentialist commitment to the basic reality of economic and historical "laws," has been unable to explain the continued viability of capitalist societies in the face of the "contradictions" implicit in capitalist production: contradictions and class interests must not only be "revealed"; they must be felicitously performed if they are to have perlocutionary effects. Applying Austin to politics leads to an emphasis on political power as control of the means of symbolic production. It points to rhetoric as a form of political action, and to criticism of discursive context as a central project of

24. I owe this hypothetical example to Charles Hedrick.

25. Note that felicity here is clearly separate from "sincerity" and "comprehensibility." The two gay persons were presumably sincere in their intention to be married. What they intended is more or less comprehensible to members of the wider community, but their act was nonetheless infelicitous in the context of the wider community, which does not acknowledge the validity of the status change asserted by the ceremony.

26. Cf. J. S. McClelland, *The Crowd and the Mob: From Plato to Canetti* (London: Unwin Hyman, 1989).

political theorizing: those in power seek to create and maintain a stable context in which rhetorical statements by appropriate speakers will act in predictable ways; theorizing this relationship points out the contingency of the context in question and thus the possibility for major revisions in what speech acts will be felicitous and who will be an appropriate speaker. If, in a democracy (unlike most other forms of government), political power (i.e., the control of the means of symbolic production) is at least *potentially* discontinuous with economic power (i.e., the control of the means of economic production), then the sort of approach I am advocating might be particularly well suited to the historical study of democracy and its critics.[27] In Athens, where the ordinary people held political power, members of the wealth elites could be genuine political critics.

In *Mass and Elite*, I attempted to define the conventions whereby the debates and proclamations performed in Assembly and courtroom could and did "do things" in Athenian society. In trying to understand the relationships of power between elites and masses of ordinary citizens, it is important to decide whether those conventions were the product of elite or demotic discourse. Was democratic knowledge simply a form of false consciousness or mystification that enabled an elite to control and exploit the lower classes of citizens?[28] I argue to the contrary, that the sociopolitical conventions dominant in late fifth- and fourth-century Athens were the product of a historical development whereby the citizen masses *defined themselves* as Demos and the Athenian political order as *dēmokratia*.[29] As a result of this process, the Demos gained control of the public language employed in classical Athenian political deliberations. Thus the primary context for felicitous speech performance in Athens was defined by popular, not elite, ideology. And hence democratic knowledge and demotic social conventions sought to extend a form of rhetorical and even epistemological hegemony over all members of Athenian citizen society, including the elites.

The hegemony of popular ideology and public discourse was the basis of Athens' political order. Athens was a democracy, not just be-

27. By "traditional Marxist theory," I mean studies that focus on economic production and de-emphasize the state and ideology, e.g., G. A. Cohen, *Karl Marx's Theory of History: A Defense* (Princeton: Princeton University Press, 1978). Other forms of Marxist analysis, e.g., that of Antonio Gramsci, Fredric Jameson, Terry Eagleton, and Louis Althusser do, of course, focus attention on politics and ideology.

28. See Terry Eagleton, *Ideology: An Introduction* (London: Verso, 1991), 29–30: ideology types four and five.

29. For "capital-D" Demos, as the whole of the "imagined" citizenry, see Josiah Ober, "The Nature of Athenian Democracy," *Classical Philology* 84 (1989): 322–34.

cause the ordinary citizen had a vote, but because he was a participant
in maintaining a political culture and a value system that constituted
him the political equal of his elite neighbor. Through publicly performed speech acts, democratic institutions were implicated in an ongoing process of defining and redefining the truths used in political
decision making and of assimilating local knowledges into an overarching democratic knowledge. It was that process and that overarching knowledge that elite Athenian critics sought to expose as problematic.

POWER AND RESISTANCE

Though my respect and admiration for certain aspects of the
Athenian political regime are by now clear, it is obviously essential to
avoid adulation. Accepting ideology (often defined as the ideas of the
dominant classes) as an important part of historical context, socialist
theorists since Antonio Gramsci have emphasized its hegemonic role
in obscuring "objective" material interests and in promoting stability
in repressive regimes, a stability that primarily benefits the ruling
class.[30] Whether or not we adopt Gramscian categories, it is clear that
the Athenian citizen did benefit materially from the democratic regime in ways denied to noncitizens.[31] Thus, even if she accepts that
demotic values operated to control the behavior of and to limit exploitation by elites *within* the society of the citizens, a modern critic might
well argue that Athenian society as a whole was elitist, unjust, and
unattractive, by defining what I have described as "democratic knowledge" as a hegemonic ideology that maintained the privileged position
of a minority population of native-born, adult males at the expense of
oppressed noncitizens.[32]

How would an Athenian critic have responded to this line of reasoning? Plato famously suggested (*Republic* 562b–563c) that the excessive liberating tendencies of democratic culture extended well beyond
the citizen body, to women, slaves, and even domesticated animals (cf.
Pseudo-Xenophon, *Athēnaiōn Politeia* [= *Constitution of the Athenians*]

30. Eagleton, *Ideology*, offers an overview; on cultural hegemony, see Joseph V. Femia,
Gramsci's Political Thought: Hegemony, Consciousness, and the Revolutionary Process (Oxford: Oxford University Press, 1981).

31. E.g., by his virtual monopoly on the right to own land (and thus to secure loans on
land) and to be paid for various forms of government service. The advantages of citizenship
were multiplied during the imperial era—see Moses I. Finley, *Democracy Ancient and Modern*,
2d ed. (New Brunswick: Rutgers University Press, 1985), 76–109—but were always considerable.

32. See Ober, "*Polis* as a Society," for further discussion of the issue of social justice.

1.10–12). And in the *Ecclesiazusae*, Aristophanes comically turned over control of the Athenian state to citizen-women. It must, however, be said that, on the whole, Athenian critics of democracy (at least those who wrote texts that survive) were only peripherally concerned with the oppression of noncitizens. Nonetheless, various Athenian critics of democracy *were* concerned with showing that democratic ideology was a sort of mystification that obscured truths about the world—truths that were historically objective (Thucydides), natural (Aristotle), or transcendental (Plato). The attempt to establish disjunctions between knowledges founded on these various forms of "real" truth and democratic knowledge, with its emphasis on socially constructed truth, played a key role in Athenian political criticism. Thus, although the Athenian critics were far from "politically correct" by any conceivable modern (or postmodern) standard, documenting and assessing the success of their diverse and sustained criticism of knowledge-as-power might contribute to current political debates by establishing that resistance to power need not be futile.[33] Athenian critical texts may therefore be extremely important subjects even for students of political history and theory who remain utterly unconvinced by the ideas developed in those texts.

If critical resistance was not ultimately futile, neither was it easy. For the prospective Athenian author of a text systematically critical of democratic culture (as opposed to the local critic of democratic practice), the issue was not how best to describe "what is functionally or instrumentally wrong with how this regime works." Rather, faced with the democratic tendency to monopolize the terminology of politics, he confronted the more basic problem of finding a vocabulary capable of being adapted to the expression of his criticism.[34] How to break free of the equation between democracy and legitimate political rule? How

33. For criticism of Foucault's lack of attention to resistance, see Charles Taylor, "Foucault on Freedom and Truth," in *Foucault: A Critical Reader*, ed. David Couzens Hoy (Oxford: Blackwell Publisher, Basil Blackwell, 1986), 69–102; Edward W. Said, "Foucault and the Imagination of Power," in ibid., 149–55; and Sheldon S. Wolin, "On the Theory and Practice of Power," in *After Foucault* 179–201. There is a growing concern among students of Foucault's work to point out that he did in fact account for resistance, especially in his later work; see, e.g., Colin Gordon, "Governmental Rationality: An Introduction," in *The Foucault Effect: Studies in Governmentality*, ed. Graham Burchell, Colin Gordon, and Peter Miller (Chicago: University of Chicago Press, 1991), 1–51. For Foucault himself on the problem of resistance, see "Is It Useless to Revolt?" (trans. James Bernauer) *Philosophy and Social Criticism* 8 (Spring 1981): 1–9, and "Questions of Method," in *Foucault Effect* 82–86.

34. It will be clear by now that I disagree with the theory, put forth by, e.g., Nicole Loraux, *The Invention of Athens: The Funeral Oration in the Classical City*, trans. Alan Sheridan (Cambridge: Harvard University Press, 1986), that Athenian democracy itself was subverted by the continued power of aristocratic discourse; see my *Mass and Elite in Democratic Athens: Rhetoric, Ideology, and the Power of the People* (Princeton: Princeton University Press, 1989), 289–92.

to explain why a rational reader should not find Athens' political system any more attractive than does the writer? How to articulate an alternative politics that the reader could be persuaded to prefer and (perhaps) actively to support?

Modern political theory might seem to suggest that the obvious starting point for the Athenian critic of democracy was the issue of sovereignty: Who actually rules and in whose interest? versus Who *should* rule and in whose interest? But the ugliness of the oligarchic governments of 411 and 404, regimes that in fact attempted to narrow the criteria for citizenship in Athens, may have tended to encourage late fifth- and early fourth-century critics to seek other lines of approach.[35] Although Aristotle was crucially involved with the question of who did and should constitute the political authority, Plato focused on the *source* of popular authority: democratic knowledge itself. He offered a fundamental challenge to democracy by bringing into question the basic assumptions on which democratic knowledge rested; he questioned the validity of mass wisdom as a basis for judgment, the efficacy of public rhetoric as a prelude to decision making, and the felicity of the speech acts performed by public bodies. A second line of approach, emphasized especially by Thucydides, was to query the nature and function of the demos's *kratos* (i.e., political power itself). Given the interrelationship of knowledge and power, these two approaches can be seen as closely related; an attack on democratic knowledge undermined the demos's *kratos*, and an attack on the nature or use of *kratos* by the demos might in turn destabilize democratic knowledge.

Before the Athenian critic of democracy could offer an alternative to democratic knowledge and practice, he had first to identify a *point d'appui* that would be recognized by his intended readers (probably elite, but not necessarily antidemocratic) as legitimate. The problem was most frequently addressed by attempting to exploit the audience's recognition of incongruities in the matrix of assumptions and values that constituted democratic knowledge (as in the Socratic elenchus) or of contradictions between democratic ideals and the outcome of democratically arrived-at decisions (e.g., Thucydides' account of the Mytilenian Debate). Closely related was the search for new genres in which criticism could adequately be expressed. Finding a gap, or a "lack of fit," in democratic knowledge, and developing (or adapting) a literary genre suitable to exploiting inconsistencies were difficult tasks

35. The centrality of the issue of sovereignty in modern theory is, in any event, an artifact of the political conditions of early modern Europe; see Ober, "Nature of Athenian Democracy."

in light of the democracy's hegemonic tendency to obscure contradictions and its close relationship to the existing genres of drama and public oratory.[36] Various solutions, only gestured at here, were devised by individual authors in the last decades of the fifth century and especially in the fourth.

In the *Constitution of the Athenians*, Pseudo-Xenophon took as his *point d'appui* the gap between the "real" interests of the elite and the interests protected by the democratic regime. Employing the trope of irony, he worked within (and perhaps originated) an editorial genre: a here-and-now discussion of actual political action and policy which freely employed the existing language of the democracy and which allowed the logic of the democracy to "speak for itself." In the hands of this author at least, editorial irony proved problematic. Pseudo-Xenophon's irony seems unable to stand up against the democratic discourse he introduces into his text. The reader comes to feel that the author has nothing better to offer than the system he claims he will not praise but evidently cannot help admiring. Not surprisingly (to those who take the power of ideology seriously) the tactic of allowing the vocabulary of democratic discourse and the assumptions of the dominant democratic ideology free rein in the text leads to a general collapse of the intended force of the author's criticism.

Thucydides took over from Herodotus the embryonic genre we call historiography and gave it a definitively political and critical stamp. By claiming to have reconstructed the "real" meaning and objective causes of the dramatic course of events that began in the mid-430s, Thucydides attempted to demonstrate the comparative ignorance and foolishness of the collectivities that made Athenian policy, as well as the incompetence of the democratic politicians who misled the masses and were misled by them in turns. Thucydides' political history sets up a contest between his austere, seemingly objectively based, historical way of knowing and emotion-laden, hopelessly contingent democratic knowledge; between his difficult, closely argued, written text and the easy-listening, illogical orations of Athenian politicians; between his readers, who were in the process of being educated in the complexity of political realia and Athenian Assemblymen, who thought only of power and their own pleasure. The narrative describes the horrors attendant on the confrontation between the great force (*dunamis*) generated and wielded by a *dēmokratia* and the stubborn, brute realities of a protracted war.

36. See J. Ober and Barry S. Strauss, "Drama, Political Rhetoric, and the Discourse of Athenian Democracy," in *Nothing to Do with Dionysos? Athenian Drama in Its Social Context*, ed. John J. Winkler and Froma I. Zeitlin (Princeton: Princeton University Press, 1990), 237–70.

For Aristophanes, genre was less of a problem; for the forms of comedy were well established. Moreover, the comic poet's audience expected him to criticize Athenian society. In *Ecclesiazusae* Aristophanes takes as his point of departure a comic "alternate Athens" and the incongruity between politically constituted identities and perceptible referents. He asks a funny question that has profound critical bite: Could Athenian women be constituted "males" if the Assembly enacted a decree that they, rather than biologic men, were to have the rights and responsibilities of citizenship? The play exposes the contradiction between Athenian belief in the power of the citizenry to constitute political realities by legal enactment, on the one hand, and in the naturalness of a world in which men alone were empowered political agents on the other.

Plato took the debate over politics to a more exalted plane. In the *Republic* he shifts from Socratic elenchus (in Book 1), a form of debate which assumes an interlocutor with real opinions (i.e., a connection to the ideological context) and which owed something to Athenian traditions of public debate, to a new generic variation of the dialogue form (in Books 2–10).[37] In the later books, Socrates expounds to students a metaphysical and ontological argument for a utopian, authoritarian political order ruled by a class of philosophers who had "left the Cave" and so had gained a rigorous and accurate knowledge of reality. This approach enables Plato to work out a positive political program based on a formal distinction between mere opinion (*doxa*) and actual knowledge (*epistēmē*). Viewed from the perspective of the *Republic*'s ontological epistemology, the problem was not merely that democratic knowledge failed to account for objective facts accessible to the careful observer (per Thucydides). Rather, the problem was that democracy's claims to be a legitimate way of knowing about society and a just system for making decisions were false because it had no way of testing appearances by reference to an external, metaphysical Truth (i.e., the Forms). A political regime based on mass opinion (the lowest sort of *doxa*) was thus not only likely to be sloppy in its judgments and capricious in its behavior; it was wrongly constructed by definition. The entire performative process of the speech act is ruled out of court and replaced by a reference-based morality. Justice becomes a fixed and absolute standard. Politics becomes a matter of foundation (an unrevisable although not indestructible order is built

37. I owe this insight into the distinction in literary forms to a paper by Mary Blundell, delivered at Princeton University in March 1992.

on the foundation of Truth), rather than a matter of practice (a revisable order exists in the action of felicitously doing).

Isocrates' *point d'appui* in the *Areopagiticus* is his fellow Athenians' nostalgia for the better conditions widely assumed to have pertained in the days of their ancestors. His approach is in some ways similar to that of Pseudo-Xenophon in that he adopts the overtly democratic genre of symbouleutic oratory and borrows political language from democratic ideology. But like Thucydides and other Athenians involved in the "ancestral constitution" (*patrios politeia*) debate, he employs a "historical" perspective. His ostensible goal is to recuperate Athens' pristine and ancient form of government and society—which turns out to be a highly hierarchical and paternalistic system that he specifically names *dēmokratia*. In appropriating genre, vocabulary, and name from the regime he intended to criticize, Isocrates demonstrates an audacious pride. He is confident that his rhetorical *technē* will allow him to transubstantiate democratic political slogans into an essentially aristocratic system of political values.

In terms of genre and critical stance (as in other ways), Aristotle's *Politics* is a work of synthesis. His point of departure is human nature. The final goal of the text (as we have it) is to derive the best possible regime from widely accepted postulates about human nature. While granting democracy a relatively high level of instrumental success in the regulation of class tension and recognizing the validity of mass wisdom in certain sorts of decision making, Aristotle's teleological naturalism allows him to conclude that workers simply cannot achieve true political *aretē*. The citizens of the best polis will thus naturally have to be an association of leisured aristocrats, thereby obviating the need to solve the intractable problem of proportionate equalities. The citizens' formal and normative education will ensure that decision making is based on formally rational "practical reasoning" (rather than democratic knowledge) and that their society, having achieved the telos toward which the polis was naturally tending, will not require revision.

Even after a much fuller exposition of the content of Athenian political criticisms than I have attempted here, we will be left with two supremely difficult questions: What were these texts *meant to do*: what was their intended effect on readers? And what *did they do*: what practical effect did they have on the form or content of Athenian democracy? The general term *critic* covers a broad range of intentions. Are we dealing with an irreconcilable enemy of the democratic order, or a democrat who believes that current practice is inconsistent with the highest democratic ideals? I would tend to push Pseudo-Xenophon and Plato in the direction of the first category, Aristophanes toward the second, and leave Thucydides, Isocrates, and Aristotle somewhere in between. But attempting to fix authors on a hypothetical political spectrum is hazardous: Athenian political texts are complex and multivocal. The illocutionary force of a critical text need not be limited to the hortatory, admonitory, subversive, or openly revolutionary; Aristophanes (for one) manages to fit all of these voices and more into the scope of a short play.

The lines of communication between elite critics and the demos, between those partially outside and those inside the democratic regime, remain obscure.[38] Yet our current inability to trace simple cause-effect relationships between text and political change does not (in and of itself) invalidate the proposition that criticism is a precondition to revision. It has often been pointed out that Plato's utopia in the *Republic* could never have been realized in the real world. But the "practical" workability of theoretical notions is beside the point. By describing a hypothetical counterregime or a counterknowledge, based on a set of countertruths, the critical theorist helped to establish and maintain a discursive space outside the dominant regime. The literary speech act performed felicitously within the society of elite intellectuals might or might not ultimately achieve felicity in the broader political society of Athens. The actual effect on democratic practice of a given author's criticism can seldom, if ever, be measured. But just as the Assembly brought a particular reality into being through the performative act of enunciating a *psēphisma*, so the critic expanded the ground in which resistance to ideology was possible and fundamental change conceivable. And thus (perhaps unwittingly) the critic helped to guarantee the potential revisability of the democratic regime through the performative act of constructing an alternative political paradigm. Once again, a comparison to Marxist theory may be instructive. Whether or not the theorist succeeds in changing society in accordance with her own ideals, she provides conceptual resources in the form of original and challenging uses of existing terminology. Those cultural resources may be found useful even by advocates of change who reject the substance of the theorist's argument in that they help to make (or keep) thinkable the possibility of a world profoundly different from the one we now inhabit.

Finally, what does the phenomenon of criticism of democracy in late fifth- and fourth-century Athens have to tell us about critics of

38. I hope to explore this issue in future work on the theoretical content of certain Athenian dicanic orations; see above, n. 15.

modern democracy? Does the history of Athens lead us to conclude that conservative complaints on the subjects of "democratic hegemony" and popular culture should be read as part of a grand tradition of resistance? Should the conservative critic of democracy therefore be regarded as a particularly admirable, even essential, feature of modern political life? This would be the case *only* if modern societies were democratic in an Athenian sense of the term, that is, if the mass of ordinary citizens maintained an active control over most aspects of ideology, public discourse, governmental institutions, and the political agenda. Given the sovereign authority of the modern state, the thinness of modern practices of citizenship, and the top-down structure of mass communications and media, the idea that the citizenry could exert any sort of hegemony in a modern liberal democracy seems, on the face of it, chimerical.

Yet the notion that "democracy" once *did* and still *should* mean "the power of the people" is remarkably stubborn. And that notion may provide exactly the point of departure needed by the truly essential critics of modern democracy: those who refuse to accept that everexpanding, hierarchical governmental and corporate power (and the knowledges they produce) are an inevitable and natural outgrowth of social complexity—or that they are desirable for a citizenry that hopes to live in a society characterized by justice, freedom, dignity, and equality. Given the residual revisability of democratic culture, it is perhaps not excessively utopian to hope that criticisms by educated elites of "democratic hegemony" might, some day in the future, once again be read as productive forms of resistance.

S. SARA MONOSON

6 Frank Speech, Democracy, and Philosophy: Plato's Debt to a Democratic Strategy of Civic Discourse

Why did the Athenians value frank speaking? What do Plato's texts have to say about this democractic practice? How might these questions color our reading of the discussions of democracy in Plato's texts? Certainly Plato's texts deliver fierce criticism of democratic politics, especially the functioning of institutions such as the courts, Assembly, and theater. But are Plato's dialogues unceasingly hostile to everything democracy represents and produces, as is usually thought?[1] Must we read them as an enemy attack on democracy? This essay pursues these questions at their point of intersection.

I propose that the pattern of Plato's texts' treatment of the Athenian democratic principle of frank speech—parrhesia—supports the view that these texts exhibit a complex engagement with practices that the Athenians themselves identified as constitutive of democracy. In particular, I show that Plato drew on this local democratic practice to develop his critical vision. I argue, in short, that Plato's texts defend the idea of parrhesia and appropriate this democratic strategy of civic discourse for philosophy. This essay thus provides important evidence for the accuracy of an unconventional interpretation of Plato's attitude toward democracy which is now emerging from scholarship. This work urges us to recognize that Plato's texts display profound interest in core democratic practices and to consider the significance

I thank W. R. Connor, George Kateb, Alan Ryan, J. Peter Euben, John Wallach, and Richard Dagger for their comments on an earlier draft of this essay.
1. See, e.g., the use of Plato in Robert Dahl, *Democracy and Its Critics* (New Haven: Yale University Press, 1989).

of this complexity in his political thought. In particular, it argues that the genre of writing Plato originates, the dialogic form, both is rooted in and departs from specifically Athenian norms and practices of political education and ethical teaching associated with the performance of tragedy.[2] This scholarship shows that clarifying the way in which the dialogic form of composition and the content of the texts are related to tragedy illuminates the connectedness of Plato's thought to the tradition he was criticizing: while the texts clearly urge the reader to adopt a highly skeptical attitude toward democracy, they also prompt the reader to worry that certain democratic practices actually inform and support that skepticism.

The stakes involved in characterizing the attitude of Plato's texts toward democratic practices as complex, engaged, and at times, ambivalent are political as well as intellectual. This new interpretation challenges the use to which the "authority" of Plato has been put by late twentieth-century conservative critics of democracy in the United States, especially the efforts of these critics to claim Plato as their own.[3] Moreover, recognizing this measure of complexity in Plato's thought raises the possibility that his texts may be of interest to democratic theorists for something other than a classic statement of opposition to democracy. In particular, it directs us to the fact that Plato's texts treat democracy not only as a set of deeply flawed institutions (a form of government) and as troubling patterns of social behavior (freedoms) but also as a cluster of cultural norms, practices, and ideals that are morally exciting for their ability to sustain serious, reflective, and critical investigations and conversations about how men and women should lead their lives individually and in concert with others as citizens. I am concerned here to retrieve an Athenian expression of this last, educative understanding of democratic practice as well and to retrieve Plato's engagement with it.

Before discussing Plato's texts, I present an account of the Athenian understanding of frank speech and its place in Athenian democratic ideology; I then move to set out the complexities of the treatment of parrhesia in Plato's texts. This presentation permits me to articulate fully the Athenian view of parrhesia and thus to situate Plato's texts adequately. Also, readers concerned with Athenian democratic ideol-

2. Martha Nussbaum, *The Fragility of Goodness: Luck and Ethics in Greek Tragedy and Philosophy* (New York: Cambridge University Press, 1986), 122–35, and J. Peter Euben, *The Tragedy of Political Theory: The Road Not Taken* (Princeton: Princeton University Press, 1990), 236.

3. E.g., Allan Bloom, *The Closing of the American Mind* (New York: Simon and Schuster, 1987).

ogy and practice, but not necessarily Plato's interaction with it, will find that material accessible in the first section.

Parrhesia in Athenian Democratic Ideology

It is clear from the literary evidence that the Athenians closely linked the practice of democracy with that of free speaking. But precisely what role did the Athenians believe free speech performs in democratic political processes? Precisely how did the Athenians understand the connection between free speech and democracy? I maintain that they viewed a pervasive cultural ethic specifically of frank speaking to be a necessary precondition for the flourishing of certain political institutions, in particular, the Assembly.

The Athenians celebrated free speech as a fundamental ideal of democratic politics. Evidence of their seriousness about free speech is, moreover, abundant in the literary record. Assembly meetings opened with the proclamation Who wishes to speak?—a ritual affirmation of the right of all male citizens to address the Assembly (as well as to attend and vote). In addition, although tragedy was performed for grand civic occasions, the content of the performances often subjected Athenian political life to rigorous scrutiny. Comedy not only displayed colorful (and off-color) language but developed biting political satire. Orators also did not shrink from delivering stinging criticisms of policies adopted by the demos and of the moral character of those on whom the demos relied for leadership. Philosophy too proffered harsh political criticism. Much has been written, moreover, about the formal scope (legal, moral, and artistic) of free speech at Athens as well as about the extent to which the democracy actually tolerated the speech it professed to value. The focus is often on the degree to which it is possible to maintain that, despite the absence of talk about rights in ancient Athens, the Athenians implicitly did recognize a personal right to free speech and understood the protection of such a right to be among the objectives of democracy. I focus on a different issue—how the Athenians represented to themselves the connection between free speech and democracy—which I approach by looking at the way parrhesia figures in the patriotic self-image of Athenian democracy.

Parrhesia is a complex idea with a long history in ancient Greek thought.[4] Speaking with parrhesia (*meta parrhēsias*) meant, broadly,

4. The evolution of the idea and practice of parrhesia in Greek philosophy was the subject of a remarkable series of lectures by Michel Foucault in 1983. He showed that parrhesia

"saying everything." More specifically, it meant speaking one's own mind, that is, frankly saying what one thinks, especially uttering a deserved reproach. The term *parrhēsia* could refer to speech in varous spheres of life—the theater, personal relations (most important, in friendship), and political deliberations. In the theater it pertained mostly to comedy, specifically, hurling insults at identifiable individuals and ridiculing Athens.[5] In personal relations it referred mostly to candid speech among friends and associates.[6] It could also be thought to characterize the openness and easiness of daily life. Demosthenes mentions that slaves at Athens enjoy more parrhesia than citizens of other poleis.[7] Parrhesia also appears in orators' descriptions of the kind of speech ideally expected of them in their role as advisors to the demos.

In each of these contexts, parrhesia is consistently and closely associated with two things: criticism and truth telling. To speak with parrhesia was to confront, oppose, or find fault with another person or with a popular view in a spirit of concern for illuminating what is right and best.[8] Parrhesia implied, therefore, a claim on the part of the speaker to be capable of assessing a situation and pronouncing judgment on it. This implication of intellectual autonomy was so much a part of its meaning, moreover, that we find it made quite explicit: speaking with parrhesia is equated with "telling the truth as one sees it." This truth claim did not, it needs to be stressed, entail any assertion of a view's alignment with an absolute, transcendent standard. Rather, it asserted a specific relation between the speaker and his view, that is, that the speaker sincerely and strongly holds his view to be right. The main work the truth claim did was to assert the honesty and personal integrity of the speaker and the apparently critical import of his logos—not the certain flawlessness of the logos itself.

That Athenians claimed the idea and practice of parrhesia to be an

---

was linked to truth telling and argued that tracing its changing meanings in Greek philosophy provides an account of a genealogy of the critical attitude in Western philosophy. "Discourse on Truth: A Study of Parrhesia" (Lectures delivered in English at the University of California at Berkeley, 1983, transcribed by Joseph Pearson, Department of Philosophy, Northwestern University).

5. On comedy, see Max Radin, "Freedom of Speech in Ancient Athens," *American Journal of Philology* 48 (1927): 215–30. See also Aristophanes *Acharnians* 500ff., where it is mentioned that Cleon accused Aristophanes of ridiculing Athens in front of foreigners. The term was also sometimes used in a pejorative sense to suggest abusive speech on the comic stage.

6. Isocrates uses it to describe a quality of friendship; see *To Demonicus* 34, *To Nicocles* 3, 28, and *To Antipater* 4–5. Aristotle also uses it to describe how one ought to behave with friends (*Nicomachean Ethics* 1165a29).

7. Demosthenes *Third Philippic* 3.

8. Demosthenes *Third Olynthiac* 32, *Fourth Philippic* 54, and *Against Aristocrates* 204; Isocr. *To Nic.* 3 and *Panathenaicus* 96; Euripides *Electra* 1055–60; Aristophanes *Thesmophoriazusae* 540–43.

essentially democratic ideal is very clear from several sources.[9] Why? What work did it do in the construction of a patriotic self-image of democracy? It worked at Athens to assert the excellence of democracy in two significant ways. First, it forcefully articulated some of the meaning of the Athenian conception of freedom (*eleutheria*). Second, it expressed an idealized version of Assembly debate. Frankness could be considered a virtue in many settings or political meetings. But parrhesia conjured up a particular set of associations that the Athenians sought to identify specifically with the conduct of Assembly debate. I go on to map the political concerns that help explain the importance of parrhesia in this context, but the net result was that the idea and practice of parrhesia was thought to be at the very heart of Athenian democracy's coherence as a politeia.[10]

The association of unrestrained speech, and specifically the term parrhesia, with freedom is very strong in Greek literature. Aeschylus's *Persians* names an unguarded tongue a sign of freedom (591–94). Euripides' *Hippolytus* closely links being free with the practice of parrhesia, and both with Athenian citizenship (421–23). A fragment of Democritus also confirms an intimate connection between freedom and parrhesia.[11] It might be tempting to think that the Athenians typically made this linkage largely because of the intellectual freedom that the practice of parrhesia presupposes. But once we recall that Anaxagoras, Protagoras, Diagoras, and perhaps Diogenes of Appolonia had to run for their lives and that Socrates did not flee and was killed, this account of the root attraction of parrhesia for the ordinary Athenian democrat becomes far less tempting.[12] I think it is more plausible to attribute the prominence of parrhesia in the popular Athenian understanding of freedom to its contribution to the representation of the sharp contrast between democratic citizenship and

9. Plato *Republic* 557b; Demosthenes *Funeral Speech* 25–26; Euripides *Ion* 671–75 and *Hippolytus* 420–23.
10. What follows is not a general discussion of free speech at Athens but of the concept of parrhesia in particular. For a broader discussion of the Athenian understanding and practice of free speech, see Robert J. Bonner, "Freedom of Speech," in *Aspects of Athenian Democracy* (New York: Russell and Russell, 1933), 67–85; Kenneth J. Dover, "The Freedom of the Intellectual in Greek Society," *Talanta* 7 (1976): 24–54; Arnaldo Momigliano, "Freedom of Speech in Antiquity," in *The Dictionary of the History of Ideas*, ed. Philip Wiener, vol. 2 (New York: Scribner's, 1973), 252–63; and Radin, "Freedom of Speech."
11. Democritus frag. 226 Diels-Kranz (*Die Fragmente der Vorsokratiker*, ed. Hermann Diels, rev. Walter Kranz, vol. 2 [Berlin: Weidmann, 1952]).
12. Momigliano, "Freedom of Speech in Antiquity," 258. See also John Stuart Mill's comments on the Athenians' suspiciousness of intellectual life in "Grote's Plato," in *Collected Works*, ed. J. M. Robson, vol. 11 (London: Routledge and Kegan Paul, 1963), 398–99; and Gregory Vlastos, "Why Was Socrates Condemned?" in *Socrates, Ironist and Moral Philosopher* (Ithaca: Cornell University Press, 1991), 293–97.

life under a tyranny. The Athenians expressed the excellence of democracy to a great extent through its contrast with the Athenian experience of tyranny (the Peisistradae) as well as their knowledge of Persian despotism. The practice of parrhesia in politics and personal life at Athens was treated as a sign, indeed as a proof, that the Athenians had defeated tyranny at home, fought off the threat from abroad, and were now in fact living as free citizens.

An intolerance of parrhesia marked tyranny of both the Hellenic and Persian varieties in the Athenian view. A tyrant's arbitrary, unaccountable, and absolute power virtually precluded assuming the risk of saying anything other than what the tyrant wished to hear. When a person dared to speak his own mind to the tyrant, moreover, it was considered surprising and strange. Aristotle, for example, names Peisistratus's willingness to listen to a common man's parrhesia as evidence of the mildness of his tyranny (*Athēnaiōn Politeia* 16.6).[13] Speaking freely among even one's neighbors was dangerous, as the possibility of betrayal to the tyrant was ever present. Silence was normally expected of the subjects of a tyranny. An intolerance of parrhesia was a symptom of the watched character of daily life. A citizen of a democracy, in contrast, was expected to have and to voice his own critical political opinions.[14] Being free meant being able to hold those who exercise power accountable, that is, at the very least, being able to expose lies, name abuses, and demand change. The principle of accountability was, moreover, absolutely central to the Athenian understanding of the distinction between the democratic and tyrannical exercise of power.[15] The connection between unrestrained speech and being free also celebrated the termination of guarded, suspicious relations among neighbors, which had been characteristic of life under tyranny. The coupling of freedom and parrhesia in the democratic self-image therefore functioned to assert two things: the critical attitude appropriate to a democratic citizen, and the open lifestyle promised by democracy.

It is important to recognize that the celebration of parrhesia in democratic politics did not carry any demand for a notion of "protected speech." Quite the contrary was the case. Speaking with parrhesia in the democratic political context retained a strong association with risk. The risks did not normally include execution, but they cer-

13. *Aristot. Ath. Pol.* [= *Constitution of Athens*]. See also Plato *Rep.* 567b–d and Euripides *Bacchae* 668–71 for the intolerance of parrhesia under tyranny.
14. Critical opinions in religious matters were not quite as welcome, we should remember; see Dover's discussion of impiety charges in "Freedom of the Intellectual."
15. See, e.g., Aeschylus *Persians* 210–20, and Aristotle *Politics* 1295a20.

tainly included humiliation and fines, for example. These risks were not thought to undermine or even conflict with the right of free speech; rather, they affirmed that the speaker could be held accountable for the advice ventured. The strong association of political parrhesia with danger can, moreover, illuminate what made it so valuable an idea for the democrats. The free democratic citizen presupposed by the ethic of parrhesia was daring and responsible, self-confident and eager to enter the fray, the very antithesis of the slavish subject of a tyranny.[16] The risks emphasized that participation in democratic politics, forming and expressing an interpretation of the public good, was a difficult endeavor. Success at it—as an individual leader or a collective body—was to be praised and admired. The coupling of freedom and parrhesia suggested the daring called for by democratic politics. It asserted the excellence of democracy, then, by naming a particular virtue it cultivates in citizens (critical intellectual autonomy in political matters) and suggesting the glorious possibilities for citizens of democratic polities.

Parrhesia also figures in the Athenian patriotic representation of good Assembly debate, which depended, first of all, on meeting certain formal conditions necessary for decisions to be democratically legitimate (e.g., equal access to the Assembly, the right to speak at the meeting, and majority rule). But the Athenians also worried about whether democratic debate could produce wise decisions, and it is in this connection that critical parrhesia is tremendously important. Demosthenes, in fact, claimed that a democracy is in grave danger when no one dares to speak out truthfully and critically in the Assembly.[17] Precisely what part the concept of parrhesia played in articulating the substantive conditions under which debate could be thought to generate wise decisions is a complicated story, however, requiring a digression on a related but distinct conception of free speech, namely, *isēgoria*.

Isegoria referred to the equal right of all citizens in good standing to address the assembly and was a central element in Athenian democratic thought. Herodotus used it as a synonym for democracy.[18] In it, the twin democratic ideals of freedom and equality merge; it ex-

16. See Euripides *Phoenician Women*, lines 386–94, where, in the middle of a discussion of the miseries of an exile's lot, the subject of parrhesia comes up. Polyneices states, "The worst is this: the right of free speech (parrhesia) does not exist," to which Iocasta responds, "That is the slave's lot—to be forbidden to speak one's mind" (*Euripides: Orestes and Other Plays*, trans. P. Vellacott [New York: Penguin, 1972]).

17. Demosthenes *On Organization* 15.

18. Herodotus *Histories* 5.78; see also Pseudo-Xenophon ["Old Oligarch"] *Athēnaiōn Politeia* [= *Constitution of the Athenians*] 1.2.

pressed the thought that each citizen has an equal right to conduct his life as a free being, that is, to engage in political activity, where "political activity" means to offer an interpretation of the public interest for consideration by the collectivity.[19] It is therefore a richer democratic principle than the more formal equal right to attend and vote in the Assembly; for, as Josiah Ober has suggested, it enabled citizens to be far more actively engaged in the deliberative process, in effect transforming the ordinary man's experience of political life.[20] Isegoria implied a participatory ethic.[21] Isegoria was, accordingly, especially important for democratic Athens's assertion of the legitimacy of Assembly decisions. The opportunity for active participation in debate was part of the formal apparatus (along with equal access to the Assembly and majority rule) the Athenians relied on to give credibility to the claim that individual citizens are meaningfully implicated in the decisions of the Assembly and therefore morally obligated to obey them. This claim was ritually affirmed at each Assembly meeting, as the proceedings began with the question Who wishes to speak?[22] The language announcing decisions also affirmed the claim: the announcement read not "The majority wants . . ." but, rather, "It seems best to the demos that . . . ,"[23] suggesting the entire citizen population is implicated in the decision.

The Athenians relied on a celebration of free speech generally to do more ideological work in the Assembly as well. The general, nontechnical notion of free speaking figures importantly in the Athenian view of how it is that democratic deliberations manage to produce *wise*, as well as legitimate, policy. Some words from Pericles' Funeral Oration assert this connection. In the Hobbes translation they read: "We Athenians weigh what we undertake and apprehend it perfectly in our minds, not accounting words for a hindrance of action but that it is rather a hindrance to action to come to it without instruction of words before" (2.40).[24] This passage suggests that the Athenians val-

19. See Euripides *Suppliants* 438–42, where the equal right to address the assembly is linked to the positive exercise of freedom.

20. Josiah Ober, *Mass and Elite in Democratic Athens: Rhetoric, Ideology, and the Power of the People* (Princeton: Princeton University Press, 1989), 79.

21. Note that Ps.-Xen. identifies the main reason democracy at Athens was in no real danger of attack: it had no significant population of the "disenfranchised" to rise up. He of course ignores the population of slaves, metics, and women; but his point that citizens are well-integrated and implicated in the life of the polis is significant (*Ath. Pol.* 3.12–13).

22. Aristophanes *Acharnians* 45.

23. See E. L. Hicks and G. F. Hill, *Greek Historical Inscriptions* (Oxford: Oxford University Press, Clarendon, 1901), nos. 73–75.

24. Thucydides *The Peloponnesian War: The Complete Hobbes Translation*, with notes and new intro. David Grene (Chicago: Chicago University Press, 1989).

ued the general practice of free speaking in the Assembly for its role
in the education of action, chiefly collective action. I move now to take
a closer look at precisely how the particular concepts of isegoria and
parrhesia figure in the representation of the work of educating action.

Isegoria was understood to do some of the work of educating action, that is, producing wise policy and public confidence. It affirmed,
for example, that ideas matter in Assembly debate, not necessarily the
status of the speaker or the artistry of his presentation. Consider the
following passage from Demosthenes' *First Olynthiac*:

> Oh Athenians, I believe that you would prefer it to great wealth if it
> could be made clear to you what would be the best policy in the
> matters now under discussion. This being the case, it is proper for
> you to listen intently to all those desirous of giving advice. For not
> only might someone come forward with a carefully thought out pro-
> posal, and you, having heard it, might decide to adopt it, but I con-
> sider it part of your good fortune that other speakers may be in-
> spired with suitable suggestions on the spur of the moment, so that
> from among many proposals it will be easy to choose the one most
> in your own interest. (1.1)[25]

Isegoria also implied the airing of various and conflicting proposals
and therefore the expression of differing opinions before a binding
decision was taken. In this way, it could contribute to intelligent debate and thoughtful decision making. In addition, isegoria gave rise to
the practice of skillful oratory. The right to speak did not guarantee
one a hearing. As Robert Bonner notes, "It was no easy matter to
address several thousand people in the open air, even when all were
orderly and attentive, but if, like the Athenian assembly, they were
always volubly critical and often unruly and tumultuous, the difficulty
was materially increased."[26] Skill was necessary on most occasions, especially if one wished to offer new, critical, or unusual advice. We
know from Plutarch, for example, that even Demosthenes' first effort
at addressing the assembly was a disaster.[27] The Athenians delighted,
however, in excellent oratory, for the most part taking enormous
pleasure in hearing competing views argued intensely and beautifully,
and expecting the competition among orators for the respect and admiration of the polis to increase the likelihood that the arguments
brought before them were clear and informed.

25. Trans. borrowed from Ober, *Mass and Elite*, 317.
26. Bonner, "Freedom of Speech," 75.
27. Plutarch *Life of Demosthenes* 5.

Isegoria had, however, severe limitations as a guarantor of intelligent debate. It gave rise to what the Athenians themselves perceived to be the greatest threat to the ability of democratic deliberative processes to discern the public interest and produce wise decisions: manipulative and deceptive oratory in the service of a speaker's personal ambitions rather than the public interest. By pandering to the whims and desires of the people, a clever orator could elevate himself to a position of leadership. He could also perhaps direct public policy so as to benefit his own pocket or to suit his own private purposes. Expert oratory could, then, corrupt the deliberations and lead to the neglect of the public interest and, perhaps, to disastrous decisions and actions. The Athenians recognized this danger and were intensely suspicious of expert oratory, even as they expected and enjoyed the display. The "evils of flattery" topos commonly employed by orators is good evidence for the Athenians' awareness of danger and willingness to be reminded of their vulnerability.[28] The Athenians also attempted to safeguard themselves from the influences of a deceitful orator in practical ways. For example, meetings of the Assembly opened with the pronouncement of a curse against those who would deceive the people.[29] Citizens who had committed certain offenses (prostitution, for example, or maltreatment of parents) were considered untrustworthy and stripped of their right of public address.[30] In addition, Athenian law provided for the prosecution of individuals who "deceive the Assembly" and abuse the public confidence. Persons could be charged, tried, and punished for having offered insincere (perhaps bribe induced) advice or simply for what proved later to have been unwise advice (e.g., through the prosecution of a *graphē paranomōn*, which, roughly, meant charging that the advice had been unconstitutional). The practice of isegoria had raised the possibility of wise democratic decision making, *and* it had erected serious obstacles to its realization.

Thus though the notion of isegoria was clearly of great importance in the Athenian democratic self-image, it could not, on its own, ideologically suggest the positive ability of democratic deliberations to produce wise as well as lawful decisions (to educate action). An appeal to isegoria in the course of debate could not adequately confront and allay Athenian suspicions of expert oratory. The efforts of orators to link their critical arguments to the idea and practice of parrhesia ap-

28. See Ober, *Mass and Elite*, 323.
29. Bonner, "Freedom of Speech," 76.
30. See Aeschines *Against Timarchus* 28ff., where he lists the offenses that could result in the loss of one's right of public address.

pear, however, to have had precisely this aim in mind. For example, Demosthenes often explicitly identifies his efforts to criticize a common Athenian viewpoint with the ideal of speaking with parrhesia and contrasts his speech with flattering, deceitful, or self-promoting oratory. The closing of the *Fourth Philippic* is typical: "There you have the truth spoken with all parrhesia, simply in goodwill and for the best—no speech packed by flattery with mischief and deceit, and intended to put money in the speaker's pocket and control of the polis into our enemies' hands."[31] An appeal to the ethic of parrhesia was in fact a strategy speakers employed to negotiate and reduce the Athenians' suspicions of expert oratory. An appeal to parrhesia was an economical way of affirming two things that were absolutely necessary to a defense against these suspicions: the personal virtue and integrity of the speaker, and the priority of the public interest over personal pleasures.[32]

The invocation of parrhesia asserted the personal integrity of the speaker in a number of ways. It identified the speaker's motivation as a commitment to truth and to the exposure of truth. There was no claim to have uncovered certain, indisputable truth, but rather a view supremely worthy of confidence. But just as important as this truth claim was the suggestion that the speaker willingly embraces considerable risks by speaking—risks to his reputation, financial well-being, and personal safety. When one spoke out in the Assembly, one risked being disliked, shouted down, humiliated, fined, or brought up on any one of a variety of charges, some of which could carry stiff penalties. The climate of personal risk was, in fact, emphasized by the orators. The presence of the risks made more credible the orator's claim to be saying what he thinks is true and right, that is, what he thinks is in the best interest of the polis in contrast to what might benefit him personally. Demosthenes, for example, chooses to close his *First Philippic* by reminding his audience of the risks he has run by speaking with parrhesia: "I have spoken my plain sentiments with parrhesia. Yet, certain as I am that it is to your interest to receive the best advice, I could have wished that I were equally certain that to offer such advice is also to the interest of the speaker. . . . But, as it is, in the uncertainty

31. *Demosthenes*, trans. J. H. Vince, vol. 1, Loeb Classical Library (Cambridge: Harvard University Press, 1962); see also Demos. *Third Olyn.* 3, *First Phil.* 51, *On the Chersonese* 32, *Third Phil.* 3–4, and *On Org.* 15. Isocrates too cites his commitment to parrhesia to distinguish his speech from mere flattery; see *Antidosis* 43.8–44.1 and *Panath.* 96.

32. The importance of the integrity of the speaker to the Athenians' consideration of the merit of his proposal is apparent from the extent to which orators attack each other on precisely these grounds. The personal invectives are, at times, quite extreme. See, e.g., Demosthenes *On the Crown* and Aeschines *Against Ctesiphon* as a pair.

of what the result of my proposal may be for myself, yet in the conviction that it will be to your interest to adopt it, I have ventured to
address you."[33] He uses an acceptance of risks to bolster his claim to
be offering thoughtful, justified criticism, not just wielding a malicious attack or delivering deceitful, manipulative advice or acting on a
bribe. The appeal to parrhesia perhaps even associates his speech with
the exercise of a moral obligation.[34]

Associating debate with the practice of parrhesia affirmed the virtue of the hearers as much as it did that of the speaker. The performance of the role of speaking with parrhesia (*epi tou bēmatos parrhēs-
ian*) and giving priority to the promotion of the public good required
the collaboration of the hearers.[35] To the extent that the hearers willingly suffer criticism, reflect on their opinions, and generally listen to
others, *their* public-interestedness (that is, their placement of the public good before that of personal pleasure) is on display as well as that
of the speaker. Demosthenes' appeal to parrhesia at the beginning of
his *For the Liberty of the Rhodians*, for example, affirms the importance
of political parrhesia to debate and good outcomes and indicates that
the cooperation of the hearers is essential: "Your duty, men of
Athens, when debating important matters, is, I think, to give parrhesia to every one of your counsellors."[36]

In addition to asserting the personal integrity of the speaker and
the moral virtue of the hearers, the ideal of speaking with parrhesia
in the Assembly affirmed the usefulness of rigorous, critical appraisal
of proposals before the Assembly and, perhaps of more importance,
of the subjection of the apparent will of the demos to interrogation.
The Athenians believed that a proposal or view that could garner the
confidence of a large number was likely actually to be the best available alternative.[37] But their belief in the truth or accuracy of a majority decision was predicated on a certain expectation of the quality of
debate preceding the vote. The Athenians did not expect the collective desires of the many to translate magically into an intelligent collective will. They merely considered a proposal that could gain the
reasoned confidence of many more likely to be good than one favored
by a few, or only one. They assumed a proposal able to withstand the
separate scrutiny of many persons would most likely be best. This is

33. Trans. Vince, *Demosthenes.*
34. Cornelius Castoriadis, "The Greek Polis and the Creation of Democracy," *Graduate
Faculty Journal* 9 (1983): 98.
35. Demosthenes *On Halonnesus* 1.
36. Demos. *Rhodians* 1, in Vince, *Demosthenes.*
37. See Ober, *Mass and Elite*, 163–65.

problematic of course, because persons do not normally conduct entirely separate and independent evaluations when they meet in the Assembly. Nevertheless, the Athenians did patriotically represent a majority decision as the most commonly held opinion and not as the opinion of the mass. The association of critical parrhesia with Assembly debate, therefore, helped establish confidence in the collective wisdom of the demos. A vote taken after speeches delivered in a spirit of parrhesia could represent not simply the uncomplicated preferences of the majority but the considered judgment of citizens. As a result, such a decision could be thought to be wise and worthy of the confidence of the demos. Even a common criticism of democracy in the ancient sources stresses this point: the complaint is that when things go badly, the people fail to remember that they—and not only a solitary, individual advisor—had chosen the policy in question, had deemed it best. The policy had represented the best judgment of the demos at the time. Consider the speech of Diodotus in Thucydides, for example. He pleads with his audience to recognize their share of the responsibility for decisions: "When at any time your affairs miscarry, you punish the sentence of that one only that gave the counsel, not the many sentences of your own that were in fault as well as his" (3.43.4).[38]

It needs to be stressed, in conclusion, that the ideal of parrhesia celebrated in the Athenian patriotic self-image implied an intimate relation between a speaker and the words spoken. One's critical and bold speech was taken to express—perhaps to expose—something of who one is, what one cares about, how one has chosen to live. One's convictions were on display when one spoke with parrhesia. Such exposure was, moreover, a risky business. Too, when one seriously *listened* in the spirit of parrhesia, one's convictions hung in the balance. Parrhesia must not, therefore, be confused with mere audacious speech,[39] with playing the devil's advocate, or even with bold speculation. That the speaker and audience had personal stakes in the views uttered was a crucial characteristic of the ideal of democratic parrhesia.

Parrhesia clearly did a considerable amount of work in the Athenian patriotic self-image. In particular, celebrating parrhesia asserted some of the substantive qualities of a free citizen, expressed strong

38. Thuc. *Peloponnesian War: Hobbes Translation.*
39. Parrhesia was sometimes used in a pejorative sense to mean mere audacious or hot-tempered speech; see, e.g., Euripides *Orestes* 905; Foucault, "Discourse on Truth," 34–41; and Isocr. *Panath.* 218. This pejorative sense is not, however, the content of the ideal as celebrated in the Athenian patriotic self-image.

opposition to the return of tyranny, projected an image of both the kind of speech ideally expected of those who chose to step forward and advise the Assembly and the kind of critical attitude ideally to be adopted by all citizens. In addition, it is represented as central to the health of democratic deliberations and the ability of democratic institutions to foster inquiries into the public interest.

PLATO'S APPROPRIATION OF PARRHESIA FOR PHILOSOPHY

Soon after Socrates begins to develop an explicit critique of democratic politics in *Republic*, Book 8, he makes an intriguing comment to Glaucon and Adeimantus. "Because it contains all species of regimes," he states, "a man wishing to organize a city, as we were just doing, must go to a city under a democracy" (557d4–9).[40] The inclusion of "as we were just doing" indicates that Socrates is referring to their efforts to organize a city in speech, that is, to conduct an intellectual project like that "reported" in the previous books in the text of the *Republic*. This comment thus raises the attentive reader's interest in the relation between democracy and philosophy. It subtly challenges the assumption that philosophy and democracy are thoroughly at odds. It suggests, in fact, that democracy to some extent sustains an environment conducive to philosophy.[41] In the treatment of parrhesia, I argue, Plato explores the complexity of the relation between democratic practice and philosophy.

Plato's texts mingle a repudiation of democratic politics with a subtle affirmation of the celebrated democratic ideal of parrhesia.[42] They defend the democratic conceptualization of parrhesia and appropriate it for philosophy. Moreover, the texts do not simply appropriate the term while substantially altering its content. Rather, they work with the common Athenian understanding of parrhesia. Plato draws on the ideal of parrhesia both in his representation of the practice of philosophy and in his account of the fundamental failure of democratic politics to deliver on its promise of parrhesia.

40. *The Republic of Plato*, trans. Allan Bloom, with notes and an interpretative essay (New York: Basic Books, 1968). Subsequent quotations are from this edition.
41. Which is not the same as providing an environment conducive to the political empowerment of philosophy; the many factors that combine to prevent this from happening are the subject of Book 6 and arguably much else in the Platonic corpus.
42. It is important to note that Plato does not show the same interest in isegoria, a term that stresses the equal opportunity of all citizen males to address the Assembly and not the specific character of the speech.

Plato links parrhesia and philosophy in works from every period of his life. Three times in the *Laches*, a very early dialogue, he relies on the notion of parrhesia to describe some of the psychological preconditions for conducting philosophical inquiry (178a, 179c, 189a). In fact, he indicates that a moral attachment to the democratic ideal of parrhesia can ready one for philosophy. The first two appearances of the term, for example, refer to Lysimachus's eagerness to search for some help in determining how to educate his son. The third refers to Laches' eagerness to converse with Socrates. Moreover, though the participants do not settle on a satisfactory answer to the question posed at the beginning (What is courage?), they do in the end explicitly affirm the usefulness of the Socratic method. We can observe, moreover, that the *Laches* as a whole illuminates what conducting a philosophical investigation entails and that the concept of parrhesia figures prominently in it. In the *Gorgias*, a middle-period dialogue, Plato relies on parrhesia on six different occasions to explain the psychological disposition needed if one is to participate in a serious search for the truth as distinct from a competition for rhetorical victory (487a, 487b, 487d, 491e, 492d, 521a). In the *Laws*, a late work, Plato again links a commitment to the ideal of parrhesia to the progress of a serious intellectual inquiry into political matters. Three times he has speakers appeal to the company's understanding of the importance of parrhesia to justify the expression of painful criticism in the course of the development of an argument (806c8, 806d2, 835c4). On one occasion in particular he represents the Athenian Stranger's entire project in the dialogue (his effort to "say what is in his opinion best for the city and the citizens") as "giving extraordinary honor to parrhesia" (835c).[43] Moreover, in the *Eighth Letter*, written near the end of his life, Plato even speaks of his own advice concerning the affairs of Syracuse in the aftermath of Dion's death as being offered "with all parrhesia" (354a).[44]

In the *Republic*, we find that features of the practice of parrhesia (though not the term itself) are clearly implicated in Socrates' efforts

43. Note also that Plato does, on occasion, make use of other common meanings of parrhesia. For example, the outspokenness of Alcibiades in the *Symposium* 222c1–2; the speech of an intoxicated person in the *Laws* 649b2–3, 671b3–4, and *Phaedrus* 240e5–6; and candid speech among friends in the *Charmides* 156a8.

44. I think there is good reason to accept this letter as genuine. See Ludwig Edelstein, *Plato's Seventh Letter*, vol. 14 in *Philosophia Antiqua* (Leiden: Brill, 1966); John Harward, *The Platonic Epistles* (New York: Arno, 1976); and Glenn R. Morrow, *Plato's Epistles: A Translation with Critical Essays and Notes* (Indianapolis: University of Indiana Press, 1962). See also Robert S. Brumbaugh, "Digression and Dialectic: The *Seventh Letter* and Plato's Literary Form," in *Platonic Writings/Platonic Readings*, ed. Charles L. Griswold, Jr. (New York: Routledge, Chapman and Hall, 1988), 84–92.

to construct a "city in speech." In Book 5, Plato highlights the fact that Socrates is speaking especially boldly, that he is daring to venture where the argument leads, that he is daring to say what he truly thinks. The term *parrhēsia* does not appear in these passages, but other constructions emphasize that a willingness to speak frankly is necessary for the progress of the philosophical investigation at hand. The characteristics attributed to Socrates at these moments echo some of the characteristics patriotically associated with one who dares to speak with parrhesia. The moments are Socrates' introduction of the possibility of women guardians (450cff.) and of the idea of the philosopher king (473cff.).

The introduction of the idea of women guardians is full of references to the great risks one runs when one speaks uncommon or radically critical things. Allusions to the *Apology* abound. What interests me here is the mention of the specific risks the speaker runs and of the daring the speaker will exhibit. Socrates clearly identifies the risks he is about to assume: the proposal will seem impossible and his credibility will be doubted (450c); he will prove mistaken and cause harm to his fellows, albeit involuntarily (450e–451a); and he will be laughed at (451a). His articulation of the risks reminds the reader of the practice of speaking with parrhesia. It recalls Assembly oratory in which the speaker appeals to the ethic of parrhesia and highlights the great risks he is undertaking in order to emphasize his personal integrity. The characteristically Socratic worry about being mistaken also recalls the politician who appeals to parrhesia to indicate that he is offering his understanding of the truth in all seriousness, but not as an absolute certainty. The worry about eliciting laughter also fits with an evocation of the ethic of parrhesia. Although I have not focused on it in this essay, it was on the comic stage that the limits of Athenian toleration of parrhesia were pushed most aggressively. In addition, the interlocutors' assurance that he should assume the risks because "your audience won't be without judgment, or distrustful or ill-willed" (450d) also serves to evoke the practice of parrhesia: it suggests the attitude expected of the hearers in a parrhesiastic encounter. And, finally, Glaucon's exhortation to "be bold and speak" (451b5) reminds the reader of the ethic of parrhesia.

The introduction of the idea of the philosopher king also subtly manipulates the ethic of parrhesia. Socrates begins the passage by noting that what they must do next is "seek out and demonstrate what is badly done in cities today and with what small change . . . a city would come to this [ideal] manner of regime" (473b). He then states briefly and forcefully that the small change he has in mind will likely drown him in a wave of laughter and ill repute but that nevertheless "it shall be said" (473c7, trans. modified). He then addresses his readers and interlocutors in the imperative: "Consider what I am going to say" (473c8–9). The risks he identifies at this point include not only being laughed at but something more akin to the risk undertaken by orators: losing one's standing with the public. He then emphasizes his determination to say what he thinks, that is, to come forward to name the one small change that can illuminate the transformation of the city. That "small change," of course, is the marriage of philosophical knowledge and political power. When Socrates reiterates the need for this "small change" in Book 6, moreover, he again emphasizes that he is speaking in the spirit of parrhesia. He refers to the argument he made as "fair and free speech (*logon kalon te kai eleutheron*) of the sort that strains every nerve" and recalls that when he spoke he "was frightened; but, all the same, compelled by the truth [to continue]" (499a).

Plato represents Socrates as speaking with parrhesia as he presents the ideas both of the philosopher king and of women guardians. Even as he discusses two profoundly antidemocratic institutions, he manages subtly to express an intellectual debt to a democratic value; for he clearly recognized that democracy claimed parrhesia as a defining feature of its politics. In Book 8 of the *Republic*, Socrates describes democracy as "a city full of freedom and frank speech (*eleutheria* and *parrhēsia*, 557b)."[45] Because Book 8 delivers perhaps the most severe of Plato's critical arguments about democratic politics, it is striking that this critique relies on Athenian understandings of the importance of parrhesia to express democracy's flaws. In particular, the critique proposes that democracy fails precisely because it cannot in fact nurture or even tolerate the practice of speaking with parrhesia, despite what it professes. We can, of course, disagree with Plato on this score. But the accuracy of Plato's portrayal of Athenian democracy is not what is at issue here. Rather, it is the possibility that at least some of the language and conceptual apparatus he marshals in his most scathing critique of democracy derives from Athenian democratic ideals themselves.

The general context of the key passage from the *Republic* (557bff.) is Socrates' account of the degeneration of regimes and souls. In particular, it is the account of the democratic manner of life and its deterioration into tyranny. At the start of the passage, Socrates asks, "Is

45. James Adam notes on *Republic* 557b that parrhesia was a "watchword" of democracy; see *The Republic of Plato*, ed. idem, 2d ed. (New York: Cambridge University Press, 1965).

democracy not first of all a city full of freedom and parrhesia?" Adeimantus replies, "That is indeed what is said." Yet what follows is a description of a democratic polis completely lacking in the practice of critical parrhesia understood as the frank expression of one's considered judgment. Democracy is portrayed as a regime in which citizens practice no discrimination—they treat all views and desires as equally deserving of attention and pursuit. In addition, Socrates directly criticizes freedom and, to a lesser extent, equality. The ideal of parrhesia, however, is not implicated at any point in the critical argument.

The absence of any attack on parrhesia in this part of the text is striking. Frank speaking was a highly celebrated, and highly controversial,[46] democratic principle. The absence of any objections to the ideal is especially intriguing, moreover, because a well-known attack on democratic parrhesia would fit in quite well with a line of reasoning pursued here. Parrhesia on the comic stage, for example, was attacked as nothing more than baseless, abusive speech, speech uninformed by any thoughtful point but uttered simply for the pleasure of the hearers or for the fun of raising a ruckus. Parrhesia in the Assembly was criticized by Isocrates (who defends it in other places) as speech hardly tied to any commitment to the exposure of truth and practice of intelligent criticism, or to the project of discerning good from bad choices; rather, it was reckless.[47] Such views of parrhesia could have formed part of Plato's case against a lack of interest in discrimination which he takes to be characteristic of democracy, but he does not develop such an attack in the Book 8 passage. Instead, he relies on the patriotic conception of parrhesia in the very construction of his critique. I will plot how this works by looking at sections of it in turn: the metamorphosis of oligarchic man into democratic man; the description of the fully democratic man; and the transformation of a democratic regime into a tyranny.

A curious dynamic between true and false speech is at work in the account of the emergence of democratic man from oligarchic man (559dff.). The mainspring of this transformation is the growth in the variety and quantity of desires experienced by the young individual. Democratic man emerges when the oligarchic norms imposed by his father, which once regulated his desires and their satisfaction, lose their hold, liberating all desires and declaring them equally deserving of satisfaction. The completion of the change is signaled, moreover, by the young man's attachment to the ideals of freedom and equality,

46. See the attack on free speech (both isegoria and parrhesia) in Ps.-Xen. *Ath. Pol.* 1. 6–9.
47. *On the Peace* 14. See also Eur. *Orest.* 905, where parrhesia is used to suggest ignorant outspokenness.

ideals that celebrate the defeat not only of oligarchic standards of discerning good from bad desires but of any and all standards of discernment whatsoever.

Democratic individuals live "in accord with a certain equality of pleasures . . . fostering all on the basis of equality" and consider this life "sweet and free." Such a life is much admired, Socrates admits, chiefly for the variety the individual can experience (561e). But Socrates does not attribute the change from oligarchic to democratic man simply to the onslaught of desires and the rejection of oligarchic standards. He also names the fact that the young man's soul was "bereft of true speeches"[48] (*logoi alētheis*, 560b9) at the very moment when he was confused and suffering inner turmoil. These speeches, "the watchmen and guardians in the thoughts of men who are loved by the gods" (560b9–10), were absent from his mind. Instead, when conflict was raging inside his mind, he was supremely vulnerable to the influence of "false and boasting speeches" (*pseudeis ka'alazones logoi*, 560c2). In fact, Socrates remarks that these false speeches closed his mind to any help he may have received in gaining some new direction. Socrates states that the boasting speeches "close the gates of the kingly wall within him" (560c3–4) to any help possibly forthcoming from strengths residing within his self, or from older men. Socrates continues by arguing that the boasting speeches purge moderation and order "from the soul of the man whom they [the pleasures] are seizing . . . they [boasting speeches] proceed to return insolence, anarchy, wastefulness and shamelessness from exile, in a blaze of light, crowned and accompanied by a numerous chorus" (560d9–560e4). This may allude to Alcibiades' return to Athens and the procession to Eleusis that he orchestrated in 407 B.C. If we make this identification, moreover, then among the "older men" whose help this boastful, democratic man resists we would certainly include Socrates.[49]

At this point it is necessary to consider to what "false speeches" is intended to refer and their relation to the idea of parrhesia. We can immediately rule out the kind of false speech (lies, myths) of the sort promoted for the education of children in Book 2 (376eff.) and in the presentation of the "noble lie," also called the "myth of the metals" (414bff.). The false speeches at work in ushering in a disorderly soul are in no way useful, medicinal, or noble. They are destructive and tend to incite the passions. Uttering such false speeches is distinctly unlike speaking with parrhesia. It is not to counsel critical evaluation

48. "Speeches" is awkward here but I have opted for it because it is necessary to convey the sense of *logoi*, which suggests not just words but accounts and arguments.

49. I am grateful to W. Robert Connor for pointing out this allusion.

and scrutiny of all known alternatives, or to express one's considered judgment; it is instead to recommend disregard for standards.

I suspect that "false speeches" refers to the (boasting and false) words of politicians and perhaps poets. This interpretation would fit with the attack on these forms of speech that runs throughout the entire text (as well as tying up with the *Apology*) and with an explicit connection made later in the Book 8 passage itself. In Book 6, for example, slanderous speech against philosophy is one of the reasons given for the city's failure to recognize the political value of philosophy—and therefore for continued suffering. The slander (*diabolē*)— that philosophy is a useless, if not vicious, activity—is perpetrated, moreover, by those who themselves seek to exercise power (rhetors, poets) though they lack the knowledge necessary to do so in a way beneficial to the polis.[50]

In the Book 8 passage, democratic political leaders are represented as catering to the growing desires of the people rather than attempting to direct or educate them. This sort of speech on the part of the politicians figures centrally in the account of the demise of democracy and the emergence of tyranny (564eff.). In his discussion of the tyrant's rule at the end of Book 8, moreover, Socrates explicitly recalls the earlier decision to banish the poets from the ideal city. The poets, he says, "extol tyranny as a condition equal to that of a god" (568b4– 5) and, "gathering crowds, hiring fine, persuasive voices, they draw regimes toward tyrannies and democracies" (568c2–4). The role of false speeches in the emergence of democratic man and the striking remark about the soul of the young man being "bereft of true speeches" function to raise doubts about the ability of the political leaders and the poets—those citizens relied on in a democracy to speak with parrhesia and provide the citizens with an encounter with "true speeches"—to perform the task of educating action.

How are we to understand the references to "true speeches"? Socrates gives no explicit indication of exactly what they are or where they are to come from. We can infer from the work they are capable of doing—establishing some inner order and averting the eventual danger of suffering a tyranny—that "true speeches" would have to guide a critical review of the alternatives facing an individual. The educative work that true speeches are expected to perform is further indicated in the description of the fully democratic man. Socrates states that the democratic soul "will not admit true speech or let it pass into the guardhouse" (561b9–10), that is, into his mind. Socrates goes on to

50. See the image of the ship at *Rep.* 488a–e.

describe precisely what is therefore lost: any interest in discerning good from bad desires or in recognizing the need to indulge some and control others—any interest in establishing some conscious order—is rejected outright. Instead, the democratic man holds that "all [pleasures] are alike and must be honored on an equal basis" (561c3–4). Clearly, "true speech" is speech that evaluates critically the merit of acting on any one of many and various felt desires.[51] In this way it is like the practice of both critical parrhesia and philosophy. Plato chooses this general, abstract term, true speeches, I think, to make it possible to observe what is common to these practices—a commitment to truth and a concern to discern good from bad options for action.

We can observe Plato's view of how democracy generates a need for "true speech" which it cannot fulfill in another Book 8 passage. Socrates does allow that democratic man can attain a certain kind of equilibrium. The difficulty is that this equilibrium is due purely to uncontrollable factors such as luck and aging (561a8–10). Socrates argues that "if he [democratic man] has good luck and his frenzy does not go beyond bounds—and if, also, as a result of growing older and the great disturbances having passed by, he readmits [moderation and order] and does not give himself over to the invading desires, then he lives in accordance with an equality of pleasures" (561a8–10). To whichever pleasures happen to come along, he submits himself, "as though it were chosen by lot" (561a–b). Such a man will do gymnastics at one moment, drink at another, and engage in politics at another (561c–d). The way Socrates concludes this part of the passage is particularly interesting. He suggests that such is the life of an *isonomikos anēr*, a man attached to the law of equality. The term *isonomikos* instantly recalls the celebrated democratic principle of *isonomia* (political equality) which was, in the democratic mind, strongly associated with the kind of order, balance, and lawfulness thought to characterize the life of a democratic citizen. It is worth noting that the text here admits that a commitment to equality *can* do the valuable, indeed essential, work of keeping things in check, providing order. The problem is that the commitment is distinctly unreliable; it requires considerable help from forces beyond human control—chance and

51. True speech may also be speech that illuminates the value of philosophy, that is, that argues for philosophy's political usefulness. This is the implication of Socrates' references in Book 6 to his own speeches aimed to counter the slander of philosophy (489d, 499a). The failure to give an adequate hearing to such speeches is named part of the reason why reasonably fine natures often do not turn toward philosophy but are lured away by the glorious possibilities associated with other pursuits (and therefore why one willing to pursue philosophy is so very rare), as well as why the city does not insist that true philosophers rule (499b8–10).

nature—to accomplish the task. This fact strikes Plato as acutely problematic. And the texts offer only one way of adequately addressing
the need for order: some exposure to true speech—that is, the active
intervention of the intellect.

Next let us look at the curious way the issue of parrhesia surfaces in
the account of a democratic regime's slide into tyranny (562a7ff.).
Socrates begins the passage by emphasizing the extreme attachment
to freedom characteristic of democracy. He names the greediness for
freedom as the chief cause of the slide (562b–c). But it is important to
recognize that the greediness for freedom is not itself the agent of the
disastrous change; the citizens do not all become tyrannical and anar-
chic. Rather, the climate of greediness provides the condition under
which the people swiftly fall victim to the vicious designs of a few or
of one.

The argument begins with a description of how this greediness af-
fects daily life. The first thing Socrates mentions is the corruption of
politics. The liberation of the insatiable desires of many make it possible for a "bad winebearer" to become a leader (*prostatēs*), in which case
the city gets drunker (562c9–d2). Freedom will spread to everything,
including private relations and the behavior of beasts, causing anarchy. Distinctions will be unmaintainable. Citizens, metics, and foreigners will be indistinguishable one from another (562d–563a).
Slaves will be no less free than their owners, and there will be freedom in the relations among men and women (563b). The description
of the excesses of freedom is interrupted at this point by an odd but
telling comment by Adeimantus and a response by Socrates. "Won't
we," Adeimantus interjects, "with Aeschylus 'say whatever just came to
our lips?'" (563c1–2). Socrates responds, "Certainly, I will speak in
such a manner" (trans. modified).[52] He then goes on to utter the daring (because offensive) remark that even beasts are free in a democratic city. They move about the city virtually unrestrained, "bumping
into whomever they happen to meet on the road" (563c). The comment about the uninhibited character of the speech Socrates and Adeimantus are practicing and Socrates' affirmation of his intention to
continue to speak in this manner remind the reader of the issue of

52. See Adam, *Republic of Plato*, 248, on this passage. He discusses the possibility that it
links up with Aristot. *Nic. Eth.* 1111a9ff. If so, the passage could further imply speaking in a
manner that reveals some important truth. It would also fit with the Socratic profession of
ignorance even at the moment he utters elements of a positive doctrine. Aristotle is discussing
the possibility that a man can be ignorant of what he is doing. He cites people who inadvertently reveal a secret and plead, "It slipped out of their mouths . . . as Aeschylus said of
the mysteries" (*The Basic Works of Aristotle*, ed. and trans. Richard McKeon [New York: Random House, 1941], 966).

parrhesia. If only fleetingly, the possibility that Socrates and his interlocutors are practicing parrhesia comes to the fore. They are speaking
out, they are saying what they think, following the argument where it
leads, exposing truth. In the midst of the anarchy that is democracy,
they are trying to practice parrhesia, to name the problem and suggest a course of treatment.

The concluding remark of this passage is even more telling. Socrates adds that the radically democratic city in which beasts behave as
they wish—the one about to generate a tyranny—is a city "full of
freedom" (*mesta eleutherias gignetai*). This comment repeats the exact
same phrase that Socrates had used to introduce democracy pages
earlier but with one glaring change: a city described as full of freedom and parrhesia (*mestē eleutherias kai parrhēsias*, 557b4–5) is now a
city full of freedom only. I think this omission is deliberate. It implicitly denies the patriotic claim that Athens is a place full of parrhesia
because it proposes that parrhesia is not truly practiced by those on
whom the Athenians rely for it. As long as the city rejects philosophy,
it is a city full of freedom untempered by the critical power of parrhesia and is therefore also a city in great danger. Plato thus defends
rather than rejects the ideal of parrhesia. He argues, moreover, that
the very regime that professes to honor parrhesia actually lacks it.
Democracy generates a need for something it cannot provide or tolerate.

Next consider the role of parrhesia in the account of how a tyrannical regime evolves. Socrates maintains that tyranny has its origins in
the development of conflict among the various members of the city
brought about by the greed of some. He begins by observing that
people will not assemble to conduct business without receiving some
compensation. The leaders of the people, in order to promote themselves, aim to satisfy the appetite of the people by contriving to take
from the wealthy. The wealthy defend their interests, believing the
people to be deceived by slanderers. They become committed oligarchs out of the experience, however, and enter into political rivalries with the leaders of the people, or plot to overturn the government. The people, eager to defeat the oligarchs and egged on by their
leaders, move to protect the democracy and satisfy their greed by fostering a strong leader. A tyrant, Socrates proposes, then "grows naturally, he sprouts from the root of leadership" (565d1–2). A leader's
chief resource in the democratic context, we must remember, is his
speech. Leaders are those who successfully persuade the Assembly
time after time, gaining for themselves a position of authority with the
people. Plato is here implying, then, that speech is the primary instru-

ment by which a tyrant initially promotes himself. The emerging tyrant is an example of a deceitful speaker manipulating the felt desires of the people to gain personally.

Socrates' account of the emergence of the full tyrant offers, moreover, a scenario in which the deceitful speech of the politician plays a central role. A leader brings an unjust charge (deceitful speech) against a wealthy man, seeking to seize his wealth to satisfy the greed of his followers. The leader in effect murders the man and starts rumors about the cancellation of debts and redistribution of land (more deceitful speech). This action incites the wealthy to seek to slay this emerging tyrant, or to turn the people off him by means of strong, even slanderous speech. If they fail, however, the leader is likely to become a full tyrant, as he has already tasted blood. He tricks the people (more deceitful speech) into allowing him to form a private bodyguard and is then firmly installed.

Where is the celebrated practice of parrhesia in this story? Parrhesia, truthful political criticism, was supposed to be the Athenians' front line of defense against the potential for the abuse of the power of speech and the consequent threat to the integrity of the democratic political order. The patriotic self-image celebrated parrhesia for its capacity to perform precisely this role. The answer is that it is absent from Plato's account. In his view, people just rode along, they did not name the abuses or criticize the prosecution of policy. They were instead either drunk with booty or possessed of minds closed by the influences of deceitful speech. Once the tyrant is well established, moreover, Plato makes very clear that the powers of true persuasion and critical speech—the promise of parrhesia—are no match for the unaccountable use of physical force and violence. The fate of those who desperately turn to parrhesia at this point is another strong statement of the costs of its neglect at an earlier time.[53] A citizen suspected by the tyrant of having "free thoughts" (*eleuthera phronēmata*, 567a5–6)[54] or of being discontented with the tyrant's rule will simply be killed (sent to fight in a drummed up war). Even a person from the tyrant's inner circle who attempts to address him with parrhesia in an effort to resist the perpetration of horrors will simply be killed.[55]

53. The link between the failure to practice parrhesia and the development of severe problems recalls Demosthenes' warning (*On Org.* 15) that democracy is in danger when citizens fail to practice parrhesia.

54. The use of the phrase "free thoughts" is noteworthy for its suggestion that a norm of intellectual freedom is presupposed by the ethic of parrhesia.

55. Socrates' description of the death of this individual at 567b is, I think, a reference to the fate of Theramenes during the period of the Thirty Tyrants. See Aristotle's defense of him in *Ath. Pol.* 28.5, 32.2, 33.2, 34.3, 36–37.1.

This particular account of the slide into tyranny would not necessarily have struck the average Athenian democrat as odd. Quite the
contrary. Fear and suspicion of political leaders was common. The
Athenians worried about deceitful oratory and the virtue of their advisors, that is, the strength of their advisors' commitments to the priority of the public interest over the promise of private benefit. The
Athenians considered their city to have reliable mechanisms in place
to check these threats (among these would be a commitment to parrhesia), and we may want to agree that they in fact really did and that
Plato is wrong in pressing the absence of true parrhesia and the extreme vulnerability of a democratic polity and a democratic citizen.
Nevertheless, the point to stress is that Plato's arguments utilize Athenian democratic understandings of parrhesia in the construction of
his radical critique of democratic politics. Plato's critique is to some
extent constituted by this Athenian democratic ideal.

The way Plato works with the idea of parrhesia in the well-known
criticism of democracy in Book 8 presses the importance of raising a
particular question when evaluating the functioning of a democratic
order: Are the institutions that the polity relies on for the development and expression of critical, frank speech really adequate to the
task? Plato's discussion of the issue manages, moreover, to affirm the
political value of free speech while denying that known institutions of
democracy can actually deliver it. The institutions democracy relies on
to foster and showcase parrhesia cannot, in his view, do the job. Instead, he paradoxically proposes, only philosophy can carry out this
important political work. But one need not accept his conclusion
about philosophy's exclusive claim to the practice of "true parrhesia"
in order to agree that he raises an important issue: evaluation of established or imagined political institutions should be driven by the
following question: Do they promote or impede the practice of critical
and reflective political speech? Following the Athenian understanding
of the demands of parrhesia, we should recall, such an evaluation
would involve scrutiny of the kind of attitude demanded of hearers as
well as speakers.

Plato's reliance on and appropriation of the Athenian understanding of parrhesia raises questions about the accuracy of an assumption that directs most discussion of treatment of democracy in
his texts. He is often taken to have had nothing but contempt for
Athenian democratic principles and practices. His political theory is
commonly thought to be an unrelenting attack on everything democracy prizes and celebrates. Of course his works are not "friendly" to

democracy, but the treatment of parrhesia in the texts indicates that Plato was in significant ways engaged with practices of Athenian democratic politics and not, as most commentators assume, simply and unequivocally against them. His treatment of parrhesia, along with the relation between the dialogic form of composition and the performance of tragedy (another practice of Athenian democracy) as analyzed by others,[56] shows that Plato's thought is significantly indebted to the Athenian democratic tradition he criticizes and sometimes appears (on the surface) to be repudiating.

This perspective on Plato's political thought calls into question the use to which Plato's texts have been put by conservative critics of democracy in the United States in the last decades of the twentieth century. Plato's texts emerge as politically complex and as resistant to easy classification as unequivocally antidemocratic. In fact, this perspective on Plato's work should interest democratic theorists precisely because it directs attention to how his texts engage an element of the Athenian democratic tradition that our own predicament is making increasingly important for us to contemplate: Athens' multiple and extremely sophisticated strategies of civic discourse and deliberation.

56. Euben, *Tragedy of Political Theory*, and Nussbaum, *Fragility of Goodness*.

J. PETER EUBEN

7   Democracy and Political Theory: A Reading of Plato's Gorgias

There is a tradition, almost as old as democracy itself, that says that "the people" must be saved from themselves as well as from their overly ardent and indulgent defenders. Demos-kratia, the power, rule, and mastery of "the people" is a disease that must be cured. For the *Federalist Papers*, the prescription was a redefined republicanism that would correct democratic excesses while becoming, for the lovers of liberty, an exemplary alternative to Athens, whose instability gave legitimacy to the partisans of order. For "democratic revisionists" of the 1950s and 1960s, the prescription was a plurality of elites, "slack" in the system occasioned by voter apathy, and periodic elections, all of which allowed "the system" to work. For the Trilateralists of the 1970s, ungovernable democracy could function when ruled by "responsible elites." For liberal democrats of the 1980s, it could flourish only within a constitutional framework of rights and laws.

The first political theorists may be said to be the foundation of that tradition. Though Thucydides' Pericles gave an eloquent justification for democratic culture, and the historian himself admired the enormous power that culture made possible, he thought Periclean Athens to be the rule by one man and preferred the "moderate" democracy/oligarchy of the 5000. Though one can find passages in Aristotle's *Politics* that are favorable toward democracy (such as the argument for the superiority of collective wisdom over that of a single man), he regarded democracy as a corrupt regime except perhaps for an agrarian version, whose virtue lay in the political participation it made unlikely. And of course there is Plato's *Apology of Socrates*, in which the latter claims that he does philosophy with anyone he meets in the city, insists that philosophy is a gift of Apollo to Athens, and makes the truly remarkable claim that everyone can live the life of a thinking citizen. It is largely on the basis of the *Apology* (and *Crito*) that Socrates has been regarded as sympathetic to democratic Athens, if not democracy in general.[1] But the bulk of the Platonic corpus finds Socrates a persistent, even relentless, critic of democracy. And insofar as Plato has shaped "the" discourse of political theory, the animus against democracy found in his work is inscribed in the scholarly tradition that continues to frame contemporary views of democratic politics and culture.

It is hardly surprising, then, that Plato should be invoked to help legitimate the conservative political and educational agenda of the 1980s or that, in part because of this, liberal and radical critics should find further reason to criticize if not dismiss him. But if the conservative antidemocratic reading of Socrates is exaggerated or even mistaken in crucial ways, then that reading becomes co-optation, and liberal or radical criticism of Plato based upon it, premature. What reasons could one have for taking this view? I offer one general consideration as preface to a particular consideration of the *Gorgias*.

It is usually accepted that there were no theoretical defenders of democracy in ancient Greece, or at least none whose writings we have (unless one accepts Protagoras's views in Plato's dialogue by that name

1. The most notable contemporary defender of a democratic Socrates is Gregory Vlastos; see his *Socrates, Ironist and Moral Philosopher* (Ithaca: Cornell University Press, 1991) and "The Historical Socrates and Athenian Democracy," *Political Theory* 11 (1983): 495–515. Vlastos argues that such admittedly "unforgivable, intemperate allegations of wrongdoing against Athenian political life" do not undermine "the credibility of [Socrates'] insistence in the Crito that [he] finds the constitution of Athens 'exceedingly pleasing' to him and prefers it to that of any city, Greek or barbarian." He goes on to note that Socrates never attacks any democratic institution other than payment for public office and insists on the radically democratic enterprise of interrogating *all* the people he meets (not just citizens) and then concludes by saying that perhaps Socrates' greatest achievement is the democratizing of moral philosophy. ("Historical Socrates and Athenian Democracy," 507, 508.) Socrates, he insists, is "demotikos," one who is well disposed toward the people; "philodemos" rather than "misodemos" (*Socrates, Ironist*, 18, n. 69). But Vlastos's Socrates is demophilic because he is a moral philosopher rather than a political theorist. He is not a *political* theorist because Socrates' doctrine is "properly speaking a moral one though it clearly has far-reaching political implications"; he is not a political *theorist* because "he has no political *theory* at all" (*Socrates, Ironist*, 13, 237). It seems to me these assertions may beg the questions Socrates (or Plato) was trying to raise. In times of crisis what does it mean to "do politics?" Certainly the challenge of feminism and social movements generally has been to insist that politics is different from government and that it happens in places where those with power insist it does not. As to Socrates having no political *theory*, it is worth noting that the person who most insists on the separation of philosophy and politics is Callicles. Vlastos is right to claim there is not political *theory* in the *Gorgias if* the *Republic* defines what it means to have one. The question, again, is whether that is the only way to be theoretical. On these matters, see John R. Wallach, "Socratic Citizenship," *History of Political Thought* 9 (Winter 1988): 393–413.

as a faithful historical rendering).[2] If we understand "theory" as the kind of philosophical and historical enterprise it became after Thucydides and Socrates, the statement is largely true. But if we take a more expansive view of political theory, we can see anticipations and elements of it in Greek tragedy and recognize how tragedy together with comedy constituted an institutionalized democratic tradition of self-critique upon which Plato (and Thucydides) drew both substantively and structurally.[3]

Read against the context of tragedy, Socrates becomes a character in a drama as much as a historical figure, and the argument of a dialogue like the *Gorgias* resides as much in its architecture as in its explicit argumentation, both of which complicate the view of Socrates as antidemocratic. Read against the frame of Aristophanic comedy, Socrates' criticisms of Athenian politics seem both familiar and tame. That juries of ordinary citizens gave prizes to comedies that were as critical of the intellectual sophistication of the demos and of the political acumen of their cultural and political leaders as anything Socrates says in the *Gorgias* gives a certain historical plausibility to Socrates' claim (in the *Apology*) that his becoming a gadfly was part of Apollo's gift to Athens.

Drama was not only a vehicle for cultural self-critique; it contained (or posed) questions about its own status as such a vehicle, extending its reflections on Athenian political culture to itself as part of that culture.[4] In the *Clouds*, for example, Aristophanes parodies the pretensions of philosophers whose attachment to the new postmodern education of ultraunorthodoxy dissolves all foundations, as well as the mindless attachment of old educational reactionaries to foundations that have lost their hold and point. But he also includes himself in these parodies, so that the "subtext" of the play—the way comedy has affinities with both the new and old education—moves with and against the action and plot of it. Something similar happens in the *Gorgias*.

2. Some critics take it that way because they think Socrates respectful of Protagoras. As I do not, the argument for historicity must rest on other grounds, and they, as usual in such cases, are inconclusive.

3. See the discussion of this issue in Maria Lugones and Elizabeth V. Spelman, "Have We Got a Theory for You! Feminist Theory, Cultural Imperialism, and the Demand for 'the Woman's Voice,'" *Women's Studies International Forum* 6 (1983): 573–81.

4. I have made this argument in *The Tragedy of Political Theory: The Road Not Taken* (Princeton: Princeton University Press, 1990). I do not want to exaggerate the continuities between drama and philosophy. It is important to keep in mind that tragedy and comedy were performed in the theater as part of officially sanctioned festivals. As such, they were a regular part of public life in a way philosophy was not. There was no accepted "form" or forum within which something called "philosophy" was expected to be performed.

It is not unusual for a Platonic dialogue to call attention to the conditions of its own existence. Sometimes Socrates explicitly warns an interlocutor that something is missing, illegitimate, or problematic about what is going on in the argument; other times he provides implicit but clear signals to the reader even when the interlocutor misses it. (Plato uses more complex strategies to signal what Socrates misses.) But the *Gorgias* is distinctive in the degree to which it makes the preconditions for dialogue the subject of dialogue. It interrupts the flow of discussion to point to what is assumed or omitted from it, discourses about discourse, and lets us know it is using terms with overlapping and inconsistent meanings. At least in the *Gorgias*, Socratic dialogue is presented not only as a mutually beneficial, freely chosen search for truth but as a form of power that marginalizes other voices. As the generally decorous struggle between Socrates and Gorgias over the relative merits of rhetoric and dialectic becomes a battle between Socrates and Callicles over who will have power in the dialogic and political communities, and as Socrates unsuccessfully attempts to reestablish the mutuality he so pointedly stipulates as the necessary condition for any successful search for an answer to the question of the best life, the *Gorgias* suggests that no knowledge is innocent of power and no morality is wholly independent of political struggle.

The point is made precisely at the moment when Socrates assures Gorgias that what matters in their discussion is being committed to the argument and to truth, no matter where it may lead or who "wins." Dialectic is not a battle; intellectual freedom and power are not matters of victory but of a collective triumph over ignorance and confusion. Only if one welcomes refutation will arguments about significant matters not degenerate into fruitless vituperation; only then can one be liberated from wrong opinions about the most important matters. Yet these pronouncements on the preconditions for philosophy turn out to be nonnegotiable demands. Gorgias accepts them only because he is embarrassed not to and to go against the entreaties of the assembled company, who want the conversation to continue. The moment is revealing in two ways: it shows how truly dependent rhetoricians are on their audience despite their claims to be powerful, and it shows Socrates willing to use the intimidation of numbers.

If the dialogue does show norms being decided politically rather than being derived epistemologically,[5] and if even philosophy is political, then the boundary separating philosophy (or dialectic) as the co-

5. See Wendy Brown, "Feminist Hesitations, Postmodern Exposures," *Differences* 1 (1991): 63–84.

operative search for truth from rhetoric (or eristic) as the verbal combat in which one tries to vanquish the other, is far more permeable
than it seems. Perhaps that is why Socrates appears willing to become,
at least momentarily, what he criticizes in his opponents.

A dialogue about deception and disguise, one that constantly interrupts itself to talk about what is and is not happening within or
around it, that elaborates criteria of success it then fails to meet or
draws distinctions it then violates, is a warning against any literal reading of it. But what does all this have to do with whether the Socrates
in the *Gorgias* is "an authentic democrat"? Few dialogues seem more
relentlessly critical of Athenian democracy. There are Socrates' contemptuous references to the multitude and rejection of jury pay, his
conception of political leadership as "psychic engineering," his general indifference to the question of "who enjoys the political rights
and prerogatives of citizens," and perhaps most significant, his dispar-
aging dismissal of the pantheon of revered Athenian leaders, whom
he regards as inept, corrupting sychophants. Having made the Athenian people worse rather than better, those leaders had, absurdly,
"educated" the hoi polloi to ostracize or throw them out of office.[6]
The worst offender was Pericles, whose introduction of public fees
made the Athenians *argous* (lazy and idle), *deilous* (cowardly, miser-
able, and worthless), *lalous* (talkative and chattering like the flapping
of bird wings), and *philargurous* (avaricious and covetous) (515e). If
someone were an animal trainer who had transformed horses or dogs
into vicious animals dangerous to himself, everyone would admit that
he was an inept, self-destructive animal trainer. Why then not admit
that Pericles was an incompetent political leader for the same reasons?
Indeed, as far as Socrates is concerned, it is he, not Pericles or Cimon
or Miltiades or Themistocles, who is the only Athenian who attempts
and practices "the true art of politics" (*alēthōs politikē technē*, 521e).[7]

I have no intention of reading such criticisms of democracy out of
the dialogue. They are too persistent and explicit to be explained
away by any (overly) ingenious interpretation. But I do offer a reading against the grain in a way that complicates the conventional un-

6. For the phrase "an authentic democrat" and the other quotations, see Neal Wood and
Ellen Wood, "Socrates and Democracy: A Reply to Gregory Vlastos," *Political Theory* 14
(1986): 55–83.

7. Because the word *epicheirein* can mean attempted or performed, there is an ambiguity
about what exactly Socrates is claiming for himself. For two different readings see *Plato:
Gorgias*, transl. with notes Terence Irwin (Oxford: Oxford University Press, Clarendon,
1979), and Vlastos, *Socrates, Ironist*. It is on the basis of this claim that I. F. Stone, *The Trial of
Socrates* (New York: Doubleday, 1988), calls the *Gorgias* "the most intemperate of all Plato's
dialogues" and "blushes" at his "outrageous self-promotion."

derstanding of the dialogue and opens democratic dimensions of it and Socrates. I argue that at a minimum, Socrates exposes indefensible understandings of democracy and is highly critical of democracy's critics, even when, as with Callicles, they present themselves as lovers of the demos. The question of who is and who is not a friend to democracy—of when being a critic of it makes one antidemocratic rather than a "prophet" calling one's people back to the best in their tradition and toward the most promising future—is worth asking if hard to answer. I also suggest that there are ways in which the Socrates of the *Gorgias* is genuinely sympathetic to aspects of democratic culture, though—and this is no minor proviso—it must be a democracy in which individual citizens are politically educated to think for themselves against the blandishments of sychophants and manipulators. Finally, and most speculatively, I think there are elements in Socrates' consideration of leadership and the dialogue's vision of the relationship between philosophical thinking and politics that make him and it "radically" democratic.

I

The *Gorgias* is a series of linked conversations between Socrates and the great rhetorician who gives the dialogue its title; his young, ardent, but not very adept pupil Polus; and a formidably ambitious would-be Athenian politician named Callicles, in whose home the exchange takes place.[8] But the dialogue does not begin there, and the fact that it moves from a public space to the privacy of a home is suggestive insofar as it anticipates other contrasts such as those between what is external, seen, and appears to be, and what is internal or interior, hidden, and really so; between what is spoken in public and what is spoken only in private; and between what is purposely displayed and what is unintentionally displayed by that display. Various characters in the dialogue are masked or disguise themselves, thinking to deceive others, though often inadvertently conspiring in self-deception. Deception and self-deception, insincere speech and an inability or unwillingness to hear, rhetorical posturings and strategic shifts of position to protect reputation all make dialogue impossible,

8. Callicles has been regarded as a uniquely powerful character in the Platonic corpus. Thus Eric R. Dodds in his commentary, *Plato's Gorgias* (Oxford: Oxford University Press, 1959), 267, sees Callicles as representing Plato's own impulse to power: "Plato paints himself here as he might have been, as he feared to be." Similar sentiments are expressed by Werner Jaeger, *Paideia*, vol. 2 (Oxford: Oxford University Press, 1944), 138.

which is why Socrates persists in trying to make Gorgias say what he means and why, later, he welcomes Callicles' frankness.

Socrates wants to know "who" Gorgias is, which means he wants to know about what Gorgias does, what he professes to teach, and the professed power of his art. At first Gorgias is reluctant to say what he does, in part because of his precarious position at Athens. As an outsider he must attract students willing to pay his fee. But to do that he must offer something distinctive and exciting: teaching conventional morality will not do. Yet the more unconventional his moral teachings, the more trouble he is in with the fathers of the sons who are attracted to him, and the more he is likely to "produce" students who reject the conventional morality that he seems, under Socrates' questioning, to believe in, for all his amoral posturings. Because everything he says is conditioned by his strategic dilemma, we can never know what to think: Does he believe his initially radical claims to teach anyone how to realize any ends they have, or are we to believe the more conventional view he later endorses, or is too ashamed to contravene, that he must and does teach the just use of rhetoric? Does he care for anything beyond his wealth and reputation? And if he does not, what does this—and his preoccupation with strategy—say about his politics and that of the city in which so many respect him? If rhetoric is merely persuasion without giving reasons, then, on his own terms, we have no reason to believe him and many reasons to distrust him.

There is another point about rhetoric as practiced and taught by Gorgias. As a foreigner he need not live with the consequences of what he says and does the way a citizen must. He may have to be concerned with his safety, but he will not have to fight in a war his students persuade the Assembly to undertake. Socrates' objection to rhetoric is not simply that it is rhetoric but that, as practiced by noncitizens, it is disconnected from a living community of fellow citizens. That is part of what this discussion about taking responsibility for one's students is about and part of what Socrates' true art of rhetoric involves. This good rhetoric is not only grounded in philosophy; it is also grounded in the political community as well as the community of interlocutors.

In fact, Gorgias seems to be a corrupter of democratic politics. He boasts that rhetoricians, as masters of language, provide men with the greatest degree of freedom and power. To be free is to have power over the powerful, which rhetoric supplies by enabling its students to persuade judges in the law courts, councilmen in the Boule, and citizens in the Assembly no matter what the actual merits of the case may be. Indeed, because the rhetorician can control any discourse, his is truly the master art. Without the power of rhetoric, the businessman would make money not for himself but for the man who did have such power, and the physician would be helpless in convincing a patient to take medicine if the rhetorician argues against him, even though the latter is utterly ignorant of medical matters. In fact, rhetoricians need know nothing about the world except how to appear to know about it before people who do not. But that means that Gorgias's power depends on the ignorance of the people. In the same way an audience knowledgeable about medicine would remain unmoved by rhetorical displays having to do with illness or cure, a politically educated citizenry would be unmoved by rhetorical displays of leaders who lacked judgment and wisdom. The rhetorician, then, has a stake not in educating the Athenians but in miseducating them. He is a teacher of disinformation.

But in fact Gorgias has no more real power than the political leaders he claims to make powerful. This lack of power is both particular and general. It is particular in the sense that neither Gorgias nor the political leaders he would advise know what he or they are doing. Nor have they thought about the world they are constituting. Gorgias does not recognize the consequences of his "teaching" until he sees them exemplified in the persons and politics of Polus and Callicles. It is who they are that shows him who he is. When he withdraws, it may be as much because he recognizes the implications of his teachings as revealed in their character as because Socrates has refuted him (or perhaps this revelation is the most powerful refutation Socrates can make). And when he reenters the dialogue, it is as Socrates' ally against Callicles, who is presenting an implication of Gorgias's own earlier argument.

Gorgias's lack of power is general because the drive for mastery, whether in the dialogue or the polity, and the longing, whether unacknowledged or declared, to be a tyrant are self- and polis-defeating. Tyrants *and* rhetoricians are, contrary to Gorgias's boast, the least rather than the most powerful and free, "if by power (*dunasthai*) one means something good (*agathon*) for the men who wield it" (466b). They may do what they think pleases them, but that is not the same as doing what is really good for them, and all of us want what is good for us. We always suppose our ends and the means we choose are somehow good. No one wishes to act unjustly since that will harm himself, and who in his right mind wants to harm himself? Thus anyone who acts unjustly does so unwillingly and unknowingly, not realizing that, for instance, his self-aggrandizement is actually a form of self-destruction. Because rhetoric is worse than useless in helping men distinguish between what they think is good and what is truly good, inasmuch as rhetoricians misidentify and confuse our rational, if unconscious,[9] desire for justice, rhetoricians make men weaker rather than stronger and worse rather than better.

Even worse, tyrants and rhetoricians are utterly dependent on the whims of their audience. Successful manipulation of others requires a servile hypersensitivity to every changing desire or mood of the person or people being manipulated, creating thereby an unseen dialectic of perverse dependency. Later, responding to Callicles' warning and threat that if he eschews rhetorical skills that allow him to dominate others, he will be powerless against those who wish to slap his face or take his money or banish him, Socrates insists that anyone who focuses all his energies to avoid victimization will exhaust himself anticipating the possible responses of his potential victimizers; for only complete conformity to their present and future desires can ensure his escape. But if, Zelig-like, he melds into whatever surroundings he is in, instead of standing out from them, he has no identity or independent purpose and so becomes an instrument for the purposes of others. Thus Gorgias, who claims to be the master of the mastering art of rhetoric, dances to the tune of the musicians. Thus Callicles, the man who will claim nature's sanction for his domination of his city, will be a slavish leader.

Although Gorgias initially insists that rhetoric is simply a neutral technique to be used for either good or ill and that if that technique is misused, it is the fault of the student, not the teacher, he soon changes his mind about rhetoric, but not about the responsibility of the teacher. Just because the rhetorician is capable of overpowering anyone on any topic because he can win over the multitude through the force of words, thereby robbing people of the honor, "is no reason why he should do so. . . . And if a man learns rhetoric, and then does injustice through the power of his art, we should not detest his teacher and exile HIM from the city for he has transmitted his art in the expectation that it will be used rightly. If it isn't, that is not his fault, but that of his student. So if anyone is to be banished it is the student, not the teacher" (457a–c). Provoked by Socrates, Gorgias changes his view once again, now claiming that the rhetorician can and must teach the right use of the technique along with the technique itself. All of these vacillations take place in a context in which

9. See the discussion in Charles Kahn, "Drama and Dialectic in Plato's *Gorgias*," in *Oxford Studies in Ancient Philosophy*, vol. 1, ed. J. Annas (Oxford: Oxford University Press, Clarendon, 1983), 75–122.

Gorgias is likening himself and his views to the democratic leaders of Athens which Socrates will criticize in terms that precisely invert Gorgias's present claims and denials.

If Gorgias is to teach the just use of rhetoric, he must know what justice is and that he is teaching what he thinks he is teaching, which in turn presupposes that his art is truly a techne. The only way to eliminate the disjunction between what a teacher teaches and what a student learns (which is a precondition for the strong claim of responsibility) is for the teacher to possess a techne. With the systematization of knowledge a techne requires, there is less dependence on chance and a greater likelihood of intentions controlling consequences. The only way to teach justice is for the teacher to *be* just. If he is, then his student will necessarily be so, since true knowledge is a form of power over the randomness of moral and political action.

The political analogue is that a leader must be just and possess a political techne to assure justice in his citizen/students, just as Socrates (perhaps ironically) claims he could do as the practitioner of the political art. But the argument and the analogy are complicated by the fact that Socrates was tried for corrupting the young and blamed, as he is now by I. F. Stone, for having students responsible for the violent antidemocratic takeover. And then, too, the accusations Socrates brings against Gorgias were also brought against him, and the question becomes Why was he not as good at "educating" his students as he insists Gorgias be in the education of his?

More than that, one of his students was Alcibiades, whom Socrates specifically invokes as a way of establishing a common ground with Callicles. But as Alcibiades was not only Socrates' student but Pericles' as well (he was the latter's ward), they share joint responsibility for their student's excesses. And that creates a kinship between Socrates and the man he accuses of being the worst political leader of all and against whom he offers himself as the one true practitioner of the political art. Finally, there is Socrates' own "failure" in the dialogue.

A similar complication arises when Gorgias assimilates the rhetorician's view of politics and leadership with that of the democratic leaders Socrates criticizes in his exchange with Callicles. Such assimilation is obviously useful because it legitimates his presence, justifies what he is doing, and makes his potential banishment an unpatriotic act. Yet however strategic the assimilation may be, its effect is to associate Gorgias's view of politics as manipulation, deceit, and domination for selfish ends with theirs. They were not "really" men who shared a public responsibility with relatively free and equal citizens but subtle tyrants, powerful and free because above the law. Later

Polus will make this connection more explicit by identifying democratic leaders with the tyrant Archelaus, and Callicles will provide
metaphysical justification for it. Since it is this assimilation that forms
the context and preface for Socrates' critique of Athenian democratic
leaders, it is not clear whether he is criticizing Pericles or "Pericles"—
whether his dispute is with what Pericles "really" was and did or with
a particular representation of Pericles which had come to legitimate a
corrupt understanding of democratic politics. In these terms, Socrates' critique may be an effort to save his native city from a corrupting
vision of itself.[10]

II

Socrates' conversation with Polus makes explicit the implications of
positions Gorgias refused to acknowledge as his own or was too
ashamed to defend consistently. Socrates had asked Gorgias who he
was, what he taught, and what, in consequence, his art produced in
the world. Now we have an answer: Polus.

Whereas Gorgias had inserted himself into the tradition of Athenian leaders, thereby redefining that tradition as he legitimated his
activity, Polus identifies those leaders with the notoriously ruthless
tyrant Archelaus. If Archelaus is the secret ideal of all political leaders, whether democratic or not, then the difference between him and
Pericles is simply cosmetic. Pericles was, on this account, a counterfeit democrat who insinuated himself with the demos so he could
dominate them. But then there is really no point in talking about a
"democratic" leader or trying to determine who is and who is not an
"authentic democrat." If, as ancient writers and their modern counterparts claim, tyranny is a particular danger in a democracy, either
because the purported disorder leads to tyranny or because democratic citizens furtively admire the tyrant whatever their professed respect for the law, then Socrates' attempt to exorcise the glamor of
tyranny and thus break the unholy alliance between the would-be tyrant and the many who surreptitiously envy him, even at their own
moral and political expense, makes the philosopher an ally of democracy. And if such secret admiration for the tyrant causes conflict
within the city and the soul, then anyone who prevents it can make

10. I do not mean to suggest that I find Plato's implicit portrait of Athens in the *Gorgias*
persuasive. Clearly he has his own political agenda, and the dialogues, like Greek tragedies,
are never simply historical reflections. But there is independent historical evidence of an
intellectual and political crisis in the early fourth century.

the claim to be practicing the political art, which is what Socrates claims as part of his critique of the "democratic" leaders.

What is the significance of a democracy honoring a tyrant like Archelaus? Does the honoring of tyranny abroad invite similar honoring of tyranny at home—or at the very least, undermine political and moral resistance to it? If it does and did, would that mean that someone who refused to honor foreign tyrants was contributing to a political culture that resisted tyranny and the demise of democracy at home?

Given democratic leaders who seek tyranny and democratic citizens all too likely to envy them for it, it is problematic for democrats to believe what Gorgias and Polus apparently do—that justice and right is whatever the majority says it is. With so many ignorant of who they really are and what they really want; with so few aware of what freedom, power, and happiness really are; with so many confused about what it means to be a democratic citizen and about the criteria for distinguishing between democratic leaders and tyrants, voting to decide which way of life or policy is best amounts to moral and political suicide.[11]

Polus has another role in the drama; he is a transitional figure between Gorgias and Callicles. The Archelaus that Polus praises had, by treachery and butchery, "risen" from slave to tyrant. Callicles will celebrate the man who, seizing power without compunction, smashes all conventional laws and limits, thus trampling the slave morality by which the masses thwart the assertion of (his) natural superiority. Thus the abstract question of whether an alliance with and praise for a tyrant abroad might not inspire tyranny at home is given force and answered by Callicles, a putative democratic leader and would-be tyrant of Athens.

III

For a number of reasons, Callicles is the test case for Socrates (and so for me). Because dialectic requires that men not hide their true feelings and that they share some common affections, Callicles rather than Gorgias or Polus is a worthy interlocutor. Unlike them, he is outspoken and sufficiently liberated from conventional morality to ex-

---

11. This is true of dialogue and of politics. The connection is made by Polus, whose evidence that Socrates' views are strange, absurd, out of place, unnatural, and disgusting (*schetlia, huperphuē, atopa*, 467b, 473a) is that "no one would assent to them," which would be clear if Socrates were to ask "any one in the present company" (473e).

plicitly justify Gorgias's covert and Polus's overt but confused admiration for tyranny. Like Socrates, he has two loves: Alcibiades and philosophy in the case of Socrates; the Athenian demos and Demos, son of Pyrilampes, in the case of Callicles. And there is something else the two of them share: Athenian citizenship. So the stakes of this conversation are at once greater and more particular.

There is a sense in which Callicles does display the virtues for which Socrates praises him. Whereas Polus was shamed into accepting the dictates of conventional morality that doing wrong is uglier than suffering it (*adikein aischion einai tou adikeisthai*, 482d), and Gorgias was shamed into conceding that he would teach justice along with rhetoric, because both men lacked the courage of their convictions (or argument), Callicles will say what is true without fear. And whereas Socrates has self-servingly confused his interlocutors by moving back and forth between nature and convention as it suits him, and purposely debased the conversation by turning it away from concern for the true nature of things into a popular harangue (*dēmēgorika*) on behalf of the usual moral banalities mouthed by the vulgar, Callicles will do neither (482e). In truth, nature (*phusis*) and convention (*nomos*) are often opposed; while convention dictates that doing wrong is worse than suffering it, nature teaches us that suffering wrong leaves one an impotent slave, unable to help oneself and one's friends, a "man" in name only, without a reason to live and little prospect of doing so. Conventional morality is an ideology and strategy devised by the slavelike majority to ensure that they, instead of their natural superiors, have pride of place. Once we realize that praise of equality and lawfulness by the weak is a tactic in a war for power rather than an objective good as the weak pretend, then we can (or will be forced to) look to the only objective standard left: nature. And nature teaches us that what is naturally superior should dominate what is inferior, that by the "law of nature" (*nomon phuseōs*)[12] what is better, stronger, and braver (*ameinō*), whether that be a state or an individual, is rightly master over what is not; that the one whose power enables him to accomplish things (*dunatōteron*) should discard all the contrived charms, legal niceties, and moral pieties that would shape and shackle him. Standing before us in the light of day as nature intended him, he would at once be thoroughly dominant and thoroughly just in the only sense of justice that can be defended. All of us, if we are honest, admire such a man. All of us, if we were honest, would want to be Xerxes.

12. In Greek this is a new and paradoxical phrase.

Socrates does not see this because philosophy blinds him to it. Callicles has nothing against philosophy. On the contrary, if practiced at the right time of life and in moderation, it is a significant part of a good education (*paideia*). But when mature men indulge in it at the expense of gaining worldly experience, when they prattle away with lisping little boys in corners instead of debating with men in the agora or Assembly, where something is really at stake, then philosophy is dangerous as well as frivolous because it leaves one lost in the political world and vulnerable to those who are not. Out of friendship, Callicles warns Socrates that his ignorance of public life will prevent him from succeeding in any noble enterprise (including presumably that of political education) or even protecting himself against unjust accusations that may lead to his death.

How then could dialectic possibly be liberating when it leaves men helpless and confused like some blind beggar or naïve child? How can it make men powerful when it leaves them despised in their own city, an outcast among compatriots, stripped of dignity, impugned with impunity? "How," Callicles asks, "can this be wisdom, Socrates, this art that takes a man with a good nature and makes him worse, unable to help himself or save himself or anyone else from the most serious dangers. . . ?" (486c). The charge Callicles makes, that philosophy makes someone worse, is precisely the charge Socrates brings against Pericles in defense of philosophy.

Socrates professes delight with Callicles' speech because it manifests the three essential qualities for testing the validity of an argument: knowledge (*epistēmēn*), good will (*eunoian*), and frankness (*parrēsian*) (487a). He is certain that whenever Callicles agrees about "any opinion my soul proposes, then it must be the whole truth about the subject under discussion: what a man's character ought to be, what he should study and up to what point. . ." (488a–c). But there are good reasons to question Callicles' frankness, Socrates' equation of their two loves, and so the possibility of dialogue between them. To begin with, there is something paradoxical about a frankness that is necessarily strategic, often unthinking, and so inconsistent. Socrates makes this argument in his elaboration of their respective loves.

While philosophy and the Athenian demos are equally imperious, they are very different in what they insist upon and what they do to their lovers. The demos requires that Callicles agree with everything it says if he is to keep its fickle and ever-shifting affections. This not only makes him a slave to the demos; it actually deprives him of any identity of his own. Without such an identity, Socrates is not talking with "Callicles" but with some similacrum or momentary representation of "him." For Socrates to talk with *someone*, he must detach Callicles from his love and unite Callicles with Callicles' own self. Only when Callicles is a friend to himself can there be friendship between Callicles and Socrates. As Callicles' initial professions of friendship become threats of what will happen to Socrates if he continues his unseemly love of philosophy, both prospects become highly problematic.

Philosophy may be imperious but it is not capricious. It is driven not by the whims of the multitude but by something more permanent and impersonal: the demands of reasoned argument. Thus loving philosophy allows Socrates to escape the obsequiousness necessary for tyrants, rhetoricians, or demagogues and permits him to fashion his own identity. Contrary to Callicles' belief, identity is not forged by the assertion of natural superiority. Nor is it understood by means of rhetoric. Rather, it emerges, and is recognized as emerging, through dialogue and dialectic. One has an interest, then, in dialogue and dialectic because one is "self" interested, though what the self and interest are is transformed in the process.

Moreover, Callicles does not love the demos, as Socrates suggests. That becomes clear in Callicles' second speech in praise of natural superiority. Socrates gets Callicles to acknowledge that physical prowess cannot be equated with moral capacity, and this for at least two reasons. The first is that because stronger, better, and superior are not coterminous (at least as Callicles seems to be defining them), "nature" would sanction the rule by three different kinds of people. The second, more significant for my analysis, is that if stronger means better and superior, and if the hoi polloi are naturally stronger than anyone inasmuch as they make the laws that regulate the individual, then they are also better. And because the opinion of the many, as Callicles represents them, is that justice consists in sharing equally and that it is uglier to do wrong than to suffer it, their opinions are true by nature. Either one must find a way of thinking about politics, morality, and nature independent of public opinion or accept the idea that they are what the majority says they are.

In response Callicles insists that Socrates has made a substantive mountain out of a verbal molehill. Obviously he meant that the strong were qualitatively better and superior. It was never a matter of mere numbers or sheer physical dominance. Callicles is equally impatient when, in response to his redefinition of strength and superiority as a matter of intelligence, Socrates uses examples of medicine, weaving, shoemaking, and farming to prove that the most intelligent should be in control because they will *not* take advantage of others. That is not the sort of intelligence Callicles means. For him, the truly strong man is one who combines intelligence with the tenacity, boldness, and courage to convert ideas into fact and so to dominate public life. It is naturally just that such men rule the city as they wish and in their own interests. Indifferent to the mob's incantations of moderation, they prefer the power and happiness that come from giving their passions free rein. What is beautiful and just by nature (*phusin kalon kai dikaion*) is marshaling all one's resources of mind and body to fulfill one's chosen passions with impunity. That is what it means to be powerful and why it is that the many who are unable or unwilling to follow this prescription censure and limit those who are. Thus they falsely "naturalize" notions of temperance, lawfulness, and justice in ways that allow the baser or lower to rule what is higher and better. If Socrates had the courage to really face the truth, he would admit that "luxuriousness, licentiousness and freedom (*truphē, akolasia, eleutheria*), when dominant, are really virtue (*aretē*) and happiness (*eudaimonia*); everything else is empty terms, mere conventions, contrary to nature, worthless nonsense" (492c).

In this exchange, Socrates presents himself as sharing the views of justice endorsed by the hoi polloi, while Callicles brutally rejects those views, calling the hoi polloi "a mob of slaves" and a "rabble of worthless men" (489c).[13] But if Callicles despises the demos, which Socrates had said he loved, then what should we make of the initial equations of which this claim is a part and of Socrates' insistence that those equations provide a ground for a dialogue capable of determining the truth of the subjects under discussion? If the contrasts that open the discussion with Callicles are so obviously and quickly subverted, what lesson should we draw about the other oppositions that frame the dialogue? And who is and who is not being frank here? If, as seems true, no one is frank in the sense Socrates praises, then perhaps it is in the nature of dialogue for some opacity and "rhetoricity" to be present because human exchanges, whether in the form of philosophical discussion or political deliberation, are contests as much as conversations.

Moreover, if the putative lover of democracy is contemptuous of it, perhaps the putative critic of it is the real friend. At the very least, we confront a question about what caring for the demos means and how to recognize the person who does so. Clearly protestations of affection are not enough, as they may well hide the enemy within the friend,

13. For evidence that Callicles is an aristocrat who despises the poor and egalitarianism in general, see 483b–c, 490a, and 512c–d.

just as "frank" criticism of democracy's faults may obscure the friend within the seeming enemy.

Or perhaps one should put the point somewhat differently: that Socrates and Callicles both love Athens, but they love very different conceptions of it, much as I have suggested that the argument over Pericles' leadership is an argument over which representation of Pericles is to be honored. Does Callicles represent the essential nature of democracy such that there must be an ineluctable conflict between philosophy and such politics, or is he a perverse product of a democracy whose perversity Socrates and philosophy seeks to reveal?

But whether Callicles and Socrates both love Athens, it is pretty clear that the sheer fact that they have loves does not, as Socrates implied it could, provide them with a ground for dialogue, let alone agreement. In fact, their respective loves drive them in different directions, toward incompatible lives. They differ about tyranny, freedom, happiness, power, leadership, and democracy and about how political discourse as a whole should be constituted and conducted or even whether such discourse as Socrates extols is even possible. The escalating animus that marks the recurring breakdowns in the conversation and the increasingly strained efforts to rebuild it indicate how the "founding" of a dialogue, even among fellow citizens, involves interest and power. The question, of course, is whether this is ever *not* the case: whether there can be a discourse that provides a common ground while acknowledging the contestable origins of that ground, or whether we are left with more or less disguised tyrants and mute contests of force, in spite of all our talk.

The prominence of Alcibiades in the equation is an additional complication. It is not simply that there is evidence within and outside the Platonic corpus that Alcibiades shares some of the traits and views propounded by Callicles, but that, as I have already argued, Alcibiades is a figure that draws Socrates and Pericles closer together. If Alcibiades epitomizes a democracy gone wrong, and if neither Pericles nor Socrates were able to prevent him from further corrupting the city he would lead, any more than Socrates is able to prevent Callicles from pursuing his similar political ambitions, then the charge leveled by Socrates against the Athenian political leaders cannot be read literally or accepted uncritically. But how *is* it to be read?

The prelude to Socrates' critique of rhetoric consists of demeaning analogies that precipitate both the dissolution of the putative friendship Callicles claimed for him and the unraveling of whatever dialogue had been taking place between them. Socrates pushes Callicles to distinguish between good and bad pleasures, thereby undermining the latter's initial view that happiness, freedom, and power were embodied in the tyrant's life of self-indulgence, the definition of politics as domination that underlies and follows from it, and the nature of rhetoric that fails to make the distinction and so perpetuates the view and the definition.

Socrates likens rhetoric to cooking: both direct their efforts at producing pleasure without regard to the soul's best interests. Ignorant of what they are really doing, rhetoricians and cooks are unable to provide an account of their "power" or purpose, which is why the two exercises are nothing more than irrational routines that encourage a similar irrationality in their audience. Instead of improving the souls of their fellow citizens and helping define the public good as philosophy and good political leaders do, rhetoricians flatter the citizens while advancing their own private agendas. There *may* be a form of rhetoric that is not subject to such charges, but Socrates doubts Callicles has ever even run across it, at least up until now. But it can, presumably, exist, just as there can, presumably, be a way of life superior to that of the tyrant and a way of doing democratic politics different from the way Callicles and (his) Athenians now do it. If it does exist, its task would be to adumbrate that other way of life and conception of politics.

Callicles disagrees; he *has* seen such rhetoric practiced by the great Athenian leaders of the past: Themistocles, Cimon, Miltiades, and Pericles. It is this claim that evokes Socrates' argument defining the art of politics and the absence of such an art in the practices of the Athenian leaders Callicles names. These leaders, Socrates insists, were rhetoricians in the old sense, not the new one. All they did was gratify desires, not educate them, and as a result, made themselves and everyone else worse than they were before. And if a good citizen is one who makes his fellow citizens better, Pericles could hardly have been a good citizen; for among the Athenians he had supposedly improved, he had a worse reputation at the end of his leadership than he had at the beginning. (Similar stories can be told about Cimon, Themistocles, and Miltiades.) Surely there is something absurd about calling such a man a good leader, for the same reason that it would be absurd to call an animal trainer competent when the horses he trained became uncontrollable. Surely it is irrational for such leaders to whine about their unjust treatment and invoke their great services to the city when the latter turns against them. "This is a total lie. Not a single leader of a city could be unjustly ruined by the city over which he exercises authority" (519c). The situation of such a leader parallels that of a teacher who professes to teach virtue but then goes on to accuse his student of cheating him out of money or gratitude.

It is no surprise that this is too much for Callicles. He had entered the fray provoked by Polus's admission of what *he*, Callicles, is now unable to refute. He was aware at the outset that if Socrates was right, then the world as he understood it was upside down. Now Socrates seems right. Yet what is right still seems absurd, and so Callicles begins to withdraw from the dialogue, first feigning ignorance, then angrily refusing to answer at all (he now says he only answered to please Gorgias), insisting that Socrates either end the conversation, continue it with another, or do openly what Callicles implies he does anyway: talk to himself.

Yet Callicles does not, yet, fully withdraw but oscillates between sullen agreement, contemptuous dismissal, and genuine attraction to Socrates.[14] Although the conclusions seem absurd and are totally at odds with Callicles' initial assertions, the life he has chosen to lead, and the kind of man he has already become, something about what Socrates says and who he is draws Callicles back into the discussion despite defeats and frustrations. "I do not know how it is," Callicles says later, "but your words attract me, Socrates. Yet as with most people, you do not quite convince me" (513c).[15]

Socrates believes he knows why: love of the demos makes Callicles resist him and dialectic. If Callicles could be distanced from that love, he might accept dialectic as a competition in which participants vie with each other to discover a common good (*koinon . . . agathon*) that benefits them all. Though Callicles (among others) supposes Socrates to have answers to his questions before he asks them, so that "dialogue" is merely a masked monologue, Socrates denies this. "You must remember," he assures him, "that I have no more knowledge than you do when I ask and speak but rather join in a common search with you; so that if my opponent has any substance in what he says, I will be the first to acknowledge it" (506a). If Callicles learned this lesson, if he came to understand that, at least in the case of dialectic, there is such a thing as the general interest, he might, then, become a political leader similarly dedicated to the good of the whole city. In this sense and way, philosophical argument could be a form of political education and the art of dialectic a kind of political art, at least insofar as politics too can or should be deliberation about a common good. Of course it remains to be seen whether politics, or more point-

14. Callicles is deeply divided between admiring the courageous independent life of the philosopher, which he initially believed to be effeminate, and the life of the tyrant, which he initially thought courageous and independent but now sees as slavish. He can neither talk with Socrates nor stop talking to him, and so Socrates' "failure" may not be one.

15. When Callicles interjects (481c), he asks Socrates if he was joking, because if he was "serious and what you say is true, won't human life have to be turned completely upside down and everything we do seemingly the opposite of what we should do?"

edly, democratic politics, can be that way and whether dialectic is an appropriate "political" ideal.

Political authority depends on the possession of the political art, which, like the art of any craftsman, is guided by a definite form or end (*eidos*) in the organization of the city or soul. Only a man who possesses that art can be just, temperate, and virtuous; only he is free and able to choose what desires are worth satisfying, when, and how. It makes no more sense to allow a diseased soul to decide on what is good for it than to allow a fevered body to decide what food or drink it needs.

By suggesting that Callicles lacks this art and these virtues, Socrates challenges the former's capacity to judge who is and who is not a political leader. Callicles knows no more about the matter than the rhetoricians he admires know about the world they propose to master. Thus how can he, with his view of power that would destroy the community he hopes to rule, decide what constitutes good leadership? How can a man who embraces the endless torment of trying to slake every whim and who regards his fellow citizens as potential enemies and is an enemy to himself and to the gods, rightly assess which rulers are worthy of emulation? What proof have we that Callicles has the slightest idea of what is entailed by leadership and could himself lead? He cannot name any citizen who became less unjust, licentious, or stupid because of being associated with him or even identify a teacher who has become so. If Callicles' own life is in disarray (which it must be if he admires tyrants), then he is an unlikely candidate to make the life of another more orderly, less likely still to put collective life in any order. Callicles has never asked himself about his qualifications for pursuing the career in public life he thinks is his due. Given who he is, what he aspires to be, and what he admires, Socrates' challenge of and to him can hardly be deemed antidemocratic. Indeed, Socrates' exposure of Callicles, his critique of tyranny, and his insistence that, however deficient the many are en masse, individually they are the equal of supposedly "superior" men, all suggest the opposite.[16]

But what about the idea of a political art whose aim and skill lie in "making" citizens as good as possible, "prescribing for them as a physician" in accordance to some agreed upon procedures that every craftsman adopts to produce his "product?" Surely it is preferable to have political problems dealt with by men who have mastered a rational and dependable method rather than by the haphazard, irrational, hit-or-miss approach that must characterize the many. Experts

16. Vlastos argues this in *Socrates, Ironist*, 18.

cannot be seduced by the blandishments of self-serving political leaders and ignorant rhetoricians. But then is this not precisely a kind of antidemocratic social engineering, a rule of experts possessing special knowledge rather than rule by the people, based on their shared knowledge?

Socrates does put forward some such view, and in some of its forms it does seem antidemocratic. He also seems to believe that possessing the political art means that no accidents of character or situation can excuse a statesman who fails to control the actions of those he leads or a teacher who fails to control the actions of his students. Socrates is not just oblivious to such complexities; his rendering of the circumstances Athenian leaders confronted is perversely selective. Finally, Socrates does regard majority rule as an absurd way of deciding any issue of import. Surely all of this substantiates the claim that Socrates is antidemocratic. It even suggests that he is politically simpleminded in the way most moralists are.

Socrates objects to voting under any circumstances and by any group of people, including oligarchs and audiences present at philosophical encounters such as we see in the *Gorgias*. No one who appears before a crowd can be a political educator, not because the hoi polloi are individually incapable of learning how to think seriously about political and moral matters but because the dynamics of a crowd, particularly one subject to the rhetorical skills of a Gorgias, erodes the capacity to think. One could put Socrates' challenge this way: What must people know and what sort of character must they be assumed to have before counting votes makes sense? Supposing they do not know enough or do not have the "right" character? And who is to judge and how can "we" not judge? The answer to that challenge, given by even the staunchest democrats, has often relied on such notions as false consciousness, manufactured consent, the general will, democratic centralism, ideal speech situations, and a broad imperative to unmask or demystify, all of which in certain cases presuppose something like a political techne.

But what about the claim to mastery promised by the new form of rhetoric? It is worth recalling that this claim emerged as a counter and political obverse to the claims to mastery proclaimed by Gorgias, Polus, and Callicles. Rhetoric as Gorgias practices it promises political mastery for private, antipolitical aims; teaches its students how to reduce others to one's will and to a means; persuades by flattery rather than on the basis of facts, which it needs to obscure in order to maintain its control; and exacerbates the disharmonies in the soul and the divisions in the city. Political techne, on the other hand, promises comparable mastery for shared ends, treats others as ends or as temporary means so they *can* be treated as ends, and convinces others on the basis of knowledge and so reduces disharmonies and divisions. But there is evidence that this polarity between rhetoric and expertise which frames the argument is itself inadequate and reductive and that the posited control, of which both boast, is impossible and undesirable. What is that evidence?

Socrates offers at least three different analogies between a possible political art and other arts, and each has a different political implication. One likens political techne to a craft like shoemaking, where the material worked on is utterly passive. The second likens political techne to animal training. Here the "object" of the skill is animate but only peripherally "participates" in its own "domestication." An unbridgeable inequality between the material and the artist remains.

Now one thing that distinguishes a techne from a mere knack is its ability to render a rational account of its aim and procedures. Presumably that account does not much interest the leather or a dog. But it does interest a patient, which suggests how the third analogy, that between a doctor who prevents or cures illness of the body and a political craftsman who prevents or cures political and psychic illness, is of a different order. In medicine the "material actively participates in its own physical regeneration." As opposed to Gorgias, Socrates supposes that a good doctor-patient relationship means that the former "would himself persuade his patient to accept treatment, not by using rhetoric but by explaining to him the cause of his symptoms and the rational basis of the prescriptions proposed."[17] But even more significant, a healthy man would be allowed to do what he wants, and this, admits Terence Irwin, who is otherwise unsympathetic to a "democratic" Socrates, "would have surprising results for Socrates' claims about political authority: it would apparently make the expert's control only temporary."[18]

Still, this seems an exaggeration that does not quite meet the objection. For Socrates, even here, apparently conflates political education, "the joining with one's equals in assuming the effort of persuasion and running the risk of failure" in common deliberations about public matters, with education that permits "the dictatorial intervention based on the absolute superiority of the adult" and relies on some blueprint to ensure success. Hannah Arendt regards this confusion

17. Dodds, *Plato's Gorgias*, 211.
18. Irwin, *Plato: Gorgias*, 216. Even if there is no political techne or expert (*technikos*), the search for him and for the grounds of his expertise may lead us to knowledge of how to act politically and morally which we could not have gained in other ways.

and the very idea of politically educating adults as "coercion without the use of force."[19] Even political artists as doctors will not do. One could say, using Arendt's own categories,[20] that the man with political techne is not a ruler but a lawgiver; and in times of severe moral and political crises, a lawgiver may need to give laws not to the whole community but to its members singularly, so that they can become more of a community, at least to the extent that they can then engage in political deliberation and moral discussion.

But all these qualifications and emendations still accept the idea that Socrates regards some form of political techne as necessary and desirable. But it is not clear that he in fact does. If there is any ultimate authority in the dialogue, it is dialectic itself. Now however much Socrates may depart from the canons of dialectic as he explicitly defines them, and in whatever ways Plato signals its insufficiencies, or we, following Nietzsche and Jean-François Lyotard, regard it as enervating or covertly tyrannical, dialectic does require the active participation of the interlocutors in a way even the doctor-patient relationship does not. Moreover, dialectic can be taught and practiced by any intelligent person of good character, a claim Callicles cannot accept. Indeed for Callicles, politics is all a matter of leadership, not citizenship. But then a different dimension of Socrates' critique of "Pericles" appears, one less directed at the latter's failures than at the paradox of "democratic leadership" or authority. In this dimension, Pericles is not a good political leader because leadership as usually constructed and practiced deprives citizens in a democracy of the responsibility for shaping the conditions of their intellectual and political lives. In arguing this, I am not denying that Socrates castigates democratic leaders for catering to, rather than educating, the desires of the citizenry, though I think much of that criticism is directed at a particular construction of those leaders popular among antidemocrats like Callicles. I am arguing that his objection may be deeper and more provocative; that the very emphasis on leadership itself is part of the problem. In these terms, Socrates' claim to be the sole practitioner of the art of politics means that he alone refuses to accept a kind of leadership (in politics and in the dialogue) that deprives (or relieves) citizen-interlocutors of their moral, political, and intellectual responsibilities.

For another thing, if Socrates possesses political techne in the way

19. Hannah Arendt, "What Is Education?" in *Between Past and Future*, enlarged ed. (Baltimore: Penguin, 1968), 176–77.
20. See, e.g., her distinction between poiesis, which is a legitimate activity for the lawgiver but not for the political actor, and praxis, which is appropriate only in the public: Hannah Arendt, *The Human Condition* (Garden City, N.Y.: Doubleday, Anchor, 1959), sec. 27.

Pericles did not, what do we make of his failure with Callicles in the dialogue and with Alcibiades and Critias outside of it? It may well be that such "failure" is essential for the success Socrates cares for, which is not the kind of success that seems mandated by the political art he praises in opposition to the one celebrated by his interlocutors. For the art we see demonstrated by Socrates in the dialogue (or by Plato through it) does not "produce" good citizens in the sense a craftsman produces good shoes. If the point is to have us not just think what Socrates thinks but to think like him—which Socrates encourages by simultaneously asserting his ignorance and being confident in his arguments—then there can be no passive acceptance of doctrinal instruction, whether emanating from the ministrations of an expert, the lessons of a teacher, or the injunctions of a political leader. This combination of confidence and assertion of ignorance pushes readers to think through "the central affirmations, denials, and reasoned suspensions" of the dialogue.[21] It may even push them outside the boundaries of dialectic and in the process call into question the identification of philosophy with dialectic and perhaps that of Plato with Socrates as well. One might even say that the architecture of the *Gorgias* is more inclusive than its arguments, or provides a counterpoint to them.

Socrates' "failure" with Callicles—the contradictions between the idea of authority as posited by dialectic and that presupposed by the notion of expertise and the tension between his claim that there are truths and his insistence that he is uncertain of them—is reiterated and rooted in the tension inherent in the movement of language, which marks the *Gorgias* as a whole. The dialogue holds out the promise of constructing a consistent, rigorous moral language out of the complex and inconsistent materials present in ordinary speech—a language that would permit new possibilities for self and community to emerge. But the hope remains unfulfilled, perhaps necessarily so, because self and community cannot be "rigorous" and consistent the way argument can. Here again the seductions of mastery are explored and even extolled, but also exposed and dissipated. In Mikhail Bakhtin's terms, the dialogue presents two competing verbal-ideological worlds: one in which language works as a centripetal force moving to impose a firm, stable linguistic meaning and performance on the discussion; the other in which it pushs toward decentralization and segmentation, as fissures and discontinuities disrupt the exchanges.

21. The quote is from Vlastos, who goes on to talk about disavowals voiced "at the conclusion of entirely successful eclectic argument in which Socrates has, to all appearance, proved his thesis to the hilt" (*Socrates, Ironist,* 84, 50).

"Every utterance of a speaking subject," Bakhtin writes, "serves as a point which both forces are brought to bear. Thus language is full of contradictions, tensions between two embattled tendencies."[22] One might even say that this movement of language is itself democratic.

IV

Dialectic as Socrates employs it emerges as critical of the enemies of democracy, including those who may not know they are, because they have been seduced by ideas of power and leadership that would destroy democratic culture. By standing against the vision of freedom and happiness celebrated by Gorgias and Callicles, Socratic political art enables men to develop those qualities of mind and character that make democratic citizenship possible. Dialectic insists that participants in the conversation take responsibility for what they say and do, that they render considered judgments rather than ceding responsibility to others. Citizens must think for themselves and make informed judgments about the character of their own lives as well as (and in order to) make such judgments about would-be leaders. All this contrasts with the miseducation for private gain implicitly endorsed by Gorgias as well as by many political insiders of our own day.

But dialectic is more than a tool for criticizing democracy's enemies; it is, as this discussion has implied, an idealized analogue of democratic deliberation, a fact that gives further substantiation to my claim that Socrates has good reasons to announce that he is the one true practitioner of the political art.[23] As participators in the dialogue must take responsibility for what they say and are, so must citizens. And as every participant in the conversation is or should be the educator of every other, so too should every citizen think of himself as a political educator as well as a political learner.

As we saw, Socrates insists that neither dialogue nor politics can be a war of all against all because both require a common search for something larger than self-interest or self-aggrandizement. As participants in dialectic welcome refutation because it reduces the divisions

22. Mikhail Bakhtin, *The Dialogic Imagination*, ed. Michael Holquist, trans. Caryl Emerson and Michael Holquist (Austin: University of Texas Press, 1981), 272.

23. Referring to the *Gorgias*, Dodds says that "philosophy is politics by other means" (384, quoting V. De Magalhaes-Vilhene, *Socrate et le legende platonicienne*). There are obvious dangers in regarding philosophical dialogue as even an ideal analogue insofar as such an ideal elides inequalities of power and the presence of conflict, which remain dimensions of politics. My argument is that Socrates does not elide them but, in fact, suggests the "political" dimension of philosophical dialogue.

in the soul and increases the likelihood of arriving at the truth, so participation in political deliberation should involve a willingness to accept "defeat" if a better policy for the whole is proposed, thereby reducing divisions within the city. Similarly, to be a friend to oneself and to one's fellow citizens requires comparable qualities and commitments: the full recognition of the value of self and other in a universe of two is analogous to recognition of the value of self and others in the context of citizenship. When Socrates speaks of truth as larger than the particular interests of those engaged in its pursuit, or insists on pushing ahead for the sake of the argument rather than for the sake of any individual involved in it, he may be proposing a political ideal.

But this is too neat and too easy. Not only does Socrates (or Plato) hold out philosophy as a political ideal; he also—perhaps uniquely in this dialogue—politicizes philosophy. When Socrates speaks of (or we see) the fragility of sustaining conversation, or the difficulty of arriving at mutually satisfactory definitions (not to mention agreement about what constitutes a worthy life); when we see Socrates' failure or the way philosophical distinctions give way to explosions of anger, it becomes clear that establishing a dialogic community, no less than a political one, involves complicated negotiations of power. Insofar as philosophy is politicized in this way, it becomes less a search for truth than for truthfulness, in the sense of mutually establishing acceptable grounds for speech and action and opposing their reduction to rhetorical strategies of manipulation. But if it is politicized, philosophy cannot then ignore the way such grounds (as well as the conversations made possible thereby) are established within larger cultural contexts. Nor can it ignore particular subtexts that inscribe inequalities of power or "nonrational" factors elided by divorcing philosophy and politics. In almost all other dialogues, and some of the time in this one, Socrates refuses to accept any desires, interests, or identities of actual people as a legitimate source of justification for political practices and institutions because people are too misguided, self-destructive, and ignorant. In other places, such "false consciousness" is either transformed or made harmless by reasoned argument or appropriate myths, but I think the *Gorgias* holds out another, more democratic possibility despite Socrates' failure with Callicles. The possibility is that "false consciousness" may be lessened, if not dissipated, by a form of education that is politically and philosophically democratic because the risks of dialogue are mutual and the grounds for accommodation remain debatable, including what the mix of knowledge and power is at any moment.

But there is yet another voice in the *Gorgias*, one that creates a problem for any putative analogy between dialectic or philosophy and politics. It is a voice that reminds us of the conditions of Socrates' death. At several points in the dialogue, Callicles warns Socrates about what will happen to him if he insists on pursuing philosophy at the expense of more manly pursuits, such as politics and rhetoric. Socrates shows disdain for any threats about being tried, not because he thinks himself immune to future prosecution but because of the knowledge he has of the reasons he would be put to death: he is one of the few, if not the only one, who attempts the true art of politics; and his trial will be "like a physician tried before a jury of children on the accusation of a cook" (521e) and condemned because the medicine he prescribes to cure their illness is not sweet enough. In place of the "services" rendered by Themistocles and Pericles, which actually did corrupt the young, *he*, Socrates, will be accused of doing so because, spurning such "services," he will make the young question their lives and traditions, in public as in private. This, and the fact that he has never said or done anything unjust to man or gods, is both his service to the city and his defense. If he is convicted for this service, he will face death with the composure appropriate for a man who will come before the judges in Hades unburdened with the evils that afflict the men Callicles praises and the man he would become.

The harshest judgments made and the worst punishment administered by these judges will be against those whose repeated acts of extreme injustice have left them incurable. Almost certainly these men will be "tyrants, kings, despots, and politicians," those whose exercise of irresponsible power has been so admired by Polus and Callicles. By suffering the most painful and fearful torments, they will finally render a real service, as object lessons, for those who secretly admire or would publicly emulate their lives of counterfeit freedom, power, and happiness. Though highly unlikely, it is not altogether impossible to find a good man among statesmen, one who can justly manage what public affairs are entrusted to him (526b). Such a man deserves the greatest respect for resisting the temptations to do wrong that inevitably plague the life of power. Such a man was Aristides.[24] Outside of such exceptional men, the other man most worthy of respect is the

24. The mention of Aristides just confuses things further. That Socrates praises any political leader is significant in suggesting that the kind of political techne he admires may have existed in the past (but see Irwin, *Plato: Gorgias*, 247). Demosthenes links Pericles and Aristides, and though Plutarch contrasts Aristides' rectitude with Themistocles' deviousness while suggesting they were rivals if not bitter enemies, other sources insist they became allies. Still others blame Aristides for being *overly* democratic in opening up the franchise to men who did not meet a minimum income requirement.

philosopher who has lived a life dedicated to the cultivation of truth while declining to meddle in the affairs of others. Concerned above all to present a healthy soul to the ultimate judges, the philosopher willingly relinquishes the honors and power coveted by others.

The myth of the trial in the court of Hades provides a transcendent dimension to the dialogue and the argument, making the projected trial of Socrates and the techniques advocated by Callicles to avoid it or prevail in it, seem insignificant by comparison. It also recasts as it summarizes the issues of the dialogue, such as the relation between nature and convention,[25] philosophy and rhetoric, the life of justice opposed to the life of tyranny. And it returns us, dramatically as well as substantively, to the opening scene with its contrast between what is public and private, what appears or seems to be and what is really so. Finally, the myth concludes a journey that has become a theodicy.

Perhaps Callicles will be intrigued by the idea of the greater advantage offered by living a good life, or be momentarily intimidated by the vision of horrific punishment meted out against the kind of man he wishes to be. More likely, as a realist, he will not be sufficiently moved by it to change his mind. We cannot know, because he is silent and Socrates is left, still and again, to talk alone. In dramatic terms, the dialogue has become a monologue, and Socrates a mirror image of Gorgias, who was so confident in his abilities that he was unable to hear others and so, himself.

Socrates invites his recalcitrant interlocutors to be his companions on a journey that will lead to happiness in this life and the next. Only after they have completed their journey and practiced virtue together will it be appropriate for them to engage in public life or to deliberate about whatever may interest them. But in their present condition, miseducated, misinformed, and ignorant as they are about the subjects of the greatest importance, it would be presumptuous to make

---

25. The beginning of the *Gorgias* was about disguise; the end is about nakedness, with everything revealed. The myth is also a response to Callicles, not only because Socrates throws the latter's words back in his face (cf. 525a and 486a–d) but because it is only on the day of judgment, when standing naked before naked gods, that we can know what Callicles claimed to know: the nature of men. He has proven himself a creature of culture, not nature, and what he says and does makes sense only within already established social and moral relationships. On this whole issue, see Alasdair MacIntyre, *A Short History of Ethics* (New York: Collier, 1966), 188: "What Callicles calls our 'natural' beliefs represent for Socrates the artificial values imposed upon us from without by such corrupting influences as a Gorgianic rhetorical education. . . . What Callicles dismisses as society's merely conventional values represent for Socrates what men believe by nature." Thus philosophy liberates us from those conventional notions of what is natural. See also Richard McKim, "Shame and Truth in Plato's *Gorgias*," in *Platonic Writings/Platonic Readings*, ed. Charles L. Griswold, Jr. (New York: Routledge, Chapman and Hall, 1988), 139.

the claims or express the aspirations that have characterized the interlocutors. Rather, they should take the truths revealed by their discussion as a guide to pursuing virtue and justice, abandoning the path
Callicles extols; for his way "has no value whatsoever" (527e).

V

Yet if Socrates were right, the *Gorgias* would be far less than it is:
polyphonous, and provocative, forcing its readers to confront the tensions and conflicts it seems so anxious to resolve, intriguing them with
a heretical ambivalence at the heart of its surface confidence. Callicles
is neither silenced nor banished but remains present, not just on the
margins, warning philosophy of its own ignorance, but at the center
as well, mocking philosophy's denial of its will to power. Occasionally,
as with Nietzsche, Callicles has his revenge; and when he does, the
concluding myth and last lines of the dialogue become rewritten.

The *Gorgias*, perhaps uniquely among Platonic dialogues, has an
extraordinary generative capacity. It gives birth to configurations that
confound its form, to energies that trespass its explicitly stated boundaries, and to voices that "interrogate" its closures, much like the democratic culture we see portrayed, either admiringly or critically, in
drama, Herodotus, and Thucydides.

It was said that the Athenians never stopped talking. Neither does
the *Gorgias*, a hardly surprising fact, given how much it owed to vital,
if imperfect, democratic culture.

III

ATHENIAN
IDEALS
AND
CONTEMPORARY
ISSUES

CHRISTOPHER ROCCO

8 *The Tragedy of*
   Critical Theory

The title of my essay is both provocative and ambiguous. It is provocative because it juxtaposes ancient tragedy to contemporary Critical Theory in a way that suggests the former can contribute to an understanding of the modern themes and concerns that occupy the latter. That the Greek polis and its thought can help us make sense of our times is implausible today, not only because freedom for a few male citizens was based on institutionalized slavery, the exclusion of women from public life, and pronounced social inequalities, but also, and perhaps more important, because Greek thought was innocent of the complexities of a structurally differentiated and functionally interdependent modern society. Better to leave the ancient polis and its contents to the philologists and historians of antiquity: the problems generated by the modern nation-state demand a commensurately modern social and political theory. Why turn to the Greeks and tragedy when there are so many other sources more appropriate and more easily appropriated? Surely it makes more sense to read a modern text (and modern social transformations) in the theoretical tradition initiated by Marx, Durkheim, and Weber. This essay directly challenges such assumptions, though not because modern social theory is irrelevant either to Critical Theory or to the modern social developments that concern it. Rather, I argue that Max Horkheimer and Theodor Adorno's *Dialectic of Enlightenment* reinserts the ancient sense of the tragic into their theorizing in a way that alerts us to the tremendous losses suffered in the name, and for the sake, of modernity—losses that liberal and radical theorists alike have largely ignored.

My purpose is not to argue that such theorists have been wrong in their analyses and assessments of modernity, so much as incomplete. If Charles Segal is right, then Greek tragedy can help "modern man . . . to confront the darker side of his own existence and explore beneath the surface of his own highly rationalized, desacralized, excessively technologized culture"[1] and so provide a useful corrective to the pervasive view of history as unmitigated progress.

My title is not only provocative but ambiguous as well; "The Tragedy of Critical Theory" suggests at least two meanings. First, it alludes to a heroic struggle fought by the Critical Theorists against the regressive advances of enlightenment: what Horkheimer and Adorno saw to be the irresistible development toward total social integration. The story of Critical Theory, then, constitutes both a theoretical and a political tragedy. Horkheimer and Adorno came to see social freedom and enlightened thought not as moments of a reconciled totality but as opposite poles of an irreconcilable dialectic. Nevertheless, the authors faced this pessimistic conclusion with heroic intransigence, themselves admitting that "critical thought (which does not abandon its commitment even in the face of progress) demands support for the residues of freedom and for tendencies toward true humanism, even if these seem powerless in regard to the main course of history."[2] Against all theoretical and political opposition, Horkheimer and Adorno never stopped resisting forces of integration that appeared to them as implacable as archaic fate.

Critical Theory, however, has more than just a tragic history to recommend it. It also has a tragic consciousness. Horkheimer and Adorno are thus more than tragic figures caught in a web of fate not wholly of their own making. They are also playwrights of a sort, composing a drama about the vicissitudes of enlightenment. The "tragedy" of Critical Theory thus refers to the tragic elements and the tragic sensibility that Horkheimer and Adorno bring to their theorizing. The *Dialectic of Enlightenment* is thus a modern tragedy, even though its authors were convinced that the culture industry made tragedy impossible. That it *is* a work of tragedy in such an antitragic climate makes the *Dialectic* untimely, and, if we are to believe Nietzsche, it is precisely this untimeliness that recommends it.[3]

---

1. Charles P. Segal, "Greek Tragedy and Society: A Structuralist Perspective," in *Interpreting Greek Tragedy: Myth, Poetry, Text* (Ithaca: Cornell University Press, 1986), 23.

2. Max Horkheimer and Theodor W. Adorno, *Dialectic of Enlightenment: Philosophical Fragments* (1947), trans. John Cumming (New York: Seabury, Continuum, 1969), Preface to the 1969 ed., ix.

3. For Nietzsche, the point in studying the thought of the classical past was its ability to

I am suggesting, then, that Horkheimer and Adorno's *Dialectic of Enlightenment* constitutes an example of how the themes, style, and language of Greek tragedy can provide a point of reference and a source of inspiration for theorizing in and about the present. As I have indicated, this means reading a work of contemporary theory in terms provided by Greek tragedy and as a modern tragedy, a tragedy of enlightenment. I elaborate similarities, first in structure, then in content, and finally in aim, shared by both Greek tragedy (as that is represented by Sophocles' *Oedipus the King*) and *Dialectic of Enlightenment* to give substance to my claim that there is a use, in our time, for the thought of the classical polis.[4]

I

By structure I mean not only the obvious characteristics of a work's form—whether it be a play, a dialogue, a novel, or a treatise—but also its style, sensibility, and tone; the kinds of images it uses and evokes; the texture of its language and the architecture of its composition; the rhetorical strategies it employs to persuade its readers (or audience) and the way in which these *form*al elements work with or against a text's explicit or surface argument.

The *Dialectic of Enlightenment* recalls the structure, style, and sensibility of Greek tragedy in at least five ways.[5] First, unlike a philosophical or theoretical treatise, but like tragedy, the work of Horkheimer and Adorno embodies a dramatic or dialogic form. In collaborative effort, the authors join two distinct voices in a single work. As they themselves acknowledge, the vital principle of the book is "the tension between the two intellectual temperaments conjoined in it."[6] The two

act "counter to our time and thereby . . . on our time and, let us hope, for the benefit of a time to come" ("On the Uses and Disadvantages of History for Life," in *Untimely Meditations*, trans. R. J. Hollingdale [London: Routledge and Kegan Paul, 1983], 60).

4. My reading of the *Dialectic* is a rather sympathetic one. I am not overly concerned to defend some of its more contentious claims, for instance, that German fascism is to be deduced from the logic of the dominant ratio itself, that modernity has abolished the individual, or that the culture industry lacks critical content. There is something of the true and the false in those claims, and they deserve consideration on their own merit elsewhere. I am more concerned here that the work of Horkheimer and Adorno be taken seriously again; that it be read in the context of Greek tragedy; and that Greek tragedy and classical thought in general be recognized as valuable sources for thinking about contemporary problems. The value of *Dialectic of Enlightenment* lies in its ability to teach us *how to think* about the world of people and things, which, like Greek tragedy, it does by both precept and example.

5. Martha C. Nussbaum, *The Fragility of Goodness: Luck and Ethics in Greek Tragedy and Philosophy* (New York: Cambridge University Press, 1986), makes this argument, 122–32, for the relationship between Greek tragedy and Plato's dialogues.

6. Horkheimer and Adorno, *Dialectic of Enlightenment*, ix.

different voices united in the book achieve the plurality of positions, viewpoints, and arguments that define tragedy's concern with moral communication and debate. Multiple voices lend the *Dialectic* a certain multidimensionality that contributes to an open-ended and on-going model of communication, rather than a declamatory, authoritative, or monologic model. By presenting multiple positions and so multiple points of engagement, Horkheimer and Adorno encourage the reader, in Martha Nussbaum's analysis of tragedy, to "enter critically and actively into the give and take of debate much as a spectator of a tragedy is invited to reflect about the meaning of events on stage."[7] The *Dialectic* thus asks the reader to take sides and make judgments just as tragedy encouraged its spectators to judge the action of the characters in a drama. Horkheimer and Adorno, of course, ask us to reflect on the meaning and consequences of enlightenment and judge them for ourselves.

Second, in tragedy, great and heroic deeds or terrible suffering are called forth as responses to real-life events and crises.[8] Theoretical reflection in the *Dialectic* is likewise a response to a lived crisis of fundamental importance. As a response to the rise of fascism in Europe, the Stalinization of the revolution in Russia, and the commodification of everyday life in the United States, the *Dialectic* attains an immediacy and urgency usually lacking in "objective" theoretical texts yet present in Greek tragedy. Tragedy also makes plain the stakes involved in human action and debate, providing a set of motivations for entering into debate or pursuing a course of action by revealing how and why characters undertake a discussion and what sorts of problems call forth reflection.[9] The *Dialectic* similarly shows us the stakes involved in theoretical reflection. If, as the authors say, enlightenment gives itself over to method, which is inimical to thought as such, and if, in the correct application of method, the answer is already decided from the start, then there is no mystery and no desire to reveal mystery. To the extent that enlightenment ruthlessly extinguishes the awe and wonder that accompanies multifaceted experience, and so that which nourishes the theoretical faculty itself, enlightenment as event and crisis prompts the authors to become theoretical in the first place.

Third, like tragedy, Horkheimer and Adorno suspect any attempt to construct a single, unitary, or comprehensive account of the world. The *Dialectic* is concerned (again following Nussbaum's account of Greek tragedy) to "display to us the irreducible richness of human

7. Nussbaum, *Fragility of Goodness*, 126.
8. Ibid., 130.
9. Ibid., 127.

value" (134) against social forces that would reduce both humans and their values to problems of economic exchange and bureaucratic administration. Tragedy wished to present the " complexity and indeterminacy of the lived practical situation" (134) in all its diverse richness, variety, and multiplicity. *Dialectic of Enlightenment* likewise honors the particular, the individual, and the concrete in all its complexity and suspects those overly general, abstract, determinate, and reductionist accounts that simplify the world. The ancient playwrights and the authors of the *Dialectic* share a suspicion of what Michel Foucault would later refer to as total or global theory.[10]

The architecture of the book further reflects this concern with concrete particulars and the suspicion of unitary, hierarchical, and functionalizing knowledge. Comprised of a number of mutually referential essays and subtitled *Philosophical Fragments*, the *Dialectic of Enlightenment* breaks off inconclusively in a series of notes and drafts. The aphoristic structure of the work thus reiterates its concern with the particular fragment and individual detail and further reinforces its warning against succumbing to the tyranny of the kind of knowledge that would unify all experience. But a fragmentary style is not fragmented, nor does it mean a lack of theoretical coherence. Like the best Greek tragedy, which simultaneously denies and presents the world as wholly intelligible,[11] the philosophical fragments of the *Dialectic* are mediated by a thematic unity that make it an excellent example of the very order it supposedly rejects. Horkheimer and Adorno have managed to create a theoretical form that achieves that very diversity-within-unity that has always eluded enlightenment itself.

Fourth, the *Dialectic* shares with Greek tragedy the form of an elenchus, or cross-examination.[12] Like a play that charts the course of a character's most confidently asserted claims about himself and the world around him, claims that further developments subsequently prove wrong, Horkheimer and Adorno show us how enlightened thinking blinds itself to the meanings and consequences of its own achievements and how its grasp of, and control over, practical problems is irreversibly deflated. In their narrative, enlightenment follows the course of a tragic reversal: its unreflected assumptions about its

10. See esp. the essays "Truth and Power" and "Two Lectures" in Michel Foucault, *Power/ Knowledge: Selected Interviews and Other Writings, 1972–1977*, ed. Colin Gordon, trans. Colin Gordon et al. (New York: Pantheon, 1977), 76–131.

11. Timothy Reiss, *Tragedy and Truth* (New Haven: Yale University Press, 1980), puts it this way: "And, one may feel prompted to ask, if tragedy is a negation of the possibility of a systematic order of knowledge, how is it that it is itself one of the finest examples of this supposedly impossible order?" (21).

12. Nussbaum, *Fragility of Goodness*, 129.

own truth and value are undermined. Reason may have once promised the subject control and mastery, but now it ruthlessly controls
and masters the subject itself.

Last, and perhaps most important, Horkheimer and Adorno work
as much through poetic images, associations, tones, textures, and sensibilities that evoke the "passional knowledge"[13] of Greek tragedy as
through theoretical argument. Like tragedy, the *Dialectic* engages not
only our wits but our passions as well, appealing as much to the power
of our emotions as to the power of our reason. To read the *Dialectic* as
a tragedy means to read it as a lament, as a weeping or crying over the
tremendous destruction wrought by modernity. It is a mournful re-
membrance of what has been overlooked, ignored, rejected, and refused; over countries, homes, places, people, and identities that have
proven expendable. The *Dialectic* continually invokes the lives that
have been damaged, lost, or destroyed and the experiences that have
been repressed, subjugated, or smoothed over by the functionalist coherence of a system that must either expand or perish. Exiles themselves, Horkheimer and Adorno experienced firsthand the literal and
metaphysical homelessness of modernity their book describes. If the
passional knowledge of tragedy is the kind that comes through suffering, then the wisdom contained in the *Dialectic of Enlightenment* is truly
tragic.

II

Not only do the ubiquitous images of light and darkness, sight and
blindness that pervade Sophocles' *Oedipus the King* invite sustained
comparison with Horkheimer and Adorno's *Dialectic of Enlightenment*.
No classical text better illuminates the contemporary one, for other,
more systematic and substantive reasons as well. Both the *Dialectic* and
Oedipus the King focus on the ambiguous relationship between human
intelligence and power, and both consider that issue through the
themes of civilization and savagery and identity and difference.

Sophocles' *Oedipus the King* is about the fine line that separates civilization from savagery, the city from the wild. Oedipus is the paradig-
matic civilizing hero, a man who uses the powers of intellect and reason to vanquish the threat of undifferentiated chaos. By solving the
riddle of the Sphinx, he triumphs over untamed nature; with his solution he enthrones "man" as the measure of all things, and himself as
master of Thebes. When Oedipus boasts that he destroyed the death-

13. Ibid., 122.

dealing Sphinx alone and with unaided intellect, he asserts that rational mastery of the world upon which all the greatest achievements of
Greek civilization were thought to rest.[14] Yet Oedipus transgresses the
very boundaries he seeks to establish. For all his civilizing power, he
remains a creature of the wild, unable to banish the "nature" within
himself. Rescued from the mountain fastness of Cithaeron, he becomes a beast himself, killing his father in the wild, committing incest
at the very hearth of the city, finally banished from the human community that nurtured him. Oedipus is himself a savage, a destroyer of
civilized values and the city that embodies them, his will and intellect
mortal threats to the hard-won human order of the polis.

By dramatizing the dialectic of civilization and savagery, Sophocles
suggests that civilization is a precarious achievement and its reversion
to savagery a persistent and imminent possibility if not an inescapable
reality. Human intellect and reason possess the power to lift us out of
nature *and* return us to barbarity. In the case of Oedipus, the assid-
uous and unwavering application of reason reveals not human progress but bestial regression. Every step Oedipus takes in his search for
the murderer proves the power of his intellectual progress to be the
progress of a tyrannical power. Reason, and the mastery it brings,
constitutes the obverse side of a savage tyranny. As Segal reminds us,
all the achievements of human civilization centered on Oedipus "come
to reflect the ambiguity of man's power to control his world and manage his life by intelligence."[15] Oscillating between intellectual mastery
and ignorance, between godlike omniscience and fateful resignation,
Oedipus lacks an appropriately political kind of knowledge. In terms
of the play as a whole, this means a collective and deliberative, rather
than a singular and analytic, knowledge; one that is simultaneously
active and shaping *and* passive and receptive, a knowledge that reflects on the conditions of its own possibility and heeds its mortal
limits. Oedipus and Thebes, however, lack the kind of knowledge
tragedy itself inculcates in its citizen audience.[16] As long as they do,
they are bound to repeat an endless pattern of incest, trapped within
the inexorable dialectic of civilization and savagery.[17]

14. Charles Segal, *Tragedy and Civilization: An Interpretation of Sophocles* (Cambridge: Harvard University Press, 1981), 3.
15. Ibid., 232.
16. On the educative function of tragedy, see the essay by Stephen Salkever, "Tragedy and
the Education of the Demos," in *Greek Tragedy and Political Theory*, ed. J. Peter Euben (Berkeley and Los Angeles: University of California Press, 1986), 274–303.
17. On the eternal return of the same in the Oedipus plays, see Froma I. Zeitlin, "Thebes:
Theater of Self and Society in Athenian Drama," in Euben, *Greek Tragedy and Political Theory*,
101–141.

Horkheimer and Adorno's book is also about the dialectic between civilization and savagery, reason and tyranny, enlightenment and myth. The authors of *Dialectic of Enlightenment* had in fact set themselves "nothing less than the discovery of why mankind, instead of entering into a truly human condition, is sinking into a new kind of barbarism" (xi). Horkheimer and Adorno confronted the fact of material progress and social regression: the indefatigable self-destructiveness of enlightenment. Kant had laid the philosophical foundations of a purely formalistic reason; Sade and Nietzsche, the "black writers of the bourgeoisie" (117), mercilessly elicited the implications of enlightenment by insisting that formalistic reason is no more closely allied to morality than immorality and by denying the possibility of deriving from reason any fundamental argument against murder (118); but it was Hitler and the fascists who brought enlightenment to its logical conclusion in a return to outright barbarism.

Consistent with the central thesis of their book, Horkheimer and Adorno interpret the Holocaust as a deadly combination of myth (anti-Semitism) and enlightenment (bureaucratically and rationally organized mass murder), the savage reversal of civilization into barbarism. That rationalism should culminate in collectively legitimated mass murder was not an isolated anachronistic irruption of savagery into modern civilization but the crystallization of its organizing principle. The "irrationalism" of anti-Semitism proceeds from the "nature of the dominant *ratio* itself, and the world which corresponds to its image" (xvii). The thesis that civilization and savagery are inextricably linked finds tragic testimony in the methodically administered destruction of whole nations.[18]

Horkheimer and Adorno sought the cause for the destruction of all civilized values—for barbarism on a hitherto unprecedented scale—in the triumph of scientific method and its extension into, and domination over, all spheres of life. This thesis differs from theorists on the left such as Georg Lukács as well as from those on the right such as Karl Popper and Friedrich Hayek.[19] Whereas Lukács argued that the

18. Adorno elsewhere characterized modernity's psychological principle as "frigidity," that is, as the capacity to see one's fellows devoured by the monster without experiencing guilt or physical pain. Hannah Arendt comes to a similar conclusion but names that singular condition thoughtlessness: the inability to think from the standpoint of somebody else made it possible for Eichmann to efficiently organize mass murder; see *Eichmann in Jerusalem: A Report on the Banality of Evil* (New York: Viking, 1964), 49. On the linkage of civilization and savagery, cf. Walter Benjamin's "Every document of civilization is also a document of barbarism" (*Illuminations*, ed. Hannah Arendt, trans. Harry Zohn [New York: Schocken, 1968], 262).

19. Georg Lukács does not deal with fascism directly (though Horkheimer and Adorno use his concept of rationalization as reification to interpret the reversal of enlightenment in the

commodity form and the reification it necessarily brings were specific to capitalist economic organization, both Popper and Hayek blamed socialism and the labor movement: Popper because Marxism had replaced the "piecemeal social engineering" of liberalism with historicism and utopianism; Hayek because socialism had introduced the ideas of planning and state intervention into the successful functioning of competitive capitalism. But fascism becomes possible not only as a result of the wholesale reification of society, through either the market or centralized planning. Nor is it merely the truth of a liberalism stripped bare to reveal the naked inequalities and oppression inherent in the apparently free exchange of the market. Rather, fascism paradoxically embodies elements of both myth and enlightenment. In its attempt to free men from the imperatives of nature, it enslaves them to a second nature. The fault lies as much with the methods of the natural sciences (the practice of systematization) and their counterpart in epistemology (logical positivism) as with the market and capitalist relations of production (though domination certainly intensifies under these latter historical conditions). Horkheimer and Adorno radically question the pursuit of both unreflective science and systematic logic and attempt to expose the structure of formal reason as a structure of domination in order to understand the entwinement of enlightenment and myth, of reason and madness, that accompanied German fascism.

The authors of *Dialectic of Enlightenment* suggest a connection between the intellectual mastery of nature and tyranny over men and women. Reason, which once worked by concepts and images, now refers to method alone. Indifferent to the qualitatively and individually unique, insensitive to multiplicity and particularity (7), impatient with tradition and history as well as with religion, metaphysics, and philosophy, the domination of discursive logic in the conceptual sphere tends to domination in actuality. The aim of enlightenment is the subsumption of all particulars under the general, "the substitution of formula for concept, rule and probability for cause and motive" (5). But all systems of knowledge obscure as much as they reveal, exclude as they include, foreclose human possibilities as they disclose the secrets of nature and enslave the subjects they originally intended to liberate. Blind to the course of its own progress, enlightenment pays for each

---

Dialectic); see *History and Class Consciousness: Studies in Marxist Dialectics*, trans. Rodney Livingstone (Cambridge, Mass.: MIT Press, 1971), esp. the essay "Reification and the Consciousness of the Proletariat," 83–222; Friedrich Hayek, *The Road to Serfdom* (Chicago: University of Chicago Press, 1944); and Karl Popper, *The Open Society and Its Enemies* (Princeton: Princeton University Press, 1950), 85.

and every advance in material production with the increased impotence and pliablity of the masses. The unprecedented increase in economic productivity of all kinds promises greater social justice, yet the technical apparatus and the groups that administer it "assume a superiority disproportionate to the rest of the population. Even though the individual disappears before the apparatus which serves him, that apparatus provides for him as never before" (xiv). Promising the subject control and mastery, enlightenment ruthlessly controls and masters the subject. If enlightenment aimed originally at freeing man from fear of mythical powers, it has replaced those archaic forces with a new myth of things as they actually are, in order to justify a correspondingly new kind of terror. Fear of departing from the charmed circle of facts, terror of the unknown, and hatred of the unknowable identifies the modern self with its archaic counterpart. Enlightenment behaves like Sophocles' Oedipus: it surely did liberate the species from the awe-ful power of nature but also brought with it a new plague. Both remedy and poison, savior and destroyer, civilized and savage, farsighted in its commanding vision yet blind to the ambiguity of its own identity, actions, and consequences—enlightenment is not only *deinon*, (awesome, terrifying) but *pharmakon* (remedy, poison) as well.

To the extent that the *Dialectic* is concerned with the self-destruction of enlightenment's emancipatory intent *and* with the precarious divisions that separate civilization from savagery, it recalls the moral judgment of Sophocles' *Oedipus the King*. In their attempt to make Auschwitz intelligible, Horkheimer and Adorno evoke the moral sensibility of tragedy where the poverty of current linguistic expression proves inadequate to the unprecedented nature of the new barbarism. Adorno used to speak of a "universal context of guilt," a phrase that alludes to the impossibility of completing anything in the spirit in which it was conceived. No matter how generous or radical the intent, our best plans go wrong. We act in order to extricate ourselves from the ravages of enlightenment in its capitalist and fascist phases, only to entangle ourselves in them ever more deeply. Like Oedipus, we continually reinforce the power of a fate whose hold we seek to break. Even when the traditional theories of virtue have collapsed under the weight of rationalist skepticism, when we ought to, but cannot, do anything right, we still must act and be judged for our actions. The *Dialectic* refuses to abandon the moral language of guilt and responsibility at a time when the forces of fate, congealed in the logic and power of immense economic and bureaucratic systems, seems unassailable. Horkheimer and Adorno anticipate that other German émigré, Hannah Arendt, who looked to the moral language of Greek tragedy in order to understand the unprecedented nature of the Holocaust. Insisting that Eichmann be tried for his specific deeds and not his motives, Arendt reiterates the tragic self-judgment of Oedipus: we are responsible for our particular deeds no matter how generously, nobly, or—as in the case of Eichmann—how indifferently they are conceived.[20] The authors of the *Dialectic* and Arendt agree with Greek tragedy that we must decide and act in a world we never made and that such decisions and actions are tragic.

Oedipus's answer to the Sphinx's riddle, "It is man," revealed his unique ability to apprehend unity amid the multiplicity of forms, to rationally organize the data of experience. He reduced all "problems" of difference to their lowest common denominators, the better to solve them. Impatient with multiple meanings, diverse or contradictory voices, and plural points of view, Oedipus imposed his unitary vision on the world to the exclusion of varied and variegated possibilities. The unity he achieved, however, was attained at the expense of a plurality that makes a polis possible in the first place. By insisting that words and the world have only one meaning, by reducing the complexity and flexibility of language, by diluting the richness and harmonizing the differences within Thebes itself, Oedipus liquidated the distinctions that constituted the city he set out to save.

Horkheimer and Adorno's book is also about the dialectic between identity and difference, uniformity and individuality, the one and the many. They explore that dialectic through a consideration of enlightenment's will to unity, the production of a uniform and characterless "mass" culture, and through the problem of "system" in both theory and practice.

Enlightenment's tendency to reduce the many-faceted and contradictory nature of experience to a singular unity apprehensible under the laws of formal reason already finds its expression in the ancient enlightenment. Just as Xenophanes derided the multiplicity of deities as so many false projections of humans themselves, so too does the most recent school of logic denounce the words of language as false coins better replaced by neutral counters. "On the road to modern science men renounce any claim to meaning": there is no difference between the totemic animal, the dreams of the ghost-seer, and the absolute Idea.[21] The rich multiplicity of forms is reduced to position and arrangement; history, to fact; things, to matter. Science, guided

20. Arendt, *Eichmann in Jerusalem*, 278.
21. Horkheimer and Adorno, *Dialectic of Enlightenment*, 5.

by method, "makes the dissimilar comparable by reducing it to abstract quantities. To the enlightenment, that which does not reduce to numbers, and ultimately to the one, becomes illusion; modern positivism writes it off as literature" (7). From Parmenides to Russell, unity is the slogan: "the destruction of gods and qualities alike is insisted upon" (8). The modern enlightenment, replete with experimental science, formal logic, and advanced method—all of which provided a schema for the calculability of the world—brought to fruition that extirpation of distinctions which the disenchantment of nature had always sought.

Enlightenment, however, is as democratic as the logic it employs. Not only are qualities dissolved in thought, but "men are brought to actual conformity as well" (12). Those who are not find their way into "total" institutions that increasingly resemble society itself. Whether through the market or the state apparatus that protects its clients from the dislocations caused by the former, our society is ruled by equivalence. "We were given our individuality as unique in each case, different to all others, so that it might all the more surely be made the same as any other" (13). Equivalence, exchange, abstraction—all tools of enlightenment—treat individuals as did fate, the notion of which they reject: they liquidate them. The false unity of the individual and the collectivity nevertheless shows through. The more homogeneous society becomes—the more its members are subjected to the repetition, standarization, and uniformity of productive and administrative processes at all levels and in all spheres of existence—the more that society disintegrates. "Men are once again made to be mere species beings, exactly like one another through *isolation* in the forcibly united collectivity" (36). Then, as now, movies and bombs hold the whole thing together.

The regression of enlightenment to ideology (myth) evident in the products of mass culture provides Horkheimer and Adorno occasion for reflecting on the demise of autonomous art (tragedy included) and on the corresponding abolition of the individual (154). The culture industry proves to be our counterpart to the tragic world of the Greek theater.[22] Unlike Greek tragedy, however, the culture industry aims not to encourage moral reflection, invigorate substantive debate, or elucidate those distinctions that make judgment possible but, rather, to stultify, stupefy, and create a "culture" of unthinking, pliable masses. The products of the culture industry have lost any power

22. The term *culture industry* was first used by Horkheimer and Adorno, who preferred it to *mass culture* because of the latter's populist connotations. They oppose *mass culture* not because it is democratic but precisely because it is not.

to contradict the audiences' expectations, question their norms of thought, or challenge their standards of intelligibility. Culture industry commodities have little or no critical function. Television, music, and film all encourage an attentive, but essentially passive, passionless, and uncritical reception, which they induce through patterned and predigested products: programs "watch" *for* their audiences as popular music "hears *for* those who listen."[23] Mass media images thus reproduce and strengthen, rather than question, existing social and cultural boundaries. The result is not an image of society rent by contradiction but the false identity of society and individual which urges the smooth integration of the latter into the former. If any passion is evinced, it is a passion for identification. In the context of culture-as-industry, tragedy, which once meant protest, now means consolation.

Where Greek tragedy valued and displayed the irreducible richness and complexity of human life, enlightenment treats culture as the ancient tyrant treated Thebes: science disproves the old oracles of religion, metaphysics, and philosophy daily; increasing social differentiation and technological specialization produce chaos while the culture industry "now impresses the same stamp on everything. . . . Films, radio and magazines make up a system which is uniform as a whole and in every part."[24] The culture industry obliterates distinctions and refuses to produce or sanction anything that in any way differs from its own rules, its own ideas about consumers, or above all, itself. It makes everyone the same, collapsing plurality and individuality into unity, uniformity, and anonymity, thereby destroying rather than sustaining the distinctions and differences that Greek tragedy (and political community) necessarily presuppose. The culture industry promotes that reduction, in thought and society, against which Sophocles warned: the incestuous repetition of the same that forever turns back and in upon itself, a repetition and standardization devoid of the exogamous relations and energy necessary to revitalize a people or a culture.

Yet mass culture does not shrink from suffering; for "tragedy made into a carefully calculated and accepted aspect of the world is a blessing" (151). If tragic suffering is to be shown, it must be adequately integrated into the system that can profitably use it. Tragedy thus becomes an institution for moral improvement, as suffering justifies the world that made it necessary. Tragedy has to resemble fate and is reduced to the threat to destroy anyone who does not cooperate with

23. Theodor W. Adorno, "On Popular Music," with George Simpson, *Studies in Philosophy and Social Science* 9, no. 1 (special issue) (1941): 48.
24. Horkheimer and Adorno, *Dialectic of Enlightenment*, 120.

the higher powers: "Tragic fate becomes just punishment for those who resist becoming whatever the system wants" (153). The culture industry discards tragedy by integrating both it and the individual. The substance of Greek tragedy was the opposition of its heroes to society. The need to identify, to fit in, to find refuge in the collectivity remained unfulfilled in ancient tragedy, and the tension between hero and society, unresolved. Oedipus and Antigone both defied the conventional codes of their communities and suffered for it. Today, the "miracle of integration" has brought such would-be heroes into line: the individual must find refuge in society by identifying with it and renouncing his or her individuality. The tension in tragedy dissipates into the false identity of society and individual. Whereas Greek tragedy refused final narrative closure and kept the "individual" alive, the productions of the pleasure industry affirm reconciliation and refuge and thereby defeat tragedy. "This liquidation of tragedy confirms the abolition of the individual" (154).

Horkheimer and Adorno further elaborate the dialectic between identity and difference, uniformity and individuality, with reference to what they call "the system." In the tradition of western Enlightenment, from Descartes and Leibniz to Kant, reason refers to the unified organization of data: rationality requires the consistent and coherent construction of concepts. This unity, consistency, and coherence is *the system*. Unity resides in agreement: " the resolution of contradiction is the system *in nuce*" (82). As there is to be complete harmony, uniformity, and homogeneity among the elements of the system, thought as such is reduced to the creation of unified, scientific order and the derivation of factual knowledge from principles. Thinking must make system and perception accord by reconciling the antagonism between the general and the particular, the concept and the facts. Just as the facts are predicted from the system, so must they also confirm it. All systems are closed and exclusionary.

Horkheimer and Adorno regard Hegel's philosophy as an example of a closed system despite his dialectical critique of Kant. In the anticipatory identification of history and philosophy—totality in system and society—Hegel contravenes his own prohibition against making the conscious result of the whole process of negation into an absolute (24). Nonetheless, systems interpret the world and, in that regard, are necessary components of our lives. They call for an orderly organization and presentation of experience without which we could not survive. But more often than not systems claim their concepts to be adequate to their object, which they claim to have identified fully. In systems thinking there is a kind of paranoia to embrace the whole: a system tolerates nothing outside of itself. Fear of the unknown, of departing from the rigid organization of facts, proves to be the psychological principle behind the Enlightenment penchant for system. But reality does not go into its concept without remainder. Systems inevitably enter into conflict with the "objects" they purport to grasp. The multiplicity of qualities disappears in the system, only to return later to contradict it. History defies systems, as the fate of Hegel's philosophy demonstrates and the dialectic of enlightenment attests. If history does have any unity, it is given not by any systematic construction but by suffering.[25]

Conceptual systems find their homologue in society. The tendency in contemporary social institutions toward total organization is the historical counterpart to systems thinking; the particular is subsumed under the general concept as the individual is subsumed under the "plan." "Being is apprehended under the aspect of manufacture and administration. Everything—even the human individual, not to speak of the animal—is converted into the repeatable, replaceable process, into a mere example for the conceptual models of the system."[26] Individuals are interchangeable parts in an economic and bureaucratic apparatus bent solely on self-preservation. The difficulty is to make sense of the world of people and things while doing it the least violence, a task Sophocles' *Oedipus the King* dramatized in all its tragic dimensions. Horkheimer and Adorno similarly both construe and deny the kind of thinking that allowed Oedipus initially to save Thebes and subsequently threaten it with ruin. Their alternative to systems thinking resembles what Arendt called representative thinking, the capacity to think from the standpoint of somebody else.[27] This capacity is precisely what conceptual (and social) systems deny by treating their constituent elements as objects rather than as subjects, because "to be an object also is part of the meaning of subjectivity; but it is not equally part of the meaning of objectivity to be a subject."[28]

Systems are thus theoretical *and* political problems, facts that help explain why *Dialectic of Enlightenment* is so difficult to read and why it has been so ruthlessly criticized as both a theoretical and a political "failure." If the point is somehow to avoid the chaos that the complete absence of system induces *and* the collapse into unity and uniformity

25. David Held, *Introduction to Critical Theory: Horkheimer to Habermas* (Berkeley and Los Angeles: University of California Press, 1980), 216.

26. Horkheimer and Adorno, *Dialectic of Enlightenment*, 84.

27. Arendt, *Eichmann in Jerusalem*, 49.

28. Theodor W. Adorno, *Negative Dialectics*, trans. E. B. Ashton (New York: Seabury, Continuum, 1973), 183.

CHRISTOPHER ROCCO

that a total system requires, then the *Dialectic* pursues a number of strategies to this end. I have already mentioned how the *Dialectic* consciously avoids, as an act of resistance against the system, a language that would too easily accommodate itself to current linguistic and conceptual conventions; how the two voices conjoined in the text practice the dialogue it recommends; how the emphasis it places on specific qualities, individual characteristics, and unique distinctions rejects the tendencies toward systematic unity in theory and society; and how the structure of the book, a whole composed of fragments, reiterates and performs the authors' concern to achieve a plurality within unity; and finally, how, by looking to the archaic sensibility and language of tragedy, the *Dialectic* finds there a source of energy to reinvigorate our theoretical and political language. In all these ways, Horkheimer and Adorno attempt to mediate the distance between two poles of an irreconcilable dialectic, between too much unity and too little.

There is another way, however, in which the *Dialectic* mediates between the poles of identity and difference. Earlier I argued that the disintegrating structure of the *Dialectic* reiterated its theoretical claim concerning the transition to the world of the administered life. On another level of articulation, the structural armature of the work deliberately opposes its theoretical content. The *Dialectic* seems to offer a systematic or "total" critique of rationalization. Yet if rationalization, as actuality and ideology, is total, then how can the authors know it? Have they not effectively tied their hands by relinquishing the ground on which to base their claims? What critics see as a contradiction or impassable aporia in theory construction,[29] I see as a deliberate textual strategy to undermine the book's own impulse toward total critique and so avoid just such a premature closure as its critics fear. The *Dialectic* offers a comprehensive critique of reason and at the same time deliberately dismantles the very theoretical totality it forwards. It is precisely the structure of the book, its disintegration into fragments, that questions its own substantive claims and opposes the impulse toward totalized critique. The structure of the *Dialectic* reverses the direction of its theoretical intentions by joining in opposition two ways of pursuing social critique. The disintegrating structure of the book thus reverses its theoretical claims in order to reverse the reversal of enlightenment itself.

29. Jürgen Habermas, *Theory of Communicative Action: Reason and the Rationalization of Society*, trans. Thomas McCarthy (Boston: Beacon, 1984); Seyla Benhabib, "Modernity and the Aporias of Critical Theory," *Telos* 49 (Fall 1981): 39–59, and *Critique, Norm, and Utopia: A Study of the Foundations of Critical Theory* (New York: Columbia University Press, 1986), 147–85.

III

My final reason for reading the *Dialectic* in terms of Greek tragedy has to do with a set of intentions and strategies they share. I am referring here to the way in which both use the past in an "untimely" fashion in order to raise timely questions about the cultural and political regimes they respectively inhabit. Greek tragedy performed this critical task in at least two ways. First, it juxtaposed dramatic content to ritual context. As part of a religious festival, a tragic performance was an occasion for the city as a whole to "reconsecrate, remember and rededicate itself to sustaining its traditions of collective life."[30] Yet the content of the dramatic performances radically challenged the accepted traditions in which the ritual was embedded. Tragedy presented a world torn by conflict and contradiction. In the language of structural anthropology, all the codes—ritual, religious, sexual, familial, and political—are either inverted or violated. The acceptable relationships between parents and children, men and women, rulers and ruled, public and private, citizen and foreigner, are all strained to the breaking point. Tragedy suspends the normal intelligibility of the world and so calls forth reflective questioning concerning the order that is given us and that we create.[31]

Second, tragedy expressed an ambivalent and critical attitude toward the city's presently constituted order through the formal structure of the performance itself, through the tension between the two elements that occupied the tragic stage. On one side was the chorus, representing the collectivity of democratic citizens, while opposite it was a legendary warrior king like Oedipus, representing the heroic and mythical past.[32] The juxtaposition of present democratic citizenship represented by the chorus of trained citizens and past heroic kingship embodied in the aristocratic Oedipus, questioned present democratic achievements and past dynastic beginnings alike. A second set of oppositions also cut across the first. Whereas the citizen chorus chanted its songs in the archaic lyric of a past heroic age, a legendary

30. See "Introduction," Euben, *Greek Tragedy and Political Theory*. Jean-Pierre Vernant puts it this way in "Tensions and Ambiguities in Greek Tragedy," in *Tragedy and Myth in Ancient Greece*, ed. Jean-Pierre Vernant and Pierre Vidal-Naquet, trans. Janet Lloyd (Brighton, E. Sussex: Harvester, 1981), 9: "Tragedy is not only an art form; it is also a social institution which the city, by establishing competitions in tragedies, set up alongside its political and legal institutions. The city established, under the authority of the eponymous archon, in the same urban space and in accordance with the same institutional norms as the popular assemblies or courts, a spectacle open to all the citizens directed, acted and judged by the qualified representatives of the various tribes. In this way it turned itself into a theater."
31. Segal, *Interpreting Greek Tragedy*, 46.
32. Vernant and Vidal-Naquet, *Tragedy and Myth*, 9–10.

warrior king like Oedipus spoke his lines in the contemporary idiom of Athens. Projected into the mythical past, Oedipus embodied the character and performed the deeds of a legendary king while seeming to speak and act in the immediate present. Through such juxtaposition in formal structure of the play, Sophocles refused to glorify the past even as the play turned the present into a problem that the past could illuminate from within the tradition of a public festival.

Dialectic of Enlightenment likewise suspends its readers between past and present in a way that neither glorifies the former nor reifies the latter, even as it positions itself within the tradition it criticizes. Horkheimer and Adorno juxtapose past and present, myth and enlightenment, by reading Homer's *Odyssey* as a configuration of modernity and the most recent historical developments as a return to archaic barbarism. The authors of the *Dialectic* thus echo the way in which Greek tragedy brought mythical past and enlightened present together in a unity of opposites on stage.

Their reading of the *Odyssey* sets out to assess the social and psychic costs of modern rationalism against the background of reason's prehistory in archaic myth: "No literary work testifies more eloquently to the interconnectedness of enlightenment and myth than Homer's which is the fundamental text of European civilization."[33] Their reading reveals that, contrary to enlightened thinking, the opposition between myth and enlightenment is not absolute. On one hand, the epic poem is already rationalized: it bears Bacon's "right mark." On the other hand, when enlightenment posits itself as the absolute other of myth, it enthrones itself as a new myth. By juxtaposing the archaic past of Homer's epic to our own modern present, the *Dialectic* undermines the opposition between reason and myth and so questions our confidence in the progress of reason and the superiority of modern cultural accomplishments it brings.

As it does so, it recalls Sophocles' play and that other civilizing hero, Oedipus: On one level the *Odyssey* is about the triumph of human skill and intellect over the powerful and dark mythical forces that populate a hostile world. Odysseus, alone and unaided, relies solely on his native intelligence and cunning to overcome the dreadful obstacles that bar his way home, while his less enlightened companions perish. On another level, Horkheimer and Adorno read the *Odyssey* as a reflection on the highly ambivalent nature of human intellect and power. In Homer, the authors of the *Dialectic* already find that entwinement of reason and myth that marks the modern structures of economic

33. Horkheimer and Adorno, *Dialectic of Enlightenment*, 45–46.

and political domination. Odysseus rules the ship on the return voyage not solely because of his superior skill but also because of his aristocratic standing. In Odysseus, the man of reason and the king, two strands of a theory of legitimacy emerge. He grounds his rule in both unaided intellectual achievement and hereditary entitlement, in both enlightenment and myth.[34] Under pressure of circumstance, Odysseus abdicates as king in order to take the helm as a bureaucratic expert exerting political domination in the name of rationality, whose goal is self-preservation. By reason of this victory over myth, both Odysseus and modern political systems enthrone the myth of reason.[35]

The dialectic of the Homeric enlightenment reveals more than the entanglement of myth and reason. Horkheimer and Adorno read the *Odyssey* as a prehistoric portrait of modernity: the epic appears as the "historico-philosophic counterpart to the novel" and Odysseus as the "prototype of the bourgeois individual."[36] Individuation of the autonomous self and regression to undifferentiated chaos form the poles of an unreconciled dialectic. In his encounter with Polyphemus, Odysseus must deny his identity in order to preserve it. He tricks the Cyclopes by giving his name as No-one (*oudeis*), a word sufficiently homonymous with Odysseus to delight the listener with a pun and simultaneously conceal and reveal the identity of the hero who barely escapes the rocks hurled at his boat. Risk taking, renunciation, and the sublimation of the instincts into art are further elements of bourgeois life prefigured in Odysseus's encounter with the mythical forces of nature. The principle of risk in the encounter with the Sirens allows Odysseus to listen to their deadly sweet song while his crew members close their ears. Had he not hazarded to listen, the voyage would have been safe and uneventful. But the risk Odysseus took was a calculated one in which he could be sure of a favorable return (in both senses of that word). The ropes that bound him to the mast also saved him from the danger of mortal pleasure. The counterpart to bourgeois risk taking is either renunciation or sublimation: renunciation because Odysseus may listen to the Siren's song, yet as soon as it appears within his grasp, the crew members secure his fetters ever more tightly, "just as later the bourgeois foregoes happiness the more tenaciously the more he realizes that his increasing power has put it within

34. Here is another instance in which a theme from *Oedipus the King* resonates with Horkheimer and Adorno's reading of Homer: we find the same confusing juxtaposition of hereditary entitlement (myth) and superior intellect (enlightenment) as grounds for political rule in Sophocles' play.
35. Christian Lenhardt, "The Wanderings of Enlightenment," in *On Critical Theory*, ed. John O'Neill (New York: Seabury, 1976), 41.
36. Horkheimer and Adorno, *Dialectic of Enlightenment*, 43.

his reach"; (34) sublimation because Odysseus mediates the bodily felt tension between his desire for emancipation from the forces of nature and the urge to regress to prerational pleasure in the same way that the modern bourgeois will reconcile the antagonism between work and pleasure; that is, through the contemplation of art.[37] The episode with the Sirens gives mute testimony to the dialectic of power and impotence.

Thus far Horkheimer and Adorno have exposed self-denial, repression, and sublimation as the archaic elements in modern ego formation and individuation. At the midpoint of the excursus on Homer, however, lie the concepts of equivalence and commodity exchange nascent in the archaic practice of sacrifice: "While economic exchange may be viewed as a secularization of sacrifice, it is equally true that sacrifice is the magical prototype of rational exchange."[38] The *Dialectic* here juxtaposes the commodity system of present day capitalism to the archaic practice of sacrifice in order to reveal the irrationality of the former. Odysseus proves himself capable not only of deceiving the gods about what he owes but also of bargaining intelligently to reduce his liability. According to Christian Lenhardt, "The benevolence of the deities is expected to have something to do with the *specific magnitude* of hecatombs": sacrificial offerings are not wholly exchangeable. The cunning of Odysseus's intellect explores the elasticity of that magnitude, thereby releasing the price system of mythical sacrifice from its rigid structure and subjecting the mythical contract to the "forces of the market." The bourgeois principles of exploitation and equivalence are thus already well entrenched in the mythical world of the epic. Odysseus merely enlarges the scope of these principles through deceit and enlightened bargaining, thereby "exposing the relativism inherent in the notion of equivalence" and demystifying the "natural" mechanism of exchange.[39]

The Homeric epic also enacts the transformation of sacrifice into self-sacrifice and so provides prescient allegory for bourgeois renunciation. The sacrifice to which Odysseus subjects himself in the Sirens episode, "the denial of nature in man for the sake of domination over non-human nature and over other men,"[40] already points to the loss of freedom men and women will experience in an excessively technicalized and rationalized world. Odysseus's encounter presents the paradox of triumphant reason familiar from the *Oedipus the King*:

37. Lenhardt, "Wanderings of Enlightenment," 44.
38. Horkheimer and Adorno, *Dialectic of Enlightenment*, 49.
39. Lenhardt, "Wanderings of Enlightenment," 47.
40. Horkheimer and Adorno, *Dialectic of Enlightenment*, 54

"Man's domination over himself, which grounds his selfhood, is almost always the destruction of the subject in whose service it is undertaken; for the substance which is dominated, suppressed and dissolved by virtue of self-preservation is none other than that very life as functions of which the achievements of self-preservation find their sole definition and determination: it is, in fact, what is to be preserved" (54–55). Enlightenment, whether archaic or modern, turns back and in on itself in a paradoxical process of loss: the practice of self-renunciation gives away more of life than it gives back. The mastery of nature is paid for in self-repression and the repression of others: just as Oedipus virtually destroys the city he set out to liberate, and Odysseus both saves and wastes his life and the lives of his crew, so too does enlightenment threaten with destruction that which it set out to preserve.

Throughout the first "Excursus" on the *Odyssey*, Horkheimer and Adorno juxtapose archaic elements to modern phenomena. The discovery of self-denial, repression, the sublimation of instincts, and renunciation through self-sacrifice in Homer evoke in us a highly ambivalent attitude. We cannot denounce them without denouncing ourselves, yet we surely want to dissociate ourselves from the cruelty and barbarism of the archaic past. But that is precisely what Horkheier and Adorno will not allow. When we consider our own present, it appears as wholly barbaric and irrational as the remote past of the epic. The *Dialectic* juxtaposes the archaic past to the most recent historical developments in order to show, as Lenhardt says, that "the social situation of modern man is strikingly dissimilar yet reminiscent of the first attempt to survive by establishing an order based on reason."[41] Horkheimer and Adorno's strategy thus works in two directions at once: it aims to free us from a reified present in which political and economic structures appear natural *and* it works against any nostalgic return to a falsely idealized past. Horkheimer and Adorno criticized contemporary reason as myth while they simultaneously presented historical progress as the return of the "ever-identical," as a new disposition of myth. They pointed to the most recent history (anti-Semitism, fascism, monopoly capitalism) as a regression to archaic barbarism, and they interpreted the epic of the Odyssey as an expression of the most modern, with Odysseus as the "prototype of the bourgeois individual."

Contrary to the interpretation of Jürgen Habermas, the juxtaposition of the archaic past to the events of the present is no undialectical

41. Lenhardt, "Wanderings of Enlightenment," 48.

attempt "to follow the (largely effaced) path that leads back to the origins of instrumental reason, so as to *outdo* the concept of objective reason."[42] Nor is it an attempt to construe the process of rationalization as a negative philosophy of history. Instead, as Susan Buck-Morss puts it, Horkheimer and Adorno seek to "read an archaic image as a configuration of modernity"[43] in a way that will open up the present to critical assessment. They make the archaic appear meaningful in the light of the present, while the very newness and modernity of the present they reveal as significant in light of the archaic. Like Greek tragedy, the *Dialectic* juxtaposes the moments of a seemingly overcome past to the most barbaric, most irrational phenomena of the present in order to demythologize the present and the past's hold over it. Their juxtaposition of the archaic to the modern thus worked to establish neither a historical origin for a noninstrumentalized reason nor a negative philosophy of history but rather to criticize the present by undermining our faith in the myth of history as progress.

IV

If my presentation has been persuasive, then Horkheimer and Adorno's *Dialectic of Enlightenment* exemplifies what a dialogue between Greek tragedy (and by extension the thought of the classical polis) and Critical Theory can accomplish. The authors of the *Dialectic* sought "a form of linguistic expression" which would resist assimilation to the systems of bureaucratic domination and economic production of late capitalism.[44] The themes, style, and language of Greek tragedy provide the necessary point of reference for revitalizing a theoretical and political language all but completely degraded and devalued by the proliferation of method, technique, and calculative reason. The *Dialectic* looks to the archaic sensibility of the tragic consciousness in its relation to myth, fate, and morality in order to locate an outside point of leverage from which to comprehend and resist the ever more tightly sealed "systems" of mass deception (the culture industry) and outright barbarism (the Holocaust). The *Dialectic* thus stands to the present as Greek tragedy stood to the ancient city. It "uses" the past, Greek tragedy included, to provide us with a critical view of our own enlightened selves, much as Greek tragedy provided the polis with a

42. Habermas, *Theory of Communicative Action*, 1:382.
43. Susan Buck-Morss, *The Origins of Negative Dialectics: Theodor Adorno, Walter Benjamin, and the Frankfurt Institute* (New York: Free Press, 1977), 59.
44. Horkheimer and Adorno, *Dialectic of Enlightenment*, xii.

critical consideration of its own public and private life.[45] Since Horkheimer and Adorno learn in part how to "use" the past from Greek tragedy, they reject the easy nostalgia of conservative cultural criticism, together with its wholesale assimilation of the past to the present, as a negation of the past's critical potential. Greek tragedy (and theory) can surely help to loosen the hold that modern forms of life exert on us, but a return to the past is neither possible nor desirable. Like tragedy, Horkheimer and Adorno's narrative account of atrocity offers no consolation for the entanglement of history, savagery, and civilization save the wisdom that comes through suffering.

45. I do not mean to overdraw this analogy. The differences between 20th-century social theory and ancient tragedy remain crucial. Critical Theory has no festival context, and modern intellectuals tend to criticise their societies from the margins, not, like a tragic performance, from the center of the city. Nonetheless, I think I have pointed to some important and instructive similarities in structure, substance, and aim they both share despite (or because of) their radical differences.

BARRY S. STRAUSS

9 The Melting Pot, the Mosaic, and the Agora

On the face of it, those of us who believe that Athenian democracy is an inspiration to the pursuit of democracy in America run into a stumbling block: that is, the exclusive nature of Athenian democracy. Consider, for instance, testimony from journalist James Fallows's recent book, *More Like Us: Making America Great Again.* Fallows cites a 1988 letter from a friend pessimistic about America's new racial and ethnic diversity: "None of the great outpourings of human civilization was, so far as I know, prompted by immigration. In fact, Attic Greece, Imperial Rome, Han China, Renaissance Italy, Bourbon France, Imperial England all were products of a racially and culturally homogeneous people. . . . With the most depressing regularity, it seems that great cultures have been the products of single peoples."[1] While disagreeing strongly both with Fallows's friend's conclusion about immigration and culture, and with his characterization of Imperial Rome (an extremely diverse place, in fact), I concede that the evidence tends to support his description of Athens as a homogeneous society. Certainly, Athenian citizenship was highly restrictive. In democratic Athens in its heyday (fifth and fourth centuries B.C.), only adult men who could prove descent from an Athenian father and an Athenian maternal grandfather could themselves be citizens. All other men and all women and children had inferior statuses of various sorts, the most extreme of which was slavery.

1. James Fallows, *More Like Us: Making America Great Again* (Boston: Houghton Mifflin, 1989), 205.

252

Consequently, Athens seems to be primarily of negative significance for contemporary America. Society has become increasingly diverse and for various reasons, for instance, the increasing liberation and assertiveness of long-resident ethnic, racial, and religious groups, a large nonwhite emigration since 1965, and decolonialism. How can America—a polyglot society with one of the most varied and ambitious mixture of peoples, races, and religions in human history, a country of some 250 million people—learn to be more democratic from Athens—a country of at most 50,000 citizens at its population peak? What can a country struggling to achieve equality learn from one where citizenship was based on heredity and gender?[2] What can a "nation of immigrants" learn from a country where immigrants were almost always forced to accept second-class status as permanent resident aliens, with virtually no hope of "naturalization"? Whose orators took pride in their fellow citizens' supposed pure birth, unsullied by intermarriage with outsiders? Whose public art proclaims not the universal rights of humanity, but the triumph of an idealized human species, Greeks, over supposedly half-bestial barbarians, Persians?

Indeed, many thinkers have found in Athens precisely the opposite of an inspiration to greater democracy; they have found instead a demonstration of the importance of maintaining a measure of elitism even within a democracy. Tocqueville, for example, was not at all troubled by reaching the conclusion that, as the majority of the inhabitants of classical Attica lacked citizen rights, Athens was not a democracy but "merely an aristocratic republic."[3] On the contrary, he used the Athenian example to warn nineteenth-century Americans against what he saw as a dangerous popularization and commercialization of their culture. Athenian literature, with its aristocratic spirit, provided an exemplary counterbalance, "a prop on the side on which we are in most danger of falling."[4]

To put it bluntly, what are nice friends of democracy like us doing in a place like Athens?

To be sure, slave-owning, imperialist, gender-exclusive Athens is far from standing as an example of who democracy can be *for*; but it may yet be a useful model of how democracy can *work*. Students of democratic institutions may admire, for example, the boldness with

2. Though sometimes referred to in contemporary texts as "citizens" (sometimes only as "city-women"), Athenian women could not participate in the political institutions of the democracy. They had considerable informal power, but legally they were under the protection of a man (usually the husband or father).

3. Alexis de Tocqueville, *Democracy in America*, vol. 2, trans. Henry Reeve, rev. Francis Bowen, ed. Phillips Bradley (New York: Knopf, Vintage, 1945), 65.

4. Ibid., 67.

which Athenians filled most public offices not by election but by lottery (with hearings held to weed out the unfit and terms limited to one year). They may also appreciate the Athenian fondness for magistracy by committee. I certainly do; having served a stint on the local zoning board, I am struck by the value of the committee system as a way to introduce amateurs to the responsibility of public office. Advocates of national service will take note of the Athenian insistence that all able-bodied citizens share the burden of military service.

Useful examples all, and there are others; but they do nothing to bring us closer to solving the challenges of a multiracial and multicultural democracy. No democrat today can be an admirer *tout court* of Athens; its flaws are too many and too obvious. I have, for example, heard students criticize the Athenian ideology of autochthony— the notion that Athenian citizens were born of the soil itself: "Attica . . . has always been inhabited by the same race of people" (Thucydides *History of the Peloponnesian War* 1.2)—as an eerie precursor of sinister, modern notions of "blood and soil." Particularly in the fifth century B.C., when Athens was an imperial power, Athens's very high opinion of itself from time to time edges uncomfortably close to something like the idea of a Herrenvolk. Consider the words of Pericles' Funeral Oration (430 B.C.):

> Taking everything together then, I declare that our city is an education to Greece, and I declare that in my opinion each single one of our citizens, in all the manifold aspects of life, is able to show himself the rightful lord and owner of his person, and do this, moreover, with exceptional grace and exceptional versatility. And to show that this is no empty boasting for the present occasion, but real tangible fact, you have only to consider the power which our city possesses and which has been won by those very qualities which I have mentioned. Athens, alone of the states we know, comes to her testing time in a greatness that surpasses what was imagined of her. (Thuc. 2.41.1–3)[5]

An Athenian's alleged unbroken descent from the soil itself made him not only different, but better, than others: so Athenian patriots believed. "We are the only true noble authochthonous people of Attica, the manliest race"; so Aristophanes has one of his choruses declare (*Wasps* 1076–1077), in imitation of standard patriotic rhetoric. In the

5. *Thucydides: History of the Peloponnesian War*, trans. Rex Warner, rev. ed. (Harmondsworth: Penguin, 1972), 147–48.

funeral oration of 338 B.C. attributed to Demosthenes (60.4–5), the speaker argues, referring to Athenian ancestors, "They alone of all mankind inhabit the land from which they sprang and passed it on to their descendants. The following assumption may thus be made: Those who came into their cities from elsewhere and were called citizens are like adopted children. These men [to whom the oration is dedicated] are legitimate children born of the seed of their fatherland."[6] In the *Menexenus* (245c–d), which contains a parody of an Athenian funeral oration, set during the Corinthian War (395–386 B.C.), Plato goes even further: "So firm and healthy are the nobility and freedom of the city and the natural hatred of barbarians among us because we are pure Greeks, unmixed with barbarians. The descendants of Pelops, Cadmus, Aegyptus, Danaus, and many others live with us, being barbarian by nature and Greek by custom only. We ourselves are Greeks and live unmixed with barbarians. Consequently, there is instilled in us a hatred of the foreign nature."[7] Indeed, although humanism was a strong current in classical Athenian thought, the modern western notion of universal human rights probably owes a great deal more to such ideas as the status of all of us as god's children or the universal kingship of one deity or the Augustinian belief in the equality of us all as sinners; in other words, it may have deeper roots in Jerusalem than Athens.

And yet, as Lady Macbeth said of the murder of Banquo, "Who would have thought the old man to have had so much blood in him?" Look closer at the sacred bones of the West's first democracy, and we find the traces of blood and flesh. Not only that, we find a human and humane side of Athenian culture that subverts the confident arrogance of the Athenian division of the world into male Athenian citizens and everyone else. In a great advance from previous work, recent studies of Athenian history have encouraged us to explore the power and positive contributions of women and minorities to democratic Athens. They have encouraged us to find in Athenian ideology not so much the sound of the male citizen elite locking the door and throwing away the key as that of a cacophony of voices. Athenian ideology is not an accurate and straightforward image of a homogeneous society but, rather, a mask, substituting a new, civic identity for the diverse and divisive backgrounds that in fact characterized the citizenry. Read thus, Athenian ideology (as expressed in oratory,

6. *Amazons: A Study in Athenian Mythmaking*, trans. W. Blake Tyrrell (Baltimore: Johns Hopkins University Press, 1984), 114.

7. Ibid., 116.

drama, and art) is not merely a study in unity and stability but also an expression of tension and ambiguities. In short, Athenian ideology addresses some of the very same questions that face American ideology in the ever-more-diverse society of the late twentieth century.

Naturally, this is not the way things might have looked to a classicist a hundred years ago, when the shadows of nineteenth-century racism and imperialism fell over the historiography of Athens. Athens is a scripture that has been cited by many a devil. The Nazis, for instance, were thrilled to "come home" to the Athenian Acropolis after the Wehrmacht's conquest of Greece in 1941, convinced as they were that Athens' racial purity was the key to its greatness. More recently an American sometime-Nazi, David Duke, has cited his devotion to western civilization as the one constant theme in his checkered résumé.

Athens is worth a second look, nonetheless. As historians, we need to set the record straight; as citizens, we need to learn from other societies that have faced the challenge of diversity. Let us begin with a closer look at the apparent monolith of Athenian homogeneity and exclusivity. Then, having established the actual complexity and diversity of Athens, both in ideology and practice, let us consider its significance for multiracial democracy in contemporary America.

Racial exclusivity, first of all, was not the sole element in autochthony,[8] which also implied love for the land and, with it, respect and admiration for the hardy peasants who scraped a living from Attica's relatively infertile soil. Autochthony, moreover, could be interpreted as an antiexpansionist doctrine. After the Peloponnesian War (431–404 B.C.) and the collapse of the Athenian empire, autochthony was revised to fit a postimperial mood. Consider the version of Lysias in his Funeral Oration after the Corinthian War (395–386 B.C.) It was well known in antiquity that many Greek city-states had been founded by conquest; the original inhabitants had been expelled or enslaved. Athens' archenemy Sparta, whose ancestors had settled on land belonging to other Greeks, was considered one of the worst offenders. Athenians, however, were supposedly the sole and original inhabitants of their land, so they could have committed no such misdeeds. Lysias (2.17) says, "It was most fitting that our ancestors, moved by a single resolve, fought for justice: for the beginning of their way of life was just. For unlike most peoples they were not collected from everywhere nor did they settle another people's land after driving out the

8. On autochthony, see Nicole Loraux, *Les enfants d'Athéna: Idées athéniennes sur la citoyenneté et la division des sexes* (Paris: 1981), now *The Children of Athena: Athenian Ideas about Citizenship and the Division between the Sexes*, trans. Caroline Levine (Princeton: Princeton University Press, 1993).

inhabitants; since they were autochthonous they possessed the same mother and fatherland."[9]

In any case, autochthony was not the sole component of Athenian ideology. Athens was also considered, somewhat paradoxically, a sanctuary for the defenseless, a haven for suppliants. Myth highlights several well-known cases of aristocratic refugees seeking help from evildoers abroad, but the self-conception of Athens as the friend of suppliants persisted into the historical era. For example, the Athenian expedition of 461 B.C. to help Sparta after an earthquake and a revolt by helots (roughly, serfs) was remembered fifty years later as the response to a Spartan suppliant who came to an Athenian altar and pleaded for help (Aristophanes *Lysistrata* 1137–1146). The best-known suppliant myths were those of the survivors of the Seven Against Thebes, of the Herakleidai (children of Herakles), and of Oedipus in exile; these were celebrated in drama, oratory, and art. In each case, Athens accepted a suppliant or suppliants and risked military force to defend them against their persecutors. Retelling the myths, dramatists show the suppliants throwing themselves on the mercy of Athenians and on their amour propre: consider, for example, Euripides' *Suppliant Women*. The leaders of the Seven have fallen in battle before Thebes, but the enemy forbids the retrieval and burial of their bodies, a violation of civilized custom. Heartbroken, the mothers of the Seven go to Athens for help. "City of Pallas!" their chorus addresses the Athenians, "You revere right, despise crime, and are ready / Always to help ill-fated men" (Eur. *Suppl.* 377, 379–380).[10] Sophocles' *Oedipus at Colonus* shows the ill-fated Oedipus seeking sanctuary in Athens. At first he is nearly rebuffed by the elders of the Athenian country-district of Colonus. He takes them to task:

Is this the reputed godliness of Athens,
City of justice, where, if anywhere,
The suffering stranger should look for refuge and help? (260–62)[11]

Our appreciation of paradox grows when we consider that historically, Athens allowed suppliants not merely to plead their case but to settle, sometimes in considerable numbers. Foreigners settling in Athens? Indeed, the closer one looks at the reality of Athens' autochthony claim, the weaker it becomes. Even in the fifth century B.C.

9. Modified from the trans. of W. R. M. Lamb, *Lysias*, Loeb Classical Library (Cambridge: Harvard University Press, 1930), 39.
10. *Euripides—IV*, trans. Frank Jones (Chicago: University of Chicago Press, 1958), 72.
11. *Sophocles: The Theban Plays*, trans. E. F. Watling (Harmondsworth: Penguin, 1974), 79.

there was a revisionist view, put forward by the historian Hellanicus. (*FGrH* 323a F161) There were indeed good reasons for skepticism. First, Attica had traditionally allowed powerful exiles to settle. Herodotus claims that some of the most prominent families of Athens's history were descended from foreigners: the sixth-century tyrants Peisistratus and his sons from Pylos in the Peloponnese; the tyrannicides Harmodius and Aristogeiton from Eretria or even Phoenicia, via Boeotia; the late sixth-century oligarch Isagoras possibly from Caria (in southwestern Anatolia); and the fifth-century generals and politicians Miltiades and his son Kimon from Aegina (Herodotus *Histories* 15.55, 57–58, 65–66, 6.35). The historian Thucydides was descended from Thracians.[12]

Second, in the period of land hunger and migration during the eighth and seventh centuries B.C., many people probably came to farm in Attica, an attractive destination both because it was relatively underpopulated and because the settlers were accepted. There are numerous indications of such settlement in the sources, one of the most interesting of which is Plutarch's statement that Solon finally restricted immigration in 594 B.C. because of overcrowding (Plutarch *Solon* 22.1). Restricted, that is, but not stopped: he may have (the tradition is uncertain) encouraged immigration by foreigners who had been permanently exiled from home or who came to Athens to practice a particular trade and were willing to move their whole families with them (Plut. *Sol.* 24.2). By mid-sixth century, the position of some immigrants grew uneasy, either because they had come to Athens in violation of Solon's restrictions or because conservative Athenians refused to accept them. Fearful for their future, Athenians "of impure birth" flocked to the banner of Peisistratus, a popular champion and would-be tyrant who took power in 561 (Aristotle *Athēnaiōn Politeia* [= *Constitution of Athens*] 13.5).

Third, previous immigrants prospered, and new immigrants came to Athens under the tyranny of Peisistratus and his sons, during which many of Solon's laws were relaxed (561–556, 545–510). Some new immigrants were artisans and workers, some refugees in the wake of Persia's conquest of the Greek cities of the Aegean coast of Anatolia in 547, some mercenaries brought by the tyrants, some freed slaves from abroad or their descendants.

It is obvious, therefore, that, contrary to Athenian claims, Attica had *not* "always been inhabited by the same people." Probably only a

12. In this paragraph and in the next several pages I follow the arguments of Philip Brook Manville, *The Origins of Citizenship in Ancient Athens* (Princeton: Princeton University Press, 1990).

minority of Athenians in the classical period (fifth and fourth centuries B.C.) were descended from immigrants, but it was a significant minority. Whenever an immigrant married a native, the circle of nonautochthonous Athenians widened.

Here the story becomes both dramatic and relevant for modern democracy. When, in 510 B.C., a Spartan army drove out Peisistratus's son and successor and ended the tyranny, Athens's nobles assumed that they could turn the clock back and reestablish control of the regime, which would become an oligarchy. Ordinary people, however, particularly immigrants and their descendants, had grown used to the privileges they enjoyed under the Peisistratids. In 508 they drove out the oligarchs and the Spartan army supporting them. Under the leadership of the reformer Cleisthenes, they established the foundation of what would become, in two generations, Athenian democracy—the first democracy in history. The status of the immigrants assumed crucial importance in Cleisthenes' reforms.

The would-be oligarchs of 510 had struck at Peisistratus's supporters by sponsoring a revision of the list of Athenians, in order to excise those of "impure birth" (Aristot. *Ath. Pol.* 13.5). Immigrants and their descendants lost status and privilege, and it is likely that they became fervent supporters of change. Cleisthenes spoke to their needs by establishing a radical, new definition of Athenian nationality: a civic definition.[13] Old institutions and old ideologies were swept aside and replaced by a new way of defining "Athenian." The traditional units into which Athenians were divided were abolished and replaced by 139 local "peoples" (demes), generally corresponding to existing localities, and ten new tribes, named for legendary Athenian heroes. The purpose, according to Aristotle, was to mix the population up so that more people might share the citizenship (Aristot. *Ath. Pol.* 21.2). The "peoples," not the oligarchs, decided who was an Athenian, and generosity on their part was mandated. "No investigation of tribes" was the reply to anyone who quibbled about someone's ancestry (Aristot. *Ath. Pol.* 21.2). For legal purposes, Athenians were given new names, based not on the traditional patronymic (e.g., Themistocles, son of Neocles) but on their local "people" (Themistocles of Phrearrhia); the new "demotic" names, like the new tribes, deemphasized ancestry. It thereby became possible to grant citizenship both to foreigners and even to freedmen (Aristotle *Politics.* 1275b34–37). The ten tribes, in which new and old immigrants alike were

---

13. See the argument of Christian Meier, *The Greek Discovery of Politics*, trans. David McLintock (Cambridge: Harvard University Press, 1990).

mixed, served as the basic units of the army, of a new Council of Five Hundred (divided into ten tribal sections of fifty members each), of participation in festivals, and even of seating in the theater. They effected, in short, a considerable reorganization of Athenian society.

Cleisthenes' reforms are not to be reduced to a sop to the "immigrant lobby"; breaking the power of the local gentry, counteracting regionalism, and increasing the influence of his own family were as, if not more, important to him. Nor does this extremely brief account do justice to the breadth or complexity of Cleisthenes' reforms. We have seen enough, however, to establish several crucial points. The citizens of fifth- and fourth-century Athens were not all descended from a common, homogeneous group. Autochthony, therefore, was a myth. In many ways, it is an offensive myth, one meant to keep outsiders out. Yet an examination of Cleisthenes' reforms suggests that it was part of a larger, and salutary, myth: the civic myth.

Faced with diversity, the Athenians embraced an artificial unity. People whose ancestors might have come from Corinth or Sicily or Anatolia now belonged to tribes named after traditional Athenian heroes, such as the legendary kings Kekrops or Aigeus or Erechtheus. Their offical legal names recalled the map of Attica, comprising 139 localities in an area of about one thousand square miles. In short, immigrants and their descendants were guaranteed equality in the form of a new "all Athenian" identity.

In modern terms, this was a highly assimilationist solution to the problem of ethnic diversity. It was not a multicultural or "mosaic" solution, which encouraged immigrants to cultivate their original and diverse customs. It was, rather, a unicultural or "melting pot" solution, but one with a twist. The melting pot argument in America has assumed that the customs of different immigrants could be blended together to create a new and hybrid whole. The Cleisthenic solution, in contrast, demanded that immigrants completely renounce their various ancestral traditions. By accepting autochthony, they had to mask their foreign origins entirely. Yet the Cleisthenic solution also demanded a degree of renunciation from Athenians of native descent, for they had to renounce their traditional tribes and patronymics and to accept people of immigrant ancestry as equals. They had, in short, to give up privilege.

It was a moment of generosity, granted under the pressure of self-interest: the need to close ranks in the face of civil strife and foreign invasion. Unfortunately, the moment was not to be repeated. After Cleisthenes, although Athenians allowed immigration to continue, they closed the gates to naturalization. Within fifty years, the citizen body was officially made a closed descent group. New immigrants were now restricted to a second-class status as metics (resident aliens). Although they were free to prosper economically, metics could not own land or participate in politics, and they had to pay a special tax as well as serve in the military. Citizen became an exclusive, priviliged status in a formally stratified society.[14]

As in more recent times, so in Athens, attitudes toward immigration were thus cyclical: relatively open before 500 B.C., relatively closed afterward. Ironically, what began as a myth, that is, the homogeneous origins of the Athenian civic body, eventually became accepted as truth: first by Athenians, then by later students of history. Contemporary nativist attitudes, so powerful in the 1990s in places like France and Germany (and not entirely dormant in the United States either), similarly seem to confuse appearance and reality. In this essay I have attempted a more accurate historical appraisal, in the hope that readers might draw profitable lessons from the actual, as opposed to the ideologized, Athenian experience.

Those lessons are several. First, Athens shows that we are not alone. Although the United States is probably more diverse, ethnically and racially, than most societies in history, it is neither the only society nor the only democracy to be characterized by diversity. It is true that most of the immigrants to Athens were Greeks, and perhaps physically indistinguishable from native-born Athenians; but the considerable cultural differences among the Greek city-states should not be underestimated—and these differences loomed even larger to contemporaries. Immigrants spoke different dialects of Greek from native Athenians, worshipped similar but not entirely the same gods, and had somewhat different customs: small things *sub specie aeternitatis* but not at the time. Although it was a city-state with an ideology of homogeneity, therefore, the reality of Athens's society was considerably more complex. There may be a general lesson here for historians. Rather than starting from the assumption that a given society was unitary, historians might start from the skeptical position that societies *present themselves* as unitary even though they are in reality highly diverse. The history of Athens suggests that ideologies of autochthony and unity are just that: ideological. One begins to suspect that far from being the historical exception, diversity is the rule. The issues facing contemporary America, therefore, are neither unique nor insoluble but part of a common human experience.

14. On Pericles' citizenship law of 451–50 B.C., see Cynthia B. Patterson, *Pericles' Citizenship Law of 451–50 B.C.* (New York: Arno, 1981).

Second, there is much that is attractive about the civic solution to diversity that emerged under Cleisthenes, because it required both immigrants and natives to sacrifice traditions in favor of a new, artificial commonality. Both groups had a stake in a common enterprise. Perhaps Plato had Cleisthenes in mind when he wrote in the *Republic* (early fourth century B.C.) about the need for the citizens of the ideal polis to believe in the myth that they were all brothers and "born of the earth" (414e). Plato calls this myth a "noble lie" (414b); the same might be said of Cleisthenes' civic ideology. By making citizens the figurative sons not of human fathers but of the localities of Attica, by promoting a civic rather than a biologic identity, Cleisthenes averted civil war. He also laid the groundwork for democracy by getting the Athenians to agree on a common identity.

Third, Cleisthenes created institutions that translated the noble lie into action. Athenians of different ethnic origin and from different parts of Attica all mixed together in ten tribes that formed the framework of the military (the army in Cleisthenes' day, but within a generation, as Athens became a sea power, the navy too), the Council, and various religious and theatrical rituals and festivals. These institutions had the added advantage of making the civic myth seem more real. Any artificial mythology, created at a stroke, always runs the risk of falling flat because it lacks legitimacy. Cleisthenes succeeded because he translated his myths into action, because he was lucky enough to have the victory over Sparta of 508 with which to inspire people, and because he was shrewd enough to take pains to seek legitimacy. He consulted the Delphic oracle, for example, about the ten eponymous heroes of the new tribes, all of whom were figures that already had some status in mythology—although, of course, the resulting structure was novel.

A "noble lie" of common identity, artificial civic myths, and institutions in which to make "mixing" (dare one say integration?) a reality are three principles that could go far toward building a new society out of America's great ethnic and racial diversity. One can hardly imagine how much a common commitment to mixing with each other might energize American society. Furthermore, the novel mix could be built of multi- rather than unicultural elements. Unlike Athenians, Americans would not have to adopt a civic ideology that honors only the heroes of the majority (still people of European descent as of the 1990s). American civic ideology could instead pay proper honor to the diverse mythologies of the numerous peoples who make up the country. The only caveat would be an underlying emphasis on commonality, but mixing would go far toward meeting that need.

Mixing must be encouraged on every level, from school to sports to work. The military can play a particularly important role in this regard. A two-year national service requirement (ages 18–20), with extremely few exemptions granted, would encourage the intermingling of Americans from every walk of life. Still, it is all too easy to imagine soldiers breaking into ethnic, racial, or regional social groupings; indeed, that would be the likely result unless social mixing were encouraged, both in ideology and practice, from an early age. National service should be an important stage in creating the civic community, but it cannot be the beginning. Festivals, contests (from sporting events to spelling bees), choruses, artwork, radio and television programs, sermons, pop songs, seminars, comic books, theater, parades, Sunday supplements—in short, the widest possible range of activities and media should be drawn into the task of emphasizing the ties that create an American civic community.

Particular emphasis might be placed on the modern equivalent of Cleisthenes' dictum "No investigation of tribes!" One way to do this, if admittedly an extreme one, would be simply to mandate that in public discourse, everyone have a demotic name. A country as big as America would perhaps need 13,900 demes rather than Athens's 139, but a system could be worked out. So, for instance, Bill Clinton might become Bill Arkansas, Jesse Jackson become Jesse District of Columbia, Geraldine Ferraro become Geraldine Queens. Another expedient might be explicit encouragement of studying someone else's group: Cajuns investigating Chinese-American culture, or Mexican-Americans exploring African-American history, or Hispanic-Americans learning about America's Hibernian heritage.

None of this is to say that civic ideology and its institutional manifestations alone can solve the problems of American democracy. Without finding new ways of creating wealth, without improving American global economic competitiveness, without improving education, and without diverting resources toward improving the status of what has become a virtually permanently impoverished 10 or 20 percent of the population, it will be difficult to make democratic participation a reality. But the creation and enhancement of civic ideology might provide an impetus toward the solution of other problems, simply because it would put the problems of society on center stage.

To sum up, the exclusivity of Athenian democracy is a subject rich in paradox. Although it would be rash to say that modern America is entirely comfortable with diversity, ancient Athens was clearly far more troubled by it and thus felt the need to elaborate a myth of autochthony. Ironically, that myth has often been accepted as a real-

ity: "proof" of the importance of keeping society racially homogeneous. In fact the Athenian experience offers a very different lesson.
Democracy can thrive in a diverse society as long as people of different origins and customs are united by myths of community. Democracy and diversity will coexist nicely—indeed, each will energize the
other—as long as citizens have a civic identity in public life. If people
have a "demotic" identity, if there is "no investigation of tribes," if
there is "mixing" throughout the life cycle and in a variety of enter-
prises, then democracy becomes a reality without homogeneity. American ideology can make use of Athens's "noble lie" of community without accepting the ignoble lie of autochthony. We have progressed
from Athenian exclusivity, but the Athenian notion of civic identity
still has much to teach us.

WARREN J. LANE

AND ANN M. LANE

10   *Athenian Political Thought and*
      the Feminist Politics of
      Poiesis and Praxis

Athenian democracy was an order of governance and culture,
an organization of power as well as ethics. Inhabiting a liberal political
culture of diminished citizenship, Americans tend to see power and
ethics as separable, even disparate. Attending to the multisided character of ancient democratic experience can help us reassess the costs
we incur by our modern political practices.

Contemporary feminist political thinkers such as Nancy Hartsock,
Jean Elshtain, and Kathy Ferguson, among others, have perceptively
inquired into the separation of power and ethics, particularly as manifested in the prevailing forms and ideals of bureaucratic power. Their
studies analyze fundamental features and presuppositions of these
formations as well as identify modes of activity and association that
could counter and potentially supplant hierarchically oppressive practices and arrangments.

We argue, however, that such feminist theorizing, despite its critique of the power/ethics split, has overlooked crucial strands of classical thinking about power as oriented toward praxis (doing) as opposed to that centered on poiesis (making). Overlooking the classical
resources, feminist analyses of power have not avoided serious ambiguities. Thus what is often regarded by feminists as the strongly positive, nonhierarchical expression of power manifest in human competence and caregiving is, we suggest, often covertly hierarchical. Lack
of critical attention to such latent shortcomings—ones to which Athenian political thinking was well attuned—has come, in turn, to jeopar-
dize the coalitions that white feminists seek with women of color and

265

working-class women. But before turning to an examination of the ambiguity within the feminist theorists' conception of power and its implications, it is helpful first to consider the Greek conceptions that assist an analysis of power's dual sociopolitical potential.

Jean-Pierre Vernant has called attention to the important problematizing of collective power and decision making in many Greek city-states in the sixth and fifth centuries B.C. There appeared at this time a vivid metaphor for political power, political space, and interhuman concourse which aptly characterized the democratization of political life. Lawgivers, reformers, historians, and poets spoke of collective power located *es meson*—at the center of the people. The image was that of a circled assembly of people who faced a center, to which all had rotating access as temporary speakers addressing and addressed by their peers, as the assembly visibly and openly discussed, criticized, and decided issues of public concern.[1]

The various discussions in the dramatists and Herodotus of the resituation of collective power from an overhead to an in-between position indicate the fundamental antithesis between hierarchical and shared power. Collective power not rightly communalized is regarded by these ancient critics as the improperly exclusive preserve of a favored few, or elite, who occupy the apex of the societal pyramid. These notables may be kings (in the Greek sense of hereditarily defined heads of aristocratic families and clans), tyrants (in the neutral Greek sense of a usurper of those exercising traditional prerogatives), or oligarchies composed of the wealthy and often the well-born. Although, from a fifth-century Athenian standpoint, power at the middle defined democratic Athens's opposition to other types of regimes, in principle the metaphor could also define the contrast between more broadly based and more narrowly defined oligarchies. The *es meson* metaphor thus delineates a collective democratizing process, but it prescribes neither its scope nor its overall consistency.

The emergence in Greece of a problematic of collective power which opposed its shared or hierarchical expressions was a political development of great significance because it provided an idiom of

1. The richness of this metaphor for public deliberation and its political implications are explored by Jean-Pierre Vernant, *Myth and Thought among the Greeks* (Boston: Routledge and Kegan Paul, 1983), chaps. 6 and 7, and *The Origins of Greek Thought* (Ithaca: Cornell University Press, 1982), chaps. 4 and 8. Cf. G. E. R. Lloyd, *Magic, Reason, and Experience* (Cambridge: Cambridge University Press, 1979), 242, n. 60, on relevant passages in Aeschylus and Euripides. As Vernant implies and H. W. Pleket asserts, the "essence of 'isonomia'" of political equality (the byword of Athenian democratizing reforms from the time of Cleisthenes) was the placing of power at the center of the people; see Harry W. Pleket, "Isonomia and Cleisthenes: A Note," *Talanta* 4 (1972): 65.

understanding and practice which could be brought to bear in the communal restructuring of power. As the political history of Athenian civic crises, institutional change, and leadership makes evident, this idiom was pertinent to diverse sectors of judicial and political affairs of the sort in which a traditional or even an antitraditional hierarchically exercised power of decision making was popularly challenged and reconstituted.

Athens, over much of the course of three centuries, displayed a unique ability to mold both its local institutional assemblies (of deme, phratry, tribe) and its politywide institutions (of assembly, councils, and lawcourts, as well as their officeholding requirements) toward a realization of visible power sharing and away from hierarchy. This resilient and extensive regime of democratized power among Athenians did not rely on compartmentalization of politics from the remainder of social life. On the contrary, one could say that what existed at the collective, macropolitical level consistently drew upon and reinforced micro-level sociopolitical considerations. Athenian politics were thoroughly entwined in the fabric of ordinary experience. This interplay is primarily responsible for the multidimensionality of Athenian democracy.

Of particular importance among the micro-level experiential considerations at Athens was a culturally defined understanding of human agency, its potentialities and priorities. This understanding was oriented by a ranked contrast between the action and association pertinent to praxis and those relevant to poiesis. Roughly translatable as the contrast between "doing" and "making," the Greek terms—developed by Aristotle in the context of his politics—defined highly divergent constellations of activity and association.

The praxis-poiesis contrast taken up by Aristotle not only has immediate Sophistic precedents but also draws upon a tradition of Athenian thinking to which Solon, in the early sixth century, was a major contributor. In his elegies, which became part of the oral education of later Athenian youth, Solon dwells on a comparison between people's potential for civically minded or justice-championing activity, on the one hand, and on the other, private aims of wealth and status whose myopic pursuit destroys a city's well-being.

The Solonic contrast—between activities that further justice and political harmony and those lesser yet often necessary activities whose potentially exaggerated importance undermines civic life—is addressed to all free Athenian males regardless of hereditary position or wealth. The Solonic distinction and ranking of forms of activity became a basis for ordinary people's assimilation of an understanding of how

their endeavors were implicated in the life of the city. Moreover, Solonic language lent commoners the intellectual means to identify and
criticize self-serving claims to rule by their social superiors. The differentiation of ways of action and the establishing of priority, conceived poetically by Solon (amid reforms that created practical occasions for the exercise of civic capacities by new, commoner male
sections of the population) provided a vocabulary available to all male
members of the polis regardless of class. In Solon's view, people could
attain (especially through actual participation in democratic practices)
the multifaceted agency he poetically delineated. A citizenry could
achieve a heightened level of sensitivity to the demands of the democratizing collective power his reforms inaugurated and resist any upsurge of hierarchical power that, unconstrained, might rob a polity of
its chances for communal well-being.[2]

I

Visibly shared and democratic forms of power, as opposed to hierarchical forms of association, are of fundamental concern to American feminist political thinkers. Such concern arises not only out of a
feminist critique of masculinist ideologies and arrangements. Wom-
en's attention to class, ethnicity, race, and anti-Semitism as they affect
power relations throughout American institutional life also prompt
this concern, as do possibilities for wide-ranging coalition formation
to contest oppressive structural relations.

In recent years, feminist political thinkers have emphasized the notion of empowerment, rejecting the primacy of power as dominance
and control in favor of power as human capacity or agency.[3] They
have stressed women's capacity and competence to organize themselves, as in self-help health clinics, workplace antiharassment cam-
paigns, and antibattering shelters. Yet their analyses of "capacity" and
"competence" can be problematic. Whose capacity and competence do
the thinkers really focus on in these examples? Who is empowered by
such activities? And who is precluded from empowerment? In oppressive situations, the exercise of agency on the part of some women may
not empower all women. Is there a secret connection, not always dis-

2. On Solon and his self-conception as educator of his city, see Werner Jaeger, *Paideia*,
vol. 1 (Oxford: Oxford University Press, 1944), chap. 8, and William G. Forrest, *The Emergence of Greek Democracy* (New York: McGraw-Hill, 1966), chap. 6.

3. E.g., Nancy Hartsock, *Money, Sex, and Power* (New York: Longman, 1983); Elizabeth
Minnich, "Thinking As We Are," in *Between Women*, ed. Carol Ascher et al. (Boston: Beacon,
1984), 171–85; and Janice Raymond, *A Passion for Friends* (Boston: Beacon, 1986).

cerned by feminists, between some forms of asserting competence and some forms of oppression?

The extensive critiques of feminist activities coming from women of color, poor, and working-class women indicate both the political-cultural complexity of those activities and the need for democratically inclined feminists to realize when their actions are complicitous with the prevailing, privileged order. The ancient Greek concepts of poiesis and praxis, particularly as retheorized by Hannah Arendt, can be useful to contemporary feminist thinkers in making such judgments.

In the 1950s and 1960s, Arendt, a German-Jewish political theorist, drew on Aristotle to explore power dynamics in the Russian, German, and Hungarian revolutionary movements as well as in the refounding of Israel. She argued that there was a recurrent tension between party or administrative hierarchical tendencies on the one hand and popular councils' democratizing, confederative tendencies on the other.[4] Arendt's analysis is equally relevant to understanding contemporary political resistance movements, such as the ecology movement, ethnic solidarity movements, and western feminism.

Arendt observed how often movement participants mistook their "ministering" to others' needs (poiesis) as the model for sociopolitical life. She witnessed how such a caretaking mentality (e.g., attention to what was called the "social question" or a preoccupation with "survival") destroyed peer relations and a democractic political vision.[5] The importance of attending to people's needs notwithstanding, she argued, the sustenance of the movement depends on equal attention to the political relations between those doing the attending and those being attended to. Although caretaking seems to offer a liberating, alternative vision of interindividual existence, it actually distorts clear political thinking. Thus, it is not caretaking, emphasized by so many feminist political thinkers, but the "networking" dimension of women's experience (praxis), which, Arendt would argue, can generate a democratic feminist sociopolitical vision.

Feminists' new awareness of agency is in part a retrieval of a nondominative sense of power already latent in Anglo-American usage. As Bernice Carroll has observed, dictionary definitions between 1933 and 1966 reveal a sharp shift in ordinary language usage about

4. See Hannah Arendt, *The Origins of Totalitarianism* (Cleveland: World, 1958), and *On Revolution* (New York: Viking, 1963).

5. For a telling example of how a damaging paternalism can easily coexist with caretaking in an important political movement, see Renny Golden and Michael McConnell, *Sanctuary: The New Underground Railroad* (Maryknoll, N.Y.: Orbis, 1986), esp. 168–70.

power.[6] This period covers the rise of fascism, World War II, the Cold War, and the nuclear peace. In the decade of the thirties, both the *Oxford English Dictionary* and the *Webster's International* defined power as the "ability, whether physical, mental or moral, to act: the faculty of doing or performing something." The second definition was an "exerted ability to act or produce effects . . . strength, might, energy, vigor, force." Only the fourth definition contains our now conventionally accepted usage: "the possession of sway or controlling influence over others, command, ascendancy." In the dictionary of the sixties it is this last notion, further elaborated as "dominion" and as "ability to compel obedience," that becomes the premier definition. The more traditional sense drops into second place. And, as Hartsock points out, it is this lapsed sense that feminists have resuscitated in their thinking.[7]

In recovering the older, agential meaning of power, theorists such as Carroll and Hartsock rely heavily on the phrases "energy and competence" and "capacity and effectiveness." Although these phrases rightly alert us to the mistake of conceiving of power always as domination, they offer no clue about how to differentiate caretaking from participatory power. Hartsock collapses all distinctions of power into mere "competency." Her discussion of power, nonetheless, usefully points us toward Arendt's conception of human agency. Hartsock notes that Arendt stresses the significance of "equals" who share a world and its affairs. Such peers "share words and deeds," "speak and act together," and "act in concert" to shape their situations. Arendt, spelling out the intimate connection between power and the sociopolitical bonds of community, argues that the quality of solidarity among a community of peers is as important as the issues they are dealing with. Reflecting on the student movement of the 1960s, Arendt observes that the participants failed to recognize that the ultimate value of their struggle lay in participation itself.

Hartsock's discussion importantly contributes to the feminist reassessment and selective assimilation of the ideas of Arendt, who directly explores the unprecedented organizational, imperialist, and technocratic perils of modernity and the challenges it made to democratic thinking and practice. Both Arendt and Hartsock elaborate an affirmative sense of power and understand the conditions that promote or inhibit it, but Arendt, more fully than Hartsock, articulates

6. Bernice Carroll, "Peace Research: The Cult of Power," *Journal of Conflict Resolution* 4 (1972): 585–616.

7. Hartsock, *Money, Sex, and Power*, 210–26.

for us the ambiguities of agency and furnishes clues for identifying its varieties.

II

Arendt revived and elaborated the classical Athenian distinction between praxis and poiesis from her early *Origins of Totalitarianism* to her late *Life of the Mind*.[8] Following Aristotle, she claims that praxis makes people most fully human; for it involves participatory acts among peers which create their sociopolitical world—people collectively determining their own lives.[9]

Poiesis has two senses: instrumental, as in the production of things, and ministrative, in the sense of caring for the needs of people, animals, and other living things. Poiesis attains its consummation and meaning in some self-subsistent end. Thus, for instance, productive activity achieves its determinate end in a cabinet built or a loaf of bread baked. A result (bread) is realized outside the activity (bread making) that brought it into being. Poiesis must cease in order for its end to exist. The Athenian and Aristotelian usage of poiesis, however, included not just instrumental activity but also ministrative activities such as doctoring, training athletes, generalship, ship navigation, and shepherding a flock.[10] We could add to this list raising children as well. These forms of poiesis also have their completion and meaning outside themselves. In the Athenian view, "He who builds a ship or attempts to cure a sick man has ultimately achieved nothing so long as the ship is not finished or health is not restored."[11]

In contrast, praxis achieves its fulfillment and meaning only in the performing of the activity itself, only so long as the activity unfolds in time. For Athenians, praxis centered on participatory interaction conducted among peers through words and deeds. Like dancers performing a dance, praxis manifests itself only in the course of its performance. When the activity ceases, it no longer possesses efficacy or engages its participants.

---

8. Arendt's most extensive treatment of the contrast can be found in *The Human Condition* (Chicago: University of Chicago Press, 1958). Helpful comments can be found in Nicholas Lobkowicz, *Theory and Practice* (Notre Dame: University of Notre Dame Press, 1967), chap. 1.

9. See, esp., "Action," in Arendt, *Human Condition*, 175–247.

10. Moreover, for the asocial implications of poiesis, see Arendt, *Origins of Totalitarianism*, 475.

11. Nicholas Lobkowicz, "On the History of Theory and Praxis," in *Political Theory and Praxis: New Perspectives*, ed. Terence Ball (Minneapolis: University of Minnesota Press, 1977), 18.

Poiesis and praxis consequently generate different forms of human relationship. In its instrumentalism, poiesis is asocial, requiring removal from others for concentration; in its ministrative (caretaking) aspect, it is hierarchical because it involves specialized knowledge, intervention in and over another's life, and the application of skill not possessed by the one cared for. To the contrary, praxis, as embodied in participatory actions, promotes horizontal, peer ties—mutual empowerment.

Unlike us, the Athenians saw the easy compatibility of ministering to the needs of others and dictating to them.[12] In contrast to the asocial and hierarchical implications of poiesis, in Athenian and Aristotelian usage, praxis realizes a life of common empowerment among friends and citizens. Friendship in Athenian political culture was esteemed as one of the greatest goods of human life.[13] It sustained personal life as well as the political community itself.[14] The chorus of Antigone credits friendship with giving solidarity to political life—the cosmic law required for civic morale.[15] For Aristotle, "political community depends on friendship . . . a [polity] aims at being, so far as it can be a society composed of equals and peers who, as such can be friends and associated."[16] Friendship was also the genuine touchstone of justice: "When [people] are friends they have no need of justice, while when they are just they need friends as well, and the truest form of justice is thought to be a friendly quality."[17]

Martha Acklesberg has clearly indicated the significance of Athenian and Aristotelian understandings of friendship for currrent feminist thinking and practice.[18] She has analyzed the liabilities of women's resort to familial idioms of "sisterhood" to define themselves and

12. For an example of the interchangeability in Greek language and thought of the ministrative exercise of power, see the array of linked usages under the entry *"poimen"* (shepherd) in the *Liddell-Scott Greek-English Lexicon* (1968), 1430.

13. For the interconnection of kindredship, friendship, and citizenship as depicted in Athenian drama, see Warren J. Lane and Ann M. Lane, "The Politics of Antigone," in *Greek Tragedy and Political Theory*, ed. J. Peter Euben (Berkeley and Los Angeles: University of California Press, 1986), 162–82.

14. Aristotle *Nicomachean Ethics*, trans. David Ross (Oxford: Oxford University Press, 1954), 1155a14–15.

15. Sophocles *Antigone*, in *The Complete Greek Tragedies*, trans. Elizabeth Wyckoff (Chicago: University of Chicago Press, 1954), no. 355. For commentary, see Lane and Lane, "Politics of Antigone," 178–79.

16. Aristotle *The Politics*, trans. Ernest Barker (Oxford: Oxford University Press, 1962), 1295b7–8.

17. Ibid., 1155a24–26.

18. Martha Acklesberg, "Sisters or Comrades? The Politics of Friends and Families," in *Families, Politics, and Public Policy*, ed. Irene Diamond (New York: Longman, 1983), 339–56, and "Women's Collaborative Activities and City Life," in *Political Women*, ed. Janet Flammang (Newberry Park, Calif.: Sage Publications, 1984), 242–59.

pointed out the merits of a Greek idiom of friendship in its personal and civic application. Furthermore, she appreciates the power of friendship and neighbor networks among poor urban women to provide self-confidence as well as cross-ethnic and cross-racial solidarity for facing community-related political issues. Yet despite the Greek argument available to her, which opposes friendship and nurturance, Acklesberg uses friendship and nurturant values interchangeably.

Academics, political actors, and officials now easily confound participatory activity with notions of cooperation, interdependence, supportiveness, and nurturance—notions deeply enmeshed in ministrative practices and understandings. It is therefore more necessary than ever that people pursuing an alternative vision of sociopolitical life closely examine the current feminist idioms pertaining to "maternal thinking" and "caretaking." Such idioms endanger coalition friendships because they encourage, for example, the best intentioned white, middle-class activists to uncritically adopt a stance of political condescension toward prospective partners when they are poor women and women of color.

In friendship, participants not only assert their own perspectives and initiatives but find opportunities for further action put at their disposal by coparticipants, creating the bonds of trust essential to mutual empowerment and a broad distribution of power. It is vital moreover that the role of initiator rotate among all parties. Rotation demonstrates trust in others and disavows any intention to make others dependent or to undermine their self-confidence, thus permitting them to codetermine the content and quality of interaction. No one then becomes confined to a specialized capacity.

As Janice Raymond rightly observes, genuine friends or peers are not abstract equals according to some formal standard. They are, on the contrary, persons "capable of meeting the requirements of a situation or task."[19] Peership here becomes a matter of repeatedly proving one's moral and practical mettle in a perpetual test posed by the inevitable contingencies and ambiguities of sociopolitical interaction. Peership conceived not formalistically but as an actively reaccomplished status creates bonds of intense solidarity. And experiences of solidarity enhance trust in one another's capacities to act well. Over time, these accumulated experiences invest bonds with enduring value.

Such a peer milieu provides a desirable model of interindividual life to extend beyond existing hierarchical confines into wider social life. Thus, for example, the broader separatist institution building of

19. Raymond, *Passion for Friends*, 229.

American feminists in the nineteenth and twentieth centuries took as its elemental unit the peer formation of friends. These localized networks of relations provided participants with an appreciation for democratized conduct and inspired them with an intimation of an alternative mode of interindividual life. Networks also made possible yet wider confederative mobilizations of people. Movements' loss of contact with these crucibles of peer solidarity presage loss of morale and organizational rigidification. Indeed, feminist movements have not always been successful either in sustaining such peer formations as building blocks or in recreating their effects at higher levels of organization.[20]

III

Even Kathy Ferguson's important and compelling *Feminist Case against Bureaucracy* exhibits the difficulties inherent in an overly ministrative conception of agential power which are seen in the work of other feminist theorists. For Ferguson, feminist political thought must come to grips with the dominative implication of bureaucracy if that theory is meant to liberate women and men. But she also thinks a radical analysis must acknowledge women as both staff and clients of bureaucracy. Failure to do this results in ignoring the gender-rooted legacies that help sustain bureaucracy. Moreover, that failure also forces theory to lose touch with resources buried in women's experience which might otherwise be applied to criticizing bureaucracy and projecting a counter vision.

Ferguson makes two provocative arguments in her book, one pertaining to a structural syndrome, the other to alternative values. It is her view that modern bureaucracy is a medium that gives new, increased play and prominence to a syndrome of conduct hitherto associated with middle-class women in their traditional dealings with a patriarchal order. The syndrome, a way of simultaneously defending oneself from and accommodating the requirements of subordination, is a complex of stereotypical attitudes and behaviors foremost among which are "gentleness, nurturance, sympathy, patience . . . expres-

20. See, e.g., Nancy Cott, *The Bonds of Womanhood* (New Haven: Yale University Press, 1977); Estelle Freedman, "Separatism as Strategy: Female Institution Building and American Feminism," *Feminist Studies* 5 (1979): 512–29; Blanche Cook, "Support Networks and Political Activism," *Chrysalis* 3 (1977): 44–61; and Jo Freeman, *The Politics of Women's Liberation* (New York: 1975).

sive[ness] . . . attentiveness to others [and] nonassertiveness."[21] With their skill in learning and displaying these "feminized traits," middle-class women have adapted to gender-based asymmetries of power in a manner that has now become, through the proliferation of bureau-cracies, the widespread practice of staff and clients enmeshed in such organizational power relations.[22]

Ferguson's second and more important argument addresses the values and experiences that generate a liberatory alternative to the contemporary, bureaucratic hierarchization of our lives. Bureaucratic dominance is characterized by asymmetric power relations, the wielding of specialized knowledge, enforceable norms, rationalistic thought, and vocabularies of abstract right and duty. These features decontextualize, depoliticize, and fragment the everyday interactions of people, whether personnel or clients. Subordinate persons turn to feminized, defensively adapted performances as their only available means of making their situation tolerable. Such performances, though quite understandable, do not challenge, even obliquely, the perpetuation of hierarchy itself.

This feminizing stance toward subordination, which is so rooted in the middle class, is unexpectedly widespread and prominent because of the proliferation of bureaucratization. But Ferguson believes the corrective to it—and to the bureaucratic outlook—lies in the gradual diffusion of a different aspect of women's lives: genuine "caretaking and nurturant experience."[23] She rightly insists that liberatory counterideals "and alternative forms of relation and organization" are as firmly centered in women's experience as the feminizing adaptation itself (xi). In her view, women are eminently qualified to think through and exemplify caregiving ways that can be blended into movement-related forms of resistance to dominative power.

21. Kathy Ferguson, *The Feminist Case against Bureaucracy* (Philadelphia: Temple University Press, 1984), 93.

22. As intriguing as Ferguson's argument is that the spread of bureaucratic organization in societal life draws upon traditionally middle-class feminized ways within the gender order to sustain both its internal system of ranks and its external client relations, it is a thesis that calls for additional inquiry. As Wendy Brown, "Challenging Democracy," *Women's Review of Books*, November 1984, 16–17, has acutely observed, the very analogical breadth of Ferguson's analysis of feminizing conduct—one which many contemporary dominated groups make use of— also obscures what is particular to any one of these groups. Ferguson makes an interesting acknowledgment about the role class plays in susceptibility to the feminizing syndrome, but the insight has no significant place in her overall analysis. Brown also comments that it would be instructive to know the importance Ferguson attaches both to the sexual objectification of women by men and to male misogyny as a means of differentiating the feminized conduct of women from that of other subordinate or oppressed groups.

23. Ferguson, *Feminist Case against Bureaucracy*, x.

Ferguson suggests, morever, that once significant numbers of women appreciate this responsibility, they will develop many localized protest sites embodying caretaking values. She believes politically conscious women will emerge throughout bureaucratized society and not merely in highly visible, co-optable loci of resistance. Women foremost, but also men, can, through education and encouragement, rise to a critical awareness of the oppositional perspective latent in experiences of genuine female caregiving and use this experience's rejection of "the terms of self-understanding embedded in bureaucratic discourse" (x–xi) to foster a successful counter vision and an ongoing resistance.[24]

Ferguson, however, never finds a convincing way to sort out true caretaking from counterfeit, feminized performances. Indeed, problematic assumptions underlie her confidence that such a sorting is possible. She observes that differential class affiliation operates to render women of the middle class, whether black or white, more adept at and more prone to resort to feminizing adaptations than their lower-class counterparts (97, 207–8). The latter lack bourgeois ideology's training in the "female virtues" of dependence and passivity, according to Ferguson. The very deprivations of poor women's lives make an appeal to these feminized virtues ineffective. The arrangements for living established by poor women include general caretaking activities ordinarily distorted by sentimentality among middle-class women.

Thus Ferguson implies that deprivation insulates against the social artifice that impedes realization of a more complete form of life, which amounts to a classist version of the noble savage ideology. She suggests that poor women hold the clue to the essentials of a female activity that more privileged and status-preoccupied middle-class women must seek to comprehend. Lower-class women and their experiences thus appear to offer the key to sociopolitical salvation for their middle-class counterparts. Academics in this scenario crack the cipher lodged in poor women's seemingly mute existence, helping them to transcend that existence. This argument not only fosters a condescending relation between educated middle-class feminists and lower-class women but bases itself on a repugnant assumption: the moral-intellectual insights accruing to one group of women rest on the necessary deprivation endured by another group.

In short, caretaking activity itself cannot sustain the countervaluative impetus Ferguson assigns it. Because caretaking looms large not only for Ferguson but for other feminists such as Sara Ruddick, Jean

24. Ibid., 175, 249 n. 44, iii.

Elshtain, and Carol Gilligan, on whose work she draws (though in Ferguson's case, with far more radical political intentions), we need to recognize the collusive ties caretaking must forge with larger hierarchical contexts.

Ferguson defines caretaking as nurturant tendance, as devoted solicitude toward "others" and their "diverse needs" (158–59). The affectionate tending by mothers of children, who have special requirements for preservation, growth, and acceptance, "only partially captures that which is unique to the experience of women as caretakers" (171). Women's attentiveness to the diverse needs of people involves them in the relatively invisible, prestigeless rounds of "domestic and familial labor." Such labor, Ferguson observes, is more rooted in "the maintenance of processes than in the production of products" (163).

As Iris Young similarly expresses it, the female home- and family-centered world oriented by a "concernful dealing with processes of life and death" contrasts with the male public world dominated by utilitarian meanings and activities centered on "making, planning, calculating, and achieving."[25] Everyday, home-centered activities include, says Young, not only "birthings" and "caring for young children" (one's own and those of others) but also "caring for the sick, infirm, or aged; sitting with the dying and preparing bodies of the dead." In these latter undertakings, women use implements and materials to establish "an environment of comfort, nourishment or cure," not for achieving specific ends of production. Giving care calls for knowledge of when to intervene and when to stand aside; it requires a spirit of attentiveness rather than a desire to "succeed at any cost" (25–27).

Ferguson's emphasis on homemaking tasks that establish an "environment of comfort," satisfying the needs of family members, has the effect of extending the meaning of caretaking beyond that of children in a narrow sense. But there persists a danger, Ferguson acknowledges, that caretaking will be too closely and inappropriately identified with only the model of mother-child relations. She does not wish to see the inequalities latent in such a relationship interjected into an already heavily hierarchized society, and therefore she stresses that

25. Iris Young, "Is There a Woman's World?" (Paper delivered at The Second Sex— Thirty Years Later, New York University Conference, September 27–29, 1979), 25–27. This distinction between female and male spheres of activity, which Ferguson and Young refer to, has its roots in the ideologies of gender spheres of the nineteenth century. On this gender ideology, see Cott, *Bonds of Womanhood*. On continuities in gender ideological assumptions among nineteenth-century, early twentieth-century, and second-wave feminism, see Nancy Cott, "Feminist Theory and Feminist Movements: The Past before Us," in *What Is Feminism?* ed. Juliet Mitchell and Ann Oakley (New York: Pantheon, 1986), 34.

caretaking, properly conceived, is not a product of an enlarged maternal practice. She argues consequently that caretaking arises from women's role not as mothers but as daughters. Being a beneficiary of maternal solicitude, and undergoing a lengthy apprenticeship in its practice as a daughter, render the latter especially attentive to caretaking. This rearing and training is a lasting legacy whether or not the daughter decides to become a mother.[26]

Ferguson's linking of nurturance to women's apprenticeship as daughters rather than to maternalism uncouples her views from the traditionalist feminist positions that move readily toward conventional pro-family, anti-gay, anti-abortion policy positions.[27] Ferguson's distinction enables her to present caretaking as a "characteristic" mode of thinking and acting belonging to women generally; one which, irrespective of maternal status, they can carry beyond the confines of the family into society at large. Freed from any exclusive anchorage in motherhood, the capacity for nurturance of others is seen as the experiential touchstone for an alternative, antihierarchical understanding and practice of life available to women and men.[28]

However impressive caretaking activity's outward divergence from the more legalistic aspects of bureaucracy (structured roles, abstract rights, impersonal rules) may be, caretaking unfortunately shares with bureaucracy a hierarchizing of interaction. Women's concernful dealings with processes, to which Ferguson refers, focus on those needs that people cannot meet by themselves. The asymmetric power relation built into ministrative activity linking solicitous caregiver to needful recipient implies dangers unacknowledged by Ferguson when she looks to caretaking as a liberatory resource.

26. Ferguson, *Feminist Case against Bureaucracy*, 171.
27. See Judith Stacey's analysis of the later writings of Betty Friedan and Germaine Greer and her overall assessment of Jean Elshtain, in "Are Feminists Afraid to Leave Home? The Challenge of Conservative Pro-Family Feminism," in Mitchell and Oakley, *What Is Feminism?* 208–37.
28. As her own extensive treatment of feminizing conduct makes abundantly clear, Ferguson is thoroughly aware of the ways in which genuine caregiving can be deformed under constraining hierarchical conditions, whether patriarchal or bureaucratic (*Feminist Case against Bureaucracy*, 166–77). Moreover, Ferguson makes no attempt to deny that children can be ill-treated and abused by mothers or that nationalism and racism can make their own invidious use of caretaking in ways that can be enthusiastically endorsed by women. She does not seek to drape women's moral sensibilities in sentimentalized oversimplifications that disguise potential, contextually rooted moral disabilities and blindness. That such ideologically and institutionally based oversimplifications have, however, invaded women's thinking about themselves—not only in nineteenth-century suffragist views of race and class but also in twentieth-century German feminists' attitudes toward the Nazi party and Jewish women—heightens the importance of establishing an adequate critical standard that feminists can apply to distinguishing the liberatory from the counterfeit potentialities of women's experience and makes the lack of such a critical standard in Ferguson's account more serious.

We have already noted how Ferguson views a feminizing caretaking stance as a defensive adaptation to subordination and a counterfeit expression of an ostensively genuine form of such activity.[29] But there are no less serious limitations in the "true" variant of caretaking. These limitations are not the consequence of externally imposed constraints; nor are they the product of either the masculinist or the bureaucratic settings in which caregiving ordinarily operates, as Ferguson assumes in her treatment of this activity's deformation. Rather, as the Greeks understood, the limitations are centered in the inherent dynamic of this activity. This is not to say that ministrative activity is somehow immoral or unnecessary. The point is that the characteristics of various ministrative modes of agential power need to be discerned so that they will not usurp the place of those participatory modes of agency more suited to common empowerment. When we make distinctions sensitive to forms of power, we are more likely to enhance participatory possibilties while ensuring access to necessary caretaking.

Ferguson's last chapter—on the elements of an alternative, liberatory feminist vision and practice of interindividual life—tangentially discusses friendship, participatory activity, and peer ties. Drawing on Acklesberg, Ferguson rightly perceives in friendship a challenge to any simplistic distinction between private and public life as well as a principle and form of political association. As in the Athenian-Aristotelian understanding of friendship discussed above, Ferguson sees that the equality, trust, freedom, and mutualities essential to friendship should inform all levels of political association and furnish a visionary touchstone for the creation of a genuinely meaningful way of life.

Ferguson's remarks on friendship are brief, confined to one place in her analysis, and little connected to her overall concerns with caretaking activity, so why does she raise the issue at all? Despite her own emphasis on women's experience as daughters as the source of their caregiving capacity, she remains suspicious that the mother-child rela-

29. One further variant of counterfeit caretaking not encompassed by Ferguson's notion of feminization is that which Jessie Bernard terms the "taking care syndrome." This syndrome pertains to women who regard grown men as "just little boys grown tall who (have) to be taken care of . . . protected from their own inadequacies" and shielded from the humiliating knowledge of being the object of such protection. This stance of preemptive and aggressive solicitude may be regarded, in some part, as an adjustment to a masculinist order by much-abused women who have developed a consoling self-deception about themselves. But the syndrome also bespeaks an attitude of condescension that virtually precludes the possibility of overtures from men being taken seriously when they are intended as invitations to participate in association as peers. See Jessie Bernard, *The Female World* (New York: Free Press, 1981), 425–27.

tion, with its pervasive inequalities, will too readily become the model for caretaking within larger sociopolitical formations. Western patriarchal and sentimentalized conceptions of motherhood—conceptions shared by men and women—make likely such a misidentification of liberatory sources, and that, she observes, would, at best, ensure a "benevolent despotism" in sociopolitical affairs.[30]

Perhaps Ferguson introduces friendship into her analysis as a final safeguard against the adoption of a maternalist model for caregiving in sociopolitical life. Friendship provides counterimages and counterexperiences that remind people they do not want a benevolent maternalist despotism in sociopolitical existence. Ferguson wants caretaking to be "connected to the more equal and reciprocal relations of friendship" (173), but she sees no contradiction between caretaking and friendship. This is problematic. The "connection" she makes between divergent modes of activity and association necessarily implies the subordination of friendship to caretaking. Friendship is reduced in her schema to an afterthought, a protective measure improvised against the culturally powerful maternalist conception of caretaking ever present in masculinist society. Encapsulating friendship in caregiving, she seeks to make solicitude flow from each party, in turn, to satisfy the needs of the other. She thinks, in the end, that rotation of caregiving will suffice to establish true interdependence.

Although interdependence may indeed be preferable to rationalized and impersonalized relationships, the subservience of friendship to ministration disallows that pivotal sharing of words and deeds generative of common empowerment, and it discourages attention to the conditions fostering such interaction. Moreover, it insufficiently insulates people against vulnerability to increasingly subtle forms of co-optation issuing from the wider bureaucratic context.

IV

We believe the hierarchization of interaction generated by caretaking represents the elemental aspect of this practice's collusive relation with the bureaucratic order to which it is supposed to stand as an alternative. But these interior limitations with their microcollusive connections to extant hierarchical forms have a macrocollusive counterpart. As Michel Foucault has pointed out, the historical and institutional organization of ministrative functions by the church, and subsequently the state, in western society has enormously enlarged the

30. Ferguson, *Feminist Case against Bureaucracy*, 172.

scope, complexity, innovative impetus, and prestige of ministrative activity in our lives.[31]

Foucault provides us with insight into a certain configuration of power which, if not adequately comprehended and checked, assumes through its focus and manner of organization an insidiously dominating guise. He designates this often subtly managerial and shepherding power "pastoral." Its earliest, most institutionally and ideologically developed locus was the Christian church and the relation it established between priest and laity.[32] The priest was the knowledgeable spiritual shepherd, the devoted, watchful caretaker and protector of the souls of his parishioners and of the spiritual welfare of his parish. The all-male priesthood was educated and trained to minister to the spiritual needs of congregants who could not themselves satisfy these needs as they traveled the path of repentence on earth.

With the coalesence in Europe by the sixteenth century of centrally organized, territorial, monarchical states, Foucault perceives ministrative service and discourse not eliminated from the church but incorporated preeminently in the state. The new ascendancy of the state as the primary site of pastoral power meant that the pastoral function "was no longer a question of leading people to their salvation in the next world, but rather ensuring it in this world."[33] The focus of organized caretaking shifted from the ultimate spiritual welfare of Christians to the secular welfare of political subjects. Not souls but public health, city planning, the production of wealth, urban food supplies, means of transportation, safety from invasion, and public order became paramount objects of care for state officials who tended the worldly welfare of whole populations. Foucault provides a sweeping analysis of the diffusion, proliferation, and oblique interlocking of ostensibly benign ministrative agents and arrangements directed to the professional supervising of the vast human, material, technical, and cultural resources whose expert deployment alone sustained the welfare of the state.

Foucault shows how diverse fields of study pertaining to geography, economics, demography, irrigation, forestry, public health, and social custom either became dissociated from older moral and religious frameworks when they were pursued as adjuncts to state administra-

31. Despite her familiarity with Foucault and her perceptive use of Foucauldian ideas, Ferguson has not explored the relevance of his analysis of pastoral power and the pastorate for an understanding of bureaucracy.

32. Michel Foucault, *Omnes et Singulum: Towards a Criticism of Political Reason*, 1979 Tanner Lecture on Human Values (Salt Lake City: University of Utah Press, 1981).

33. Michel Foucault, "The Subject and the Power," in *Michel Foucault*, ed. Hubert Dreyful and Paul Rabinow (Chicago: University of Chicago Press, 1982), 214–15.

tive concerns, or were developed specifically to enhance officials' management of affairs. The state encouraged the formation of scientific
societies, schools, and professional associations that would contribute
to fields of knowledge whose very content and manner of conceptualization made them amenable to official use and the exercise and ex-
tention of ministrative functions.

The modern social welfare system is, for Foucault, only the latest
development of the civil ministrative system that has been a central
part of state functioning since the sixteenth century. The depoliticizing and disempowering impact on people generated by the upsurge
and diffusion of ministrative endeavors requiring systems of super-
and subordinative relations, should not, however, be taken to mean,
as Foucault himself cautions, that political struggle was eliminated
from societal affairs or that the myriad clientele of pastoral elites were
utterly pacificed. Historically, both the church's and the state's ministrative functioning has been the object of sometimes violent political
conflict. Monastic communities inspired by ideals of early Christian
piety and charity often spearheaded ecclesiastical reform aimed at
making pastoral power throughout the church a more vibrant reality
in human life. Similarly, peasant and urban-based rebellions have
arisen from a desire to see the restoration in practice of a ministrative
ideal and order from which an existing regime was thought to have
grown hypocritically remote.

Reformative caregiving cannot challenge hierarchy at a fundamental level, however, nor promote itself as the moral nucleus for a form
of life that can viably replace it. Today's feminists have, in the example of premodern and early modern advocates of reformative ministration, a reminder that though such values and activity can spur people to a more conscientious exercise of their ministrative functions,
caretaking has always been unable to inspire genuine sociopolitical reconstruction along participatory lines.

V

Arendt has written that subordinated peoples and groups retain in
their cultural depths a "hidden tradition," a legacy of valuable ideas
and practices that can nourish not only their members but, when re-
cast, the life of the larger society.[34] If this valuable hidden resource
within women's experience cannot be identified with caretaking (and
we have tried to indicate why it cannot), an alternative source must be

34. Hannah Arendt, *Jew as Pariah*, ed. Ron Feldman (New York: Grove, 1978), pt. 1.

sought. One alternative that can lead us out of the impasse created by the problematic quality of caretaking is the lateral, networking dimension of women's experience. In contemporary usage, "networking" designates a capacity for forging connections with others—connections that in any sociohistorical instance may move in either a reactionary or a public-minded direction.[35] Women who network and become fully aware of the wider sociopolitical implications of what they are doing will encounter each other ultimately as coparticipants—the initiators by word and deed of practices formative of common empowerment and peer bonds. Lateral connections among peers have a participatory dynamic that sets them off both from women's more usual vertical ministrative involvements aimed at ameliorating need and from patriarchal vertical connections that bind a woman to some implicitly or explictly privileged male figure, whether father, brother, husband, lover, boss, ritual officiant, or citizen-activist.

We should distinguish here the networking dimension as manifest among peers from its other possible manifestations (in a convent, a cult, or a conventional political grouping) where women might also be linked primarily to other women. These latter manifestations may involve women in extradomestic ties that yield power and value not otherwise attainable in a society where gender ideology and gender-linked structures firmly divide a lesser domestic status from a higher public one. We wish, however, to stress not so much the extradomestic character of the connections women establish as the embodiment in those connections of the principle of friendship, its participatory understandings and practices, and a concern for the conditions under which it can flourish.[36] Associations that do not build self-consciously on these participatory activities and understandings, however meritorious they may be in other respects, fail to radicalize the lateral, or networking, possibility inherent in such associations. Radicalization raises the question of whether networking women take the participatory principle internal to the life of their milieu out into the affairs of the world they seek to act upon.

Feminist anthropologists, social historians, and sociologists have shed much light on aspects of women's networking experience.[37] But with the exception of Acklesberg and bell hooks, little has been done

---

35. See Karen Sacks, "Networking: When Potluck Is Political," *Ms*, April, 1983, 97–98.

36. See Estelle Freedman, "Separatism as Strategy: Female Institution Building and American Feminism, 1870–1930," *Feminist Studies* 5 (1979): 512–29.

37. E.g., Michelle Rosaldo, Louise Lamphere, and Rayna Rapp among anthropologists; Carole Smith-Rosenberg, Nancy Cott, and Temma Kaplan among social historians; and Carol Stack and Joyce Ladner among sociologists.

by feminist political thinkers to build on fundamental sociohistorical and ethnologic work in order to better comprehend women's cultural resources and their movement-forming, coalitional, and democratizing possibilities. Thus, in spite of the engaged spirit and merits, for example, of Ferguson's political insights into the connection between bureaucracy and the patriarchal-based feminizing adaptation, her account of the experiential underpinnings of a feminist alternative vision falters because of her exaggerated regard for one limited dimension of women's multifaceted exercise of power. The recommendations that Ferguson makes in her concluding chapter in behalf of caretaking are unpersuasive in view of the social, historical, and ethnologic inquiries into the networking aspects of women's lives. These studies provide a broad basis for questioning the scope, implications, and especially the privileged status accorded caretaking by many feminists.

This is not to say that networking can stand by itself, unexamined, as a source for a feminist counter vision and practice. Networking and the formations arising from it can lead to democratization or hierarchization, so criteria are needed for judging them. But such criteria depend on a degree of clarity about the ambiguities of agential power yet to be achieved.

The problematic of agential power as it enters into and seriously unsettles feminist networking activity is evident, for example, in the effort of activists to shelter battered women. The antibattering movement illustrates the disjunction within networking activity which can spring from a venture in which middle-class, (usually) white women, who may or may not have undergone battering, organize themselves to serve battered women, many of whom are poor women of diverse ethnicities.[38] The degree to which decision making includes the voice and views of the more marginalized women requesting shelter is a crucial issue, as is the adequacy of the counseling and outside support extended to them with respect to ethnic and class affiliations. The appeal to a principle of sisterly solidarity as the impetus to networking may cogently capture for shelter activists and organizers their distance from official male obliviousness to and casualness about women's abusive home situations. Such an appeal may also reflect activists' removal from reliance on liberal representative and procedural means in their collective deliberations. But networking that manifests even sincere sisterly concern does little itself to highlight important and multi-

38. On the shelter movement, see Susan Schechter, *Women and Male Violence* (Boston: South End Press, 1982).

faceted differences between activists and battered women—differences with implications for the organization and policies of any shelter as a whole.

Sisterly concern as the basis for networking, when not sustained by a critical conception of alternative values and practices, readily transforms itself into a form of annexation in which a "dilated I or We" assimilates indistinctly perceived others to itself.[39] The temptation to such annexation is strong in feminism and springs from two sources. The first is the familiar assumption that women share an overriding unity of condition because of victimization by males. This presumed unity can trivialize particular sociocultural and historical legacies that might enable different ensembles of women to redefine their marginality affirmatively. The second source of a feminist impulse to annex those whom they would assist derives from the contemporary valorization of caretaking activity itself and the weight of western cultural tradition, which, especially since the nineteenth century, has lent enormous stature to such ministrative activity as essentially female. Sisterly concerns and networking practices informed only by caregiving ideals easily overlook the sociocultural diversities among shelter seekers. The differential sociocultural affiliations of women seeking shelter mean that each group stands in a different relation of marginality from the prevailing society and its traditions and that in some groups, multiple fronts of marginality converge whereas in others they do not. Furthermore, women from different classes have more or less experience with settings in which they exercise participatory initiatives and responses that significantly qualify their own caretaking activities. The resourceful self-confidence such participatory experience encourages may render otherwise harried poor women particularly aware of the maternalistic implications of some forms of shelter activist assistance.

The urgent need of battered women for assistance helps promote obliviousness on the part of activists to sociocultural diversities. When these urgencies combine with caretaking ways possessing their own hierarchizing import, the likelihood of socially prejudicial attitudes entering into organization and policy is further increased. Ministrative preconceptions prompt activists to conceive themselves as guardians of their client's welfare and furnish activists with a mandate to preemptively define needs and intervene peremptorily to remedy them. Inattentive to their own short-circuiting of the imperatives of

39. Rosalind Delmar, "What Is Feminism," in Nancy Cott, *What Is Feminism*, 30.

peer interaction, activists, Susan Schechter notes, react with impatience and resentment toward those aid seekers who seem to challenge their good works ungratefully.[40] In reality, however, it is the activists' unwitting transformation of ministrative relations, unconstrained by participatory considerations, into covertly dominative relations that is the true source of aid seekers' grievances.

The issues raised by the example of the antibattering movement occur everywhere in the women's movement where sociocultural diversity must be met and negotiated. Many feminists have posed the question of how an awareness of a diversity of affiliations and voices and a commitment to such diversity can be sustained within the exercise of power which networking requires. There is at least one theoretical resource for facing up to the challenge of making diversity compatible with the exercise of participatory power called for by networking at its best; it resides in the Aristotelian and Arendtian contrast of praxis and poiesis. The heuristic value of this distinction lies in its reminding us of the difference between participatory and ministrative forms of agential power and their respective forms of interaction. These interactional patterns display opposed orientations toward human diversity: The former recognizes diversity as an element that can be integrated in the interaction formative of common empowerment. The latter disallows diversity as a distraction or irrelevance to the effective execution of a need-servicing task.

That ambiguity which often afflicts the feminist reconception of power's affirmative aspects—ambiguity which, in the case of Ferguson (among others), leads to a theoretically unwarranted restriction of agential power to its ministrative expression—has its movement-focused counterpart in the equivocation pervading women's very practice of networking. Networking calls for an exertion of agential power, but the terms in which this activity is conceived (as the antibattering effort illustrates) have a formative bearing on the quality of relationships that result. The Aristotelian-Arendtian idiom of action offers an analytic of power that feminists can draw upon to disentangle and reintegrate their own multiple commitments—to assist those in need and to establish solidarity bonds with them. The very nature of the caretaking ideal in feminist thinking and the amplification it receives from the culture at large in a right-wing political climate, means it is more incumbent than ever on feminists to disassimilate themselves from caretaking's condescending inattentiveness

40. Schechter, *Women and Male Violence*, 281–86.

to sociocultural differences and its collapsing of interactional possibilities.

The reactionary Reagan and Bush regimes pressured women to retreat from the cause of gender politics and coalition-based struggles on myriad fronts of political concern to women and men. Judith Stacey notes that within feminism itself, "conservative pro-family feminis[t]s" like the later Betty Friedan or Jean Bethke Elshtain and Carol MacMillan, have "already shifted the terrain of feminist discourse in a more defensive direction." She concludes that such theorists "redefine feminism in a way that undermines its radical potential."[41] This self-injurious potential is evident as well in broader feminist theoretical endeavor.

Thus feminist theory's reconception of agential power in preeminently ministrative terms serves unwittingly to legitimate bureaucratically organized ministrative offices. Indeed the current emphasis on caretaking by theory helps lend credence to the idea of women as natural bureaucrats. Women's special ability for and skills in nurturing and providing for others' needs, developed in mother-daughter relationships Ferguson cites, could be further cultivated and enlarged in application for the benefit of the prevailing order through proper professonal training. As Judy Auerbach ironically observes, women are perfectly suited to become professional managers of settings requiring humanization. Though not exactly environments conducive to "comfort, nourishment, or cure," such ostensibly humanized settings would increase employee productivity, efficiency, and where appropriate, corporate profits. Though from an official vantage point, women would be regarded as insufficiently enterprising and aggressive for top-level positions, they would appear well suited to middle-level managerial posts. Auerbach notes that graduate schools of management have not been slow to see the importance of the caregiving ethic for themselves and their clients.[42]

It is particularly important, therefore, for feminists to address and make explicit the ambiguities buried in their own affirmative interpretations and exercises of power. Clarity of sociopolitical self-understanding is critical for feminism to escape complicity with the very structures and practices it wants to undo. Once feminist political thought recovers the divergent implications of power and association indigenous to the praxis-poiesis idiom, it will have a means of interrogating the quality of its own networking activity and policies and

41. Stacey, "Feminists Afraid to Leave Home?" 231.
42. Judy Auerbach, "On Gilligan's *In a Different Voice*," *Feminist Studies* 11 (1985): 149–61, esp. 158.

educating its adherents to the democratizing impulse—*es meson*, the centering of power—carried by participatory action and coempowerment. The theoretical reappropriation of the Aristotelian-Arendtian idiom by feminists would help guarantee that "the hunger for equals," which Adrienne Rich perceives as animating radical feminist ventures, will be genuinely pursued and truly satisfied.[43]

43. Adrienne Rich, "Conditions for Work," in *On Lies, Secrets, and Silence* (New York: Norton, 1979), 214.

CHARLES W. HEDRICK, JR.

11 *The Zero Degree of Society:*
Aristotle and the
Athenian Citizen

In my experience as a teacher of Athenian democracy, easily
the most controversial and difficult topic has been the relationship
between Athenian citizens and others within their society; this has certainly been a central concern of professional scholarship during the
past twenty years. Specifically, it is troubling that a state that we call
"democratic," which many acknowledge as the source and origin of
many of our contemporary political ideals, should limit citizenship as
restrictively as did ancient Athens. True, freedom and equality were
ideals of Athenian citizenship, as they are for the American citizenry
today. In Athens, however, citizenship was restricted to native free-
born adult males— in all likelihood, something considerably less than
a quarter of the total population of ancient Attica.[1] All these men may

The translations from Aristotle's *Politics* are taken, unless otherwise specified, from *The
Politics of Aristotle*, ed. and trans. Ernest Barker (Oxford: Oxford University Press, Clarendon,
1970).
  1. It would be useful to know how many people were and were not citizens of ancient
Athens, or even approximately what percentages belonged to each status category. Unfortunately, estimates of the Athenian population and its breakdown are notoriously variable and
controversial. I think that Mogens H. Hansen has done the best that can currently be done with
the numbers: *Demography and Democracy: The Number of Athenian Citizens in the Fourth Century B.C.*
(Herning, Denmark: Systime, 1986). As a rough estimate (based largely on probably unreliable
military conscription figures from antiquity), we might say that the number of citizens in the
fourth century B.C. hovered somewhere around thirty to fifty thousand. Citizen population in
the fifth century B.C. may have been somewhat greater. For the other categories of the person,
there is virtually no evidence worthy of the name. Slaves most likely outnumbered citizens in
ancient Athens, perhaps by as many as two to one, perhaps more. Noncitizen natives, women,
and children certainly outnumbered adult males, but by how much it is impossible to say. No one
can give a reasonably based approximation of the numbers of resident aliens in classical Athens.

well have been equal and free in many respects, but the majority of
the population, including women, children, metics, and slaves, most
certainly was not.

In modern America, we have extended the full citizenship to virtually the entire adult population. By the standards of our universal
franchise, ancient Athens looks very little like a democracy. If our
political objectives are to link the ideal of democracy with the promotion of *social* equality and freedom among all those who are subject to
the state's laws, and not just the *political* equality and freedom of citizens, then it is arguably a strategic error to grant the coveted title of
"democracy" to Athens—as perhaps it would be to grant the title to
America today.[2] Regardless of the name we give to the Athenian state,
however, the cohabitation of the ideals of a radical equality and freedom of citizens with the practical and blatant political inequality and
constraints imposed on everyone else in Athenian society is disturb-
ing: Is this simply another contradiction between ideology and social
practice? Or is there a less apparent connection between the two?

It is difficult to know where or how to begin discussing the specifically democratic, Athenian ideology of citizenship and society. Clearly
the issue can be approached from various perspectives, using a variety
of critical tools. In the best of all imaginary worlds, we would have
that chimera, the "representative attitude" of some "typical Athenian," exposited in exhaustive, inclusive detail, to guide us. No such
essay, of course, exists or ever could have existed. The extent to which
any text or, for that matter, any individual's attitudes, ever represents
more than itself or can be used as " typical" of some larger ideological
trends, is always debatable. In the case of the Athenian democracy, no
examples of systematic reflection or self-justification whatsoever have
survived, never mind some general "representative essay" on the nature of citizenship and society. In fact it is unlikely that such texts
were ever written. As has often been noted, until relatively recently
there has been no such thing as democratic theory, only democratic
practice;[3] theory, in fact, is arguably in itself antidemocratic.[4]

In sum, although it is impossible to be certain of the details, no one would dispute that the
noncitizen population of Athens was considerably greater than the citizen population.

2. For the problem of the relationship of a democratic political system to its citizens
versus its relationship to those others who are subject to its rules, see Robert A. Dahl, *Democracy and Its Critics* (New Haven: Yale University Press, 1989), chap. 9.

3. The absence of a democratic theory in ancient Greece was noted some years ago by A.
H. M. Jones, in his famous essay *Athenian Democracy* (Oxford: Blackwell and Mott, 1957), 41.
See further Dahl, *Democracy and Its Critics*, 1–14.

4. On the general antipathy between theorizing and democratic practice, see Sheldon S.
Wolin, *The Presence of the Past: Essays on the State and the Constitution* (Baltimore: Johns Hopkins
University Press, 1989), particularly the essay entitled "Tending and Intending a Constitu-
tion: Bicentennial Misgivings."

In this essay, I have chosen to analyze a theoretical treatise, Aristotle's *Politics*, as a way of beginning a discussion both of it and of Athenian citizenship and society. The juxtaposition of the *Politics* and Athenian society might be criticized for any number of reasons. Aristotle is obviously anything but a "typical Athenian." Although he lived in Athens for much of his life, he did so as a metic, a resident alien, and so could not participate in the political life of the state. Nor could the *Politics* ever be imagined as something approximating a "representative statement" of Athenian democratic ideology. To begin with, Aristotle is clearly critical of democracy as a political form. Furthermore, though the essay is avowedly based on a body of empirical evidence, including Athenian practices, it is nevertheless intended to deal with politics at a more general and abstract level; many of Aristotle's remarks do not apply at all to specific political practices of Athens. This shortcoming is part and parcel of any theory: the greater the level of generalization and abstraction, the more exceptions to it will be found. Finally, it might be argued that Aristotle's arguments are not only too general and abstract—governed by the imperatives of typology and category—to be historical; they are also too structured and totalizing to be democratic or to fairly represent the processual ideals of democracy: theory subordinates everything to its goals; democracy is oriented toward a practice.

This last criticism may well apply to any systematic analysis, including (need it be said?) what I have to offer here. Nevertheless, being a modern scholar, I do not know how else to think—and thinking may be precisely the problem here. Certainly I have found it useful and convenient to use Aristotle's theories as a guide to Athens' practice and as an object for my criticisms, but perhaps I should have some other criterion of judgment and justification than convenience and utility. Despite certain inaccuracies and overgeneralizations, I find that Aristotle's comments represent an interesting way of thinking about citizenship generally and about Athenian practices of exclusion in particular. The Athenians never verbalized a reply to modern critics or to Aristotle in any systematic way. I do not pretend to reconstruct here what they did not say. Yet their answer, it seems to me, surely would not have taken the form of still another reasoned treatise or article; it would rather have been found in their everyday behavior, which was doubtless less consistent and more pointless than the schematic and categorical descriptions and criticisms of their detractors.

We hear that in his cosmology the sixth-century Ionian philosopher Anaximander had the earth floating in the center, equidistant from everything, supported by nothing. Because of the equality, or correspondence (*homoiotēs*), of its position in relation to its surroundings, because of its balance (*isorropia*), the earth was free, ruled (*kratoumene*) by nothing. The earth did not fall, quite simply because its position was autonomous and universally correspondent, so it had no reason to fall anywhere.[5]

Anaximander imagines the universe as a sphere, with the earth resting fixed at the center. As Greek geometers from Thales to Aristotle to Euclid knew, the sphere, like the circle, is a shape "which is in every way equidistant from the middle to the extremes."[6] This Euclidean formulation gives the same priority to the center which Anaximander gives to the earth: the sphere is described from the center out, not the edges in. Obviously enough, however, the extremes and center of circle or sphere are linked in a relationship of *mutual* correspondence. The periphery of the circle is circumscribed from the center, but the center is equally located by the periphery. Nevertheless, the imagined priority of the center is maintained: it is the fulcrum, the position of correspondence, autonomous, ruled by nothing. In a sense, the center is conceived as not only inside the circle but outside too: in a position independent of its circumference, whence it can define and govern the arc of its periphery.

The correlation between the geometric schema of Anaximander's universe and Greek political thought is well known. The state and its citizens can be envisioned as a circle, in which power is deposited at the center, equidistant and so equally accessible to all. Herodotus uses precisely the metaphor of circle and center to define *isonomia*, democratic political equality (3.142). Jean-Pierre Vernant and others have traced the use of this image in political thinkers from Solon to Plato,[7] and even in the practices introduced by the Cleisthenic reforms to the "constitution" of Athens.[8] It is not only Anaximander's geometric fig-

5. For Anaximander's thought, we rely on the doxographical tradition, that is, the collection of "opinions" attributed to early philosophers by later writers. For Anaximander's cosmology, the crucial citation is provided by Aristotle, *De caelo* 295b10. This, and other fragments of Anaximander, are most easily consulted in the collection edited by G. S. Kirk, J. E. Raven, and Malcolm Schofield, *The Presocratic Philosophers*, 2d ed. (Cambridge: Cambridge University Press, 1983). The classic essay on the cosmology of Anaximander is by Charles Kahn, *Anaximander and the Origins of Greek Cosmology* (New York: Columbia University Press, 1960).

6. See Euclid 1, def. 15.

7. For a general and accessible statement, see Jean-Pierre Vernant, *The Origins of Greek Thought* (Ithaca: Cornell University Press, 1982).

8. See Pierre Lévèque and Pierre Vidal-Nacquet, *Clisthène l' Athénien: Essai sur la representation de l' espace et du temps dans la pensée politique grècque de la fin du VIe siècle à la mort de Platon* (Paris: Belles Lettres, 1963); see also Jean-Pierre Vernant, *Myth and Thought among the Greeks* (Boston: Routledge and Kegan Paul, 1983), particularly the essays in sec. 3, "The Organization of Space."

ures of circle and center, however, which are mirrored in Greek political thought. The qualities that define the autonomous center of his cosmos, equality and freedom from rule, are also the ideals for the status of the citizen in many Greek states, particularly in democratic ones such as Athens.

The society of the ancient Greek polis is dominated by the citizen, the *politēs*. The fulcrum of such a society, the central "first principle" and positive term from which other social facts are defined, must equally be the citizen. Other statuses of the person within the state, judged against this great autonomous standard, are peripheral, contingent, imperfect, defective. Their qualities are not characterized as positive and inherent—in a word, autonomous—as are those of the citizen but are typically defined in negative terms: they are as a group, to use a common modern term, "*non*citizens." At the same time, however, the identity of the citizen is bound up with the exclusion and domination of noncitizens: citizens are defined in opposition to those who are not citizens, so their very self-conception, their freedom and equality, is at stake when the social discrimination between citizen and noncitizen is violated. Noncitizens are necessary to citizens because they are the immediate and specific manifestation of what citizenship is not. They thus serve to remind every citizen, through innumerable daily contacts and concrete interactions, of precisely who he is. The status of the citizen, in other words, is dependent on those who are excluded from citizenship. Exclusion is the process that makes possible the self-realization of the citizen in ancient Greece. The essence of the free and equal citizen, then, is the sum of all social exclusions. The great positive ideals of citizenship, freedom, and equality are not, however, consequently to be thought of as simply empty, contradictory ideals; rather, they are precise and accurate descriptions of the peculiar vacuousness of the identity of the citizen, a vacuousness that is the product of his dominating centrality in relationship to all the "others" who live on the periphery of political society.[9]

ATHENIAN SOCIETY: CITIZENS

In reviewing the various political statuses that constitute ancient Athenian society, it is usual and appropriate to begin with the citizen. The reason for this priority is clear: in Athens, as in the Greek world

9. It would not be an error to recognize some affinities between this description of the processes determining the construction of social identity and Jacques Lacan's theory of the "mirror stage" and the development of individual identity: see *Ecrits: A Selection*, trans, Alan Sheridan (New York: Norton, 1977).

at large and elsewhere, citizenship is by definition the status "bestowed on those who are *full* members of a community."[10] Having provided this definition, the various groups of noncitizens must accordingly be thought of as less than full; their salient characteristics will be their lacks, the omissions by virtue of which they fall short of the perfection of citizenship. The citizen, then, may be defined and discussed in the same way that moderns often discuss the individual: as a plenitude, a kind of positive social term, the meaning of which not only is self-sufficient and independent but also determines and guarantees the status of others.

Aristotle provides a clear, ancient statement of the priority of the citizen. His attitude is typical of ancient and modern thought about citizenship. At the beginning of the third book of the *Politics*, he remarks that to understand the state we must begin by understanding the citizen: "A polis, or state, belongs to the order of compounds in the same way as all other things which form a single whole, but a whole composed, none the less, of a number of different parts. This being the case, it clearly follows that we must inquire into the nature of the citizen (i.e., the part) before inquiring into the nature of the state (i.e., the whole composed of such parts)" (1274b–1275a). The insistence on the explanatory priority of the part to the whole here is curious, and significant. As we will have occasion to see later, Aristotle normally insists on the priority of the whole, which give a teleological shape and purpose to its various elements. Nevertheless, the point here is clear: the state, or polis, is made up of citizens, and it is from the citizen that discussion must begin. Aristotle then proceeds to limit the definition of citizenship by enumerating residents of the polis who are not citizens: "We may leave out of consideration those who enjoy the name and title in some other than the strict sense. . . . Nor can the name of citizen be given to those who share in civic rights only to a certain extent. . . . We may dismiss children. . . . and the elderly" (1275a). Aristotle here is citing groups who do not enjoy citizenship "in the strict sense" or "only to a certain extent" in order to describe the citizen; the identifying characteristics of these groups, in other words, are deficiencies, but deficiencies only to the extent that they are judged against and subsidiary to the ideal plenitude of the citizen.

10. T. H. Marshall, "Citizenship and Social Class," in *Class, Citizenship, and Social Development: Essays* (1964; reprint, Chicago: University of Chicago Press, 1977), 92. It would be pointless to multiply examples from modern scholars; see, e.g., the standard introduction to the Athenian democracy, Mogens H. Hansen, *The Athenian Democracy in the Age of Demosthenes: Structure, Principles, and Ideology* (Oxford: Blackwell, 1991), 88: "Metics and slaves lived alongside of the citizens in the city-state, but the state itself was a community of citizens only, and of male citizens at that, for women were also excluded from political rights."

At the same time, however, the presence of these imperfections and defects serves to clarify the status of the citizen. The clarification of this status, in fact, would be precisely Aristotle's justification for his digression into the various kinds of noncitizens. This negative form of definition is a necessary strategy, the common resort of modern scholars as well. As Brook Manville notes, for instance, "Athenian citizenship embodied an overall legal status, defined by identifiable boundaries. The boundaries become most clear when we compare citizenship to the status of various groups of non-Athenians in Attic society."[11] Despite the claim that citizenship *is* something identifiable, it is necessary to have recourse to what citizenship *is not* to identify what that something is. Boundaries, in other words, are made apparent and concrete by those excluded, not by some abstract, intrinsic, positive qualities possessed by those living within the edges. Aristotle sums up this relationship succinctly: "What we have to define is the citizen in the strict and unqualified sense, who has no defect that has to be made good before he can bear the name" (1275a).

The progression of Aristotle's argument is clear: within the society of the polis, he posits the citizen as the fixed point, the standard against which social status is measured, the point from which his own discussion must depart. The noncitizens within the state can be characterized in relation to the citizen as imperfect; they are known through their contrast with the wholeness of the citizen. This relationship is already implied in the very framing of a broad, binary distinction between a positive element, the citizen, and its defective form, "those who enjoy the name and title in some other than the strict sense." Elsewhere in the *Politics*, when Aristotle reviews the dispositions and statuses of people within the state, he clearly follows this rule: the point of comparison for him is, as indeed it logically must be, uniformly the citizen. Having made these distinctions, however, he is in the end forced to reverse his procedure. To define the citizen it is necessary to have recourse to the very social elements that have been defined in terms of the citizen. Noncitizens are distinguished from citizens by their "defects." The defining characteristic of the citizen is nothing except the absence of these selfsame defects.

There are, obviously, certain apparently positive qualities, specific practices, that seem to be the essential, positive properties of citizens. Aristotle himself, in the paragraph following this very passage, provides one of the most famous and brief formulations: "The citizen in

11. Philip Brook Manville, *The Origins of Citizenship in Ancient Athens* (Princeton: Princeton University Press, 1990), 11, with bibliog. cited in n. 40.

the strict sense is best defined by the one criterion, 'a man who shares in the administration of justice and in the holding of office'" (1275a). As a minimal statement of the general prerogatives of citizenship, there is little to dispute in this definition, whether it is applied to ancient Greece or modern America. It surely is serviceable as a definition of the citizen in ancient Athens. The Athenian term for citizen is *politēs*. Only those described by this term had the right of participation in the various formal political institutions of the state.[12] The criteria and privileges of citizenship were clearly defined. To become a citizen, one had to be male and freeborn, of legitimate birth: before the citizenship reforms of Pericles in 451, this latter requirement probably meant that one's father had to be a native Athenian; after 451, both father and mother had to be native Athenians.[13] Credentials and qualifications for citizenship were checked and rechecked by an elaborate series of examinations.[14] Notably, at age eighteen, boys were examined and, on approval, registered on the lexïarchic registers, that is, lists of citizens kept by the various small towns, or demes, of Attica.[15] Once admitted to these registers, boys were allowed some of the privileges of citizenship: specifically, they could attend meetings of the assembly and vote. They did not, however, achieve complete citizen status until sometime later, after they had reached the age of thirty-one; henceforth they were permitted to serve on the Council, or Boule, of Athens and to hold office.

This brief account of Athenian citizenship is, I think, in form and substance fairly representative of most contemporary descriptions. Certainly there is little controversial in its specific details. The way in which the description is organized, however, is deceptive: as it stands, it includes no reference to noncitizens. By describing citizenship in positive terms, the citizen is rhetorically removed from society; his status appears to be self-sufficient and autonomous, in no way socially contingent or contextual.

It would be possible to extend this list of the various perquisites and

12. See, however, below, n. 23.

13. Generally on the citizenship law of Pericles, see Cynthia B. Patterson, *Pericles' Citizenship Law of 451–50 B.C.* (New York: Arno, 1981); cf. K. R. Walters, "Perikles' Citizenship Law," *California Studies in Classical Antiquity* 2 (1983): 314–336.

14. For a readable survey of the events of a Greek life, see Robert Garland, *The Greek Way of Life: From Conception to Old Age* (Ithaca: Cornell University Press, 1990). On childhood, see Mark Golden, *Children and Childhood in Classical Athens* (Baltimore: Johns Hopkins University Press, 1990).

15. See David Whitehead, *The Demes of Attica 508/7–ca. 250 B.C.: A Political and Social Study* (Princeton: Princeton University Press, 1986), 97–109.

prerogatives of citizenship in ancient Athens for many pages.[16] My point, however, can be made more briefly: none of the rights and privileges of Athenian citizenship are "essential" qualities; they are only defining characteristics of the citizen insofar as they are not allowed to noncitizens. If both "citizens" and "noncitizens" were commonly permitted to vote, for instance, then the franchise would not be a quality of the citizen, nor would it be any more significant or deserving of mention in a discussion of citizenship than, say, breathing or the ability to walk, or any of the other qualities and characteristics that humanity shares.

The prerequisites for Athenian citizenship were rigorously enforced. The Athenians policed the boundary between citizen and noncitizen ruthlessly. Demosthenes tells us, "The civic body of Athens, although it has supreme authority over all things in the state, and it is in its power to do whatsoever it pleases, yet regarded the gift of Athenian citizenship as so honourable and so sacred a thing that it enacted in its own restraint laws to which it must conform, when it wishes to create a citizen."[17] Magistrates of the city were subjected to a preliminary scrutiny to determine their bona fides as Athenian citizens. There were occasional purges of the deme registers, to remove from them those not entitled to citizenship. Severe penalties were imposed on those who falsely usurped the rights of the citizen. Specifically, a pretender might be prosecuted "for falsely passing himself off as an Athenian" and, if convicted, would be sold off at public auction as a slave. The harshness of the penalty is at first glance puzzling. What is at stake in the usurpation of citizenship to warrant such a reaction? The penalty is perhaps an index of the precariousness of the identity of the citizen. The usurpation of citizen rights is a threat to the definition of citizenship. Only by the constant effort of vigilance, by strict exclusions and maintenance of discriminations, can citizens retain the clarity of their own self-image.

ATHENIAN SOCIETY: NONCITIZENS

The categories of the noncitizen in Athenian society were numerous— exactly as numerous, in fact, as the attributes of the Athe-

16. See, above all, Manville's recent thoughtful essay, *Origins of Citizenship*, particularly chap. 1, "Introduction: What Was Athenian Citizenship?"

17. Demosthenes 59 (Against Neaera), in Demosthenes *Private Orations*, vol. 6, trans. A. T. Murray (Cambridge: Harvard, 1939), 88.

nian citizen. Social perfection, that is, the citizen, is difficult to imagine, never mind describe. Its qualities can only be apprehended and enumerated in the light of imperfection: as Aristotle says so well, the essence of the citizen is the absence of defect. It would be a mistake, however, to imagine that simply because noncitizens have tangible and easily describable failings, they are therefore something in and of themselves. As we have seen, their imperfections and defects are imperfections and defects only in relation to the perfect and blemishless citizen. Without the citizen, noncitizens would have no defect and hence no identity.

It is arguable that every community relies on an exclusionary logic to define itself. The specific character of members, however, will obviously vary from society to society, depending on the exclusions employed, the defects emphasized. To get a clearer understanding of what the Athenian citizen is, it may be useful now to describe some of the more significant (by this I mean simply larger, more numerous) categories of those excluded.

Of all the categories of the noncitizen in ancient Athens, perhaps the most salient, at least to moderns, is that of the slave.[18] Slavery existed in all Greek states, but rarely to the extent to which it is found in the classical Athenian democracy. Whereas the slaves in many other Greek states were predominantly serfs, that is, indigenous persons bound to a specific piece of property, those in Athens were chattel, who could be freely bought and sold by their masters. Furthermore, a proportionately greater number of slaves were to be found in ancient Athens than in most other ancient Greek states.[19] It goes without saying that slaves could not vote, hold office, or participate in political institutions in any other way. They had no formal rights in and of themselves, though as items of property they were protected from unlawful expropriation and malicious vandalism by the status of their owner. It would be a mistake to imagine the slaves of ancient Athens as a community of some sort—or worse, as a class; they had a huge variety of functions and statuses. Some slaves worked in teams in the silver mines; others, as domestic servants; still others labored side by side with poorer citizens as virtually autonomous skilled craftsmen. Certain slaves, the "Scythian archers," served as a police force of sorts

18. On slavery, see, e.g., Yvon Garlan, *Slavery in Ancient Greece*, trans. Janet E. Lloyd (Ithaca: Cornell University Press, 1988).

19. I am here following the views of Moses I. Finley; for further discussion and bibliography, see below, "Freedom and Equality." See, however, the remarks of Josiah Ober, *Mass and Elite in Democratic Athens: Rhetoric, Ideology, and the Power of the People* (Princeton: Princeton University Press, 1989), 24–27, who is chiefly concerned to show that the democracy itself was not per se dependent on slave labor.

for ancient Athens. The defining characteristic of the slave, what they all have in common, is not labor but the fact that they were owned, unfree. In the memorable phrase of Aristotle, slaves were "living tools," without a purpose beyond that which their master lent them, to be used as other items of property were used.

The other most notable group of noncitizens, from a contemporary perspective, is that of women.[20] Like slaves, women had some rights, but these rights extended in principle only insofar as they were dependents of citizens. Their dependency was institutionalized through the *oikos*, or family, which was nominally controlled by the adult male. The status of women is more complex, however, than this simple comparison with male citizens might suggest.[21] The Athenians distinguished broadly between two categories of free women: foreign, or *xenai*, and native, or *astai*. This division was formalized by the implementation of the citizenship law of Pericles in 451–50, which required that Athenian citizens descend from both a native Athenian father and a native Athenian mother: henceforward it was necessary to define the status of the Athenian woman clearly.[22]

Despite the distinction between native and foreign women, it must be emphasized that women were not citizens. They could not participate in the formal political institutions of the Athenian state; that is, to recur to Aristotle's definition of citizenship, they could not "share in the administration of justice and hold office."[23] The distinction between male citizens and native women is clear enough in the very terms used to describe them. The word for "foreign women," *xenai*, was simply the feminine form of the generic word for foreigner, *xenos*. Significantly enough, however, the word for citizen, *polites*, is used

20. Some samples of the work on women in antiquity: Sarah Pomeroy, *Goddesses, Whores, Wives, and Slaves: Women in Classical Antiquity* (New York: Schocken, 1975), and Pomeroy, ed., *Women's History and Ancient History* (Chapel Hill: University of North Carolina Press, 1991); Helene Foley, *Reflections of Women in Antiquity* (New York: Gordon and Breach, 1981); John Peradotto and John Sullivan, eds., *Women in the Ancient World* (Albany: State University of New York Press, 1984); Eva Keuls, *The Reign of the Phallus* (New York: Harper and Row, 1985). For an annotated study of women in Athenian law, see Raphael Sealey, *Women and Law in Classical Greece* (Chapel Hill: University of North Carolina Press, 1990). For women and citizenship, see Nicole Loraux, *The Children of Athena: Athenian Ideas about Citizenship and the Division between the Sexes*, trans. Caroline Levine (Princeton: Princeton University Press, 1993).

21. See Cynthia Patterson, "Hai Attikai: The Other Athenians," *Helios* 13 (1986): 49–67; note also David Cohen's qualifications to the practical freedoms of women in *Law, Sexuality and Society: The Enforcement of Morals in Classical Athens* (Cambridge: Cambridge University Press, 1991).

22. Before the implementation of this law, the status of the mother had presumably not been relevant to the citizenship of the offspring, and hence there was no need to control and distinguish between various types of women.

23. Note that for Aristotle this is specifically the definition of the democratic citizen; see *Politics* 1275b.

regularly throughout the classical period in the masculine form; the feminine form of the word, *politis*, is attested, but it was not commonly used to describe Athenian women; rather, it is found predominantly in satiric contexts and in utopian philosophical speculations.[24] Women in Athens, then, are not distinguished from citizens simply on the basis of gender, as female *politai*; they are also set apart, as belonging to an entirely different sociopolitical order.

Aristotle includes children and the elderly in his list of imperfect citizens. This formulation applies only imperfectly to Athens. The Athenians were unusual (at least in terms of Aristotle's theory) in that they did not discriminate against the elderly. In most Greek states, including Athens, when citizens reached the age of sixty, they no longer had the right to participate in the military (although in emergencies they might still be called up). In Athens, this change in status was not accompanied by a loss of other citizen rights; to the contrary, those over sixty became eligible to serve as special arbitrators, the *diaitētai*. In many other Greek states, however, this change did entail the loss of certain rights, most commonly the right of holding certain offices. Although this prevailing Greek attitude toward the elderly may give pause, the status of children will not seem at first glance bizarre to moderns.[25] Before the age of eighteen, young Athenian males were not registered on the lists of citizens and so could not vote. After eighteen, military training as well as some citizen privileges began. As a further qualification, certain offices were restricted to citizens over the age of thirty. It is significant that citizen status and age qualifications in Athens and elsewhere coincide with the age qualifications for army service: the citizen body and the army were coterminous.

Yet another substantial group of noncitizens in classical Athens were the metics, or resident aliens.[26] As resident aliens, metics enjoyed some of the privileges that citizens enjoyed. In particular, once registered with the state, they could participate in commerce. It is noteworthy that in Athens, metics were liable to some military service: the link between military service and citizenship is not as uniform as is sometimes imagined. The privileges of the metic, however, were clearly limited in comparison with those of citizens. They could not, for example, participate in political activities. They could not own real estate; this privilege, in the classical period at least, was reserved for

24. C. Patterson has recently claimed that the feminine of *polites* is used to describe female citizens; see "Hai Attikai."

25. For the elderly, see Thomas M. Falkner and Judith de Luce, eds., *Old Age in Greek and Latin Literature* (Albany: State University of New York Press, 1989), and Garland, *Greek Way of Life*. On children generally, see Golden, *Children and Childhood*.

26. See David Whitehead, *The Ideology of the Athenian Metic*, Cambridge Philological Society Supplementary vol. 4 (Cambridge: Cambridge Philological Society, 1977).

citizens. Nor could they represent themselves in court cases. When they went to trial, they had to have recourse to a citizen patron, or *prostatēs*, to represent them.

These are some of the major categories of the noncitizen in Athens. There are many less prominent categories, and it would be possible to continue to enumerate them: the illegitimate (i.e., bastards), for example, were excluded from citizenship,[27] as were in principle those free males who prostituted themselves.[28] It should be clear by now, however, that the Athenian citizen is a member of an exclusive minority and that the specific characteristics of the various groups of noncitizens derive from their opposition to the citizen. The general point to be taken here, though, is that in all descriptions of noncitizens, the citizen, whether explicitly mentioned or not, is implied. In describing the subordinate there is always an underlying comparison with the dominant. I would not of course deny that it is possible in principle to contrast, say, a native Athenian woman (the *astē*) with a metic or slave. Such a comparison would in fact have the salutary and subversive effect of "de-centering" the citizen from his position at the heart of society; for it implies that women or metics have some identity outside of their dependency on the citizen.[29] Nevertheless, it is only in the hierarchical comparison of the woman, the metic, and the slave with the citizen that the systematic rationale of sociopolitical status in Athenian society can be known.

The process of exclusion serves not only to separate noncitizens from citizens but to link them as well. From the perspective of the citizenry, noncitizens are not just utterly foreign; they are fellow residents of the city, sharers in its space, life, and fortunes, comparable to citizens in all respects. Their qualities then are not safely alien and unthinkable, but dangerously familiar. It is not simply that noncitizens represent the negation of the citizen; their qualities are also the qualities of the citizen, but subversive qualities that must be ruthlessly suppressed and rooted out wherever possible. Noncitizens are not just noncitizens; they are citizens too, only flawed ones.

A clear example of the ambiguity of the relationship between citizens and noncitizens is provided by the status of the youth in Athens (and the elderly in some other Greek states). They cannot simply be

27. For the status of bastards, see Cynthia Patterson, "Those Athenian Bastards," *California Studies in Classical Antiquity* 9 (1990): 40–73.

28. For prostitution and citizenship in Athens, see David Halperin, "The Democratic Body: Prostitution and Citizenship in Classical Athens," in *One Hundred Years of Homosexuality and Other Essays on Greek Love* (New York: Routledge, 1990).

29. I think that this decentering occurs in certain texts, not only in principle, but as a subversive practice in the Athenian democracy, and that this is decipherable in certain texts. This has been the point of C. Patterson's recent work: see above, nn. 21 and 24.

treated as citizens or as noncitizens. Obviously, they do not participate fully in the political life of the community, and so they are not citizens. Equally, however, it would be incorrect to categorize them with foreigners, metics, slaves, or women, because they either will be (or have been) citizens. We might say that children are potential citizens; the elderly, superannuated citizens. Aristotle makes the point best in his discussion of citizenship: "There is a sense in which the young and the old may be called citizens, but it is not altogether an unqualified sense: we must add the reservation that the young are underdeveloped, and the old are superannuated citizens, or we must use some other qualification. The exact term we apply does not matter for the meaning is clear" (1275a).

Neither would it be justifiable to dismiss metics, without qualification, as just another variety of foreigner. More important is their similarity to citizens. They are residents of the state, they contribute to the public coffers, they participate in commercial interactions with citizens. It is noteworthy that when Aristotle speaks of metics, he defines them not as foreigners but, like children and the elderly, as "imperfect citizens": "There are many places where metics do not enjoy even this limited right [of going to court] to the full—being obliged to choose a legal protector, so that they only share to a limited extent in the common enjoyment of citizenship" (1275a, trans. modified). It is not difficult to see how children, the elderly, even metics, participated to a limited degree in the political life of the city and so might reasonably be described by Aristotle as citizens—but imperfect ones. It is more difficult to imagine how those utter anticitizens, slaves and women, could in some limited way be identified with citizens. Aristotle's discussion of these groups is enlightening.

The opposition of citizen and slave is predicated on and strengthened by the reciprocal ties of owner and owned. Citizens were not owned—quite the contrary, they were the owners—and this is precisely the distinction between citizen and slave. This point is made very clearly in the first chapters of Aristotle's *Politics*, which are devoted to a justification of the relationship between citizen and slave by a contrast of the two. As Pierre Vidal-Naquet and others have shown in great detail, "The slave made the social game feasible, not because he performed all the manual labor (that was never true), but because his condition as the anti-citizen, the utter foreigner, allowed citizen status to define itself."[30] The slave is opposed to the citizen because

30. Pierre Vidal-Naquet, "Were Greek Slaves a Class?" in *The Black Hunter: Forms of Thought and Forms of Society in the Greek World* (Baltimore: Johns Hopkins University Press, 1986), 164.

the slave is owned, and this negative quality serves to establish one of the "essential" positive properties of citizenship.

Obviously enough, one can only be a master if one possesses slaves. Aristotle is clearly aware of this reliance in the determination of status. Nevertheless, he wishes to maintain the primacy and independence of the master from his slaves. In a revealing passage, he remarks, "A possession [e.g., a slave] is spoken of as a part is spoken of; for the part is not only a part of something else, it wholly belongs to it; and this is also true of a possession. The master is only the master of the slave; he does not belong to him, whereas the slave is not only the slave of the master, but wholly belongs to him" (1254a, my translation). The slave is quite literally conceived as a constitutive part of the master. The mutual reliance of part and whole should be obvious by now: no whole without parts, no parts without whole. One thinks immediately of Aristotle's opening remarks about citizenship (quoted above): as the state is an organic "whole" composed of parts, it is, necessary to begin the discussion of the state at the level of its parts, that is, the citizens; in that case, the part had an explanatory priority. Here, however, to maintain the autonomy and domination of citizen versus slave, it is necessary to stipulate the priority of the citizen as of the whole to the part, a point Aristotle is willing to maintain in the abstract.

For Aristotle, the priority of the whole is dictated by its formal unity and teleological "final cause," or purpose. The part is contingent because it lacks in itself this unity and purpose. The causal hierarchy linking these two implies a political hierarchy as well. The whole rules its subordinate parts. When Aristotle speaks of slave and master as part and whole, then, he is alluding to a general metaphysical principle: "In all cases where there is a compound, constituted of more than one part but forming one common entity—whether the parts be continuous [as in the body of a man] or discrete [as in the relation of master and slave], a ruling element and a ruled can always be traced" (1254a).

The slave is a part of the citizen, but as a part he is imperfect. Without the master, without subordinating and subsuming himself in the whole, the slave can have no purpose. The citizen too needs the slave: without this part of himself, the citizen would be unwhole and his ends unobtainable. The instrumentality of the slave is necessary if the purposefulness of the master is to be fulfilled. The relation of slave and citizen is equivocal, however. The citizen must suppress and dominate this part of himself, if he is to remain free.

As the status of the slave defines the citizen as free, the status of the

woman defines the citizen as male.[31] Aristotle explains and justifies
male domination of women using the same reasoning that he employs
to justify the domination of slaves. To begin with, Aristotle insists that
men and women are necessarily linked by the requirements of the
survival of the species:

> In the first place there must be a union of those who cannot exist
> without each other; namely of male and female, that the race may
> continue (and this is a union which is formed, not of deliberate pur-
> pose, but because, in common with other animals and with plants,
> mankind have a natural desire to leave behind them an image of
> themselves), and of natural ruler and subject, that both may be pre-
> served. For that which can foresee by the exercise of mind is by
> nature intended to be lord and master, and that which can with its
> body give effect to such foresight is a subject and by nature a slave;
> hence master and slave have the same interest. (1252a, my trans.)

Men are masters because they have foresight and so can intend the
appropriate "final end." Women, lacking foresight, cannot rule, but
the instrumentality of their bodies is nevertheless necessary to effect
the ends of men. Men, in other words, can be characterized as "the
whole" and women as "the part." Women are simultaneously identified with men as a subsidiary part and distinguished from them as
instruments without foresight. They are necessary and integral instruments: the "final end" of reproduction obviously cannot be reached
without their cooperation; at the same time, they cannot purpose this
final end themselves and, so, must be separated out and dominated.
To paraphrase one of Jacques Derrida's cuter turns of phrase, in matters of parturition, women are a part of men which must be kept
apart from men.

EXCLUSION AND SOCIETY

The focus on "exclusion" as a social dynamic is relatively recent.
Criticism of the Athenian democracy for the social inequities that occurred under its regime—perhaps even were promoted by it—is
nothing new. Since Marx, at the very least, it has been commonplace
to criticize the Athenians for their oppression of others. The materialist argument has typically been based on a notion of economic neces-

31. This point, again, has been thoroughly examined by Vidal-Naquet: see "Slavery and
the Rule of Women," in *Black Hunter*, 205–23.

sity.[32] For democracy to be possible, large numbers of citizens must have leisure to be able to participate in politics and sacrifice their time to the administration of the state. Leisure, the freedom from the need to work for the basic necessities of life, can only have been provided by the systematic exploitation of others. Democracy, it is thus argued, must always be subsidized by someone; there is a necessary correlation between the leisure for political participation and the oppression of others. Practically speaking, the ability of citizens to excercise their civic rights depends on the labor of others: the ideals of political equality and freedom were supported by political, social, and economic inequality and enslavement. As Engels once observed, "No Greek art without Greek slaves." In political terms, we can say with Thucydides, "No democracy without tyranny."[33] Slaves, women, and metics necessarily paid for the vaunted glory of the Athenian democracy with their labor.

The empirical grounds for supposing that an economic necessity dictates a correlation between the practices of democracy and social exploitation have been questioned by some, convincingly in my opinion.[34] Even more problematic than the empirical basis for the argument is the presupposition of a transcendent economic necessity, against which all social meaning is epiphenomenal: the postulate that the basic economic exigencies of survival dictate and generate the structures of society, culture, and ideology.[35] As has been pointed out repeatedly, economic practices are social, cultural, and ideological, too. An explanation that begins from a universal, ahistorical "economic necessity" has no hope of explaining anything of the specific historical circumstances in which the ideologies of economy and so-

32. See Christian Meier's sophisticated statement of this position, *The Greek Discovery of Politics*, trans. David McLintock (Cambridge: Harvard University Press, 1990), 145–46. For Athenian oppression of their allies, see, e.g., the classic discussion of Moses I. Finley, "The Fifth-Century Athenian Empire: A Balance Sheet," in *Imperialism in the Ancient World: The Cambridge University Research Seminar in Ancient History*, ed. P. D. A. Garnsey and C. A. Whittaker (Cambridge: Cambridge University Press, 1978), 103–26. For the relationship between democracy and slavery, see, e.g., Michael H. Jameson, "Agriculture and Slavery in Classical Athens," *Classical Journal* 73 (1978): 122–45.

33. When Thucydides contrasts democracy and tyranny, he is, of course, speaking not of Athenian oppression of other members of their society but of their political and economic exploitation of their "allies" by means of their empire.

34. See notably the old essay of Jones, *Athenian Democracy*, 6–7, and the more recent, persuasive, arguments of Ober, *Mass and Elite*, 23–27.

35. The hard and fast discrimination between economic "base" and ideological "superstructure" has long been an issue of contention, even among materialists. I think particularly of the work of Weber and, later, of the so-called Frankfurt school of Critical Theory: for a review, see, e.g., Mark Poster, *Critical Theory and Post Structuralism* (Ithaca: Cornell University Press, 1989).

ciety alike are fostered, only of confirming the pervasive, universal priority of economic necessity, which its advocates already know too well.[36]

The concept of social exclusion has clearly been developed out of modern research in linguistics.[37] Since Ferdinand de Saussure, it has become a truism that meaning is not inherent but is constituted through difference. Signs can only mean if they are distinguishable from other signs, that is, if it is possible to systematically exclude all the things they do not mean. Because all signs are constituted by difference, there are no positive definitions, only an unending chain of exclusions. The core of every positive value is a kind of vacuum: the intersection of all possible differences. Applying this principle to social status, we can say that status is not dictated by who is included but by who is excluded. Citizenship, then, can be imagined as the sum of social exclusions: it is not the guarantee of social differentiation, just another product of it.

The shift to an interpretation that focuses on exclusion has not occasioned any particular modifications to the general picture of the requirements of Athenian citizenship. Indeed, the insistence on exclusion in the formation of the citizenship may appear, at first glance, to be a trivial stipulation, simply another way of saying what is obvious. I think that few would deny that the positive definition of citizenship can be determined by examining who is excluded; conversely, one might equally well say that the positive definition of a category *determines* who or what is excluded; that negative exclusion and positive definition are two sides of the same coin. The focus on exclusion, however, has important political consequences; for it embeds the citizen again in society, linking his status with that of the unenfranchised, as a focus on the positive definition of the citizen does not. Athenian citizenship is not to be imagined as an a priori given, the basis of social meaning, but as itself taking its specific meaning from the social relations in which it is engaged. Consequently any appreciation of Athenian democracy must involve consideration of those excluded from its privileges as well as of those "full" participants, the citizens.

In the same way that exclusion produces identity, it produces social solidarity among citizens. As Kurt Raaflaub and others have noted, "the success of the democracy in securing the loyalty and devotion of the vast majority of citizens rested largely on its insistence on a

36. Karl Polanyi had already insisted on the "embedded" character of the Greek economy, of the mutual relationship between its structure and that of society, back in the fifties: see, e.g., G. Dalton, ed., *Primitive, Archaic, and Modern Economics: Essays of Karl Polanyi* (Garden City, N.Y.: Doubleday, Anchor, 1968).

37. There have obviously been many attempts to apply linguistic principles to the study of society. Structuralism is perhaps the most venerable of these approaches.

marked distinction between citizens (whatever their social status) on the one hand and all categories of noncitizens on the other."[38] In practical day-to-day life, a citizen would know himself and his fellows not by reciting the litany of qualifications for citizenship to himself but by contact with all of those around him who are not citizens. In Athens, and for that matter any Greek state, noncitizens will have been in the majority. All to the good. If the defining characteristics of the citizen are only defining insofar as they exclude others, then the more excluded the better. The greater the numbers of noncitizens, the stricter the penalties for the usurpation of citizen rights, the stronger the self-image and solidarity of the citizen body.

As exclusion promotes solidarity among citizens, it simultaneously produces disunity among noncitizens; for they are defined in relation to the citizen, not to each other. This disunity is also one of the reasons for the stability of Athenian society despite its social inequities. I accordingly argue against those who attempt to organize the various noncitizen groups of ancient Athens in terms of larger, overarching categories or as a social continuum of some sort. For example, in a famous article, Vidal-Naquet remarked, "The Greek city, in its classical form, was marked by a double exclusion: the exclusion of women, which made it a men's club, and the exclusion of slaves, which made it a citizen's club." He then suggested that other categories of the noncitizen should be regarded as more or less extreme cases of these two: "One might almost say a threefold exclusion, since foreigners also were kept out; but the treatment of slaves is no doubt merely the extreme case of the treatment of foreigners."[39] By organizing the various groups of the unenfranchised according to his two categories, Vidal-Naquet diverts attention from the opposition of these groups to the citizen body and to characteristics that one group might share, on a graduated scale, with other groups.[40] In Athens, I argue, all social definitions converge on the citizen. Noncitizens are effectively united only in their subordination to the citizen.

FREEDOM AND EQUALITY

The perspective on citizenship that I advance here was prompted in part by the work of Moses Finley on the freedom and equality of the

38. Kurt A. Raaflaub, "Democracy, Oligarchy, and the Concept of the 'Free Citizen' in Late Fifth-Century Athens," *Political Theory* 11 (1983): 532.

39. Pierre Vidal-Naquet, "Slavery and the Rule of Women," in *Black Hunter*, 206.

40. I am not certain how far Vidal-Naquet would press this point; see "Were Greek Slaves a Class?" in *Black Hunter*, which argues that slaves are not part of a continuum that leads up to the citizen but are utterly different from other types of noncitizen.

citizen. Finley insisted that these attributes were not to be conceived as mere intellectual ideals, divorced from their economic and social context, but as a set of specific rights and privileges that entail a concomitant number of duties and obligations among those who are not free or equal. The freedom and equality of citizens, in other words, are the products of the social relationship of citizens with others. Consequently, attempts to define them in universal terms must be doomed to failure: their specific characteristics must vary with the social relations that produce them. As Finley observed,

> The gamut of claims, privileges, powers and immunities, and of their correlative duties, 'unprivileges', liabilities and disabilities, is too vast over the whole range of human activity, and too varied not only from society to society but also among the members within any known society. The rights recognised in a given society constitute a bundle of claims, privileges, powers and immunities, unevenly distributed among the individual members, even among those who are called 'free', so that a definition of freedom encompassing them would be either a tautology or a misrepresentation of the reality. A man who possessed claims, privileges and powers in all matters against the whole world would be a god, not a man, to paraphrase Aristotle.[41]

Finley is surely right in his insistence on the social determination of equality and freedom and in his conclusion that the specific characteristics of the pair must vary from society to society. Nevertheless, I do believe that it is possible to speak in general terms about the pair. Specifically I argue that freedom and equality describe quite appropriately the zero degree of social relations, the correspondent center of the circle, where there are no significant constraints or differences, as constraints and differences are defined within a given society; to the contrary, freedom and equality describe the place whence social constraints and difference are generated.

It has often been noted that in ancient Greece, freedom and equality are attributes of membership in the state, that is, of citizenship. By contrast, in modern times, these qualities have come to be attached to the individual independent of his or her place in the community: they have become, in other words, universal *human* rights. The contradiction, so egregious to modern eyes, between the equality and freedom

41. Moses I. Finley, "The Freedom of the Citizen in the Greek World," in idem, *Economy and Society in Ancient Greece*, ed. Richard Saller and Brent Shaw (London: Chatto and Windus, 1981), 77.

of citizens and the constraint and oppression of noncitizens, would not necessarily have been a contradiction to a Greek.

Freedom and equality were certainly not the exclusive prerogatives of citizens in ancient Greece. In various senses and to various extents, women, children, metics—even slaves—might be described by Athenians as free or equal.[42] In contrast to a slave, for instance, a woman or a metic might be described as free. So Aristotle himself remarks that women are " one half of the free population" (1260b). Equality is far less often used in any sense to describe noncitizens than is freedom. Still, it is clear that a doctrine of "natural equality of men" was not unknown to Athenians.[43]

Despite these extended uses of freedom and equality, in a more restricted, political sense they are surely the exclusive property of the citizen, the hallmarks of democratic political activities and interactions, an arena from which noncitizens were excluded.[44] In the light of the standards of citizenship, noncitizens can most certainly not be described as "free and equal." As Aristotle remarks, "The authority of the statesman is exercised over men who are naturally free; that of the master over men who are naturally slaves; and again the authority generally exercised over a household by its head is that of a monarch (for all households are monarchically governed) while the authority of the statesman is an authority over free men and equals" (1255b).

The citizens of many states in ancient Greece, not only democratic ones, appealed to the virtues of freedom, equality, or both. Aristotle, however, argues that these are not simply general attributes of citizenship but, more specifically, characteristics of *democratic* citizenship. In particular, he singles out freedom as the essential and primary aim of democracy:

> The underlying idea of the democratic type of constitution is liberty. (This, it is commonly said, can only be enjoyed in democracy; and this, it is also said, is the aim of every democracy.) Liberty has more than one form. One of its forms [is the political, which] consists in the interchange of ruling and being ruled. The democratic conception of justice is the enjoyment of arithmetical equality, and not the enjoyment of proportionate equality on the basis of desert. On this arithmetical conception of justice, the masses must necessarily be sovereign; the will of the majority must be ultimate and must be the expression of justice. The argument is that each citizen

42. See ibid., 81–82, and Hansen, *Athenian Democracy*, 73–76.
43. See Hansen, *Athenian Democracy*, 81–85.
44. As many have pointed out, the idea of equality in particular is restricted to the political realm and seldom extended to apply to social or economic behavior: see ibid., 81.

should be on an equality with the rest; and the result which follows in democracies is that the poor— they being in a majority, and the will of the majority being sovereign—are more sovereign than the rich. Such is the first form of liberty, which all democrats agree in making the aim of their sort of constitution. (1317a–1317b)

Equality, like freedom, is for Aristotle a notable aim of democratic politics:

There are two conceptions which are generally held to be characteristic of democracy. One of them is the conception of the sovereignty of the majority; the other is that of the liberty of individuals. The democrat starts by assuming that justice consists in equality: he proceeds to identify equality with the sovereignty of the will of the masses; he ends with the view that "liberty and equality" consists in "doing what one likes." (1310a)

For Aristotle, it is not simply the advocacy of freedom and equality which distinguishes democracy from other forms of government in ancient Greece. Democracy is characterized by particular and extreme forms of freedom and equality: "Democracy arose from the idea that those who are equal in any respect are equal absolutely. . . . All are alike free, therefore they claim that all are free absolutely. . . . The next is when the democrats, on the ground that they are all equal, claim equal participation in everything" (1310a, my trans.).

It should not be necessary to repeat that Aristotle's attitudes may not provide an entirely (or even largely) accurate representation of the democratic attitudes of Athenian advocates of democracy. Unfortunately, no Athenian democrat has left anything like a systematic justification of his ideals. There have, however, been numerous attempts by modern scholars to reconstruct the Athenian ideals of freedom and equality from the scattered references to them in drama, poetry, rhetoric, and history.

The history and definition of freedom in ancient Greece became the subject of numerous and exhaustive discussions in the 1980s.[45] Of

45. The most important work on freedom is Kurt A. Raaflaub, *Die Entdeckung der Freiheit: Zur historischen Semantik und Gesellschaftsgeschichte eines politischen Grundbegriffes der Griechen*, Vestigia 37 (Munich: C. H. Beck, 1985). For an English summary and critique, see Martin Ostwald's review, "The Greek Concept of Freedom," *Classical Review* 38 (1988): 82–85. For a more accessible, though in some ways dated, survey of the history of freedom in Greece, see Max Pohlenz, *Freedom in Greek Life and Thought: The History of an Ideal* (1954; reprint, New York: Humanities Press, 1966). Probably the most influential work on freedom has been done by Moses I. Finley; see particularly his *Ancient Slavery and Modern Ideology* (New York:

the various Greek words for freedom, the most notable is *eleutheria*. The earliest uses of this word in a political context coincide with the rise of the notion of "citizen" in Athens in the early sixth century: the Athenian statesman and poet, Solon, uses this term to describe the prerogatives and rights of Athenian citizens.[46] By the classical period, particularly after the Persian Wars, freedom came to be one of the rallying cries of the Athenian democracy, a quality that defined civic life and the citizen.[47]

The precise meaning of freedom has been notoriously difficult to pin down. The ancient Greeks themselves sometimes provide help with the general meaning of the term, particularly when they describe freedom as *autarkeia*, self-sufficiency, or *autonomia*, independence. In practical terms, however, the Athenians most often emphasized the freedom to participate in government and the freedom to speak in public meetings (parrhesia). Aristotle's definition of political freedom as "the interchange of ruling and being ruled" (at, e.g., 1317b, quoted above) is particularly applicable to ancient Athens: as is well known, many of the magistracies of the democracy were allocated by lot and administered in rotation. Other aspects of Athenian freedom have also been emphasized: the independence of the property, person, and family from state interference, for instance, seems to have been recognized.[48]

The other great democratic ideal of ancient Athens was equality.[49] A variety of terms, mostly formed off of the root element *iso-*, "equal," are used in the surviving political texts from Athens of the fifth and fourth centuries to describe specific aspects of equality. Two formulations in particular, however, seem to have been emphasized by the democracy. The word *isonomia* was a notable slogan of the Athenian

Viking, 1980) and *Economy and Society*. See Orlando Patterson, *Freedom in the Making of Western Culture*, vol. 1 of *Freedom* (New York: Basic Books, 1991). With this, cf. Oswyn Murray, review of "Sovereignty for All?" *Times Literary Supplement*, October 25, 1991, 8, as well as O. Patterson, "The Meaning of Freedom," reply, ibid., November 29, 1991, 19.

46. The genesis of the modern ideal of "citizenship" in ancient Athens has been well discussed by Manville, *Citizenship in Ancient Athens*.

47. Raaflaub, *Entdeckung der Freiheit* is particularly good on the role of Athenian contact with the "barbarian" Persians, who serve their king as "slaves," in clarifying the concept of freedom.

48. So Hansen, *Athenian Democracy*, 77, following John Rawls, "The Basic Liberties and Their Priority," in Sterling M. McMurrin, ed., *Liberty, Equality, and the Law: Selected Tanner Lectures in Moral Philosophy* (Salt Lake City: University of Utah Press, 1987).

49. See esp. the work of Martin Ostwald, e.g., *Nomos and the Beginnings of the Athenian Democracy* (Oxford: Oxford University Press, Clarendon, 1969) and *From Popular Sovereignty to Sovereignty of Law: Law, Society, and Politics in Fifth-Century Athens* (Berkeley and Los Angeles: University of California Press, 1986). For a brief survey of the democratic meaning of the term, consult Hansen, *Athenian Democracy*, 81–85.

state from the time of Cleisthenes. In the classical democracy, the term is used to mean something like "a political equality supported by law."[50] Another notable democratic equality was *isegoria*, or "the equal right of speaking in public."[51] The notion of consensus, *homonoia*, as an aspect of egalitarianism has now been emphasized, too.[52] The specific implementation of the ideal can be seen in many of the political practices of the classical democracy: offices were allocated by allotment rather than election so that all might have an equal opportunity to serve; pay was introduced for service, so that both the poor and wealthy might equally be able to participate in government. Again, one of Aristotle's definitions appears to be quite pertinent to Athenian practices of equality: he claims that in voting "the democratic conception of justice is the enjoyment of arithmetical equality, and not the enjoyment of proportionate equality on the basis of desert" (1317b, quoted above). Athenian voting was clearly *isopsēphos*, "one man, one vote"; ballots were not weighted in favor of an aristocracy of birth or wealth.

The words *freedom* and *equality* may of course signal the enjoyment of prerogatives such as the ones I have listed here. Simultaneously, however, they suggest the disengagement of these prerogatives. Claims of "freedom" and "equality" can be seen as a kind of mystification of their own social values and function, as a means of asserting the autonomy of the citizen against others in society. Freedom, the absence of constraint, and equality, the absence of difference, suggest the intrinsicness and essentialness of the status of the citizen in isolation from society. We might imagine the free and equal citizen as the political equivalent of the idea of the individual: an entity, even a consciousness, which exists autonomous from and outside of the complex web of language and society; a thing essentially *there* and not defined by interaction with others.[53]

The connection between freedom and "essentialism" is made utterly clear in what must be the most famous discussion of modern freedom, Isaiah Berlin's classic essay "Two Concepts of Liberty." Berlin posits a basis for freedom in the human character and its natural desires:

50. See, above all, Ostwald, *Nomos*.
51. See Ostwald, *Sovereignty*, 203, and Ober, *Mass and Elite*, 72–73, 78–79. This word should of course be considered in conjunction and contrast with parrhesia.
52. Ober, *Mass and Elite*, 295–99 and passim.
53. For a critique of the poverty of the idea of freedom conceived as "universal human right" and an evaluation of the excessive concern of moderns with abstract notions of freedom, political rights, and negative freedoms, see Finley, "Freedom of the Citizen," 77–80.

I wish my life and decisions to depend on myself, not on external forces of whatever kind. I wish to be the instrument of my own, not of another man's, acts of will. I wish to be a subject, not an object; to be moved by reasons, by conscious purposes, which are my own, not by causes which affect me, as it were, from outside. I wish to be somebody, not nobody; a doer—deciding, not being decided for, self-directed and not acted upon by external nature or by other men as if I were a thing, or an animal, or a slave incapable of playing a human role."[54]

Although this paragraph is framed in terms of the individual, it can, I think, be extended to the ancient Greek ideal of the citizen. Berlin's postulation of the desire for autonomy and self-sufficiency is nothing but a desire for an essential meaning, a determinacy, against which various constraints can be measured. Further discussion can begin from this postulated base. Freedom here is not merely an attribute of the individual; it is what makes it possible to speak of the individual at all. One might say the same of the citizen.

Berlin's essay argues in part for a distinction between two kinds of freedom: the "positive freedom" to do or not do what one wishes, and the "negative freedom" from the constraint to do or not do what one does not wish.[55] The distinction between positive and negative is not, I think, valid or even particularly useful; for each implies the other. As I have argued throughout this essay, the meaning of a term can be known only by what it is not. The negative freedom from external constraints presupposes the positive freedom of autonomy of choice, as autonomy of choice presupposes the absence of constraint. The seductive danger of the concept of freedom lies in imagining that autonomy of choice can somehow exist in and of itself. Freedom means nothing without the impositions of constraint. It would be incomprehensible, unimagineable, meaningless except in the context of some such structure: it would be the state of a god, not of a person. Both the positive and negative varieties of freedom come down to a general and mutual negation: freedom is the absence of constraint just as constraint is the absence of freedom.

It is noteworthy that Berlin's description of freedom relies heavily

54. Essay originally published as a monograph, Isaiah Berlin, *Two Concepts of Liberty* (Oxford: Oxford University Press, Clarendon, 1958); reprinted in idem, *Four Essays on Liberty* (London: Oxford University Press, 1969), 131.

55. The distinction is predicated on a dichotomous relationship between autonomous individual and collective state, a distinction argued by Berlin, ibid. For discussion and bibliography of attempts to apply this scheme to ancient Athens, see Ober, *Mass and Elite*, 295–99 and esp. 295–96 with n. 7.

on negatives. He is unable simply to list the positive qualities of freedom and finds it necessary to appeal to the qualities of its opposite,
constraint. This opposition between freedom and constraint involves a
general scheme of the essential versus the contingent, the subject
versus the object. "I wish my life and decisions to depend on myself,
not on external forces. . . . I wish to be a subject, not an object." In
this opposition, one term is autonomous; the other, contingent and
defined in terms of it. What passes unnoticed is that the positive term
is vague and ill defined, relying for its clarification on what it is not: "I
wish to be *somebody*. . . . not a *thing* or an *animal* or a *slave*." The
somebody he wishes to be is animate, human, and free.

Some historians have ultimately abandoned the attempt to discover
a purely intellectual or philosophical definition of freedom.[56] Instead,
these scholars have focused on freedom as a social status among
others. It has long been noted that the ideal of freedom is intertwined
with the social status of slavery. As Aristotle remarks, "The other
form [of liberty is the civil, which] consists in 'living as you like.' Such
a life, the democrats argue, is the function of the free man, just as the
function of slaves is not to live as they like" (1317b). Already in 1954,
Max Pohlenz had made the argument: "The conception of freedom
implies its antithesis. Free men only exist where there are unfree men.
The awareness of freedom could only arise in a place where men
lived together with others who were not independent but had a master over them who they served and who controlled their lives. We
speak nowadays of free and unfree men, and so did the ancient
Greeks, but historically it was the existence of the unfree, the slaves,
that first gave others the feeling they were free."[57] Finley made the
same point even more forcefully. Freedom, he argued, was determined by the opposition of citizens to slaves; this relationship was not
"simply an issue of semantics" but one of political privilege. In his
often repeated dictum, "One aspect of Greek history, in short, is the
advance, hand in hand, of freedom and slavery."[58] The point made by
Pohlenz and Finley is, I think, indisputable, and further work has
followed their lead.[59]

One of the most important elements in the ideology of freedom is

56. So Finley, "Freedom of the Citizen," 77: "Men have for centuries exercised their minds
in vain to find a workable definition of 'freedom.' I do not propose to add yet another attempt to the mountain of failures, for I do not believe the term to be definable in any normal
sense of the word 'definition.'"
57. Pohlenz, *Freedom in Greek Life*, 3.
58. Finley, "Was Greek Civilization Based on Slave Labour?" in *Economy and Society*, 115;
see also "Between Slavery and Freedom," ibid., 121.
59. See esp. Raaflaub, *Entdeckung der Freiheit*, and O. Patterson, *Freedom*.

that it exists independently and autonomously. To suggest that freedom is linked to oppression and slavery is already a radical critique of its value. Pohlenz went further: he argued that not only was the ideal of freedom linked to slavery but it was originally generated out of the socioeconomic circumstances of slavery. This is obviously a materialist position: ideology is epiphenomenal, the base is determinant. Others have followed Pohlenz in allocating priority to slavery. In particular, Orlando Patterson has made the important and attractive argument that the idea of freedom was generated out of the experience of slavery; that is, the idea of freedom was invented by slaves, who understood its desirability.[60]

To turn the tables on freedom, not only to link it with slavery but to make it dependent on slavery, is a provocative step. For me, however, the interpretation falls short in its insistence on the priority and determinacy of economic and social factors in the production of ideology. I would prefer an interpretation that did not insist on privileging one over the other but would allow only for their mutual reliance. Finley offered an explanation that moves in this direction.[61] He argued that chattel slavery arose in connection with a complicated set of social, economic, and intellectual circumstances, circumstances that produced the Greek citizen. Slavery, then, was generated out of the ideal of freedom. The reason he assigns for this priority: demand must always precede supply.[62] Like Pohlenz and Patterson, Finley insists on seeking an origin. His origin, however, is much more problematic (some would say perverse) than a simple economic determinacy. Ideology and society are mixed for him; the priority of one over the other is moot.

The focus on slavery as the antithesis of freedom should not obscure the fact that, judged by the standards of the citizen, no member of the other categories within the Greek state is free: as we have seen, all were subject to constraints determined with reference to the freedom and equality of citizens.[63] For example, Patterson has argued (rightly, I would say) that the subordinate status of women in Athenian society also contributed to the development and refinement of

60. O. Patterson, *Freedom*, xiii, 20–44 and passim.
61. The attempt to break down the distinction between "base" and "superstructure" is often associated with names such as Max Adorno, Theodor Horkheimer, and Walter Benjamin, that is, with the so-called Frankfurt school of Critical Theory. It is perhaps no accident that Finley, in his younger days, was involved with these scholars; see Saller and Shaw, *Economy and Society*, x–xii.
62. Finley, "The Emergence of a Slave Society," in *Ancient Slavery and Modern Ideology*, 86, 89–90.
63. See Finley, "Servile Statuses of Ancient Greece," in *Economy and Society*, 146–49.

the ancient Greek notion of freedom.[64] In short, the political idea of freedom, including all of those claims, privileges, immunities, and powers that accompany it by right and principle, is the property par excellence of the citizen; the particulars of these claims, privileges, immunities, and powers are knowable as the sum of the constraints applied by citizens to the unenfranchised.

Equality can be explained by appeal to the same social process of exclusion which determines freedom.[65] Like freedom, equality may be seen as a great negation, posing as a positive autonomous quality: the absence of differences. To be sure, in practice there can be no utter exclusion of difference; it is necessary to discriminate between differences that matter and those that do not, between significant and insignificant differences. Xenophon remarked, in the course of a description of Sparta, "Nowhere are citizens so equal, nowhere are noncitizens so unequal." For the citizen, the significant differences are those that separate them from those who are unequal, the noncitizens. Equality, then, is the claim of the absence of such differences— but it can only be understood in terms of the differences it generates. There is a necessary correlation between the equality of citizens and the inequality of noncitizens.

At the heart of the hierarchical social system of Athens, then, are freedom and equality, that is, the proclaimed lack of constraint and differentiation. Absolutes such as these must exist as positive qualities at the heart of any highly differentiated society, because hierarchical differentiation must be founded on a putatively stable, positive foundation. They must be autonomous and self-sufficient because they are the putative source and basis, the fixed point that guarantees the articulation of society. The stability and autonomy of the terms are illusory, however; freedom and equality are in their essence nugatory: the absence of constraint and difference, respectively. It is one of the chief functions and priorities of the concepts of freedom and equality to deny this lurking contextuality of social status and to assert the autonomy of the citizen in society.

In a banal way, we can say that freedom and equality are one-half of the equation that opposes citizens to noncitizens, allowing the identification of either. Noncitizens are unequal, citizens are equal. Noncitizens are not free, citizens are free. At a different level, however, it is arguable that equality and freedom are effects of the system of so-

64. O. Patterson, *Freedom*, esp. chap. 7, "A Woman's Song: The Female Force and the Ideology of Freedom in Greek Tragedy and Society." Cf., however, the unconvinced remarks of Murray, "Sovereignty for All?"

65. Finley has done this to a limited extent in "Freedom of the Citizen," 77–94.

cial exclusion. They are the inversions of the processes of differentiation and constraint which generate social hierarchy. These qualities are not simply the exclusive property of the citizen body; they are the contraries of the dynamics of the social system itself. It is precisely the social processes of constraint and differentiation which support, define, and generate freedom, equality, and citizenship.

The advancement of the freedom and equality of citizens remains the goal of many modern states. Contemporary ideals of citizenship, however, are far less exclusionary than those of ancient Athens. In America, for instance, the rights of citizenship have been progressively extended until, in the late twentieth century, virtually the entire adult population is permitted to participate in the formal political institutions of the state. Immigration and naturalization standards in the modern world are considerably more liberal than they were in ancient Athens.

As the franchise has become more and more universal in modern states, the relative exclusivity of Athenian citizenship has become increasingly obvious; and for precisely this reason, there has been no shortage of critics of Athenian "democracy." Latter-day defenders of the Athenians have adopted a variety of strategies and arguments. Some have simply ignored the issue of exclusion. Others have insisted on the anachronism of foisting modern values and expectations onto the Athenians. Still others argue that modern states are not so "inclusionary" as contemporary critics seem to imagine: there has, after all, been little room in eighties and nineties America for, say, Haitian immigrants.

These arguments and justifications seem to me to overlook an important point. It is true that all states, ancient and modern, limit citizenship in some way, exclude to some extent. Nevertheless, there is a significant difference between the modern exclusion of foreigners—aliens who are not subject to the regulations of the state—and the ancient exclusion of certain native adults, who were subject to the decisions and regulations of the community. It appears to me incontestable that the modern democratic ideal of citizenship for all native adult inhabitants of a state is a basic and radical departure from the exclusionary determination of Athenian citizenship. I have been concerned here to show a connection between the "ideals" of freedom, equality, and citizenship and the social processes of exclusion in Athenian society. If it is accepted that such a connection exists, what are we to make of a universal citizenship? In the absence of exclusion, what do citizenship, freedom, and equality become? By making citizenship universal, have we finally achieved that political utopia of freedom and equality for all? Or perhaps the elimination of exclusion has also eliminated the meaning, the political significance, and the importance of citizenship, displaced it to some other social or economic region of human behavior, where a select community celebrates domination and difference in the name of freedom and equality.

JOHN R. WALLACH

12 *Two Democracies and Virtue*

At first glance, democracy stands simply for a particular organization of power. It signifies no specific ethical ideal or moral purpose, honoring nothing more than the power of "the people." Virtue, in ordinary parlance, simply designates an excellent activity. If the virtue is ethical, the standard for such excellence embodies a morally sanctioned goal or principle, but it authorizes no particular political order. Insofar as democracy designates a kind of political power and virtue denotes a certain expression of morality, democracy and virtue signify different types of human relationships and occupy distinct conceptual realms. And yet the practice of democracy and the display of virtue implicate each other; for any political order needs an ethical justification to maintain its legitimacy, and any standard for ethical excellence needs practical support to make it meaningful in the lives of its believers. Although almost no one dislikes either democracy or virtue in contemporary public rhetoric, their implication of each other today produces anxious wonder when it comes to thinking about the common good. We ask Can democracy be virtuous? Can virtue be democratic? and even Can anything common be actually good?[1] These simple, age-old, seemingly theoretical questions originated in ancient Athens. Yet they have taken center stage in an extraordinarily

1. See Friedrich Nietzsche, *Beyond Good and Evil*, sec. 43, in *Basic Writings of Nietzsche*, trans. and ed. Walter Kaufmann (New York: Modern Library, 1966), 243. For more current evidence, I may simply recall the words of a prominent political theorist who announced during a professional convention in September 1992 that "democracy has nothing to do with virtue."

complex debate about the practical future of the American political order.

In the United States, a transformation in the practical conditions of its domestic policy and foreign posture has made these questions urgent once again in the 1990s. No longer can its citizens assume, as they did in the postwar era, that its economic trajectory will rise without the concerted efforts of virtually all segments of society. No longer does the nation have, in the enemy of Soviet communism, an external threat, the mere opposition to which could be sufficient for defining its policy in international relations. These contingent bulwarks of its collective identity have disappeared, while traditional appeals to "family values," the "work ethic," and patriotism appear to be inadequate to the task of generating in American citizens an inspired, skillful devotion to a public purpose. In this context, many have suggested that as we reform our schools, health care, and economy, we are faced with a choice between enhancing the exercise of democracy among the citizenry and producing excellence or virtue in the political community as a whole.

Posed in this way, amid the pressure to perform in an increasingly competitive world economy, "democracy" typically loses. But this need not be the case. The opposition between democracy and civic virtue is not as necessary as it may appear.[2] Indeed, our belief in a necessary opposition stems from undemocratic sources of our political tradition. Moreover, the Athenians—who introduced the discourse of both democracy and virtue into the western tradition—have indicated how this opposition can be mitigated, if not removed. Let me explain how American intellectual and political traditions have fostered a belief in the natural opposition between virtue and democracy and then show how Athenian discourse about the potential for friendship between democracy and virtue may be particularly educational for American society today.

LIBERALISM AND THE PROBLEM OF VIRTUE

Like any political order, that of democracy does not immediately provide its own justification. Democratic citizens, like any citizens, must provide their own language of legitimation. In the American

2. E.g., Benjamin Barber, in *An Aristocracy of Everyone: The Politics of Education and the Future of America* (New York: Ballantine, 1992), published after this essay was composed, argues for the compatibility of democracy and "excellence" (his translation of the Greek *aretē*) as goals for U.S. public education.

democratic order, founded, more precisely, as a constitutional republic, liberalism has been the most prominent justification. It has informed the theories of the order's most influential theorists, from James Madison to John Rawls, as well as its most widely held ideology, that of equal opportunity. These theories for the elite and ideologies for the many promote ideas about the proper nature of democracy and the proper role for virtue in it, but invariably they do so in a way that makes democracy and virtue appear antagonistic to each other. Why is this the case? Why and how does liberalism constitute an antagonistic relationship between democracy and virtue? How has it done so for the American political order?

The political theory of liberalism emerged in seventeenth-century England, as the English people sought simultaneously to authorize and constrain the power of the modern state. It takes as its centerpiece the dignity of equal freedom for all citizens of political society, citizens who, because of the geographic extent and economic discipline of modern society, typically do not exercise political power and therefore are not directly regulated by the power of the modern state. Of course this is not to say the modern, even liberal, state never insinuated its regulative power into the workings of civil society. But it never established an affinity between democracy and virtue. Michel Foucault has noted that when it did so it employed an "art of government" that constituted virtue from above—which contrasts radically with the Athenians' democratic political art, which enacted the virtue of ordinary citizenship.[3] Thus, even if liberalism ultimately sanctions various arrangements of power, it is not so much a positive theory about how political power ought to be organized and directed as a negative theory about what the limits on that power are to be. Political power may be necessary, but fundamentally, its exercise must be feared. Because liberalism is about limiting political power, and democracy is a particular constitution of political power, liberalism, among other things, limits democracy. Depending on the theorist, those limits will authorize more political power (in the case of Locke) or less (in the case of Hobbes) for ordinary citizens. With respect to virtue, liberalism holds that it resides in the citizenry, and yet such virtue does not directly affect the practical exercise of political power. Peter Laslett believes that Locke's conception of human nature includes the mark of "natural political virtue," which could tend toward democracy. But Locke uses "political" to refer to sociability and, po-

---

3. Michel Foucault, "Governmentality," in *The Foucalt Effect: Studies in Governmentality*, ed. Graham Burchell, Colin Gordon, and Peter Miller (Chicago: University of Chicago Press, 1991), 87–104.

tentially, cooperation, not association and power (in order to distance his view from Robert Filmer's).[4] Because virtue, for liberals, is a function of liberty rather than power, the natural operation of democracy cannot be virtuous. Liberals may endorse a democratic political order, but the democracy they endorse only becomes virtuous by limiting the popular exercise of political power.

Such limitations are particularly apparent in the liberalism James Madison employed to justify the new American Constitution. For Madison, the practice of politics mostly involved the play of individualistic and economic interests. In the large and diverse context of early America, Madison believed that the direct, majoritarian conduct of politics—democracy—would be unstable and unwise. Yet he believed that a political order would survive only if its politics transcended interest and promoted public virtue. Because that virtue could not come from the direct political participation of its citizens, it would have to come from institutional mechanisms. In his view, the Constitution created those mechanisms in the federal, representative system of divided government. The Constitution served as a visible hand that produced public virtue out of the pursuit of private interests. It would filter the raw interests and passions of ordinary citizens into the virtuous actions of their government. No higher public purpose than the structure of power authorized by the Constitution itself was necessary to make the political order of American democracy as virtuous as it could be.[5]

But once the Constitution was established, it, like all written documents, had to be interpreted. And the light used to illuminate that document would be colored by the new issues and problems of the fast-growing young nation. Because the Constitution guaranteed conflict rather than harmony, its interpretation would need to unify the nation, constructing a constitutional ideology that forestalled political conflict. Like the Madisonian theory that informed the Constitution, that political ideology was liberal, and the collective purpose it enshrined dissociated democracy and virtue. This political ideology became the constitutive ideal of the American nation, a kind of collective myth, and is known as the ethic of equality of opportunity.

Every state needs its ideology to justify its partial claim to authorize

4. Peter Laslett, "Introduction," in John Locke, *Two Treatises of Government*, ed. Peter Laslett, student ed. (Cambridge: Cambridge University Press, 1988), 109–10.

5. For Madison's contributions on this matter in his efforts to justify passage of the U.S. Constitution, see Alexander Hamilton, James Madison, and John Jay, *The Federalist*, nos. 10, 14, 37, 49, 51, 63. See also Gordon S. Wood, *The Creation of the American Republic, 1776–1787* (Chapel Hill: University of North Carolina Press, 1969).

power over its citizens as a universal claim to social truth. Every political community needs a narrative framework for its ideology, and this appears in the form of a collective myth. Such stories about the character of the collectivity are, to some extent, necessarily conservative (they reconcile the weak and the strong to a political order over which members of each group, as individuals, ordinarily have little control) and so counsel resignation to the status quo. But if a society's collective myths only marked the practical limits conserved by the reigning patterns of wealth, law, and power, those myths would not be worth conserving; for with their only justification the preservation of injustice, they would not continue to be genuinely believed. Such crises of credibility delegitimated the collective myths of "the divine right of kings" in seventeenth-century England or the "communism" of Leninist parties in the Soviet empire during the 1980s, and revolutions ensued. But political myths of a legitimate political order lay a genuine claim on its citizens' political imagination and rational trust. More than counsels of resignation, they inspire a sense of belonging and bolster hope in the future. They project an ideal that justifies the contribution of all members of society to a community of binding beliefs and shared values.[6]

America's most pervasive and longest-standing collective myth, that of equal opportunity, and its imaginary corollary, the American dream, both typify and stretch the nature of this genre. Although no one really believes that Americans at birth or ages five, ten, fifteen, or twenty-five have or can have an equal opportunity either to reap the economic benefits American society has to offer or to hold public office, the American dream lives on because of the belief that individual effort will be rewarded; that society's middle-class deserts are available to all; that the basic structure of the American political order affords equality of opportunity by institutionalizing no barriers to the individual pursuit of happiness. This egalitarian, individualistic ethic survives because of the kernels of truth it still represents. But the ideal of equal opportunity also diverges from traditional political myths. It authorizes a community of individual means rather than shared ends, while the American dream displaces radically individual fantasies onto the nation as a whole. Neither explicitly promotes a sense of commu-

6. Friedrich Nietzsche describes this positive aspect of myth in the following sentence from sec. 23 of *The Birth of Tragedy*: "Without myth every culture loses the healthy natural power of its creativity: only a horizon defined by myths completes and unifies a whole cultural movement" (*Basic Writings of Nietzsche*, 135). For useful discussions of the notion of ideology, see Raymond Geuss, *The Idea of a Critical Theory: Habermas and the Frankfurt School* (Cambridge: Cambridge University Press, 1981), and Terry Eagleton, *Ideology: An Introduction* (London: Verso, 1991).

nity or shared values. Neither provides thread for mending a collectivity tearing at its seams.

The myth and ideology of equality of opportunity attracted the political refugees and economic immigrants who came to populate the colonies during the seventeenth and eighteenth centuries.[7] The idea assumed collective importance during the Jacksonian era, when it was associated with "equal protection of the law," and its prominence has continued ever since.[8] The notion has proven extraordinarily elastic, insofar as it informed the segregationist doctrine of "separate but equal" as well as the rallying cries of every civil rights movement in American history.[9] It now informs the arguments of the advocates and opponents of affirmative action programs, of Republicans and Democrats alike. But it has been used predominantly to extend political and economic possibilities of freedom, equality, and prosperity to widening segments of the American citizenry.

And yet the myth of equal opportunity is not really about virtue or democracy. It is not about virtue because its primary concern is rights. It would generate more choices for individuals. It does not presume to judge what decisions individuals make with their choices or to care about the capacities individuals have to make them. Indeed, it suggests that social determinants of the meaning of virtue might well inhibit efforts to fulfill the promise of equality of opportunity. Nor is it really about democracy. Though the democratic exercise of power might serve equality of opportunity, it does so only instrumentally. The goals for which opportunities are to be equal primarily concern private, not public, life—our lives as individuals rather than citizens. The ethic of equal opportunity does not necessarily valorize the exer-

7. See J. Hector St. John de Crevecoeur, "What Is an American," in his *Letters from an American Farmer* (1782; reprint, London: Dent, 1912), 39–68. For indications of this idea around the time of the founding, see Wood, *Creation of the American Republic*, 70–73, etc. For the importance in American history of the idea of equality as equality of means rather than ends, see Wilson Carey McWilliams, "On Equality as the Moral Foundation of Community," in *The Moral Foundations of the American Republic*, 2d ed., ed. Robert H. Horwitz (Charlottesville: University Press of Virginia, 1979), 183–213. For the importance of the idea of equality of opportunity throughout the history of American political thought, see J. R. Pole, *The Pursuit of Equality in American History* (Berkeley and Los Angeles: University of California Press, 1978).

8. See President Andrew Jackson's "Veto of the Bank Bill, 10 July 1832," excerpted in A. T. Mason, *Free Government in the Making: Readings in American Political Thought*, 3d ed. (New York: Oxford University Press, 1965), 449–52, esp. 452.

9. See *Plessy v. Ferguson* (1896). Note also that Chief Justice Roger Taney, who wrote the majority opinion in the Supreme Court's justification of the institution of slavery (*Dred Scott v. Sanford* [1857]), was a close friend of President Jackson and could well have contributed ideas to the president's "Veto of the Bank Bill"; for he supported the ethic of equality of opportunity in his majority opinion in *Charles River Bridge v. Warren Bridge* (1837).

cise of public power by and for ordinary citizens. As a result, even though the notion of equal opportunity does not engage questions of virtue, including the value of democracy, it still endorses a particular scheme of social ethics that privatizes our sense of virtue and instrumentalizes our regard for democracy.

The most honored elements of equal opportunity's ethical scheme are the method of competition and judgment according to merit. The notion of equal opportunity presupposes a scarcity of resources that are commonly desired. It holds that their acquisition is to be regulated by rules equally applicable to all who desire them. As a result, its principal metaphor is that of a race; and without competition, a race has no meaning. The scorecard that determines the victor must employ criteria that enable one to evaluate clearly who is ahead at the end, and these criteria are summarized in the notion of merit. Putatively objective and value-free, the idea of merit is primarily used in society to evaluate practical conflicts in which conceptions of moral virtue supposedly are not involved. It embodies a de-moralized conception of virtue.

Within the liberal ethic of equality of opportunity, merit replaces virtue as modernity's gatekeeper of social worth. But the effect of the language of merit on our society has been to sap the vitality of a democratic ethic from our private and public life. In the private workplace, it fosters the view that the highly conventional, if not problematic, relationships of power established there depend on virtually natural hierarchies of legitimate authority: what managers believe improves the amount on the bottom line automatically designates criteria of merit and expertise among workers. In the public realm, it encourages the view of politics as a horse race or contest among a few competitors, which turns most citizens into spectators.[10] The atrophied conception of democracy that results was clearly summarized by Joseph Schumpeter, when he characterized democracy as a set of institutional procedures designed to promote competition among elites

---

10. Note that Madison stated in Federalist no. 52 that candidacy for the House of Representatives "is open to merit of every description, whether native or adoptive, whether young or old, and without regard to poverty or wealth, or to any particular profession of religious faith." And in no. 57, he adds that a proper choice for a House member may be similarly open, to "every citizen whose merit may recommend him to the esteem and confidence of his country. No qualification of wealth, birth, of religious faith, or of civil profession is permitted to fetter the judgment or disappoint the inclination of the people." See Alexander Hamilton, James Madison, and John Jay, *The Federalist Papers*, ed. Isaac Kramnick (New York: Penguin, 1987), 323, 344. Would that the practical world authorized by Madison's Constitution had fulfilled the promise of his claim.

for the approval of ordinary citizens.[11] One of the major contributions of television to our understanding of democracy has been to make Schumpeter's view of democracy as the popular authorization of rule by elites emotionally compelling (the result of which has not done much good for the political power of ordinary citizens or the legitimate authority of the ruling elites).

The myth of equal opportunity, along with the criteria of merit for evaluating the activities of private citizens and the ends instrumentally served by the lawmaking of their representatives, together are the principle regulative ideals that citizens of widely varying partisan persuasions have generally approved. Without establishing a substantive standard of what counts as a good life for individuals or a just distribution of power in the political order as a whole, the ideas of equal opportunity and merit have fortified the consensus needed by the United States to legitimate its capitalist democracy as a just community of free and equal citizens.

Equal opportunity promises an equal start, not an equal finish. It sanctions equality among life choices but offers no criteria that would value some over others within the ambit of the law. To an important extent, this agnostic view about what is socially valuable and this tolerant attitude toward individual choice provide crucial supplements to an ethos of democracy in America. They dignify the life paths chosen by every single citizen, and given the enormous potential for coercion harbored within the authority of the modern state, the individualism honored by equality of opportunity protects the right of each citizen to value his or her own way of life. But as Tocqueville noted long ago, the individualism of the American character produces serious social costs.[12] Moreover, because the myth of equal opportunity indicates primarily how we would like to begin and how we ought to compete against one another rather than where we should end or, more modestly, how we should live together, equality of opportunity says nothing about the conditions (apart from the rules) in which the race occurs. Although this allows Republicans and Democrats to differ about social policies while agreeing on the importance of "equal opportunity," it does not indicate the direction in which to look in order to

11. Joseph Schumpeter, *Capitalism, Socialism, and Democracy*, 3d ed. (New York: Harper, 1950), 242, 269.

12. Alexis de Tocqueville, *Democracy in America*, ed. J. P. Mayer, trans. George Lawrence (Garden City, N.Y.: Doubleday, Anchor, 1969). On the persistence of this American malaise first noted by Tocqueville, see Robert M. Bellah et al., *Habits of the Heart: Individualism and Commitment in American Life* (Berkeley and Los Angeles: University of California Press, 1985).

solve the social problems that need to be addressed. As a result, rational support for the myth of equal opportunity has to depend on whether the relatively unregulated patterns of America's culture and political economy can assure that the various ends pursued by diverse individuals and some social groups ultimately promote a harmonious and well-ordered society. Should these historical currents stop moving in a direction that makes players acting by the rules of "equal opportunity" feel that they have a real chance for meaningful rewards, the ideology of equal opportunity could begin to lose its mythical allure. It could lose its role as an inspiring ideal of freedom, belonging, and community. It would then imprison rather than liberate our political imagination; it would be left to perform only a legitimating function for an unjustified status quo.

As the twentieth century draws to its close, the limitations of the constitutive ideal of equal opportunity have indeed become more apparent than its benefits. These limitations have surfaced in the mounting criticism since the late sixties of the theory and practice of liberalism—to the point that liberals have been desperately seeking to reconstruct their own ideology. This has occurred despite the grand intellectual project of John Rawls, whose *Theory of Justice* (1971) and *Political Liberalism* (1993) have redefined the theory of liberalism and its ideology of equal opportunity by grounding them in two principles of justice: a rigorous respect for political liberty and procedural equality and a minimum of collective or "fraternal" concern for the distribution of social benefits to the materially disadvantaged.[13]

Apart from the theoretical clarity of these principles of justice, Rawls deliberately refuses to offer a constitutive vision of what a liberal democracy ought to be for, because, in his view, that kind of determination of social excellence, of common virtue, no matter how theoretically benign, would inevitably lead to intolerable coercion and widespread division within the body politic.[14] He comes to this conclusion by critically engaging alternatives to his view which would posit an ideal of social virtue. Among these, Rawls chooses to concentrate on the monistic teleology of utilitarianism, which "extends to society

13. John Rawls, *A Theory of Justice* (Cambridge: Harvard University Press, 1971), esp. 106–7, and *Political Liberalism* (New York: Columbia University Press, 1993), which summarizes views Rawls developed in the 1980s. For an explanation of how the Rawls of the former resembles and differs from the Rawls of the latter, see my "Liberals, Communitarians, and the Tasks of Political Theory," *Political Theory* 15 (1987): 581–611, esp. 582–90.

14. Even in the more recent, historicist vein of *Political Liberalism* (133–72), the "overlapping consensus" that would support Rawls's two principles of justice cannot involve "political" purpose; it emerges from overlapping differences among competing, supposedly "non-political" views and values.

the principle of choice for one man," whose identity he represents
with an ideal Aristotelian legislator, capitalist entrepreneur, hedonistic
consumer, or Nietzschean *Ubermensch*.[15] None of these individualistic
models, needless to say, represents a sense of virtue that immediately
supports democracy. And in his view, the practical corollary of these
theoretical norms is, not surprisingly, "merit." He fears that this norm,
if politically unconstrained, would generate a meritocratic society, that
is, a society highly stratified according to putatively objective standards of performance which in fact tend to enhance elitism by promoting the advantages of current possessors of extraordinary power
and wealth.[16] Because Rawls believes these socially sanctioned ideas of
virtue would perpetuate and institutionalize arbitrary judgments of
worth that contribute to social and economic inequality, his theoretical
justification for liberal democracy embodies social virtue only in requiring adherence to his two principles of justice. Whatever other de-
terminations of virtue individuals make, including an ethic that supports democracy, they must be private. Only relegating virtue to the
private sphere can publicly maintain the dignity of pluralism and individual difference. Only public adherence to the two principles of justice can provide the rational foundation for a political community that
reconciles liberalism and democracy.

Yet this neat allocation of judgments of individual or civic virtue
into the private realm in order to preserve the authority of Rawls's
principles of justice in the public realm carries major costs. These appear in efforts that operate within his liberal framework to address a
major injustice of our time, such as affirmative action programs. Affirmative action policies are designed to enhance the chances of
groups deemed to be structurally disadvantaged by society in their
competition for scarce positions offered by educational institutions or
employers. The public controversies over these programs evidence
the difficulty liberalism has in handling questions of social worth in
American democracy. Rawlsian liberals such as Ronald Dworkin endorse the programs along Rousseauistic and utilitarian lines. As would
Rousseau, he supports them because they compensate for deficiences
resulting from the way American society fosters invidious inequalities
in the distribution of talents and abilities—inequalities determined in
light of a hypothetical, natural norm. But he also supports them on

15. Rawls, *Theory of Justice*, 24–27.
16. For the background of Rawls's point, see Michael Young, *The Rise of the Meritocracy,
1870–2033: An Essay on Education and Equality* (London: Thames and Hudson, 1958), and
John H. Schaar, "Equal Opportunity and Beyond," in *Nomos IX: Equality*, ed. by J. R. Pennock
and J. W. Chapman (New York: Atherton, 1967).

utilitarian grounds, arguing that they contribute to the achievement of a desirable social end.[17] In the technical terms of Rawls's theory, the programs serve the purposes of the difference principle without violating the civil liberty and procedural equality guaranteed by the first principle of Rawls's theory of justice. But George Sher, a critic of affirmative action, has also argued that Rawls's promotion of the liberal value of autonomous choice in fact protects the determination of worth, merit, and desert made by individuals judging claims for admission to educational institutions and employment in various jobs.[18]

Affirmative action programs offer a primary example of what a theory of justice ought to enable us to evaluate. But despite their common derivation from Rawls's theory, the perspectives of Dworkin and Sher do not engage each other. Insofar as Rawls's theory would provide clearly supportive guidelines for affirmative action, it ignores the issues of individual merit and worth that such programs ultimately involve. Yet liberals who oppose affirmative action because it violates their conception of how the public realm ought to reward individual virtue ignore the social-structural inequalities and discrimination that gave rise to these programs in the first place. In short, liberalism—the theoretical program for the American myth of equal opportunity—cannot provide a coherent justification for critical programs designed to combat existing social injustice. Inevitably, the "private" evaluation of virtue leaches into the "public" determination of justice. Yet because the result trespasses over the boundaries established by liberal theory and ideology, a sense of confusion and consternation ensues.[19] Without a more public understanding of virtue than liberalism provides, such issues will continue to lack coherent, persuasive arguments or a clear, cogent purpose.[20]

Given American society's dependence on the collective myth of equal opportunity, the most far-reaching theory of justice for liberal democracy either jettisons or subordinates the discourse of virtue for the public realm and society as a whole. But though this tactic may

17. Ronald Dworkin, *A Matter of Principle* (Cambridge: Harvard University Press, 1985), 293–315.

18. George Sher, *Desert* (Princeton: Princeton University Press, 1987). Sher's view dovetails with that of the sociological theory of Daniel Bell, "Meritocracy and Equality," *Public Interest*, Fall 1972, 29–68.

19. Michael Sandel exposes this confusion in terms of the problem of community in *Liberalism and the Limits of Justice* (Cambridge: Cambridge University Press, 1982), 72–95, 133–47.

20. In response to the Supreme Court's backtracking legitimation of affirmative action, liberals have begun to abandon support for it—ironically, in the name of equality of opportunity. See Jim Sleeper, *The Closest of Strangers: Liberalism and the Politics of Race in New York* (New York: Norton, 1990), and Paul Starr, "Civil Reconstruction: What to Do without Affirmative Action," in *American Prospect* (Winter 1992): 7–14.

appear to be theoretically necessary to maintain the coherence and compatibility of liberalism and democracy, it has been practically fruitless as a device for maintaining or generating a consensus about principles of social justice. Rawls's theory could have considerable appeal to the extent that a rudimentary consensus already exists about the basic values a society should prize and the primary direction in which the political community ought to proceed. But that consensus has been sorely weakened by, among other things, the wrenching duplicity of the country's political leaders and bloodshed of its citizenry during the Vietnam War, the subsequent constitutional crises of Watergate, and its subordinate offspring of the Iran-Contra affair, the nation's limited success in ameliorating the sufferings of black Americans and other minority communities, the erosion of economic improvement for the country's middle and lower classes, and the disappearance of the solidarity evoked by fear of Soviet communism. It is questionable whether any theory, particularly a liberal theory that forswears discussion of an ethic of civic virtue and public purpose in relationship to democratic power, can revitalize this consensus and establish a coherent political dynamic for the nation as a whole.[21]

CONTEMPORARY VIRTUE AND ANCIENT ATHENS

As a legitimating ideology for American society, traditional liberalism's discourse of rights has lost much of its persuasive force. In our increasingly cramped quarters, everyone shouting for their rights means that no one is clearly heard. As this trend has developed, a contrasting philosophical orientation has gained political salience, one that shifts public attention from the preservation of individual rights to the promotion of social virtues. A diverse range of thinkers shares this orientation, including Straussians, communitarians, and analytic purveyors of "virtue ethics." What links them all is the belief that rational discussion of social morality and political justice—in today's society, at least, if not always, to some extent—requires critical attention to the discourse of virtue.

From a liberal perspective, in which no political order naturally affirms moral principles, democracy signifies only a system of exercising power—a manner of rule rather than an ethical ideal. As no political

---

21. Some political theorists have tried to incorporate the discourse of virtue into liberalism, but they have typically done so by simply making a virtue out of Madisonian liberalism and the ethic of equality of opportunity; see Stephen Macedo, *Liberal Virtues* (Oxford: Oxford University Press, Clarendon, 1990), and William A. Galston, *Liberal Purposes: Goods, Virtues, and Diversity in the Liberal State* (Cambridge: Cambridge University Press, 1991).

regime that lacks moorings in ethical ideals can itself be a model for community, this assumption degrades the value of democracy, as it degrades the ethical value of any order of political power. It posits antipathy between democracy and virtue. Intellectuals involved in the new turn to virtue, such as Alasdair MacIntyre, share this liberal aversion to public power. Where they differ is in their belief that the private realm, which has been left relatively unregulated by liberal theory, has to be fortified with a new sense of moral purpose which would then guide public life.[22]

Yet the new discourse of virtue has not nourished democratic sentiments. In fact, it has provided a much more direct challenge than liberalism to democracy. For where liberalism provides negative or individualistic criteria for the evaluation of public power, a public conception of virtue overtly affirms a particular constellation of power and authority. Moreover, the excellence identified with the exercise of virtue is typically associated with the capacities of the few rather than the many. This has been most obviously the case with the efforts of Straussians such as Allan Bloom and Harvey Mansfield, Jr., to reshape our understanding of the worthwhile culture and political norms for contemporary American society so as to reserve influence and authority to elected and unelected elites.[23] Insofar as the virtuous would be given new power, the prospects of democracy would diminish.

In order to ground this discourse, these proponents of virtue have turned to the philosophers of ancient Greece—more precisely, the philosophers of the Athenian polis who sought to limit its democracy. To some extent, this turn to ancient Greece is altogether appropriate. Not only did these ancient Greeks launch the western history of systematic philosophy about the well-being of political community, but the principal focus for their ethical and political discussions was the notion of arete, which is best translated as virtue but also signifies, in different moments or simultaneously, excellence, worth, social value, or merit.

But remembering ancient Greek discussions of virtue need not produce ammunition against democracy. To begin with, the conventional assertion of antagonism between democracy and virtue is itself highly

22. Alasdair MacIntyre, *After Virtue: A Study in Moral Theory*, 2d ed. (Notre Dame: University of Notre Dame Press, 1984).

23. See Allan Bloom, *The Closing of the American Mind* (New York: Simon and Schuster, 1987); Harvey C. Mansfield, Jr., *Taming the Prince: The Ambivalence of Executive Power* (New York: Free Press, 1989), and *America's Constitutional Soul* (Baltimore: Johns Hopkins University Press, 1991).

questionable. Democracy as a political order requires legitimating principles, as well as standards of political excellence and social distinction, and such principles and standards do not need to be anti-democratic. Reflecting on the relationship between democracy and virtue may suggest that it is possible to formulate an ethical ideal—a conception of virtue—that would nourish, not hamper, the political order of a democracy—at least for those who wish democracy well. Why cannot a system of ethics, as well as a structure of power, be democratic? Why must the only appropriate conceptions of social ethics and virtue for democracy radically constrain it? Those who have sought to renew liberalism by reviving the discourse of virtue have highlighted the tension between democracy and virtue. But a full discussion of virtue in Athenian society would more likely educate than antagonize democracy in America.

Throughout the history of its usage in ancient Greek thought, arete signified a standard of excellence and an example for emulation to those who would achieve it. Arete was an ideal for performance. It could not be realized by merely holding a belief or expressing a point of view. It needed to be demonstrated in practice. Moreover, this standard of excellence was socially significant because the ideal was to be practically recognized by society bestowing honors on its possessors. If such recognition did not follow upon the display of arete, as was the case when Agamemnon abducted Briseis from Achilles or the better athletic performer did not win his race, an injustice was done.

While arete was originally used to designate levels of recognition and achievement that only members of the aristocracy could manifest, it always served as a critical standard that transcended the mere ascription of social rank. Thus, members of the aristocracy could desecrate as much as demonstrate the standards of virtuous behavior expected of them. Solon made this clear when he condemned the greed of the wealthy classes who had enslaved Athenian peasants. For him, the preservation of virtue in the social order required a new political system, one that would secure freedom and political voice for all Athenian citizens. By the fifth century, virtue had become associated with the critical ideals of the polis as a whole. In the Athenian polis, now constituted as a democracy, this virtue was understood to be promoted by the liberty and political equality of democracy itself.

The complementarity of virtue and democracy appears primarily in two texts: Thucydides' record of a funeral oration by Pericles which memorialized Athens just after the outbreak of the Peloponnesian War and aspects of Plato's Great Speech of Protagoras (in reality a

Sophist from Abdera and counselor to Pericles) which appears in the dialogue entitled *Protagoras*, written about forty years after the dramatic date of the speech. To be sure, Pericles' oration demonstrates gaps and problems of Athenian democracy—nearly as much as it exemplifies its worth. The address identifies the virtue of female citizens as silence; its praise of the primacy of Athens implicitly degrades all other poleis, and its eulogy for the sacrifices of fallen soldiers makes military valor—particularly as displayed by the hoplite infantry, which was comprised mostly of members of the wealthier classes—a prime constituent of the virtue of Athenian democracy.[24] As for Protagoras's speech, its theoretical foundations were insecure and exposed as such by Plato, later in the dialogue.[25] Indeed, ancient formulations of democratic virtue cannot provide a sufficient model for democratic virtue today. And yet these two texts clearly identify a range of activities that not only foster the widespread exercise of power by the demos but also signify the expression of virtue and the realization of justice. Here, the performance of the people was not evaluated in terms of criteria of merit that could be met only by individuals competing against each other. Instead, the excellence of the people involved their capacities for civic participation, cooperation, and sound political judgment about the welfare of their community.

In his Funeral Oration as recorded by Thucydides, Pericles identified for praise those qualities, those virtues, that distinguished the Athenians as a people and sustained their integrity as a commendable and coherent society. He singled out for praise Athenian practices in private life, including toleration of diverse styles of life, free and open relations among each other, and generosity of spirit. Their democracy signified a rich culture along with political institutions. But he also emphasized the exemplary quality of their public life. He cites their interest in politics:

> Here each individual is interested not only in his own affairs but in the affairs of the state as well: even those who are mostly occupied with their own business are extremely well-informed on general pol-

24. See Nicole Loraux, *The Invention of Athens: The Funeral Oration in the Classical City*, trans. Alan Sheridan (Cambridge: Harvard University Press, 1986).

25. Unfortunately, Cynthia Farrar does not pay much attention to these theoretical insufficiencies or their problematic literary context when she makes Protagoras an unambiguous democratic theorist; see *The Origins of Democratic Thinking: The Invention of Politics in Classical Athens* (Cambridge: Cambridge University Press, 1988). Whatever the relationship of Plato's Protagoras in the *Protagoras* to the historical Protagoras, the language and structure of the Great Speech ultimately were designed by Plato to serve his own philosophical purposes. The coherence of Protagoras's democratic ethic depends on its critical reconstruction by the reader; it does not lie in the text itself.

itics—this is a peculiarity of ours: we do not say that a man who takes no interest in politics is a man who minds his own business; we say that he has no business here at all.

And he applauds their skill in political deliberation:

We Athenians, in our own person, take our decision on policy or submit them to proper discussions: for we do not think that there is an incompatibility between words and deeds; the worst thing is to rush into action before the consequences have been properly debated.

This vibrant political participation by the many and the concomitant ethical rule of equality before the law does not inhibit their appreciation of individuals whose virtue will benefit the political community: "When it is a question of putting one person before another in positions of public responsibility, what counts is not membership of a particular class, but the *aretē* which the man possesses."[26] In Pericles' Funeral Oration, there is no antipathy between freedom and virtue, between political equality and political competence; and the dignity and authority of the Athenians' democratic culture and politics do not allow the differences in economic worth which characterize segments of the citizenry to gradate their sense of mutual belonging to their political community.

In Plato's *Protagoras*, Protagoras identifies the distinguishing virtue of the Athenian citizenry with a democratic capacity to practice the art of politics (*politikē technē*). This art and virtue was expressed as authoritative power; it constituted their basic right of membership in a functioning society and allowed that society to survive; it involved knowing what counts as a virtuous practice in public life:

When the Athenians (and others as well) are debating architectural excellence, or the virtue proper to any other professional specialty, they think that only a few individuals have a right to advise them, and they do not accept advice from anyone outside these select few. . . . But when the debate involves political excellence (*aretē*), which must proceed entirely from justice and temperance, they accept advice from anyone, and with good reason, for they think that

26. Thucydides *History of the Peloponnesian War*, trans. Rex Warner (Baltimore: Penguin, 1954), 240, 237.

this particular virtue, political or civic virtue (*aretē*) is shared by all, or there wouldn't be any cities.[27]

Plato's Protagoras recognized the role of specialized expertise, but he also noted the Athenians' affirmation of a commonly shared expertise, its general availability and practice so unlike the typical understanding of expertise as a specialized skill that authorizes the rule of a few over the many. Remarkably, what gave this idea practical reality was its exercise in politics by a democratic citizenry. More generally, "Protagoras" held that when it comes to the education of "private citizens" in virtue, all must share: "Everyone here is a teacher of virtue, to the best of his ability."[28] A democratic culture in the "private" realm was less structured and institutionalized than democratic practices in the "public" realm, but each complemented the other.[29]

These texts about the virtue of Athenian democracy and its citizens describe a kind of political equality that complemented rather than resisted any public recognition of virtue, and the conception of virtue so served honored rather than undermined its democratic condition. To be sure, these depictions of democratic virtue expressed myths about Athenian society as much as explicit arguments for the compatibility of democracy and virtue. Yet, unlike the myth of equal opportunity in contemporary American society, which cannot produce a conception of virtue that would apply to the conduct of democratic politics or the vocation of Americans as democratic citizens, the Athenians at least envisioned a way in which democracy and virtue might be harmonized. Insofar as democratic Athenians praised equality of opportunity, it referred to actual capacities for political participation. The notion of *isēgoria* indicated every citizen's opportunity to speak publicly in the Assembly, while the use of the lot as a method of staffing public offices meant that virtually every male citizen served on the Council for one year of his adult life. The practical dimensions of

27. Plato, *Protagoras*, trans. Stanely Lombardo and Karen Bell, with intro. Michael Frede (Indianapolis: Hackett, 1992), 322d–323a. The practical equivalents of this notion of political or civic virtue as the art of politics or political art appear at 319a, 322b–d.

28. Ibid., 327e.

29. The Greeks would not have abided the notion of "private citizen," because they tended to associate the notion of privacy with life inside the *oikos* (family) or concerned only with personal affairs. But they surely recognized a domain of social interaction that took place in public but outside the official domain of politics, and this realm included the practice of education (paideia) and ordinary social exchange in the marketplace (agora). Hannah Arendt's sharp differentiation of "public" and "private" realms in ancient Greek life and thought was exaggerated, although understandable in light of her desire to return dignity and value to contemporary life; see *The Human Condition* (Chicago: University of Chicago Press, 1958).

equality of opportunity were political and public, as well as private and economic.[30]

Of course, the way in which democracy and virtue actually were harmonized in Athenian society was not wholly reassuring. (Moreover, the notion of harmony tends to occlude the pluralism and difference that enables the individuality of citizens to thrive.[31]) And of course there was the previously mentioned exclusive and militarized character of the Athenian public realm. In addition, Athens lost the Peloponnesian War; and a three-to-two majority on a court composed of a cross-section of the Athenian citizenry condemned Socrates to death. Finally, in the train of these events and as part of a longer term development of critical discourse in the Athenian polis, emerged Plato and Aristotle. The allegiance of the two major founders of the western philosophical tradition to democracy as either a structure of power or a system of ethics was marginal at best. But it is far from clear that the actual impetus for their theoretical projects was the Athenians' efforts to reconcile democracy and virtue. Indeed, no court will return a judgment that it was democracy per se, rather than distortions of it, that resulted in these historical misfortunes and miscarriages of justice. All that we do know is that in Athens itself a legitimation crisis ensued, that its critical intellectuals devised new ethical foundations for Athenian society, and that the Athenians themselves overwhelmingly supported the continuation of their democratic life.

Athenian democrats, as well as Athenian philosophers, experienced a conflict between the actual politics of their society and their ideals of individual and collective virtue. Insofar as the practice of power and the discourse of ethics cannot be reduced to one or the other, this

30. The failure to differentiate equality of opportunity in the modern context—which primarily refers to private, individual activity in pursuit of personal gain—from the expression of equal opportunity in the ancient Athenian context—which concerned both public, political, participatory activity and private personal activity—mars the comparison of ancient and modern democratic ideas in Mogens H. Hansen, *Was Athens a Democracy? Popular Rule, Liberty, and Equality in Ancient and Modern Political Thought* (Copenhagen: Royal Danish Academy of Sciences and Letters, 1989). In the wake of the U.S. Supreme Court's affirmation of the principle of "one man, one vote" in *Reynolds v. Sims* and the Voting Rights Act of 1965, there has been increased discussion of what equality of opportunity in the political process signifies. No consensus has formed, however, about any standard that goes beyond the principles articulated in *Reynolds*, as the controversy over the nomination of Lani Guinier to the post of assistant attorney general for civil rights showed. For recent discussions of equality of opportunity in the formally political realm, see Charles Beitz, *Political Equality: An Essay in Democratic Theory* (Princeton: Princeton University Press, 1989), and Lani Guinier, "No Two Seats: The Elusive Quest for Political Equality," *Virginia Law Review* 77 (1991): 1413–514.

31. See William E. Connolly, *Identity\Difference: Democratic Negotiations of Political Paradox* (Ithaca: Cornell University Press, 1991).

conflict is inevitable. But the historical events in the late fifth century served to deepen the sense of antagonism. As a result, Athenians in the fourth century experienced a crisis in the legitimacy of their ethical and political order. The issue became how to reconstruct the beliefs and perhaps the practices of Athenian society in new and more difficult economic and social conditions. The solutions devised by Plato and Aristotle were philosophically fascinating but in their political dimensions highly problematic for democracy. Both Plato and Aristotle incorporated many dimensions of the original, Athenian integration of democracy and virtue in their own political theories. Plato emphasized the primacy of the shared life of public virtue (also championed in Periclean democracy) for the sustenance of a just and happy political community. Aristotle recognized the unique virtue of political deliberation practiced by a diverse and participatory citizenry (also recognized by "Pericles" and "Protagoras") in constituting the political decisions of a just society. But each sought to reduce the role of democracy as a constituent of the practice of virtue. By contrast, the Athenian citizenry responded to their legitimation crisis by devising institutional mechanisms for strengthening their democracy rather than limiting it. The codification of Athenian law and the introduction of *nomothetai* (citizens annually appointed from the year's jurors to consider changes in the laws) did little or nothing to weaken the power of the demos.[32] This is why the invocation of Greek discussions of virtue today is politically charged as well as intellectually stimulating.

This problematic historical context for the systematic philosophies of virtue in ancient Greek thought makes the exploration of the relationship of democracy and virtue in ancient Athens extraordinarily illuminating. It displays the kind of dramatic conflict that any society, democratic or not, must undergo. It reveals the manifold interconnections among ethics, power, and community. Unfortunately, current efforts to invoke the ancient Greek discourse of virtue in contemporary ethical and political debate radically underplay this context, and this has affected contemporary readings and uses of the wisdom of the Greeks. When contemporary thinkers dip into the texts of these philosophers and use excerpts from them as part of a theoretical foundation that would reorient our own constitutive ideals, they typically isolate the discussion of virtue from the discussion of democ-

32. See Mogens H. Hansen, *The Athenian Democracy in the Age of Demosthenes: Structure, Principles, and Ideology* (Oxford: Blackwell, 1991), 300–304.

racy. In so doing, these scholarly discussions direct our political discussions along antidemocratic paths.[33] We should not ignore the ways in which Plato and Aristotle radically questioned the virtue of democracy. But if their initial formulations are understood within the Athenian context of political criticism, if the arguments of their discourse are historically positioned in relationship to the practical conflicts of their politics, their questioning can be useful for the critical improvement of democracy itself. Our recollection of both partisans and critics of Athenian democracy can be educational for democracy today. For insofar as democratic ideals have actually shaped the history of political power, they always have been forged amid challenges to collective existence, out of the material circumstances of actual societies.

If we are to renew the constitutive ideals of contemporary American society and find a place among them for a conception of virtue that fills the void left by the myth of equal opportunity and the identity of traditional liberalism, we are well-served by recalling the efforts of the ancient Athenians to make democracy virtuous and virtue democratic. But in doing so, we need to be critically aware of the political and philosophical complexities of the story we will be telling. Even if there is no immediate support within the history or discourse of democratic Athens for anyone interested in educating democracy in America today, telling its story does not suggest that education or the promotion of political virtue must minimize democracy. To the contrary, we see the first democratic society in history, with all its limitations, finding a home, within its constitutional frame, for philosophy, virtue, freedom, and a diverse and vibrant culture. We see a political order whose close-knit character differentiated but interconnected practical and conceptual domains whose identity we have ideologically sought to separate—such as the political versus the economic, the state versus civil society, virtue versus rights—even as the increasingly publicized, interdependent, and global constitutents of modern democracies have rendered the fixed identity of these so-called spheres of life and thought, practice and discourse, obsolete.[34] We see a society in which the potential complementarity of democracy and virtue, power and ethics, equality and liberty, permeates the culture and community of citizens.

The political institutions and political criticism of Athenian democ-

---

33. For examples of how this has occurred in the appropriation of Aristotle by contemporary theorists, see my "Contemporary Aristotelianism," *Political Theory* 20 (1992).

34. A preoccupation with separate spheres is most pronounced in the work of Michael Walzer, particularly his *Spheres of Justice* (New York: Basic Books, 1983) and "Liberalism and the Art of Separation," *Political Theory* 12 (1984).

racy can enrich our understanding of the possibilities and dangers of relating democracy and virtue. Its political institutions can remind us of what a full-bodied democracy may involve, of how political practices and judgments of ordinary citizens may exhibit virtue and competence. The usefulness of this sort of understanding in public discourse has to be indirect, but it can, nevertheless, be significant. For example, among those promoting new policies for welfare or education which would reshape the American character, there is a striking absence of any discussion of the way political powerlessness deprives citizens of a sense of moral purpose. As reformers preach a new moral discipline for the poor, formulated as "the work ethic," questions about the character or distribution of political power in our public life are typically ignored. This renewed attention to a social and public, if not political, meaning for virtue has continued to foster belief in an enduring antagonism between democracy and virtue, even as the need to restructure aspects of welfare programs and our educational system could inspire us to devise new ways of making them benefit each other.[35] By contrast, the Athenians' democratic institutions, able as they were to cultivate an astonishingly sophisticated, competent culture of widespread public responsibility, suggest the American society need not become more virtuous at the expense of democracy. Or take the contemporary issue of term limits for legislators. George Will has argued that limiting the ability of citizens to reelect their congress-men and -women would actually promote "deliberative democracy" and "civic virtue."[36] In a way, the notion of term limits recalls the Athenian practice of rotation in office and might seem to be true to their deliberative democracy. But Will does not attend to the difference between term limits and selection by lot or to the fact that elections played no role in constituting the membership of the Athenians' deliberative political organs. Term limits indeed sound attractive for those interested in both democracy and virtue. But that attraction should become serious only if the limits were coupled to efforts that reduced the inequalities of wealth and power that now distort the actual political opportunities of American citizens. For only with these additional reforms would term limits actually honor the Athenians' democracy and enhance, rather than detract from, the popular virtue and exercise of political power.

35. See Lawrence Mead, *Beyond Entitlement: The Social Obligations of Citizenship* (New York: Free Press, 1986), and *The New Politics of Poverty* (New York: Basic Books, 1992); and Mickey Kaus, *The End of Equality* (New York: Basic Books, 1992).

36. See George F. Will, *Restoration: Congress, Terms Limits, and the Recovery of Deliberative Democracy* (New York: Free Press, 1992).

With respect to Athenian texts of political criticism, their typically antidemocratic partisanship was nevertheless embedded in a democratic culture. As a result, their critical discourse actually discloses how many areas of political life may be open to democratic reform. Their recognition of the ethical possibilities of politics and community enable us to see the many ways in which our society could be improved.[37]

As we now are forced by the economic straits, racial and cultural divisions, and sclerotic politics of our time, to embark on a path of renewal, the question of how to relate democracy and virtue has assumed paramount importance. The way we resolve it—and resolve it we will, one way or another—will have major consequences for many years to come. That is why the language of virtue and the discourse of political ethics should not be left to those who scorn democracy, in public or private. Democrats need to think about constructing power as well as criticizing it.[38] As we do so, we must attend very closely to the needs and wants, discourse and practices of our society, of our citizens, in order to orient democratically the new directions we take. With respect to these constitutive constraints, the authority of our stories of ancient Athens in educating our society cannot provide simple guideposts for ourselves. Indeed, to have them do so devalues the weight of our practical problems, the significance of our intellectual choices, the dignity of our values, the democracy of our democracy. But they surely can offer us myriad lessons for enabling the new American virtue to become a democratic friend.

37. The essays by Euben, Monoson, and Ober in this volume reveal just some of their critical potential in this regard.
38. This is one of the reasons why the intellectual currents of deconstruction, poststructuralism, and separatist feminism have had dubious political consequences. Their criticisms of community, identity, authority, and responsibility cannot make the need for them go away. If democrats are not going to be involved in defining their character, then antidemocrats will make sure that traditionally excluded and scorned groups and practices remain at the margin of our social life. Criticism of "harmony" from the intellectual left finds its mirror in the criticism of "disharmony" from the right. Cf. Connolly, *Identity\Difference*, with Samuel Huntington, *American Politics: The Promise of Disharmony* (Cambridge: Harvard University Press, 1981).

SELECTED BIBLIOGRAPHY

Adkins, Arthur W. H. *Merit and Responsibility: A Study in Greek Values*. London: Clarendon Press, 1960.

——. "*Polypragmosyne* and 'Minding One's Own Business': A Study in Greek Social and Political Values." *Classical Philology* 71 (1976): 301–27.

Andrewes, Antony. *The Greek Tyrants*. London: Hutchinson University Library, 1956.

Arendt, Hannah. *Between Past and Future*. Enlarged ed. Baltimore: Penguin, 1968.

——. *Eichmann in Jerusalem: A Report on the Banality of Evil*. New York: Viking, 1964.

——. *The Human Condition*. Chicago: University of Chicago Press, 1958.

——. *On Revolution*. New York: Viking, 1963.

——. *The Origins of Totalitarianism*. New York: Meridian, 1958.

Austin, J. L. *How to Do Things with Words*. Ed. J. O. Urmson and Marina Sbisà. 2d ed. Cambridge: Harvard University Press, 1975.

Austin, Michael M., and Pierre Vidal-Naquet. *Economic and Social History of Ancient Greece: An Introduction*. Berkeley and Los Angeles: University of California Press, 1977.

Barber, Benjamin. *An Aristocracy of Everyone: The Politics of Education and the Future of America*. New York: Ballantine, 1992.

——. *Strong Democracy: Participatory Politics for a New Age*. Berkeley and Los Angeles: University of California Press, 1984.

Bellah, Robert M., et al. *Habits of the Heart: Individualism and Commitment in American Life*. Berkeley and Los Angeles: University of California Press, 1985.

Bernal, Martin. *Black Athena*. New Brunswick: Rutgers University Press, 1987.

——. "Black Athena Denied: The Tyranny of Germany over Greece and the Rejection of the Afroasiatic Roots of Europe, 1780–1980." *Comparative Criticism* 8 (1986): 3–70.

Bernard, Jessie. *The Female World*. New York: Free Press, 1981.

Bloom, Allan. *The Closing of the American Mind*. New York: Simon and Schuster, 1987.

Bonner, Robert J. *Aspects of Athenian Democracy*. New York: Russell and Russell, 1933.

Burchell, Graham, Colin Gordon, and Peter Miller, eds. *The Foucault Effect: Studies in Governmentality*. Chicago: University of Chicago Press, 1991.

Carter, Laurence B. *The Quiet Athenian*. Oxford: Oxford University Press, 1986.

Cartledge, Paul A., and F. David Harvey, eds. *Crux: Essays in Greek History Presented to Geoffrey E. M. de Ste. Croix*. London: Imprint Editions, Imprint Academic, 1985.

Castoriadis, Cornelius. "The Greek Polis and the Creation of Democracy." *Graduate Faculty Journal* 9 (1983): 81–123.

Connolly, William E. *Identity\Difference: Democratic Negotiations of Political Paradox*. Ithaca: Cornell University Press, 1991.

Connor, W. Robert. *The New Politicians of Fifth-Century Athens*. Princeton: Princeton University Press, 1971.

——. *Thucydides*. Princeton: Princeton University Press, 1984.

Cott, Nancy. *The Bonds of Womanhood*. New Haven: Yale University Press, 1977.

Culham, Phyllis, and Lowell Edmunds, eds. *Classics: A Discipline and Profession in Crisis?* Lanham, Md.: University Press of America, 1989.

Dahl, Robert A. *Democracy and Its Critics*. New Haven: Yale University Press, 1989.

——. *Who Governs?* New Haven: Yale University Press, 1960.

Derrida, Jacques. *Limited Inc*. Ed. Gerald Graff. Trans. Jeffrey Mehlmann and Samuel Weber. Evanston: Northwestern University Press, 1988.

Dover, Kenneth J. "The Freedom of the Intellectual in Greek Society." *Talanta* 7 (1976): 24–54.

——. *Greek Popular Morality in the Time of Plato and Aristotle*. Berkeley and Los Angeles: University of California Press, 1974.

Dunn, John. *Western Political Theory in the Face of the Future*. Cambridge: Cambridge University Press, 1979.

Eagleton, Terry. *Ideology: An Introduction*. London: Verso, 1991.

Edmunds, Lowell. *Chance and Intelligence in Thucydides*. Cambridge: Harvard University Press, 1975.

Ehrenberg, Victor. "Origins of Democracy." *Historia* 1 (1950): 515–48.

——. "Polypragmosyne: A Study in Greek Politics." *Journal of Hellenic Studies* 67 (1947): 46–67.

Euben, J. Peter, ed. *Greek Tragedy and Political Theory*. Berkeley and Los Angeles: University of California Press, 1986.

——. *The Tragedy of Political Theory: The Road Not Taken*. Princeton: Princeton University Press, 1990.

Farrar, Cynthia. *The Origins of Democratic Thinking: The Invention of Politics in Classical Athens*. Cambridge: Cambridge University Press, 1988.

Ferguson, Kathy. *The Feminist Case against Bureaucracy*. Philadelphia: Temple University Press, 1984.

Finley, Moses I. *The Ancient Economy*. Berkeley and Los Angeles: University of California Press, 1973.

——. "Athenian Demagogues." *Past and Present* 21 (1962): 1–25.

——. *Democracy Ancient and Modern*. New Brunswick: Rutgers University Press, 1973.

——. *Politics in the Ancient World*. Cambridge: Cambridge University Press, 1983.

Fornara, Charles W., and Loren J. Samons II. *Athens from Cleisthenes to Pericles*. Berkeley and Los Angeles: University of California Press, 1991.

Forrest, William G. *The Emergence of Greek Democracy*. New York: McGraw-Hill, 1966.

Foucault, Michel. *Power/Knowledge: Selected Interviews and Other Writings, 1972–1977*. Ed. Colin Gordon. Trans. Colin Gordon et al. New York: Pantheon, 1980.

Guthrie, William K. C. *A History of Greek Philosophy*. 6 vols. Cambridge: Cambridge University Press, 1962–81.

Habermas, Jürgen. *Theory of Communicative Action: Reason and the Rationalization of Society*. Trans. Thomas McCarthy. Boston: Beacon, 1984.

Hansen, Mogens H. *The Athenian Democracy in the Age of Demosthenes: Structure, Principles, and Ideology*. Trans. J. A. Crook. Oxford: Blackwell, 1991.

———. *Was Athens a Democracy? Popular Rule, Liberty, and Equality in Ancient and Modern Political Thought*. Copenhagen: Royal Danish Academy of Sciences and Letters, 1989.

Hartsock, Nancy. *Money, Sex, and Power*. New York: Longman, 1983.

Harvey, F. David. "Two Kinds of Equality." *Classica et Mediaevalia* 26 (1965): 101–46.

Havelock, Eric A. *The Liberal Temper in Greek Politics*. New Haven: Yale University Press, 1957.

Heinimann, Felix. *Nomos und Physis*. 1945. Reprint. Darmstadt: Wissenschaftliche Buchgesellschaft, 1972.

Hignett, Charles, *A History of the Athenian Constitution to the End of the Fifth Century B.C.* Oxford: Oxford University Press, Clarendon, 1952.

Hobsbawm, Eric. *The Age of Empire, 1875–1914*. London: Weidenfeld and Nicolson, 1987.

Holmes, Stephen T. "Aristippus in and out of Athens." *American Political Science Review* 73 (1979): 113–28.

Horkheimer, Max, and Theodor W. Adorno. *Dialectic of Enlightenment: Philosophical Fragments*. Trans. John Cumming. New York: Seabury, Continuum, 1972.

Hoy, David Couzens. *Foucault: A Critical Reader*. Oxford: Blackwell Publisher, Basil Blackwell, 1986.

Humphreys, Sarah C. *Anthropology and the Greeks*. London: Routledge and Kegan Paul, 1978.

Hyneman, Charles, and Donald Lutz, eds. *American Political Writing during the Founding Era, 1760–1805*. Indianapolis: Liberty Fund, Liberty Press, 1983.

Jaeger, Werner. *Paideia*. 3 vols. Oxford: Oxford University Press, 1943–45.

Jones, A. H. M. *Athenian Democracy*. Baltimore: Johns Hopkins University Press, 1986.

Kennedy, George. *The Art of Persuasion in Greece*. Princeton: Princeton University Press, 1963.

Kerferd, George B. *The Sophistic Movement*. Cambridge: Cambridge University Press, 1981.

Knox, Bernard M. W. *Oedipus at Thebes*. New Haven: Yale University Press, 1957.

Larsen, Jakob A. O. "The Judgment of Antiquity on Democracy." *Classical Philology* 49 (1954): 1–14.

Lloyd, G. E. R. *Magic, Reason, and Experience*. Cambridge: Cambridge University Press, 1979.

Loraux, Nicole. *The Invention of Athens: The Funeral Oration in the Classical City.* Trans. Alan Sheridan. Cambridge: Harvard University Press, 1986.

Lord, Carnes, and David K. O'Connor, eds. *Essays on the Foundations of Aristotelian Political Science.* Berkeley and Los Angeles: University of California Press, 1991.

McClelland, J. S. *The Crowd and the Mob: From Plato to Canetti.* London: Unwin Hyman, 1989.

MacIntyre, Alasdair. *After Virtue: A Study in Moral Theory.* 2d ed. Notre Dame: University of Notre Dame Press, 1984.

Manville, Philip Brook. *The Origins of Citizenship in Ancient Athens.* Princeton: Princeton University Press, 1990.

Meier, Christian. *The Greek Discovery of Politics.* Trans. David McLintock. Cambridge: Harvard University Press, 1990.

Mitchell, Juliet, and Ann Oakley, eds. *What Is Feminism?* New York: Pantheon, 1986.

Momigliano, Arnaldo. "Freedom of Speech in Antiquity." *The Dictionary of the History of Ideas.* Ed. Philip Wiener. Vol. 2. New York: Scribner's, 1973.

——. "Sea-Power in Greek Thought." *Classical Review* 58 (1944): 1–7.

Naess, Arne, et al., eds. *Democracy, Ideology and Objectivity: Studies in the Semantics and Cognitive Analysis of Ideological Controversy.* Oslo: University Press for the Norwegian Research Council for Science and the Humanities, 1956.

Nietzsche, Friedrich. *Basic Writings of Nietzsche.* Trans. and ed. Walter Kaufmann. New York: Modern Library, 1966.

——. "On the Uses and Disadvantages of History for Life." In *Untimely Meditations.* Trans. R. J. Hollingdale. London: Routledge and Kegan Paul, 1983.

North, Helen. *Sophrosyne.* Ithaca: Cornell University Press, 1966.

Nussbaum, Martha. *The Fragility of Goodness: Luck and Ethics in Greek Tragedy and Philosophy.* New York: Cambridge University Press, 1986.

Ober, Josiah. *Mass and Elite in Democratic Athens: Rhetoric, Ideology, and the Power of the People.* Princeton: Princeton University Press, 1989.

O'Neill, John, ed. *On Critical Theory.* New York: Seabury, 1976.

Osborne, Robin. *Demos: The Discovery of Classical Attika.* Cambridge: Cambridge University Press, 1985.

Ostwald, Martin. *From Popular Sovereignty to the Sovereignty of Law: Law, Society, and Politics in Fifth-Century Athens.* Berkeley and Los Angeles: University of California Press, 1986.

Palmer, R. R. "Notes on the Use of the Word 'Democracy,' 1789–1799." *Political Science Quarterly* 68 (1953): 203–26.

Patterson, Cynthia B. *Pericles' Citizenship Law of 451–50 B.C.* New York: Arno, 1981.

Patterson, Orlando. *Freedom in the Making of Western Culture.* Vol. 1 of *Freedom.* New York: Basic Books, 1991.

Petrey, Sandy. *Speech Acts and Literary Theory.* New York: Routledge, Chapman and Hall, 1990.

Plato. *Plato's Gorgias.* Ed. and trans. Eric R. Dodds. Oxford: Oxford University Press, 1959.

Pomeroy, Sarah. *Goddesses, Whores, Wives, and Slaves: Women in Classical Antiquity.* New York: Schocken, 1975.

Raaflaub, Kurt A. "Contemporary Perceptions of Democracy in Fifth-Century Athens." In W. Robert Connor et al., *Aspects of Athenian Democracy*. Copenhagen: Museum Tusculanum, 1990.

——. "Democracy, Oligarchy, and the Concept of the 'Free Citizen' in Late Fifth-Century Athens." *Political Theory* 11 (1983): 517–44.

Radin, Max. "Freedom of Speech in Ancient Athens." *American Journal of Philology* 48 (1927): 215–30.

Rawls, John. *Political Liberalism*. New York: Columbia University Press, 1993.

——. *A Theory of Justice*. Cambridge: Harvard University Press, 1971.

Raymond, Janice. *A Passion for Friends*. Boston: Beacon, 1986.

Reinhold, Meyer. *Classica Americana: The Greek and Roman Heritage in the United States*. Detroit: Wayne State University Press, 1984.

Rhodes, Peter J. "Athenian Democracy after 403 B.C." *Classical Journal* 75 (1980): 305–23.

——. *A Commentary on the Aristotelian Athenaion Politeia*. Oxford: Oxford University Press, 1981.

Romilly, Jacqueline de. *Thucydides and Athenian Imperialism*. Oxford: Blackwell and Mott, 1963.

Sagan, Eli. *The Honey and the Hemlock: Democracy and Paranoia in Ancient Athens and Modern America*. New York: Basic Books, 1991.

Ste. Croix, Geoffrey E. M. de. *The Origins of the Peloponnesian War*. London: Duckworth, 1972.

Schaar, John H. "Equal Opportunity and Beyond." In *Nomos IX: Equality*. Ed. J. R. Pennock and J. W. Chapman. New York: Atherton, 1967.

Schumpeter, Joseph. *Capitalism, Socialism, and Democracy*. 3d ed. New York: Harper and Row, 1950.

Searle, John R. *Speech Acts: An Essay in the Philosophy of Language*. Cambridge: Cambridge University Press, 1969.

Segal, Charles P. *Interpreting Greek Tragedy: Myth, Poetry, Text*. Ithaca: Cornell University Press, 1986.

——. *Tragedy and Civilization: An Interpretation of Sophocles*. Cambridge: Harvard University Press, 1981.

Sinclair, R. K. *Democracy and Participation in Athens*. Cambridge: Cambridge University Press, 1988.

Stockton, David. *The Classical Athenian Democracy*. Oxford: Oxford University Press, 1990.

Stone, I. F. *The Trial of Socrates*. New York: Doubleday, 1989.

Strauss, Barry S. *Fathers and Sons in Classical Athens*. Princeton: Princeton University Press, 1993.

Strauss, Leo. *The City and Man*. Chicago: University of Chicago Press, 1964.

Trilateral Commission. *The Crisis of Democracy*. New York: New York University Press, 1975.

Vernant, Jean-Pierre. *The Origins of Greek Thought*. Ithaca: Cornell University Press, 1982.

Vernant, Jean-Pierre, and Pierre Vidal-Naquet. *Tragedy and Myth in Ancient Greece*. Trans. Janet Lloyd. Brighton, E. Sussex: Harvester, 1981.

Vidal-Naquet, Pierre. *The Black Hunter: Forms of Thought and Forms of Society in the Greek World*. Baltimore: Johns Hopkins University Press, 1986.

Vlastos, Gregory. "The Historical Socrates and Athenian Democracy." *Political Theory* 11 (1983): 495–515.

——. "Isonomia." *American Journal of Philology* 74 (1953): 337–66.

——. "Isonomia Politikē." In *Platonic Studies*. Princeton: Princeton University Press, 1973.

——. *Socrates, Ironist and Moral Philosopher*. Ithaca: Cornell University Press, 1991.

Wallach, John R. "Contemporary Aristotelianism." *Political Theory* 20 (1992): 4, 613–42.

Williams, Bernard. *Shame and Necessity*. Berkeley and Los Angeles: University of California Press, 1993.

Winkler, John J., and Froma I. Zeitlin, eds. *Nothing to Do with Dionysos? Athenian Drama in Its Social Context*. Princeton: Princeton University Press, 1990.

Wolin, Sheldon S. *Politics and Vision: Continuity and Innovation in Western Political Thought*. Boston: Little, Brown, 1960.

——. *The Presence of the Past: Essays on the State and the Constitution*. Baltimore: Johns Hopkins University Press, 1989.

Wood, Ellen Meiksins. *Peasant-Citizen and Slave: The Foundations of Athenian Democracy*. London: Verso, 1988.

Wood, Gordon S. *The Creation of the American Republic, 1776–1787*. Chapel Hill: University of North Carolina Press, 1969.

Wood, Neal, and Ellen Wood. "Socrates and Democracy: A Reply to Gregory Vlastos." *Political Theory* 14 (1986): 55–83.

CONTRIBUTORS

J. PETER EUBEN is a fellow of Kresge College and Professor of Politics at the University of California, Santa Cruz.

CHARLES W. HEDRICK, JR., is a fellow of Cowell College and Associate Professor of History at the University of California, Santa Cruz.

ANN M. LANE is a fellow of Oakes College and Lecturer in American Studies at the University of California, Santa Cruz.

WARREN LANE is an independent scholar living in Santa Cruz.

S. SARA MONOSON is Assistant Professor of Political Science at Northwestern University.

JOSIAH OBER is Professor and Chair of the Department of Classics at Princeton University.

KURT A. RAAFLAUB is Co-Director of the Center for Hellenic Studies and Professor of Classics and History at Brown University.

JENNIFER ROBERTS is Professor of Classical Languages and History at City College of New York and CUNY Graduate Center.

CHRISTOPHER ROCCO is Assistant Professor of Political Science at the University of Connecticut.

BARRY S. STRAUSS is Professor of History at Cornell University.

JOHN R. WALLACH is Assistant Professor of Political Science at Hunter College of the City University of New York.

SHELDON S. WOLIN is Professor Emeritus of Politics, Princeton University.

ELLEN MEIKSINS WOOD is Professor of Political Science at York University.

INDEX

349